The Perdiccas Years
323–320 BC

The Perdiccas Years
323–320 BC

Alexander's Successors at War

Tristan Hughes

Pen & Sword
MILITARY

First published in Great Britain in 2022
and republished in this format in 2024 by
Pen & Sword Military
An imprint of
Pen & Sword Books Ltd
Yorkshire – Philadelphia

ISBN 978 1 39902 070 1

Printed in the UK by CPI Group (UK) Ltd, Croydon, CR0 4YY.

Pen & Sword Books Limited incorporates the imprints of Atlas,
Archaeology, Aviation, Discovery, Family History, Fiction, History,
Maritime, Military, Military Classics, Politics, Select, Transport,
True Crime, Air World, Frontline Publishing, Leo Cooper, Remember
When, Seaforth Publishing, The Praetorian Press, Wharncliffe
Local History, Wharncliffe Transport, Wharncliffe True Crime
and White Owl.

For a complete list of Pen & Sword titles please contact

PEN & SWORD BOOKS LIMITED
47 Church Street, Barnsley, South Yorkshire, S70 2AS, England
E-mail: enquiries@pen-and-sword.co.uk
Website: www.pen-and-sword.co.uk

Or

PEN AND SWORD BOOKS
1950 Lawrence Rd, Havertown, PA 19083, USA
E-mail: Uspen-and-sword@casematepublishers.com
Website: www.penandswordbooks.com

Contents

Acknowledgements

My thanks go out to several figures who have been instrumental in allowing me to turn this passion project into my first book. I would like to thank Dr Simon Elliott, who kindly introduced me to Phil Sidnell, my editor at Pen & Sword, a couple of years back and set me on the road to writing *Alexander's Successors at War*. Phil also deserves special mention, as it's not every day that you meet someone equally obsessed with the Wars of the Successors in the UK. His passion and encouragement during this process have been second to none.

Nurlan Karimov and Ilkin Gambar, the brains behind the YouTube Channel Kings and Generals, I must also thank. It was they who gave me an opportunity to script and narrate a series of documentaries about the Successor Wars several years ago that further sparked my obsession for this period in ancient history.

Most important of all I am incredibly grateful to my parents, Freddie and David, who were willing to look through many drafts of my book chapters during the long days of lockdown in 2020 and offer invaluable feedback.

And finally my thanks to everyone, friends and work colleagues, for their encouragement and support during what has no doubt been one of the most difficult, but rewarding, projects I have ever undertaken.

Foreword

We are a family of eccentrics at History Hit. The CEO is obsessed with late Victorian ghost hunts, Alice, the social media genius, knows all that can be known about political satire in Georgian Britain. We all have our passions and specialisations, but Tristan, well, he takes things to a new level. Tristan came to work at History Hit years ago when we were in a tiny, airless room next to the railway tracks in Southwark. He burst on to the team like the Companion Cavalry onto the battlefield. Here was a guy with his own blog, social media pages, book, tv and podcast ideas that he was straining to get started on. A passionate young scholar in a hurry. We hired him immediately and within days he was running sizeable chunks of our operation. But however much we set him to work on the mundane corporate business of keeping the History Hit show on the road, he never lost sight of his ultimate goal, which was his first book all about the dawn of the *Diadochi*.

Now, I yield to no one in my passion for history. The ancient world is an area, if not of expertise, certainly of interest. Yet, before I met Tristan, and before I read this, I could not have told you two things about the period other than the names Ptolemy and Seleucus. I initially politely suggested that Tristan might want to look elsewhere, set up camp in some other, adjacent territory, which people might actually have heard of, like, say, Alexander the Great, 5th century BC Greece or even, well, Rome. But I quickly gave up, and I'm glad I did. Tristan has proved me wrong. Not only has he started the hit podcast The Ancients, in which hundreds of thousands of people regularly listen to in-depth pods about ancient history, with an amusing bias towards west Asia after Alexander, but now he has produced this triumphant book, which is a real gem.

He tells a captivating story of the catastrophic immediate aftermath of Alexander's death, the characters, feuds and gigantic rivalries that quickly emerged between former brothers-in-arms. In the end, Tristan has been proved absolutely right. The Successors of Alexander are as fascinating as they are important. It is wonderful to see Tristan publish this, the first of I have no doubt, many, many books in the years to come. Thankfully, the ancient world is a bottomless reservoir of subjects for future books so unlike one of his heroes, Alexander, Tristan will never have to weep as he bemoans the lack of worlds to conquer.

Dan Snow, Historian and TV Presenter
November 2021

Introduction

Alexander the Great. This Macedonian king, born more than 2,000 years ago, ranks among the most famous figures in history. And with good reason. In his short lifetime he forged one of the largest empires the world had ever seen, conquering a superpower and leaving the world changed forever. Because of Alexander, archaeologists have uncovered hallmarks of Hellenistic culture stretching from the Mediterranean to the Indus. For better or for worse, his achievements inspired many notable names that followed him. Arthurian tales of Alexander became medieval bestsellers. The whereabouts of his body remains one of the greatest archaeological mysteries of antiquity.

The legacy and achievements of Alexander the Great are astonishing, but for me it is what followed his untimely death, aged just 32, that is most extraordinary: the figures that came to the fore. Extraordinary personalities, many of whom would quickly become locked in a bitter struggle for supremacy and survival. Alexander the Great may have forged a large empire, but it was these 'Successors' that determined its fate.

Alexander's death in Babylon that fateful day in June 323 BC triggered an unprecedented crisis. Within a couple of days, Macedonian blood had stained the walls of the chamber in which he died. Within a couple of weeks, Babylon had witnessed the first siege of the post Alexander age. Within a couple of months, a major revolt had erupted on mainland Greece. Within a couple of years, theatres of conflict had arisen across the length and breadth of what was once Alexander's empire. From a Spartan adventurer attempting to forge his own empire in North Africa, to a vast horde of veteran Greek mercenaries heading home from ancient Afghanistan. From a merciless, punitive campaign against some of the most infamous brigands of the time to a warrior princess raising an army and pressing ahead with her own power play during this ancient Game of Thrones.

What followed Alexander's death was an imperial implosion. This book attempts to explain why it happened.

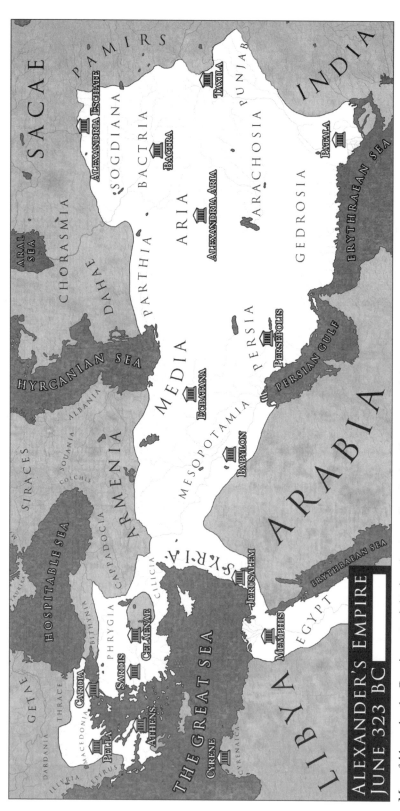

Map of Alexander the Great's empire (white) at the time of his death in June 323, with key regions and cities highlighted.

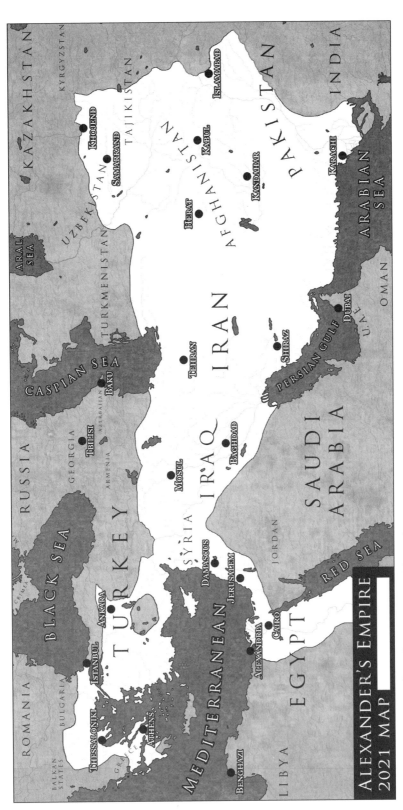

Alexander's Empire, with modern countries, cities and sea names.

Author's note

I have tried to make this book enjoyable for both the casual ancient history enthusiast and the scholar. References to the works of the historians I have used can be found *en masse* in the end notes, for anyone wanting to read deeper into the subject and the debates that abound. The limited sources mean that polarised arguments exist on many topics in this book, not least the dates.

In these cases, I have selected the argument that I find most plausible, with references to the relevant historian and his/her work in the end notes.

For certain battles and campaigns of which we have very little detail surviving, I have formulated what I believe to be a plausible series of events, explanations for which can be found in the end notes.

All dates in this book are BC unless otherwise stated. For ship names, I have decided to use the Latin rather than the Greek (the word trireme is much better known than *trieres*). All mistakes are my own.

Chapter 1

The End of an Era

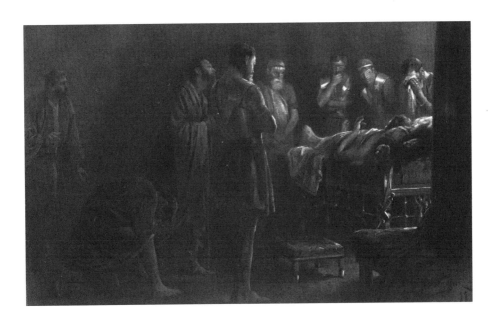

Late afternoon. 11 June 323. Babylon. King Alexander III of Macedon was dying. Surrounding the failing king's bed stood his seven *somatophylakes*, his bodyguards. Most had accompanied Alexander since his rise to power; through thick and thin these warriors had served their king, yet they were powerless to protect him from the last enemy of all. One of these men asked Alexander to whom he bequeathed his great kingdom. According to legend the 32-year-old king simply replied:

'To the strongest.'[1]

Moments later Alexander the Great died.

These seven bodyguards were now the highest-ranking individuals at the heart of Alexander's Eurasian empire. Countless times they had proven themselves on the battlefield. Although Alexander's aura had stood supreme and uncontested these *somatophylakes* reflected their king's leadership in the heat of conflict more than any others: leading from the front and dicing with death they evoked his boundless charisma. All were formidable, young and proven leaders:

Never before, indeed, did Macedonia, or any other country, abound with such a multitude of distinguished men; whom Philip (II) first, and afterwards Alexander, had selected with such skill, that they seemed to be chosen, not so much to attend them to war, as to succeed them to the throne. Who then can wonder, that the world was conquered by such officers, when the army of the Macedonians appeared to be commanded, not by generals, but by princes? – Justin 13.1.12–15

It was these *princes* that now held the fate of the empire within their hands.

The Seven

Alexander had provided a vague indication about what he wanted to happen next. Earlier in the day he had silently removed his signet ring and handed it to one of these generals. It had been a symbolic gesture. It was this man that Alexander intended should oversee the succession; it was this man that Alexander intended should manage affairs of state in the interim.[2] This man was Perdiccas.

A man with traces of royal blood flowing through his veins, Perdiccas was a member of one of the most prestigious families in Macedonia. He hailed from Orestis, a region on Macedonia's southwestern fringes where his family held great influence.[3] Perdiccas' noble background had ensured he was raised for war since childhood and by the time he had reached his 26th year, the Orestian

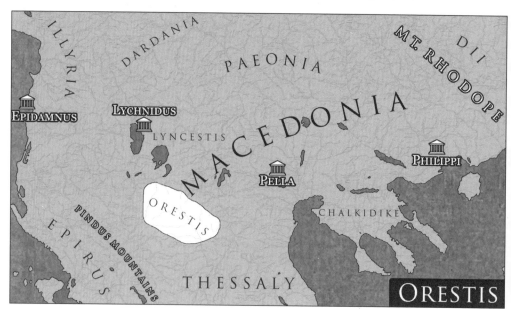

Orestis (highlighted) and Lyncestis were situated in the southwest / west of Macedonia.

prince had achieved command of one of Alexander the Great's infantry battalions, consisting of soldiers from his native Orestis and neighbouring Lyncestis.

The young man did not disappoint. Perdiccas and his *taxis* (battalion) went on to prove their worth in several engagements: from storming the walls of Thebes to accompanying Alexander on his gruelling night march across a stretch of the Zagros Mountains as they circumnavigated a strong Persian defence.[4] The battalion gained a fearsome reputation, becoming a key linchpin for the Macedonian phalanx, and the same was true for their commander. Perdiccas frequently shared the risks of his soldiers, suffering several severe wounds over the course of Alexander's campaigns. His numerous battle scars only earned him further respect and admiration from his men.

Perdiccas' remarkable feats helped elevate his status within the army. In 330 Alexander had named him one of his seven *somatophylakes,* one of his chief adjutants. Three years later Perdiccas was in command of cavalry squadrons and, by the time Alexander returned from India, such was the trust he placed in Perdiccas' capability that the king regularly provided him large sections of his all-conquering army to command on special missions.[5]

From battalion to bodyguard, Perdiccas' military career had blossomed during Alexander's campaigns. By 324 he ranked among Alexander's highest subordinates, though two generals still held higher positions: Craterus and Hephaestion. Fortunately for Perdiccas, by the end of the year, both these figures had vanished from the king's side – Alexander had sent Craterus back to Europe with 10,000 disgruntled Macedonian veterans; Hephaestion had died suddenly after a fever.[6] This offered Perdiccas opportunity to climb higher, and he was sure to do so. By June 323, Alexander had named him Hephaestion's replacement as chiliarch (vizier): the highest-ranking commander within the army, Alexander aside.[7]

Alexander's handing of his signet ring to Perdiccas provided the chiliarch a clear degree of authority among his fellow *somatophylakes,* no-doubt fuelling his ambition further.[8] But it also stoked the embers for bitter rivalry. These seven bodyguards had all willingly served under Alexander's overarching command; serving under Perdiccas however, proved another matter.

One bodyguard in particular was already wary of the chiliarch's new-found power. His name was Ptolemy, a man who was equally ambitious, and keen to make his own mark in this new post-Alexander world.

The son of a Macedonian nobleman called Lagus, Ptolemy was notably older than both Alexander and Perdiccas.[9] Like the latter, Ptolemy had served with Alexander since the start of his Persian conquest, though for many years he did not hold significant command within the army. This had all changed in 330 however, when Alexander appointed him a member of his bodyguard and by June 323 Ptolemy had cemented himself as one of the king's elite.[10]

Ptolemy prided himself on his close personal connection with the recently-deceased Alexander. Already he aimed to use this to his advantage.

Five royal bodyguards remained. Chief among them was the legendary Leonnatus, one of Alexander's most-trusted commanders and a personal favourite of the king. There was also Lysimachus, Peithon and Aristonous – all veteran bodyguards with noble backgrounds. Finally there was Peucestas, an officer who had distinguished himself with the highest valour in India when he saved Alexander's life.[11]

Together they were now the most powerful figures in the empire, facing an extraordinary situation. It was their unprecedented duty to elect the new king.

Restless Babylon

Word of Alexander's death spread rapidly throughout central Asia, but it was in Babylon itself where his passing most affected his subjects. The Macedonian veterans mourned the death of their legendary leader. To them he had been a figure larger than life: the man who had never lost a battle; the man who had led them from the highlands of Macedonia to the western bank of the Hyphasis River in India; the man who had diced with death on numerous occasions, always willing to share in the risks of combat that he regularly demanded from his soldiers. Although this cost Alexander several severe wounds throughout the course of his campaigns, his ability to always pull through had only increased his aura of invincibility among the Macedonians – a king favoured by the gods.[12]

But now that king was dead; grief and confusion welled up among the Macedonian rank and file. It was Alexander who had transformed these men from a kingdom's levy of farmers and craftsmen into the most feared band of professional soldiers in the world. What would happen to them now he was gone?

The Macedonians were not alone in Babylon to mourn Alexander's passing. Babylonians and Persians supposedly similarly paid their respects to their dead king:

The Persians had their hair shorn in traditional fashion and wore garments of mourning. Together with their wives and children they grieved with genuine feelings of regret, not for a man who had recently been their conqueror and enemy, but for one who had been a superlatively just king over their nation. They were people accustomed to living under a monarchy, and they admitted they had never had a worthier ruler. – Curtius 10.5.17

No fires burned bright that night.[13] Around Babylon, the night of 11/12 June was one of mourning. For Perdiccas, Ptolemy and the rest of the bodyguards however, thoughts about the future probably overshadowed this period of grief; it was their duty to provide leadership in this extraordinary time – their duty to reach agreement over what would happen next.

As the sun rose the next day, the mourning subsided and large crowds of soldiery gathered at the royal palace, the nucleus of power in Babylon. There Perdiccas, Ptolemy and the other generals had met to determine the fate of Alexander's Empire.[14] Only the most senior military commanders received an invite, figures such as Nearchus, admiral of the fleet, Seleucus, *strategos* of the elite Macedonian infantry called the *hypaspists* and Laomedon, a leading mercenary general and close friend of Ptolemy and Alexander. There was also Eumenes, the former personal secretary of Alexander who currently held a senior command among the cavalry. Together these figures pushed and shoved their way through a huge horde of impatient Macedonian soldiers, who had assembled in the royal courtyard and were eager to make their presence known.

As they watched Nearchus, Eumenes and the other high-ranking commanders file their way into the privacy of the intended meeting room, distress filled the hearts of the infantrymen left outside. They prided themselves as a renowned and feared fighting force, second to none. It was they who had won Alexander his heroic victories at Issus, Tyre, Gaugamela, the Jaxartes and the Hydaspes River. It was they who had sacrificed all that was dear to them in Macedonia – their homes, their professions, their loved ones – to follow their king to the edges of the known world. And now they were expected to merely look on as a small group of officers decided the future of their hard-won gains. With an irrepressible desire to prioritise their own interests in this tumultuous time, tensions rapidly heightened in the courtyard.

Suddenly the soldiers' impatience became too much to bear. Desiring to be included in the decision-making process, they burst through into the council, demanding they know what options their commanders were considering.[15]

The generals had no choice but to comply. Perdiccas and the other commanders lacked the brawn to force the intruders back and the soldiers showed no desire to depart voluntarily. In the blink of an eye the meeting had transformed from a private conclave into a very public assembly.[16]

After the situation had settled Perdiccas rose to his feet and stepped forward, placing Alexander's signet ring in full view of their new audience. The Macedonians fell silent and Perdiccas put forward his proposal for the succession.

The unborn heir

When Alexander died the Macedonian king had left no legitimate, living sons to succeed him, but that did not tell the whole story. Throughout his reign Alexander had embraced polygamy, a tradition long favoured by Macedonian kings that included his father, and forebear, King Philip II. As with Philip, these multiple marriages almost always primarily served diplomatic purposes – to help create strong, stable alliances with other powerful families both within and outside Macedonia's borders.

Alexander had made one such marriage with Roxana, the daughter of Oxyartes, a nobleman who held great sway in one of the empire's most distant, unstable regions. Although there is plausible argument that Alexander married Roxana primarily for love, the diplomatic benefits of the marriage are clear. Their union had increased Alexander's standing among his Asian subjects and also secured Oxyartes' vital support.[17] Though little is heard of her in the immediate years after her marriage, Roxana was present in Babylon at the time of Alexander's death. Most importantly, she was at least seven months pregnant.

The chances of infant mortality were high; according to one source Roxana had already born Alexander a son in India, only for him to die soon after.[18] Nevertheless for Perdiccas and the rest of the generals in June 323, Roxana's pregnancy provided potential for a legitimate heir to Alexander's throne. With this in mind, Perdiccas proposed to the troops that they await the birth of Roxana's child. If it proved a son, they would prepare him for the throne and crown him Alexander's true successor when he came of age. To manage matters of state in the meantime they would instate a regency.[19]

We can presume all the bodyguards had roughly agreed on this proposal prior to summoning the other generals for the meeting, though questions surrounding the exact nature of the regency remained.[20] Perdiccas no doubt wished himself to become sole, all-powerful regent, but for that he needed the support of his unwelcome military audience.[21] It failed to materialise. As they heard the full-extent of Perdiccas' proposal, the infantry's response was lukewarm at best. The Macedonians were not in the mood for waiting another two months for something shrouded in uncertainty. They wanted a resolution to the crisis now and showed Perdiccas little support – a huge blow for the latter.[22]

As Perdiccas floundered, other commanders sensed opportunity. They became emboldened to put forward their own ambitious suggestions to the Macedonian rank and file. It was at that moment that the ambitions of these 'princes' began to surface.

The bastard

Nearchus, Alexander's much-loved Cretan admiral, was the first to stand. The man was certainly no bodyguard, no *somatophylax*, but he held a senior rank in the military and, perhaps most importantly, he had a close relationship with the recently-deceased king.[23] All of this increased Nearchus' status and emboldened him to stand up and put forward his proposal.

Alexander's unborn child with Roxana was not the only possible candidate for the kingdom's throne. The king did have another son, then aged 4 or 5 and living in Pergamum, a city situated near Asia Minor's western seaboard. His name was Heracles, the illegitimate child of Alexander and a Greco-Persian noblewoman called Barsine. Prior to her relationship with Alexander, Barsine had been the wife of Memnon of Rhodes, perhaps Alexander's most formidable foe. Given the extraordinary times, Nearchus proposed they summon Heracles to Babylon and crown him king without delay.[24]

The admiral believed his proposal provided an immediate solution to the crisis and would break the deadlock. But it had two fatal flaws.

The first was Nearchus' clear-cut agenda. The previous year, at a magnificent ceremony in Susa, Alexander had orchestrated the marriage of his most senior subordinates to some of the highest-standing noblewomen in Asia as role models for his contentious project to unite his European and Asian subjects. Nearchus was among the chosen commanders; Alexander betrothed to his favoured admiral the daughter of Mentor, a high standing Rhodian mercenary general who had served under preceding Achaemenid rulers. Most importantly however, this unnamed maiden was also the daughter of Barsine, Heracles' mother who had been married to Mentor before Memnon (Mentor had died in c.340). For those in Babylon, the true intentions behind Nearchus' proposal were transparently clear: with Heracles as king he aimed to use his close familial connection to the monarch to achieve a senior position in the new regime. It was a power play.[25] Perdiccas, Ptolemy, Lysimachus and the other commanders in Babylon knew this all too well.

Nearchus' proposal immediately raised the ire of his fellow leaders, and worse was to follow. Nearchus had misread a crucial reason why the Macedonians had so firmly rejected Perdiccas' previous proposition. He had rightly realised the soldiery did not want any further uncertainty – they demanded a solution there and then. What Nearchus' did not realise, however, was their other reason for rejecting of Perdiccas' proposal.

A feeling of racial superiority over Alexander's Asian subjects – 'the vanquished' – was deeply ingrained among these troops and many were highly-averse to naming Heracles as their new king. They did not want this illegitimate half-Asian child, who had never set foot in the Macedonian heartlands, as Alexander's successor.[26] To them, it was an insult.

Great shouts of anger and resentment rang through the courtyard as Nearchus put forward his proposal. The admiral persisted, yet as he continued to speak in support of his ill-thought-through plan, the voices of opposition grew louder and more vociferous – the infantry vehemently clashing their spears and shields together in opposition. Eventually the disheartened Nearchus saw no option but to retrace his steps and sat down.[27]

The council

So far the army assembly had proven highly-hostile to the motions the generals had put forward, but another *strategos* soon sensed opportunity.

Ptolemy, having witnessed the uproar and anger the soldiers had shown towards Nearchus and Perdiccas, stood up to propose his preferred idea. Unlike the shouted-down Nearchus, Ptolemy fully understood why the soldiers were so angry. He slated the proposals of his predecessors, shunning them for wanting the Macedonians to serve under a half-Asian, semi-'barbaric' ruler. Instead Ptolemy proposed a radical new idea: he suggested they put aside the monarchy and form a committee to rule the empire, filled by Alexander's closest friends. Gathered in front of Alexander's throne in the royal tent Ptolemy proposed the most famous faces in Alexander's entourage decide affairs of state and rule the fledgling empire.[28]

The proposal provided Ptolemy a degree of support among the other officers, although it was not universal. Already the seeds for a rivalry between Ptolemy and Perdiccas had been sown and the former had only added fuel to the fire with his proposal.

Prior to the meeting it is likely Ptolemy had supported Perdiccas' proposal to await the birth of Roxana's child, although he remained determined to ensure his rival did not become the uncontested chief authority in the meantime.[29] That was until, however, the soldiers had burst into the meeting and forced the generals to continue discussions in public. Upon seeing the soldiers' outrage at the prospects of either delay and/or a half-Asian successor, Ptolemy had decided to change tack. Now was his chance not only to sabotage Perdiccas' plans for power, but also to entrench his position as a prominent player in the kingdom.[30]

For Perdiccas it was a stab in the back. He looked on helplessly as the soldiers started to shout their support for Ptolemy's proposal of a great council. Ptolemy's faction was winning the argument and the audience, but then another of the adjutants stood up. The shouts subsided and Aristonous walked forwards.

King Perdiccas?

Although arguably the least well-known of the seven bodyguards who outlived Alexander the Great, Aristonous evoked seniority among the generals in Babylon. Hailing from the Macedonian heartlands, his career as one of Alexander's chief advisors had been lengthy. It seems likely he had served as a *strategos* in the Macedonian army since as far back as the 340s/350s – when Philip II was in the midst of transforming Macedonia into the hegemonic power.

We know little about Aristonous' career during Alexander's reign, although one fleeting, heroic action of his survives – documented by Curtius. According to the later Roman historian, Aristonous was one of four soldiers who saved Alexander from the jaws of death during an assault on an Indian stronghold.[31]

By 323 Aristonous had gained a reputation similar in stature to the beloved Craterus: a dependable and 'traditional' adjutant, who always placed the interests of Macedonia and its monarchy above all else. The man epitomised a loyal, seasoned veteran.

Addressing the crowd Aristonous put forward his proposal:

When Alexander was asked to whom he was leaving his kingdom…he had expressed the wish that the best man be chosen, and yet he had himself adjudged Perdiccas to be the best by handing him the ring… Alexander had looked around and selected the man to give the ring to from the crowd of his friends. It followed that he wished supreme power to pass to Perdiccas.[32] – Curtius 10.6.16–18

As the veteran bodyguard finished his speech, a huge roar erupted among the Macedonians. Support for Ptolemy's previous proposal was blown out of the water; Aristonous and the soldiers urged Perdiccas to stand up and accept the kingship. They had reached their decision.[33]

Hesitantly Perdiccas stood up once more. Although not an Argead he had a well-known blood link to the Macedonian royal house and his support among the infantry and several prominent officers was clear to see. So why hesitate? According to Curtius he did so merely to feign modesty and increase the vigour of the soldiers' demands that he accept the kingship.[34] This, however, seems highly questionable. Scholars have pointed out the scene's striking similarity to a popular event in Roman history: in 14 AD the Emperor Tiberius had similarly hesitated when offered the emperorship, only to take it after persistence – an event which had almost certainly occurred during Curtius' own lifetime.[35] This seems too convenient an historical parallel. Unlike Tiberius, Perdiccas lacked the universal support to enjoy such a coronation. Significant opposition remained. Ptolemy and his supporters, who until only minutes earlier had seemingly taken control of proceedings, passively objected to the idea and formed a powerful base of opposition.

Outside of Babylon too, there was a strong possibility that several prominent figures would not take kindly to Perdiccas ascending the throne: Craterus and his 10,000 veteran Macedonians in Cilicia, Antigonus the One-Eyed, the powerful governor of Phrygia, Antipater the viceroy of Europe, and not to mention Roxana's influential father Oxyartes in the East. If he accepted the kingship Perdiccas knew there was the chance that at least one, if not all, would class him a usurper, and with Ptolemy's backing.[36]

Despite his desire to accept Aristonous' popular proposal, Perdiccas knew it was a poisoned chalice. Macedonian kingship was a messy matter and history had proven time and time again that the monarch's success depended on having strong relationships with his subjects: with the nobility, with the soldiers and with the kingdom's external allies. Perdiccas may have had support from the soldiers and some officers, but Ptolemy's hostility combined with the unknown reaction of several prominent figures throughout the empire, ensured Perdiccas felt he lacked enough support to wear the royal diadem. By accepting the kingship he knew he would be signing his own death warrant. If he could achieve the position of regent, however, then that was a different story. Then he could use his authority to cement his power base behind a façade of the king; then he could more carefully pave the way for taking the crown. Obtaining the regency was Perdiccas' aim in June 323; obtaining the kingship was not – at least not yet. So Perdiccas stepped back, spurning the calls of Aristonous and the infantry.[37]

Enter Meleager

As Perdiccas withdrew, shouts of encouragement among the infantry immediately turned to anger and resentment. Their preferred candidate had refused the kingship; once more indecision abounded. It was then that one officer among the rank and file decided to take matters into his own hands.

His name was Meleager. He had served as an officer in the Macedonian army since the reign of Philip II and had gained great respect among the infantry. Throughout Alexander's campaigns he had commanded one of the core phalanx battalions, though he had never risen further. This had likely resulted from his turbulent relationship with Alexander.

After a sumptuous banquet one night in 326, Alexander had showered his royal Indian host with a series of lavish gifts, as reward for his loyalty and hospitality. Alexander's actions drew the ire of an inebriated Meleager,

> …(he) offered (Alexander) his congratulations on having at least found in India a man worth 1,000 talents. – Curtius 8.12.17

It was not a clever move. Only three years before, a drunken, verbal attack on Alexander by Cleitus 'the Black', one of Alexander's highest subordinates,

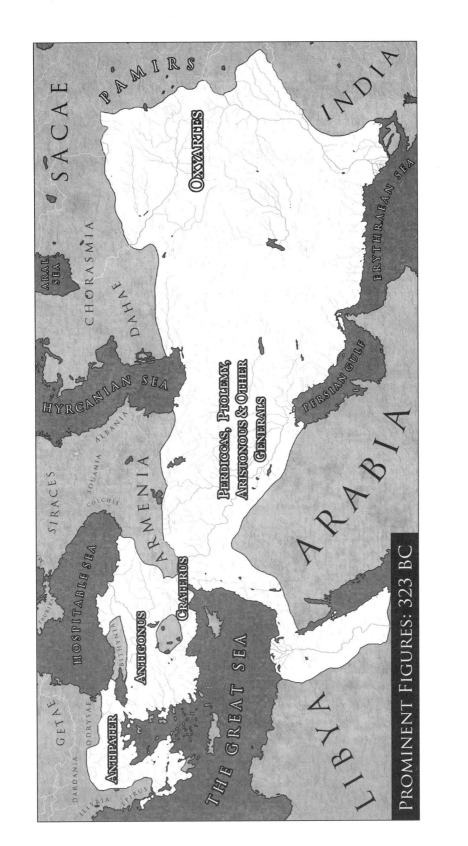

PROMINENT FIGURES: 323 BC

had resulted in the general's swift murder at the king's hand. Meleager proved more fortunate. Remembering the remorse he had felt after murdering Cleitus, Alexander let the commander's drunken quip slide, but he did not forget. *Envious men only torment themselves* he had replied, and it proved so. Throughout the rest of Alexander's reign Meleager had watched on as other commanders ascended to more senior positions, only for himself to remain among the shadows of the mediocre.[38]

Meleager's position as a battalion commander in June 323 meant he was not senior enough a general to receive an invite to the bodyguards' conclave. Nevertheless his event-filled military career and high reputation among the men ensured he represented the most authoritative voice among the irritated infantry. The rank and file looked to Meleager. Now was his moment.

Emboldened by the current crisis, Meleager stood up to address his comrades. Like Ptolemy before him Meleager had noticed the anger the soldiery felt towards delay and indecision; he also similarly had a strong aversion to serving under Perdiccas.

In one of the most remarkable condemnations of the age, Meleager delivered his damning reproach of Perdiccas:

> *God forbid that Alexander's fortune and the dignity of so great a throne come upon such shoulders! Men certainly will not tolerate it. I am not talking about those of better birth than this fellow, merely about men who do not have to suffer anything against their will. In fact, it makes no difference whether your king be Roxana's son (whenever he is born) or Perdiccas, since that fellow is going to seize the throne anyway by pretending to act as regent. That is why the only king he favours is one not yet born, and in the general haste to resolve matters – a haste which is as necessary as it is understandable – he alone is waiting for the months to elapse, already predicting that a male has been conceived! Could you doubt that he is ready to find a substitute? God in heaven, if Alexander had left us this fellow as king in his stead, my opinion would be that this is the one order of his that should not be obeyed.* – Curtius 10.6.20–23

In no uncertain terms Meleager had correctly called out Perdiccas' desired outcome. He interpreted Perdiccas' wish to await the birth of Roxana as a clear power-play. How Perdiccas aimed to become the supreme power in the empire both as they awaited the birth and, if the child proved a son, during the ensuing regency. Meleager had called out what Ptolemy, Laomedon and the rest of the 'anti-Perdiccas' faction had been fearing: Perdiccas had a plan to seize the throne.

The damnation was an extraordinary statement for an insignificant infantry officer to make, especially one whom Alexander the Great had previously disgraced. It was, however, an extraordinary time and Meleager, with the wind behind his sails, did not stop there.

After objecting to Perdiccas' ambitions in the strongest possible terms the battalion commander now exploited another of the infantry's desires: pay. The seemingly limitless wealth of the Persian Empire was within reach – wealth they had earned by the spear. In true demagogue fashion Meleager, having already riled the infantry into large clamours against a traitorous Perdiccas, announced they go and seize the plunder Alexander had promised them. With that Meleager left the meeting – dozens of supporters in tow.[39]

The unknown soldier

Meleager's speech once again flipped the assembly's mood. The infantry general had successfully exploited the soldiers' resentment for both delay and lack of pay. Anarchy seemed imminent.

So far the generals at the assembly had proposed two possible candidates for the throne with a direct link to Alexander the Great: Nearchus' proposal of the illegitimate Heracles and Perdiccas' proposal to await the birth of Roxana's child. But there was another candidate. Up to that point no-one had mentioned the man's name at the meeting. That was, however, until Meleager's impassioned speech brought the men to the brink of rioting.

Heartened by Meleager's effective intervention, a member of the Macedonian rank and file readied his proposal.[40] He was nothing special – Curtius mentions no rank, nor a name. He was an *ignotus*, an unknown. Nevertheless the infantryman shouted out his suggestion.

> *What's the point of fighting and starting a civil war when you have the king you seek? You are forgetting Philip's son, Arrhidaeus, brother of our late king Alexander; recently he accompanied the king in performing our religious ceremonies and now he is sole heir….If you are looking for someone just like Alexander you will never find him; if you want his next of kin there is only this man.* – Curtius 10.7.1–2[41]

As the *ignotus* finished speaking silence suddenly seized the entire assembly. Conflicting emotions appeared among the audience – agreement among the infantry, despair among the generals. Despite the *ignotus'* words Perdiccas, Ptolemy and the rest of the commanders had not forgotten about Arrhidaeus. How could they? The man was the elder half-brother of Alexander the Great – his father was King Philip II; his mother was Philinna of Larissa, a Thessalian noblewoman.

In Arrhidaeus' early years Philip had started grooming him as his potential successor to the Macedonian throne. This all changed, however, when the boy's health had suddenly started to dramatically deteriorate, leaving the young prince simple-minded, incapable of ruling. Arrhidaeus' illness marginalised his significance. He became an almost invisible figure. Neglected from public affairs. Cared for, but glossed over.

Everyone knew Arrhidaeus would struggle to rule effectively. Throughout his adult life, the man had shown no desire for the kingship; Alexander had never considered him either a threat or a potential successor.[42] His generals had thought the same. In a rare show of unity at this tumultuous time they had agreed before the meeting that Alexander's simple-minded half-brother was neither fit nor capable to rule. The *ignotus'* intervention, however, ensured this was all about to change following 12 June 323.

Coming to blows

Despite the generals' efforts to placate their audience's demands for Arrhidaeus, support for Alexander's half-brother only increased. Meleager, when he heard of the proposal, seized the initiative. Desiring to further erode Perdiccas' power, and at the same time elevate himself to a prominent position in the new regime, he returned to the meeting with Arrhidaeus in tow.

Ptolemy, Aristonous, Nearchus, Perdiccas and the rest of the generals could only look on as they saw the unwanted Arrhidaeus being led in blissful ignorance into the assembly's presence behind Meleager. They watched as the soldiers saluted him king, titled him Philip after his beloved father, and departed the courtyard that had just recently witnessed almost-anarchical scenes.[43]

The generals were stunned. The one thing none of them had foreseen to be the meeting's outcome had happened, and it was their fault. Their divisions and indecisiveness had emboldened Alexander's veterans to take matters into their own hands. If they were to fix the situation they realised they had to form a united front. Now was the time to compromise.[44]

Perdiccas knew this all too well – he had to make concessions on his own ambitions if they were to agree a compromise that had any chance of success with the infantry.[45] Meleager, Ptolemy and their respective supporters had already proved solid bases of opposition to his authority in the new regime – opposition that Perdiccas and his supporters knew they had to quell if they were to put down this 'mutiny'.

Peithon, another of Alexander's most senior subordinates, stepped forwards with a solution. Still he proposed they await the birth of Roxana's child (a prolonged Arrhidaeus kingship was not in their interests) but rather than there being one, all-powerful regent, he proposed they divide this power between Perdiccas *and* another military hero: Leonnatus. Together they would serve as 'tutors' for the young prince, who would observe them as they jointly managed affairs in Asia. In Europe meanwhile Craterus and Antipater – two of the most prominent Macedonians outside of Babylon – would rule these western provinces on the boy's behalf.[46]

Peithon's proposal curbed Perdiccas' power enough for the generals to reach agreement.[47] Even Ptolemy and his supporters – who only recently had denounced Roxana's unborn child as unfit to adorn the royal robes – accepted the compromise. Indeed Ptolemy's 'falling back in line' revealed his true fear. Half-Asian or no, the lineage of Alexander's successor was not as important to him as preventing Perdiccas from becoming the supreme authority. Presumably Ptolemy and his supporters made it perfectly clear they were willing to await the birth of Roxana's child, but only as long as Perdiccas had his power shared with Leonnatus.

Having finally reached agreement Perdiccas and the rest of the generals swore an oath of loyalty to Roxana's future child and prepared to announce their solution to the infantry. Of course the compromise hedged its entire existence on Roxana's child being a boy, but it is here that Meleager's demagogic speech had called out the truth:

Could you doubt that he (Perdiccas) is ready to find a substitute?

The generals would announce a male heir at any cost.[48]

Perdiccas, Ptolemy, Peithon and the rest of the generals knew that the success of their compromise relied on prying enough of the Macedonian infantry away from Meleager's faction. They knew the battalion commander and his supporters would refute their proposal there and then: Meleager rested his hopes on Alexander's simple step-brother and would no doubt insist on Arrhidaeus retaining his crown – something the generals had no intention of allowing. It was the soldiers themselves that the commanders hoped to convince. If they could pry away enough of Meleager's support, then they could deal with the troublesome battalion commander and his withering supporters without problem. All depended on their proposal's success.

It failed. Despite some initial wavering, in the end the Macedonian infantry remained loyal to the newly-instated Philip Arrhidaeus. Meleager's support stood firm while any remaining respect for Alexander's generals continued to deteriorate. The generals' refusal to even consider Arrhidaeus as king enraged the rank and file – an anger that Meleager and his followers enflamed with their rhetoric. How dare the generals swear an oath to a king other than their own – a treasonous offence![49] Riled up, the soldiers gathered their weapons,

...beating on their shields with their spears and ready to glut themselves with the blood of those who had aspired to a throne to which they had no claim. – Curtius 10.7.14

Meleager took full advantage. Equipping his arms and armour, he marched alongside Arrhidaeus at the front of the infantry column, proclaiming himself a leading member of the king's entourage in all but name. Now was the time to rid themselves of the self-interested generals.

Once again the scene was set for a showdown within the Royal Palace. Casting aside previous differences Ptolemy, Perdiccas and their supporters retreated to the chamber where Alexander's lifeless body still lay and bolted the doors. In total the defenders numbered some 600 men, but thousands of the most feared soldiers in Asia, hungry for blood, were approaching. Quickly they stormed into the chamber, Philip Arrhidaeus and Meleager leading the way. A vicious struggle erupted. Men fell to the ground with gaping wounds metres away from the legendary Alexander's corpse. The king had died barely forty-eight hours earlier, yet already Macedonian blood stained the floors of his chamber as two sides struggled for control. It was symbolic of the next forty years to come.[50]

The crisis deepens

The Cavalry	The Infantry
Perdiccas (the chiliarch)	Meleager
Ptolemy	Attalus
Nearchus	King Philip Arrhidaeus III
Aristonous	
Seleucus	
Alcetas	
Eumenes	
Peithon	
Lysimachus	
Leonnatus	
Laomedon	
Peucestas	

Diagram highlighting the two sides in the Babylon Crisis. The 'Infantry', led by Meleager, and the 'Cavalry', led by Perdiccas and the other generals.

Eventually the blood lust of the Macedonian infantry turned to remorse. The men they were attacking, these were the generals who had inspired them to success in countless battles. These were the men who had most closely emulated

Alexander's charismatic leadership style. Tempering their harsh rhetoric, they pleaded with Perdiccas, Ptolemy and the rest to lay down their arms and cease fighting. Meleager, seeing his troops stop their attack, followed suit. Relieved, Perdiccas agreed an end to the palatial clash. Swords were sheathed; the first fight of the post-Alexander period was over. But it was merely a ceasefire.[51]

Animosity between the two sides festered, particularly between Meleager and the generals. So long as the likes of Perdiccas, Ptolemy and the rest still breathed, Meleager knew his position would remain under threat. He had to rid himself of them. The only question was how?

As he considered how best to see this through, Meleager demanded his former foes remain in the chamber. But Ptolemy, Leonnatus, Peithon and the rest had no intention of being at Meleager's mercy. At the first opportunity they escaped, out of the Royal Palace and from Babylon altogether. Along with their supporters they pitched camp on the plains between Babylon and the Euphrates River to reorganise and solidify their strength. Perdiccas was the exception; he had decided to remain in Babylon. The infantry's pleas within the royal chamber had shown him that many still held a great deal of respect for their charismatic commander in chief. He remained confident that he could pry them from Meleager's grasp.[52] Meleager, however, was all-too-aware. He knew Perdiccas' continued presence within the city walls was the greatest threat to his newfound authority. But now, it seemed the gods had given him the perfect opportunity. Perdiccas – devoid of allies – was vulnerable.

That night Perdiccas awoke to find a large band of men waiting for him outside his quarters – weapons drawn. Meleager had sent them to drag Perdiccas before him in the name of the king. Perdiccas faced a dilemma; it wasn't difficult to grasp the group's true purpose. If he complied, he knew he would almost certainly not survive the night. Yet if he hesitated Meleager had given the soldiers express orders to kill him there and then. It was a death squad.

Perdiccas chose defiance. Standing in front of his intended assassins he proved to everyone why Alexander had rated him so highly as a leader throughout his campaigns.

> *He berated the messengers, time and time again calling them 'Meleager's lackeys', and the determination which showed in his expression so terrified them that they fled in panic.* – Curtius 10.8.3

Through impassioned words Perdiccas had impressively survived the assassination attempt, but it highlighted the great peril he faced if he remained in Babylon any longer. Without delay he mounted his horse and rode out of Babylon to join Ptolemy, Leonnatus and the other generals on the plain.[53]

Thousands of soldiers greeted Perdiccas as he arrived at the camp. In the meantime, his fellow generals had amassed significant support among the remaining contingents of Alexander's army.[54] The famed Macedonian Companion Cavalry – that consisted of soldiers recruited from the higher-echelons of Macedonian society – had remained steadfast in their loyalty to the generals. The same was true for Alexander's Asian battalions. By 323 these units far outnumbered the Macedonian contingents in size and strength. Included among them were some of the finest cavalrymen in the whole of Asia, hailing from noble Oriental families; Alexander had integrated these horsemen into his mounted Macedonian squadrons to form the most feared cavalry force in the world.[55]

The Asian infantry was equally formidable. During Alexander's conquest of the Persian Empire his Macedonian infantry and their perfected phalanx had developed a reputation as one of the world's most formidable fighting forces; no infantry force – Greek mercenaries, Thracian peltasts or Persian Shield Bearers – could seemingly match them on the open field.

By 323 however, a challenge to their dominance had arisen. The previous year 30,000 Asian infantrymen had joined the Royal Army. For 36 months veteran Macedonian instructors had relentlessly drilled these youths to fight in the Macedonian fashion. Equipped with c.6-metre-long *sarissa* pikes and honed to fight in dense phalanx formations they were Alexander's Asian equivalent to his veteran Macedonians. He had called them the *epigoni*, literally the 'successors'. Alexander's intention to have them replace his withering Macedonian infantry as his main force of footmen had drawn the ire of Meleager and his men. The feeling was mutual. These elite 30,000-strong infantrymen had no love for their hostile, anti-Asian Macedonian counterparts.[56]

Alongside the cavalry and the *epigoni* were several other striking Asian contingents that had pinned their colours to the generals' cause: 20,000 Persian skirmishers equipped with either bows or barbed javelins, swift horse archers from the steppes between the Caspian and Aral Seas and a powerful division of battle-hardened Indian war elephants. It was a formidable force, easily capable of annihilating Meleager's infantry.[57]

Perdiccas, Ptolemy, Leonnatus and the rest of the generals now started to use their newfound military strength to their advantage. They took command of the entire area outside Babylon's walls and cut off the city's supply routes. Babylon was under siege.

Anger grows

It was not long before dissent started to grow among the Macedonians within Babylon. A large portion of the soldiers – including some officers – still held great respect for Perdiccas and when they discovered that Meleager had orchestrated an attempt on Perdiccas' life, great anger erupted among them.[58]

A leading man behind this outrage would have been Alcetas. At the time of Alexander's death Alcetas commanded one of the Macedonian phalanx battalions; he was a senior figure among the heavy infantrymen. He was also Perdiccas' brother. Loyal to his elder sibling, Alcetas had opposed Meleager's authority, but had remained in Babylon to use his position to subtly undermine his control. His senior position among the infantry presumably provided him protection – security from Meleager, whose power depended upon avoiding internal strife among the footmen.[59]

Alcetas was not the only leading figure in Babylon attempting to subvert Meleager's authority. Eumenes, Alexander's former personal secretary, had remained in Babylon as the crisis escalated. He presented himself as a neutral figure in the *stasis*, citing his non-Macedonian birth. In fact he was acting as Perdiccas' agent.[60] Having gained the respect and admiration of the infantry – who perhaps even believed he was on their side – Eumenes urged the footmen to avoid letting this turn into all-out civil war. Instead, he encouraged compromise: open negotiations with their former generals.

Eumenes' pleas worked. Quickly Macedonian hearts turned away from Meleager and started to lean towards a negotiated settlement with their former comrades. Meleager was losing control, and in this time when inspiring leadership was essential he failed to rise to the occasion. For three days he pondered what to do, aloof from proceedings, as Eumenes, Alcetas and their supporters continued to erode the commander's influence. It proved crucial. Convinced through the power of persuasion, the infantry decided to take matters into their own hands once more. With Meleager nowhere in sight they agreed that a negotiated end to the conflict was in their best interests. They dispatched three emissaries, under the authority of King Philip Arrhidaeus III, to treat with the generals on the plain outside Babylon.[61]

They received a cold reception. Emboldened by their great strength and the discord sown among the infantry, the generals refused to negotiate. There would be no notion of compromise, unless the soldiers brought Meleager and the rest of the revolt's ringleaders to them in chains.[62] It was a bold demand, but recent events had convinced the generals that Meleager's support had withered, significantly so. Indeed they had good reason for thinking so. In the past days the generals had successfully persuaded Attalus, the most prominent infantry commander supporting Meleager, to join them. Through the mediation of either

Alcetas or Eumenes, Perdiccas had offered this seasoned warrior Atalante, his sister, in marriage to secure his loyalty. Seeing the tides of fortune were starting to shift in Perdiccas' favour, Attalus had quickly accepted.[63]

For the generals Attalus' defection was a great coup, further cementing their belief that Meleager's authority among the rank and file had all but evaporated.[64] They were gravely mistaken. As the emissaries returned and announced the generals' non-negotiable terms to the army assembly, widespread rage erupted among the infantry. Adamantly, they refused to hand over Meleager and instead readied their arms and armour for a heroic, final stand. Battle seemed imminent.[65]

Perdiccas the peace broker

The envoys had not returned to the assembly alone, however. As distress started to seize the room, the general accompanying them stepped forward. It was Perdiccas.

Just as he had been when he refused to leave Babylon with the rest of the generals a few days earlier, Perdiccas remained confident he could convince the infantry to throw off Meleager's over-arching control and prevent bloodshed. All he needed was the opportunity to make his address to the infantry. Meleager had thwarted his previous attempts with his hit squad. But now, with his enemy's support waning, Perdiccas saw his chance.

Addressing the assembly Perdiccas made his impassioned plea:

> ...he represented to them the atrocity of their conduct; admonishing them to consider against whom they had taken arms; that they were not Persians, but Macedonians; not enemies, but their own countrymen; most of them their kinsmen, but certainly all of them their fellow soldiers, sharers of the same camp and of the same dangers; that they would present a striking spectacle to their enemies, who would rejoice at the mutual slaughter of those whose arms they grieved at having been conquered; and that they would atone with their own blood to the manes of their slaughtered adversaries. – Justin 13.3.8–10[66]

The infantry sheathed their swords; Perdiccas' plea had struck deep. He had averted all-out bloodshed and had regained the respect of the infantry. Perdiccas now proposed a new compromise to heal the rift.

The key to any compromise, both parties knew, revolved around Arrhidaeus' kingship. Once before Perdiccas and the generals had attempted to ignore the new monarch's legitimacy with anarchical consequences. Perdiccas made sure they would not make the same mistake again; reluctantly recognising the soldiers' choice of Arrhidaeus as king was critical. Perdiccas had given ground on this issue, but on one major condition. He demanded that they name Roxana's child joint-king alongside Arrhidaeus, if Alexander's queen bore a son.[67]

The army assembly approved the generals' compromise, but several matters still loomed large before they could seal the agreement. Who would obtain the most prominent positions in the new regime? Most pressingly, who would receive the title of *prostates*?

This title (effectively the office of regent) offered the holder an extraordinary position – the highest in the empire beneath the king himself. Throughout Macedonian history the office had only existed when a king – due to either illness or youth – proved unable to manage affairs without aid.[68] Arrhidaeus' low level of understanding epitomised the need for such a role and Perdiccas, Meleager and the other figures in Babylon knew it. Whoever held the position of *prostates* would dictate decisions of state. Whoever became *prostates* would hold true power.

Perdiccas longed for the position, but he did not dare propose he assume it. Meleager's faction still maintained a degree of influence among the infantry and Perdiccas knew his enemies would prove highly hostile to such a compromise if he became *prostates*, the chief authority. So Perdiccas proposed another to receive the regency, a man who's loyalty to the Macedonian royal house seemed beyond question: Craterus.[69]

It was a wise choice. The great love and respect that the infantry held for the absent Craterus ensured Meleager and the army assembly soon approved Perdiccas' proposed compromise; Perdiccas' efforts had avoided all-out civil war.

Perdiccas' peacemaker efforts were soon rewarded. Having regained wide respect among the infantry, the rank and file clamoured that he retain his position as their commander-in-chief. Perdiccas agreed; his remarkable success both at de-escalating heightened tensions and at being able to compromise had allowed him to regain command over the world's most feared army.[70]

Perdiccas however made one further concession. To heal the last elements of division he appointed Meleager as his second-in-command. The man who only days before had ordered Perdiccas' cold-blooded murder now served as his highest-ranking subordinate.[71]

The generals and the infantry duly ratified the compromise Perdiccas had orchestrated before the body of Alexander the Great, 'so that its majesty would witness their decision'.[72] The army outside Babylon lifted the siege; civil war was at an end. Several had gained a lot from the struggle – Meleager and his supporters most notably. Others had lost out, particularly among the generals – their preferred outcomes having evaporated due to the need for compromise.[73] It appeared a clear diplomatic victory for Meleager's faction. But for Perdiccas and the generals, there was method in their madness. They knew something their former opponents did not.

Perdiccas had secured Meleager's trust and the appointment of Craterus as official *prostates* only increased Meleager's belief that his new position was secure. Meleager and Craterus had both commanded battalions during Alexander's campaigns; they had fought side by side in the infantry line and likely had an amicable relationship. With Craterus' appointment as regent and himself as Perdiccas' second in command, Meleager's position seemed solid.[74]

It soon proved otherwise.

'Reconciliation'

Dissent lingered. Discontented soldiers fixed their anger on Meleager's sudden (and controversial) rise to prominence. It wasn't long before word reached Meleager and Perdiccas about these pockets of resentment. Meleager was furious. To heal the rift Perdiccas therefore proposed that they hold a traditional 'purification ceremony' of the army on the plain outside Babylon. Its aim: to single-out and make an example of the troublemakers. Meleager agreed.[75]

Perdiccas, Meleager and the rest ensured the ceremony included all the traditional customs, no matter how horrific they may seem today:

> *The customary purification of the soldiers by the Macedonian kings involved cutting a bitch in two and throwing down her entrails on the left and right at the far end of the plain into which the army was to be led.* – Curtius 10.9.12

Thousands of soldiers formed up on the large plain, between the mutilated ends of the female dog.[76] The army included regiments that hailed from all corners of Alexander's huge empire: from the Peloponnese to the Paropamisadae; from Macedonia to Media. Many wielded weapons typical of their own preferred methods of warfare: 6-metre-long *sarissa* pikes, 2-metre-long *doru* spears and *xyston* lances, barbed *mesankuloi* javelins, lightweight composite bows and sharp, double-edged *xiphos* swords to name a few. For those keeping watch atop Babylon's defences it must have been an awesome sight.

At one spot on the plain stood the veteran infantry phalanx, commanded by Meleager. King Philip Arrhidaeus was visible opposite them, leading the royal *agema*, his elite cavalry squadron. Perdiccas had positioned himself next to Arrhidaeus, facing the infantry.

Nearby Arrhidaeus and his *agema* the infantry could see the powerful contingents of Indian war elephants – beasts that could crush man and horse alike under their feet. Most expected they would play no role in the ceremony. They were merely a show of force.

Suddenly the infantry grew restless. They were surrounded by their former opponents, heavily outnumbered and positioned in the centre of a vast plain. For the isolated, outnumbered phalanx the possibility of total annihilation was worryingly possible. A feeling of vulnerability swept through their ranks.[77]

Arrhidaeus, Perdiccas and the cavalry advanced towards the infantry, halting not far in front of the footmen. The King rode forward to address them – Perdiccas by his side.

Meleager watched on as the two figures advanced. It was a welcome moment. Soon the culprits who had complained about his new command would be in his custody, at his mercy. His position would be stronger than ever.

He could not have been more wrong. Meleager watched on as King Philip Arrhidaeus addressed the infantry; he watched on as Perdiccas had his chief supporters drawn out and assembled in the centre of the plain. Something wasn't right. These were certainly not the men who had opposed Meleager's command. Grave concern and confusion must have spread across Meleager's face.

It was only then, all too late, that he realised the true extent of the treachery. Arrhidaeus, at Perdiccas' urging, had sentenced Meleager's stunned followers to death in brutal fashion. The elephants were marched forwards and these thirty ringleaders were trampled to death under the feet of the beasts.[78] Meleager watched on. Helpless. Perdiccas had revealed his true colours. He had always intended to purge the army at the ceremony – a purge of Meleager's chief supporters.

The real intentions of Perdiccas, Leonnatus, Ptolemy and the rest of the generals became clear. They had never intended the compromise they had agreed to be binding. They had merely made these concessions so that they could isolate Meleager and his mutineers. With Perdiccas in *de facto* control of the army and acting chief advisor to the king (as Craterus was hundreds of miles away to the west), the compromise had provided Meleager's faction a false pretence of security. Too late did Meleager realise the generals had no intention of keeping their word. Perdiccas had orchestrated the deception with brutal efficiency – indeed it was he who had secretly instructed certain followers to openly voice their anger at Meleager's rise. He had conducted the infamous ceremony with brutal efficiency.[79]

Meleager had used Arrhidaeus' mental incapacity to be the real power behind the throne only the week before. Now he could only look on as Perdiccas used that tool against him. Before the ceremony had ended he fled. Devoid of allies and support, he hoped to seek sanctuary in a temple. But Perdiccas had no intention of letting him stay alive, and he quickly saw through what Meleager had critically failed to do days earlier. With the king's approval Perdiccas swiftly dispatched a squad to murder Meleager.

No amount of eloquent words from their intended victim dissuaded the ruffians from their duty. Without regard for the temple's sanctity, they stormed in and killed Meleager. The man who had brought the empire to the brink of civil war was no more.[80]

The Babylon Settlement

As his enemy's blood congealed Perdiccas wasted no time carrying through the rest of his plan. His control over Arrhidaeus and the royal army was clear for all to see, albeit stamped with a gruesome show of force. Now he used his newly-gained authority to continue the discussions he and his fellow generals had started over a week earlier. The most senior commanders present assembled to discover what 'prize' postings they would receive in the Empire. They believed this their deserved reward, not just for outliving Alexander the Great but also for backing Perdiccas in the preceding struggle.

With no threat of unwelcome intrusion the generals decided on new positions within the Empire. At the forefront of the agreements was Perdiccas. Quickly his comrades acknowledged him as the new *prostates* for the incapacitated Arrhidaeus. What was more they also agreed that if Roxana's child proved a son, then Perdiccas would serve as guardian for the joint monarch. In no uncertain terms the generals had bestowed the Empire's supreme authority upon Perdiccas. The commander's plan to achieve supremacy had succeeded. And who could have denied him it? It was Perdiccas who had risked his life during the past struggle to achieve reconciliation; it was Perdiccas who had masterminded the deceitful plan to isolate Meleager and his supporters; it was Perdiccas who now had control over the king and, most importantly, the army.

Perdiccas' elevation to regent was merely one of several key decisions the generals had to make. Still looming large was the question of what they should do about the absent Craterus, the *prostates* for less than forty-eight hours, and his 10,000 veterans. For Perdiccas, ensuring Craterus' force continued home to Macedonia was crucial and he quickly convinced the council to name the commander 'joint-viceroy' of Europe alongside Antipater. They dispatched official orders to their comrade's camp in Cilicia: Craterus must continue west to assume his new position. Meanwhile in Babylon Perdiccas' former position of Chiliarch lay vacant. Accepting no-one other than a close ally Perdiccas appointed Seleucus, the commander of the king's elite infantry guard and one of Perdiccas' staunchest supporters, to the position.[81]

Perdiccas and his allies controlled Babylon; the nucleus of the empire seemed secure. But the regent knew support for his faction was not universal. Although he retained the backing of a large number of generals (all hoping for favour, power and high positions in the empire), he was aware that a powerful party required placating. Ptolemy and his companions may have put aside their differences with Perdiccas to unite against Meleager, but now they had quashed this threat and witnessed the extent of Perdiccas' brutality first-hand. They demanded worthy rewards – rich postings in the Empire.

Despite the strength of his support Perdiccas knew he could not afford to become opposed by a large coalition of officers. At a time when throughout the Empire there appeared an abundance of wealth and a seemingly unlimited pool of mercenaries ready to commit their skilled services with spear and shield to the highest bidder, Perdiccas did not want to face a multi-pronged revolt. He had to compromise once again.[82]

The mechanism for this compromise was the redistribution of satrapies (governorships) that the generals then turned their attention towards. Many remained in the hands of governors that had exercised power for several years. These figures were almost immovable, entrenched in their positions due to the strong power bases they had built up: Antigonus in Phrygia, Oxyartes in the Hindu Kush and Peucestas in Persia for instance. Other regions, however, either lay vacant or were commanded by subordinates yet to establish such strong power bases. These were the people Perdiccas could replace.

One such satrapy was Egypt, among the wealthiest, most fertile and most defensible provinces in the entire empire. Cleomenes, a certain infamous Greek from the Hellenic colony of Naucratis on the Nile Delta, currently administered the region, but extortionate governing and a lavish lifestyle ensured his subjects had soon grown to despise him. Perdiccas knew they would welcome a replacement to Cleomenes' corrupt control, as did Ptolemy. The latter had fixed his eyes on acquiring Egypt for some time, recognising its potential as a strong power base, and he requested Perdiccas provide him control of the vital satrapy during the redistribution. Ptolemy had strong support among the officers present; reluctantly, Perdiccas knew he had to agree to Ptolemy's request – but on one condition: the despised Cleomenes must remain in Ptolemy's new administration, he must retain a level of authority over the region's treasury and he must serve as the new governor's second. Perdiccas hoped for friction; he hoped that a disillusioned Cleomenes would serve as his agent, his mole who would watch over Ptolemy and report any actions that may threaten the new regime. Ptolemy was all too aware of this.[83]

With Ptolemy momentarily satisfied, Perdiccas turned to providing several other figures important satrapies within the empire. Laomedon, Ptolemy's friend and supporter, received governorship of Syria – further strengthening Ptolemy's control in the south-east of the Mediterranean; Peithon, Perdiccas' power-hungry 'ally', accepted a large swathe of Media, one of the richest satrapies in the east.

Though debate over the extent of Perdiccas' authority at the time of this redistribution remains, Perdiccas made these above appointments as compromises – 'Perdiccas, in his official capacity as regent, was carrying out the desires of the *principes* (generals)'.[84] Of them all his decision to concede Egypt to Ptolemy was no doubt the one he agreed to with the greatest reluctance. Now that the Babylon Crisis was over, both knew that their greatest threat was the ambition of the other – neither wanted to be subordinate. One can imagine the apparent aggression visible between the two at the meeting.

For now, Perdiccas agreed to Ptolemy's demands – he even agreed that they should send Alexander's body to the Temple of Zeus Ammon at Siwa, Libya.[85] But in Perdiccas' eyes, just as he had done with the infantry the previous week, he only saw these concessions as temporary measures, until he had strengthened his position enough to be rid of his rival in a more permanent manner. And Ptolemy knew it.

Of the twenty-four governorships (satrapies) in the empire, Perdiccas authorised eight new appointments, almost all the appointees having been at the meeting.[86] Of these two further notable recipients include Lysimachus and Leonnatus, highly celebrated commanders that Perdiccas desperately desired to be rid of. Lysimachus was given control of Thrace, the northernmost province of the empire currently in the midst of turmoil; Leonnatus received the strategically vital satrapy of Hellespontine-Phrygia, the gateway to Asia.[87]

Perdiccas provided no such positions for his staunchest supporters however. Aristonous – the man who had previously championed the regent to take the kingship – remained in Babylon as one of Perdiccas' chief advisors, as did his brother Alcetas, and the aforementioned Seleucus.

There was, however, one exception. Eumenes, one of Perdiccas' 'inside men' during the preceding crisis received governorship of Cappadocia in eastern Asia Minor. It was far from an easy posting – the region was a 'Wild West' of the empire, where Macedonian control was non-existent and a powerful Persian nobleman ruled supreme. Nevertheless Perdiccas persisted – tasking Eumenes with winning his satrapy by the spear. To aid him, he placed the legendary Leonnatus in charge of the expedition with a sizable mercenary army and sufficient gold to raise further troops. More on this later.[88]

So the meeting ended; Eumenes, Leonnatus, Ptolemy and the other generals issued with new governorships departed the conclave and the city. For many of them a return to the heat of battle awaited.[89]

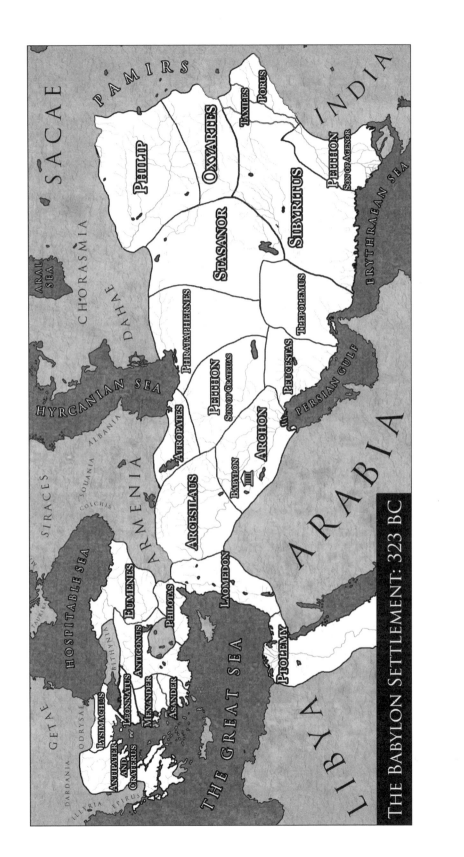

THE BABYLON SETTLEMENT: 323 BC

The Last Plans

Although his road to power had not been easy, Perdiccas had emerged the victor of the first great power struggle that followed Alexander's death. Officially affirmed as regent and with *de facto* control over the king and the royal army, he could now turn his attention to cementing his power and pursuing his own ambitions. There was, however, one last outstanding issue the new *prostates* had to address.

Alexander the Great had left behind his plans for future endeavours, having drawn up designs for several bold projects before his passing.[90] All were extraordinary, affirming Alexander's megalomaniac mindset during the months before his passing. The king had laid out plans, for instance, to build a coastal road with intermittent ports stretching along the entire southern coastline of the Mediterranean to supply his future campaigns against Carthage in the west – from Egypt to the Straits of Gibraltar.

This was the first of many extravagant plans. Alexander had intended his subjects construct a mausoleum for his father Philip that could rival in size and splendour the Great Pyramid of Giza – the tallest building in the world. He had written down orders for the erection of seven new monumental temples, to adorn some of the most prestigious sites and sanctuaries in Hellenic folklore. He had planned for the establishment of even more new cities and for the transportation of populations from Asia to Europe and vice versa, to further his desires for a cosmopolitan Greco-Asian Empire. It was delusion, without limit.

Perdiccas had no desire to attempt fulfilling any of these megalomaniacal plans, and this was especially true for one more than any other.

Prior to his passing Alexander had turned his attention to constructing the largest fleet the Mediterranean had ever seen. Numbering some 1,000 vessels he intended his shipbuilders to construct the great armada in the shipyards of Cilicia and Phoenicia, consisting almost completely of the most modern and heaviest warships of the time, equipped with artillery and manned by the finest sailors in the empire.

By June 323 work on this great fleet was already under way, funded by the seemingly limitless wealth of a Persian treasury at Cyinda in Cilicia. But it was who was supervising this project that concerned Perdiccas the most: none other than Craterus and his 10,000 veterans. Hundreds of ships still needed to be built and there was no guarantee Craterus would obey Perdiccas' order that he continue west to Europe before fulfilling Alexander's final request.[91] Desperate to have Craterus and his force out of Asia as soon as possible, Perdiccas knew he had to officially annul Alexander's last wishes.

Cilicia was situated in today's south-eastern Turkey. Cyinda was situated close to Tarsus.

Once more Perdiccas gathered the royal army. Once again he addressed the Macedonian veterans, eloquently explaining his predicament – how it was not his place to decide alone what they should do with Alexander's last wishes, but that they should make the decision together. With that, he proceeded to read out the list of Alexander's ambitious plans to the assembled crowd.[92]

The soldiers held an unquestionable love for Alexander, but even they could not stomach the extraordinary nature of the king's last plans. In what appears to be universal agreement:

> ...they appreciated how grandiose and impractical the projects were, and they decided not to put any of them into effect. – Diodorus 18.4.6

Again, Perdiccas had successfully reached his desired result through careful political planning. No longer did he need to worry about fulfilling any of Alexander's last plans.

He had enough great schemes of his own.

Further Reading

Primary Sources
Arrian *Events After Alexander* 1.1–1.9A.
Curtius 10.5–10.10.
Diodorus Siculus 18.1–18.6.
Justin 13.1–13.4.
Plutarch *Life of Eumenes* 3.

Secondary Sources
Anson, E. (1992), 'Craterus and the Prostasia', *Classical Philology* 87 (1), 38–43.
Anson, E. (2015), *Eumenes of Cardia*, Leiden, 58–77.
Bosworth, A. B. (2002), *The Legacy of Alexander: Politics, Warfare, and Propaganda under the Successors*, New York, 29–63.
Errington, R. M. (1970), 'From Babylon to Triparadeisos: 323–320 BC', *The Journal of Hellenic Studies* 90, 49–59.
Meeus, A. (2008), 'The Power Struggle of the Diadochoi in Babylon, 323 BC', *Ancient Society* 38, 39–82.
Meeus, A. (2009), 'Some Institutional Problems concerning the Succession to Alexander the Great: "Prostasia" and Chiliarchy', *Historia* 58 (3), 287–310.
Mitchell, L. (2007), 'Born to Rule? Succession in the Argead Royal House', in W. Heckel., L. Tritle and P. Wheatley (eds.), *Alexander's Empire: Formulation to Decay*, California, 61–74.
Worthington, I. (2016), *Ptolemy I: King and Pharaoh of Egypt*, New York, 71–86.

Chapter 2

The Lamian War: Part One

Alexander the Great's untimely death sparked immediate chaos in Babylon, but this was nothing compared to the wide-reaching turmoil this event would provoke further west, in Greece.

In Babylon there had been less than 10,000 rebellious soldiers. In Greece there would be tens of thousands. In Babylon any serious fighting had condensed into a relatively small-scale skirmish, with the standoff itself lasting little more than a week. Whereas in Greece, both on land and at sea, bloody battles would continue for several months, stretching from northern Thessaly to the Athenian heartlands.

This is the story of the Lamian War.

1. The Background 324–June 323

This opening segment is set during the last years of Alexander the Great's reign. Although we are heading slightly back in time, the events which happened then are vital for understanding why the Athenians revolted when Alexander the Great died. It also serves to introduce key figures in the revolt.

Athens and Alexander. Two of the most recognisable names from antiquity. The former a leading city-state that once formed the nucleus of a powerful Aegean empire. The latter a king who conquered the mighty Persian Empire and forged one of the largest kingdoms the World had yet seen. By the time of Alexander however – 336–323 – Athenian power had waned. A disastrous defeat in 338 at the hands of Alexander's father King Philip II of Macedon saw the Athenians reduced to a shadow of their past imperial self, overwhelmed by the military might of Macedon. Throughout Alexander's reign it was the Macedonians that dominated mainland Greece. They were the superpower.

For the Athenians, although difficult to accept, Macedonian overlordship proved far from disastrous. As Alexander campaigned further and further east, large tracts of the Greek mainland continued to enjoy relative independence and stability; Macedonian interference over domestic matters proved largely non-existent. This was especially true of Athens. Between 330 and 324 this prestigious city-state enjoyed a remarkable period of peace and prosperity – a 'Pax Macedonica'. Military, economic and social reforms formed the crux of this city-state's revival, healing a sense of Athenian pride that had been so deeply dented in recent years.[1]

The legacy of Lycurgus

Macedonia's uncontested supremacy provided the Athenians with the vital stability needed for them to rebuild their city's strength, but it was the shrewd stewardship of one particular Athenian that ensured this dramatic revival.[2] His name was Lycurgus, one of Athens' most cherished public figures during the latter half of the fourth century. Lycurgus had staunchly opposed the emergence of Macedonian hegemony on the Greek mainland and this opposition continued into the reign of Alexander. Still, Athenian faith in Lycurgus never faltered. When Alexander had demanded they hand Lycurgus over in 335 – following the failed Theban revolt – Lycurgus' countrymen refused to surrender him.[3]

Lycurgus would be sure to repay his countrymen's faith in full. For twelve years – between 336 and 324 – he oversaw a remarkable rebuilding and rearmament programme in Athens. Implementing radical reforms he revitalised the Athenian economy, selling off public land to private individuals and centring Athenian state revenue on individual benefaction and benevolence. It worked. Patriotic private land owners contributed substantial sums to the Athenian state, helping increase Athens' public revenue to 1,200 talents per year. This was an extraordinary sum – over twice the amount Athens had received from its allies when at the height of its power over 100 years earlier. Lycurgus' economic reforms breathed new life into a recently subjugated, demoralised Athens. He did not stop there.[4]

When Lycurgus became treasurer general in 338 the Athenian army was in desperate need of attention, having recently been decisively outclassed and overwhelmed by the Macedonian 'New Model Army' at the Battle of Chaeronea. Lycurgus had quickly set about addressing this. Using Athens' new-found wealth, citizens were enlisted, train and armed. By 323 the number of militia men Lycurgus and the Athenians could summon numbered over 5,000. These hoplites – heavy infantrymen equipped with spear and shield for a traditional type of fighting centuries old – epitomised the Athenian military revival. They were Athens' response to the feared infantry phalanx of their northern neighbours.[5]

Lycurgus did not restrict his military rebuilding to just the army. During his years in office, he had also devoted years to reconstructing the Athenian fleet, the backbone of its military power. Desiring to revive the famous, dominant Athenian navy of old, Lycurgus oversaw the extension of military docks at the Piraeus, Athens' prestigious, prosperous port. He also had a new maritime arsenal constructed, stocked full with weapons: torsion catapults, spears, stones, bows and arrows. By 324 the Athenian navy consisted of 360 triremes (threes), 50 quadriremes (fours) and 7 quinqueremes (fives) – a formidable fleet. Such was the scale of the rebuilding that even Alexander the Great had sent word to the Athenians, demanding some of these ships join the Macedonian navy. The Athenians refused.[6]

Thanks largely to Lycurgus, between 330 and 324 Athenian strength was revitalised economically and militarily. Macedonian supremacy over mainland Greece had provided Lycurgus the stability required for this dramatic transformation, but nevertheless animosity towards Macedon among certain high standing Athenians continued throughout this 'Pax Macedonica'. Hostile rhetoric remained in the speeches of leading figures like Demosthenes and Lycurgus; elaborate honours were granted to far-away anti-Macedonian warlords.[7]

Resentment towards Macedonian control did not diminish throughout this period of peace and prosperity, but neither was it widespread. Enriched landowners embraced the financial benefits this period of stability offered while certain statesmen such as Callimedon, Demades and Phocion saw the advantages of continued good terms with Macedon and of accepting the *status quo*. Throughout this 'Pax Macedonica' however, opinion remained divided amongst many Athenians. Alexander's rule had brought the city peace and prosperity, but a deep-felt desire for the return of unfettered Athenian democracy ensured that significant anti-Macedonian sentiment remained.[8]

324 – End of the Pax

In early June 324 a prominent figure from Alexander's court had arrived in Greece. His name was Nicanor, the adopted son of Alexander's famous tutor Aristotle. From Athens to Aetolia news of Nicanor's arrival soon became widespread across Greece. Not so much because of Nicanor himself, but because of the mission Alexander had given him.[9]

Earlier that year, following his return from campaigning in India, Alexander had made an unprecedented announcement that was to dramatically affect all Greek city-states under his control. All exiles from these various *poleis* were to be restored to their homelands. Banishments were to be annulled; only temple robbers and murderers were exempt from this amnesty. A seemingly gracious act, but Alexander also had a more underhand intention. This Exiles Decree was designed to hurt Alexander's enemies. To counter and destabilise prominent political groups that were hostile to him.[10]

...he (Alexander) wanted every city to contain a good number of individuals who were loyal to him, in order to counteract the revolutionary and rebellious tendency of the Greeks. – Diodorus 18.8.2

Tens of thousands of exiles would return en masse, and the home governments would have their hands too full with domestic problems to plan or support any military uprising. – Brian Bosworth *Conquest and Empire, 223*

Athens was right at the centre of Alexander's crosshairs, as were those city-states of the Aetolians situated further west. It was the Athenians and Aetolians that formed the two most significant Hellenic powers south of Macedonia. It was they that most threatened Alexander.

Wanting to further cripple their power, Alexander also announced an additional ruling aimed at the Athenians and Aetolians. It concerned the return of foreign territory. Both the Athenians and the Aetolians were guilty of seizing cities; both had driven conquered peoples into exile to suit their own agendas. The Aetolians had exiled the citizens of nearby Oeniadae, having conquered this strategic city in c.330. Meanwhile the Athenians had taken control of the island of Samos in 365, exiling its people and repopulating the island with Athenian settlers.[11]

In both cases the Athenians and Aetolians had resorted to extreme measures and placed whole city populations in exile – two cases of 'ethnic cleansing in antiquity'. Alexander saw opportunity. Demanding the return of these cities

Oeniadae and Samos, prime victims of Aetolian and Athenian expansion during the mid-4th century.

was another avenue through which to attack – and humiliate – the two most powerful states in central Greece. Not to mention he would also be ingratiating himself with the exiled populations.[12]

And so Alexander sent Nicanor to Greece to announce this Exiles Decree at the 324 Olympic Games, held at Olympia in early August. But by the time he reached Greece this festival was still a month and a half away. Nicanor had arrived with plenty of time to spare. Plenty of time during which the purpose of his mission started to spread rapidly across the mainland.[13]

As rumours of Nicanor's purpose circulated, anger erupted in many of these city-states. The decree itself was unprecedented, infringing on the autonomy that Alexander had, until then, largely left unaltered in city-states west of the Aegean Sea. Anti-Macedonian sentiment deepened.[14]

It was in Athens where rumours of Alexander's rulings seem to have struck deepest. Already Athenian exiles were amassing at nearby Megara, anticipating their imminent return to Athens when Nicanor read out the decree. Their return threatened to destabilise all the hard work Lycurgus had overseen over the past decade to rebuild the Athenian economy. This was no doubt concerning for the Athenians, as was the other impending ruling that they surrender Samos. If Alexander had hoped that his decrees would humiliate a proud and resurgent Athens, he was right.[15]

For prominent Athenians like the great statesman Demosthenes a terrifying countdown had started, ticking towards early August when Nicanor would announce Alexander's stability-shattering Exiles Decree. If this wasn't bad enough, it was then that another figure entered the Athenian political fray with an equally destabilising objective. 'When it rains, it pours.'

The fugitive

This man's name was Harpalus. Once close friend and treasurer of Alexander the Great, he was now little more than a fugitive: the most wanted man in the Empire. Harpalus, however, was a powerful rogue. Before he fled Babylon in fear of being punished by Alexander for his decadent ruling, Harpalus had embezzled a small fortune from the royal treasury – 5,000 talents of silver. Over the next few months he used his stolen funds to amass a 6,000 strong mercenary force and thirty ships, before setting sail across the Eastern Mediterranean. His destination: Athens.[16]

For Harpalus, Athens was his ideal refuge. Its revived military power, its economic strength, its animosity towards Alexander – all credible reasons why Harpalus believed Athens could be his ally against Alexander. Harpalus also had links with the city. Not only had the Athenians previously honoured Harpalus with citizenship but over the years Harpalus had become attached

HARPALUS' FLIGHT: 324 BC

to two beautiful Athenian courtesans. Harpalus hoped the Athenians would welcome him with open arms. He was to be disappointed.[17]

Rather than allow Harpalus and his army to dock at Piraeus, the Athenians turned the ships away, unwilling to allow such a large force within their walls.[18] Refused welcome, Harpalus was forced to alter his plan. He sailed his fleet southwest, clinging to the Peloponnese's eastern coastline until they reached one of the mainland's southernmost tips: Cape Taenarum. Situated slightly inland of this Cape was a famous mercenary camp – a 'sellspear' recruitment ground out of Macedonian reach. It was here that Harpalus deposited his mercenary army, alongside most of his wealth and ships.[19]

Harpalus himself had no intention of staying there however. With only a few ships and a portion of his stolen wealth he headed back the way he had come, returning to Athens. He had not given up hope of seeking refuge in Athens and now, without the intimidating presence of his 6,000 mercenaries, he hoped for a more favourable outcome. Nevertheless Athenian opposition to Harpalus remained strong. Demosthenes strongly objected to allowing Macedon's most wanted into his city. He had enough on his plate, trying to find a solution to Alexander's impending decrees on the exiles and on Samos. Ultimately however, Demosthenes' objections failed. Sometime around the beginning of July 324 Harpalus was admitted into Athens after bribing Philocles, the Athenian general in charge of Piraeus and its defences. Harpalus had bought his way into his much-needed refuge. How would the Athenians respond?[20]

Harpalus soon started pushing his anti-Alexander agenda. He capitalised on the city's growing Macedonian resentment. He targeted prominent Athenian figures that housed deep animosity towards Macedonian overlordship, an animosity further fuelled by the recent rumours surrounding Nicanor's purpose in Greece. It was not long before Harpalus gained the support of several leading Macedon-hating statesman, including the prominent and bellicose orator Hypereides. For figures such as Hypereides, Harpalus' offer to use his wealth and manpower to help fund an Athenian revolt against Alexander was too tempting to refuse.[21] This was how Harpalus, a Macedonian lest we forget, successfully ingratiated himself with leading anti-Macedonian figures within the Athenian Assembly. He had his allies, but his position remained precarious.[22]

Alexander the Great's envoys were hot on Harpalus' heels, reaching Athens not long after his admittance. They demanded that the Athenians hand Harpalus over. Let him face the King's justice. Alexander's adjutant Philoxenus, as well as his powerful viceroy in Europe Antipater and his mother Olympias all sent envoys demanding Harpalus' immediate surrender.[23]

The Athenians deliberated how they should respond. Should they hand Harpalus over? The overwhelming response was no, but the reasons differed. On one side was the war-favouring party led by the likes of Hypereides. These statesmen saw Harpalus' manpower and money as useful military assets. They wanted to use them to launch a full-scale revolt against the Macedonians. A popular plan, especially considering the growing anti-Macedonian sentiment in Athens at that time.[24]

What it lacked, however, was the support of one key voice. Demosthenes, still dominant on the Athenian political stage, objected. This was not the time for Athens to revolt he argued, but at the same time he also objected to simply handing Harpalus over. He proposed an alternative: keep hold of Harpalus and use him as a useful bargaining chip. Leverage in his planned talks with Alexander's officials over the issue of Samos and the Exiles Decree. No longer did Demosthenes see Harpalus as a mere nuisance; seeing how determined Alexander was to have Harpalus in his custody, he now saw this Macedonian fugitive as a potential 'ace up the negotiating sleeve'.[25]

They would hand Harpalus over to Alexander, but only if he relented over Samos and the exiles. For this to have any chance of success however, Demosthenes had to ensure that Harpalus was kept under close surveillance. He therefore proposed that they arrest Harpalus, confiscating his money and keeping this wanted Macedonian in their custody. It was a bold proposal by Demosthenes, opposing the popular war wish of Hypereides and his supporters. Demosthenes however, was a master at the art of persuasion and he centred his argument around the poignant Samos predicament. For many there was a deep-felt desire to retain control over this overseas territory, something Demosthenes targeted to stir emotion during his speech. Their best chance of keeping hold of Samos, Demosthenes advised, was to follow his guidance. Reject war. Trust in diplomacy. Use Harpalus as a bargaining chip.[26]

It worked.

Persuading enough of his comrades, Demosthenes convinced the Assembly to accept his proposal to incarcerate Harpalus. Harpalus' offer to supply a revolt was refused; Hypereides' faction – and war – had been kept at bay. For now.

Demosthenes had convinced the Athenians that diplomacy was their best avenue through which to convince Alexander to reconsider his rulings over both Samos and the Athenian exiles. It was now his job to see this strategy through. With Harpalus safely detained he headed to Olympia in mid-July, hoping to negotiate with Nicanor over his upcoming announcement.[27]

5 August 324 – Olympia

> *King Alexander to the exiles from the Greek cities. Although we were not and are not responsible for your banishment, we will be responsible for restoring you to your homelands. Only those of you who are under a curse are excluded. We have written to Antipater (Alexander's viceroy in Europe) about this, instructing him to use force in the case of cities that refuse to comply.* – Diodorus 18.8.4

This was the decree that Nicanor read out on c.5 August 324, as the Olympic Games came to a close. More than 20,000 people had gathered to hear its announcement – mainly exiles eagerly anticipating confirmation that

Olympia was situated in the western Peloponnese.

they could return home. Cheers erupted throughout the crowd as Nicanor finished Alexander's proclamation but, as the watching-on Demosthenes knew full well, such celebrations would not be shared by those in the cities themselves. Negotiations had failed to make any substantial progress. Despite Demosthenes' best attempts, the Exiles Decree had remained unchanged and although Nicanor did not say anything about it during his address, Alexander still expected Samos to be returned to its exiled population. Demosthenes' mission to convince Nicanor to revert the upcoming Samos ruling had failed, but in truth there was little Nicanor could have done. The man was merely the messenger; he lacked the authority to so dramatically alter Alexander's wishes, much to Demosthenes' frustration. For all intents and purposes Demosthenes' diplomatic mission to Olympia had failed.[28]

Demosthenes however, was not going to admit defeat. Having returned to Athens he still triumphed his diplomatic strategy; he still believed he could change Alexander's mind. After all, Demosthenes' Olympian mission had one silver lining. Although unable to gain any concessions from Nicanor, what Demosthenes had acquired from Alexander's agent was advice. Advice on how he, and the Athenians, could best appease Alexander to ensure that any diplomatic mission to his court had the greatest chance of success. It was this ambassadorial action that Demosthenes now proposed the Athenians pursue. Send emissaries to Alexander's court in Asia and appeal the king's rulings over Samos and the exiles. A positive outcome was far from certain, but there were two courses of action Demosthenes thought might help.[29]

1: Evicting Harpalus

The first concerned Harpalus, the Macedonian fugitive still incarcerated within the city. Having proven an ineffective bargaining chip, the man had become more burden than benefit for the Athenians. Harpalus' continued presence within the city would only serve to damage relations between Athens and Alexander. If the embassy was to have any chance of success in appealing Alexander's rulings over Samos and the exiles, Harpalus had to go. He had to leave Athens. Demosthenes saw that this became so. He allowed Harpalus' guard to relax its vigil, first reducing its numbers and then disbanding it completely. He provided Harpalus an escape route; he wanted him gone.[30]

Escape Harpalus did, hurrying down to the Piraeus and 'slipping away' by boat in late August. Harpalus was on the run once again; his story will continue in a later chapter.[31]

2: Divine Alexander

Alongside masterminding Harpalus' escape, Demosthenes also pursued another controversial course of action. The thorny question of whether the

Athenians bestow divine honours upon King Alexander was no alien topic. Although Alexander had wished it, the overwhelming majority of Athenian statesmen strongly opposed deifying this mortal king and worshipping him as a god. That was, however, until Demosthenes stood up in the Assembly and advocated that they now give Alexander the divine honours he so craved.[32]

For many of those present Demosthenes' sudden support for such an impious act was nothing short of astonishing. Demosthenes, a statesman who until then had vehemently opposed the deification of Alexander, now supported it. An extraordinary change of heart.[33]

Demosthenes had his reason. Once again it concerned the fortunes of the Athenian embassy to Alexander. Once again it came back to the basic premise of placating Alexander in any way they could. If the Athenians agreed to deify Alexander, Demosthenes reasoned, then it would surely improve Alexander's opinion of them and bolster the chance of success. If Alexander wanted to be worshipped as a god, so be it – a small price to pay if a flattered Alexander became more inclined to allow them to retain Samos and turn away their exiles.[34]

Once more Demosthenes' reasoning convinced many in the Assembly – Phocion and Demades among those that supported Demosthenes' proposal. Hypereides, standing firm in his opposition, refuted it. For years he had consistently and vehemently attacked the Macedonians as impious and he refused to condone what he saw as a sinful act.[35] Even the possibility that such stubbornness might see the Athenians lose control of Samos did not swing him or his supporters, so much so that an exasperated Demades wryly joked:

'Take care that in guarding the heavens you don't lose the earth.' – Valerius Maximus 7.2.ext.13

A clear division had emerged over whether to give Alexander divine honours, but ultimately Demosthenes won the day. The proposal was passed and the Athenian embassy set off east towards Alexander's court, bolstered by Demosthenes' recent Alexander-appeasing actions.

What followed promised to be an agonising wait. It would take months first for the emissaries to reach Alexander's court in central Asia and then for news of its fortunes to return to Athens. Nevertheless Demosthenes believed that this patient diplomatic route was Athens' best option. Bowing to Hypereides and launching Athens into a full-scale revolt against Alexander was nothing less than suicidal. They would be handing their city a death sentence. Not only were Alexander's resources immense but people feared him. They feared the young conqueror returning from the east with a vengeance, mercilessly razing prestigious cities to the ground that dared defy him. History had proven that wreaking such terrible destruction was not beyond Alexander; the king was infamous for several episodes of brutal vengeance that no doubt influenced Demosthenes' decision to pursue a path of diplomacy and flattery. What was more Alexander had been known to change his mind; diplomats had certainly convinced Alexander to revert decisions in the past. Demosthenes hoped for a similar outcome in 324/3.[36]

Far and wide across Greece, Demosthenes' diplomatic policy was pursued, with embassies departing for Alexander's court in autumn 324 to appeal the King's diplomatic rulings. Demosthenes had inevitably made enemies, infuriating the likes of Hypereides and his supporters, but he had won the argument.[37]

Demosthenes' downfall

Fast forward 6 months – c.March 323 – and much had changed in Athens. Ever since the immediate aftermath of the embassy's departure from Athens, the Athenian Assembly had been conducting an investigation into Harpalus' confiscated funds, still stowed away in the Acropolis. Not all of Harpalus' money stood accounted for and certain leading statesmen soon found themselves accused of taking bribes. The investigation lasted six months and by March 323 had reached its conclusion.[38]

At the same time news came from the east. The Athenian embassy to Alexander was returning, but they would come bearing bad news. Their appeal had not succeeded, at least not well-enough. Whether Alexander refused the Athenian appeals over the exiles and Samos outright or whether he offered a compromise where Athenian colonists on Samos were allowed to co-exist with the returning Samians is unclear but, in any case, Alexander's resolution dashed Athenian diplomatic hopes. Disappointment turned to anger; Hypereides and his supporters seethed with fury. Diplomacy had failed; Harpalus' offer had been squandered; 6 months wasted. They needed somewhere to vent their fury; they needed someone to blame. Their answer lay in the trial's conclusion.[39]

Several leading figures were found guilty of accepting bribes from Harpalus. Philocles, the man who had first allowed Harpalus into Piraeus, was exiled; Demades was fined. But it was Demosthenes that the accusers unleashed their full fury upon.[40]

For months Demosthenes had strongly protested his innocence of being bribed by Harpalus. Guilty or not his accusers did not care. Demosthenes had been the architect of the failed diplomacy strategy; he had persuaded the Assembly to accept controversial proposals such as Alexander's divinity. Demosthenes was the man Hypereides and his growing supporters sought to blame.[41]

Throughout his trial Demosthenes came under a barrage of damning attacks and accusations. Hypereides targeted Demosthenes' recent actions, twisting them to paint the accused as a corrupt traitor, as an agent of Macedon:

It was you, by your decree, who had a guard posted over the person of Harpalus; yet you did not remedy its lack of vigilance, nor, when that vigilance lapsed altogether, did you persecute those responsible. So are we to deduce that your stewardship during this crisis came free of charge?...

...you have made all the Greeks send envoys to Alexander – because they have no other option. And then there are the satraps, who for their part would willingly have come to (join) this force, each with money and all the soldiers at his disposal...

...Well! Will you be making bold, very shortly, to speak to me about friendship?.....it was you yourself who dissolved this friendship, when you took gold against your country's interests and did an about-turn. – Hypereides *State Prosecution of Demosthenes*, 12–21

Rhetorical exaggeration was deployed to further infuriate his audience, with Hypereides going so far as to accuse Demosthenes of wanting to set up a statue to 'invincible Alexander'. Fact or fiction, such a story must have infuriated the crowd and made them more inclined to find Demosthenes guilty.[42]

Dinarchus, another accuser, followed in Hypereides' wake. He attacked Demosthenes' inconsistent position surrounding Alexander's deification, labelling the accused not only as impious but polluted. A stain on the city.

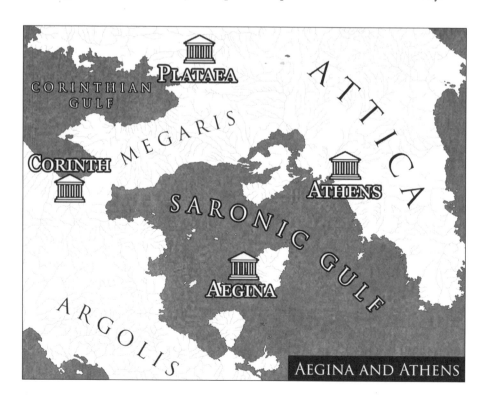

AEGINA AND ATHENS

The man is a juggler, Athenians, and a blackguard, not entitled to be a citizen of Athens, either by virtue of his birth or of his political record. – Dinarchus *Against Demosthenes,* 95–96[43]

Demosthenes was the scapegoat. Both Dinarchus and Hypereides twisted their accused's previous inconsistencies to suggest he had been bribed. A guilty verdict followed. Demosthenes was imprisoned and handed a hefty fine of fifty talents.[44]

Rather than pay the fine however, Demosthenes opted for flight. Escaping a very lacklustre guard he fled, hurrying south into exile on the island of Aegina:

He was the main victim of the Harpalus affair which he had manipulated so skilfully in its earlier phases. – Brian Bosworth *Conquest and Empire,* 220

On the warpath

Demosthenes was out of the way. As he disappeared from the scene so too did a majority in the Assembly favouring diplomacy with Alexander, favouring peace. Hypereides and his more bellicose supporters were now at the political forefront. Policy started to shift.[45]

It was not long before Hypereides and his followers began to advocate more militant, more provocative actions. Not long after Demosthenes' exile, word reached the Assembly that a group of exiled Samians had attempted to return to their island and throw out the Athenians. The attack failed; the exiles were captured, placed in chains, put on trial and condemned to death. Although this sentence was later commuted, this no-nonsense Athenian reaction was testament to their newfound militant policy to retain Samos no matter Alexander's ruling. By the spear if need be.[46]

Closer to home, the Athenians sought to strengthen their military position. Fortunately for them experienced manpower was in no short supply, thanks to another recent action of Alexander.

Disbanding the mercenaries

By early 324 the mercenary trade was flourishing. From Anatolia to distant Arachosia hired soldiers could be found across the length and breadth of Alexander's empire. Indeed, when Alexander had returned from fighting in faraway India, mercenaries formed a large component of his army. Irritatingly for Alexander however, it was not just him who had been hiring these 'sell-spears' *en masse.* In his absence many of Alexander's chief subordinates – governors and generals – had also been using their positions to hire their own mercenary armies, Harpalus chief among the guilty. Alexander's reaction was uncompromising. He demanded that these private mercenary armies be disbanded. The order was swiftly carried out and, all of a sudden, thousands of recently-employed mercenary soldiers found themselves cut adrift across the length of Alexander's Asian empire. Many of these mercenaries were 'Greek', Hellenic fighters that had ventured to Asia to serve in Macedonian employ. Naturally, their thoughts inclined towards a return to the west, to their homelands.[47]

Alexander had provided added incentive for some of these soldiers to return to Greece. This was the Exile's Decree. A significant number of the Hellenic mercenaries that had travelled to Asia and served in the private armies of Alexander's governors had been exiles. For these fortunate few Alexander's concurrent Decree offered them a clear course of action. They may have lost their employment, but Alexander's gracious decree offered them an end to their banishment. A route home. Once more it was all part of the conqueror's grand plan to destabilise opposing powers in Greece, to cause internal feuding and the disintegration of hostile anti-Macedonian political forces. In Alexander's eyes these indebted mercenaries would return to their city-states, exact their vengeance upon those who had banished them and infest their hometowns with internal turmoil. In one swift blow the strength of cities such as Athens and confederations such as that in Aetolia would evaporate. Politically, economically and socially – these city-states would be severely weakened. By offering the exiled mercenaries a route home Alexander hoped not only to reduce the number of veterans soldiers roaming his empire, but also to further damage his opponents on the Greek mainland.[48]

This decree however, only partially solved the mercenary problem. Many thousands of these hired soldiers were not exiles. Many thousands felt nothing but contempt for Alexander. In small bands they started to wander across Asia, living off the land and deliberating what they should do next. For the Greek mercenaries, a return to the west was the favoured option, with many slowly making their way towards the Mediterranean. Once they reached the sea, thousands of these soldiers boarded boats and sailed over to the Greek mainland. Following in Harpalus' footsteps, most of these mercenary-filled boats sailed to the southern Peloponnese's famous mercenary haven: Taenarum. Here they had a refuge, settled in a mercenary community several thousand strong.[49]

Throughout 324 and 323 the number of mercenaries in Taenarum only continued to increase, as more and more warbands were ferried across the Aegean to their long-awaited destination. Finding passage across the Aegean Sea was no easy feat for so many mercenary bands, but the story goes that this last sea leg of their journey was aided by one leading figure.

Enter Leosthenes

His name was Leosthenes, an Athenian who was about to become a leading figure in the mercenary world. Little survives about his background. More than a decade earlier Leosthenes' father had been forced to flee Athens and seek refuge at the court of King Philip II of Macedon. It was this family disgrace that influenced the young Leosthenes' career path.[50]

During Alexander the Great's Persian conquest Leosthenes had ventured to Asia to serve as a mercenary, but whether he fought on the side of the Macedonians or alongside the several thousand Greek mercenaries fighting for the Persian King Darius is unclear. Whatever the case, what we do know is that by 330 Leosthenes housed a deep hatred of Alexander. He returned to Athens, having wiped away his father's previous disgrace, and soon received command of an Athenian trireme, although he did not remain in 'official' Athenian service for long. Hearing that many mercenary bands were making their way west across Asia and were looking for sea transports that might ferry them over to Taenarum, Leosthenes made it his mission to provide these crossings. He did not disappoint. By the spring of 323 a sizable force of mercenaries and a large amount of wealth were at Taenarum, in no small part thanks to Leosthenes' logistical efforts. Many mercenaries were indebted to him and it was not long before they selected Leosthenes as their new leader. Far away from Macedonian territory, at this defensive bastion in the southern Peloponnese, Leosthenes now commanded a mighty veteran army – a powerful force on the Greek mainland. He had every intention of using it.[51]

It seems no surprise, given Leosthenes' strong anti-Macedonian feelings, that this commander was a friend of Hypereides. Now, with Demosthenes in exile and Hypereides' faction very much in control in Athens, Leosthenes offered Hypereides and the Athenians his services in any upcoming conflict with Macedon. Hypereides was happy to accept, although the need for secrecy was vital. Any Athenian link to Leosthenes' military preparations had to remain secret for now. Under wraps. They did not want to alert pro-Macedonian forces to their hostile intentions too soon. So the Athenians sent secret orders to Leosthenes, instructing him to start recruiting the mercenaries as if he were preparing to embark upon his own private military venture elsewhere in the Mediterranean. Leosthenes' and Athens' true intentions stayed concealed for the time being.[52]

Leosthenes' covert recruitment programme proved quick and effective. Soon he had a sizable force of mercenaries under his command – 8,000 men. Battle-hardened veterans were plentiful:

...ready for action...because they had served for a long while in Asia, where they had taken part in a large number of major battles and had become trained experts in war. – Diodorus 18.9.3

It was a formidable force, ready for Leosthenes to lead them to war once more. They did not have to wait long.

2. The Death of Alexander

In midsummer 323 a ship sailed into the Piraeus, having ferried across the Aegean an Athenian bearing extraordinary news. His name was Asclepiades and he wasted no time, upon reaching Athens proper, announcing the dramatic event that had occurred in Babylon in early June 323. Alexander was dead.[53]

At first Asclepiades' announcement was dismissed as rumour. Supposed tidings of Alexander's defeat had reached the Greek city-states in the years before, only for following reports to quickly expose them as 'red herrings'; if Alexander really was dead, Demades joked, the whole world would stink of his corpse. Such scepticism soon evaporated. As the days passed, rumours of Alexander's death in Babylon started to strengthen. More and more people rushed to announce that Asclepiades' report was true and that Alexander really was dead. For many Athenians, it was the news they had been waiting for. It triggered an outpour of clamouring for immediate revolution. This was their opportunity. With Alexander dead and his regime apparently in crisis, now was the time to rise up against Macedonian overlordship and regain their autonomy by the spear.[54]

Phocion

The veteran statesman Phocion watched on, as he saw this infectious eagerness for revolt spread across Athens. Already in his late 70s, Phocion's service to Athens was long and distinguished. A skilled orator and able commander, Phocion portrayed himself as a homage to the famous public figures of old: a new Pericles, Miltiades or Aristides. Throughout his long military career, he had fought various foes and travelled to many distant lands – from the island of Cyprus to the Hellespont. Initially he had zealously opposed the Macedonian expansion – proving a thorn in their side on several occasions. Yet following the disastrous defeat at Chaeronea, the veteran statesman recognised that Athens' best interests did not lie in fighting to the last in a forlorn war; now was the time for stability.[55]

Skilfully mediating between his home city and the Macedonians, Phocion became greatly admired on both sides: his skilful speech secured support from the Athenians while his conciliatory diplomatic tone also gained him the respect of his former foes – respect that ensured his city endured relative peace and prosperity following the Battle of Chaeronea. It was Phocion that played a leading role in creating the 'Pax Macedonica', the peace and prosperity that had proven so crucial to Lycurgus rebuilding Athenian strength. By 323 Phocion's life achievements proved his expertise both on the battlefield and in the political arena. He was one of the greatest statesmen of the age.[56]

Phocion had once been a leading advocate in fighting the Kingdom of Macedon. Fast forward to 323 however, and this wise old statesman was more cautious. Alexander may have died, but Macedon still boasted supreme military might. If Athens was to launch a revolt against the world superpower, the city-state had to avoid rushing into it before they were ready. Concerned with the necessities for war – manpower, money, logistics – he pleaded with the overeager Athenians for patience.

> *If he is dead today, he will be so tomorrow and the day after tomorrow equally.*
> – Plutarch *Life of Phocion* 22.4

Phocion's pleas fell on deaf ears. Bent on immediate conflict with Macedon, Hypereides and his allies reviewed their resources for war. Thanks to the substantial wealth they had confiscated from Harpalus, combined with that amassed by Lycurgus over the previous decade, money was not a major issue. In soldiers too the Athenians could call upon a sizable citizen army of heavily armed hoplites, not to mention Leosthenes' 8,000 battle-hardened mercenaries that boasted experience few could counter.[57]

For Hypereides and his supporters the need for secrecy was over. With Alexander's death they now openly aided Leosthenes' military preparations at Taenarum, sending the general sufficient suits of armour and money to finance his massive recruitment drive. The Athenians recognised the importance of Leosthenes' mercenaries. These experienced soldiers would form the beating heart of their land army and the Athenians were determined to see that they were kitted out with the best possible equipment.[58]

It was not long before Leosthenes' newly mobilised mercenary army left Taenarum and headed northeast towards Athens. Leosthenes himself had headed northwest, to the other major power in central Greece: the Aetolian League.

Aetolian dislike of the Macedonians was well-known and its people were natural allies for Leosthenes and the Athenians in the upcoming war. Talks between Leosthenes and the Aetolians went well, ending in the striking of a formal Athenian-Aetolian alliance. The two most powerful entities in central Greece would fight together against Macedon, both buoyed by the opportunity Alexander's timely death offered them. Once this was struck, Leosthenes hurried east to rejoin his soldiers in Attica and ready his city for war.[59]

The war debate

Even with Leosthenes' preparations, not everyone in Athens was keen on conflict. Even at this late hour, several figures still advised against it, encouraging their comrades to think again during the official Athenian war debate. Most were men of property, elite figures that were less inclined to the turmoil conflict offered and the financial burden they would have to bear funding it. Phocion stood firmly among them, no doubt aware that this dissatisfaction would prove a problem in any prolonged campaign. But Phocion also understood the new political situation in Greece. No matter the strength of Leosthenes' impressive preparations, no matter the fact that Alexander was dead, the Athenians would still be embarking on a war against the world superpower.[60]

Once again however, Phocion's voice was in the minority. Hypereides and his supporters dominated the war debate with impressive rhetoric, aided further by the presence of the young, charismatic Leosthenes. The audience's resolve for war was stiffened; across Athens rowers, dockworkers and many other lower class Athenian citizens cried out for conflict.[61] A war of words between the veteran Phocion and Leosthenes, the man of the moment, proved a highlight from the debate. Boldly and boastfully Leosthenes spoke in the Assembly, directing his verbal attacks at Phocion and his lack of support for war with Macedon:

> …*to raise a laugh against Phocion, he asked him scoffingly, what the state had been benefited by his having now so many years been a general.* – Plutarch *Life of Phocion* 23.1

Phocion refuted Leosthenes' attacks, unfazed by his opponent's attempts to mock his distinguished record of service to the Athenians that spanned more than forty years. Still resolute in his opposition Phocion gave a damning assessment of Leosthenes' clever speeches:

> *Young man, your speeches are like Cypress trees, stately and tall, and no fruit to come.* – Plutarch *Life of Phocion* 23.2

Hypereides was next to lead an attack on Phocion, asking why his opponent continued to resist war and whether there would ever be a time he offered them his support.

Phocion replied:

> *As soon as I find the young men keep their ranks, the rich men contribute their money, and the orators leave off robbing the treasury.*[62] – Plutarch *Life of Phocion* 23.2

Athenian allies (white) north of the Corinthian Gulf. The Phocians controlled the land between Athens and Thermopylae (just east of Heraclea), so gaining their assistance was vital.

No matter how witty and sensible Phocion's responses were, this war of words was a foregone conclusion. The Assembly decided on revolt and issued their militant decree. 240 warships were to be made ready for service, a mixture of traditional Athenian triremes and the larger, more modern and more powerful quadriremes.[63]

On land too, the Athenians readied their forces. All Athenians under forty were called up; of the ten tribes that made up ancient Attica, the young men from seven of these were to march with Leosthenes and fight abroad. Those from the remaining three tribes would form the home defence army, protecting Attica from enemy raids.[64]

As Athens mustered its military, diplomatic missions were also underway. North of the Peloponnese the Athenians sent envoys to nearby powers, hoping to secure their support in this war for 'Greek freedom' from their Macedonian overlords.[65] Success followed, as several agreements were struck with nearby Hellenic peoples: the Locrians, Oetaeans, Dorians and Aenianians for instance. There was also the Phocians, who agreed to ally with the Athenians thanks to the diplomacy of a certain Asclepiodorus.[66] Soon enough much of Greece to the immediate north of the Corinthian Gulf had allied with the Athenians. Further north too, an odd splattering of peoples added to the growing list of Athenian allies – Thracians, Illyrians and a group of Molossians that all shared Leosthenes' desire to destroy Macedonian hegemony on the mainland. From Aetolia to the Malian Gulf the Athenians soon had a strong set of external allies.[67]

Internally, too, the Athenians wanted the most experienced military men at their disposal. The young and dashing Leosthenes was the figurehead; old Phocion too, though opposed to war, boasted unmatched military experience and was kept on standby with the Athenian home army. Meanwhile those experienced Athenian military men currently in exile were offered a route home – redemption – if they agreed to help command the war effort.

The Athenians needed all the experienced military men on which they could lay their hands on. – Ian Worthington *Deinarchus' Philocles,* 81[68]

March to the Gates

Leosthenes did not linger in Attica long. Time was of the essence; it would not be long before Antipater, the powerful viceroy situated in Macedonia, marched south to counter this growing threat. Before the Athenians had finished readying their land army, Leosthenes and his mercenaries left Attica and headed towards the agreed defence location. A place where Leosthenes could best resist the impending Macedonian fury that Antipater was sure to unleash. One place stood out above all the rest, a place where one of history's

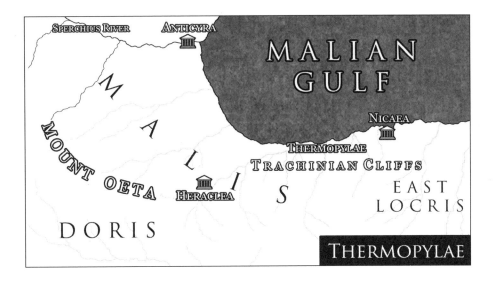

most famous battles occurred. A place entrenched in Hellenic myth and legend: Thermopylae.

Situated on the southern shoreline of the Malian Gulf, Thermopylae – 'The Hot Gates' – was a narrow pass that formed the gateway to the heart of Greece. On one side of the pass was the sea; on the other the Trachinian Cliffs towered above. With the pass being less than twenty metres wide at its narrowest point, here history had proven numbers counted for little. Discipline and formation would decide the day – as long as the infamous mountain path that circumnavigated the Gates was properly defended and the sea was in friendly hands. Here, at the site of the Spartan King Leonidas' famous last stand, Leosthenes would set up the defence.

Leosthenes' route to Thermopylae was not direct. Prior to reaching the Pass, he and his mercenaries had to make an important detour west, to Aetolia. In the time since Leosthenes had last left this region the Aetolians had stayed true to their alliance and mobilised their own powerful army to aid Leosthenes at Thermopylae. 7,000 Aetolians, professional warriors that were probably kitted out for heavy 'hoplite' warfare, awaited Leosthenes' arrival in eastern Aetolia so that he could lead them to Thermopylae.[69] For these Aetolians, simply marching to fight at Thermopylae was an extraordinary undertaking in itself. Never before, to our knowledge, had an Aetolian army ventured so far from their homeland. Together with Leosthenes and his mercenaries they marched northeast, past Mount Oeta and towards Thermopylae. Other allied contingents presumably joined Leosthenes' force en route – Locrian, Dorian and Phocian battalions – and by the time they reached Thermopylae, this elite vanguard numbered more than 15,000 men.[70]

They reached 'the Hot Gates' in the late summer/early autumn of 323. For the time being there was no opposing army in sight, but Leosthenes knew that this would not remain so for long. A Macedonian storm was brewing.

The Macedonian perspective

As the Athenians had been mobilising for war, news of their intended revolt had reached Pella, the heart of Macedonian power in Europe. Recognising the scale of the rebellion, the veteran statesman controlling the city prepared to lead out the Macedonian army once more. This was Antipater, a man long-accustomed to ruling.[71]

When Alexander the Great had embarked on his Persian Campaign in 334 he had needed a steady hand to remain at home; discontent was already brewing among the recently-subjugated Greek city-states to the south and the tempestuous Thracians to the north. To maintain control of his European possessions Alexander had therefore left them in the hands of 65-year-old Antipater. It proved a wise decision. Showing a shrewd knowledge of administration Antipater managed the troublesome European provinces with an iron first, crushing any revolts to Alexander's rule. He had no intention of ruining this reputation when news reached him in 323 that the Athenians and Aetolians were up in arms; he would not stand aside and watch his motherland's fifteen-year-hegemony over the Central Mediterranean be overthrown.[72]

Antipater was no fool. Having witnessed both the Harpalus affair and the Exiles Decree he must have known that anti-Macedonian sentiment was rising further south.[73] When news of Athens' decision to revolt reached him, an unsurprised Antipater reacted swiftly. 13,000 Macedonian infantrymen were mustered, each primarily equipped with a 6-metre-long pike called a *sarissa* and fighting in dense formations called phalanxes – impregnable against any attacker attempting to assault them from in front. Mercenaries and lighter-armed footmen supported this formidable heavy infantry force, providing critical cover for the slow-moving bulldozer that was the Macedonian phalanx.[74]

And then there was Antipater's heavy cavalry. The elite of any Macedonian army, these 'Companions' played pivotal roles in the past victories of both Philip II and Alexander the Great. Primarily equipped with a 2-metre-long lance called a *xyston* and trained to carve a gaping hole through chinks in an enemy line through their use of the wedge formation, these men were the ultimate shock cavalry. Their availability for Antipater however was in short supply:

> *Macedonia was short of citizen soldiers because of the number of those that had been sent to Asia as replacements for the (Alexander's) army.* – Diodorus 18.12.2

ATHENS AND MACEDON: 323 BC

Antipater could only muster six hundred cavalry to complement his force.

Similar to the Athenians however, Antipater could not march out of Macedonia at full military strength. The issue of home defence was paramount; already Illyrian, Molossian and Thracians had sided with the Athenians and Antipater could not leave Macedonia open to invasions from these troublesome neighbours as he marched south to deal with Leosthenes. He therefore left a significant detachment of troops in Macedonia under the command of Sippias, his subordinate. Antipater also instructed Sippias to muster more men in his absence.[75]

On the diplomatic front too Antipater was active. Prominent allies were sent south on diplomatic missions, to convince cities to resist Athenian overtures, to resist joining the revolt. Meanwhile Macedonian messengers were sent east, across the Hellespont to request aid from two prominent generals that now held significant power in this new post-Alexander world. These were Leonnatus and Craterus, famous former subordinates of Alexander the Great who both controlled powerful armies in western Asia. More on them later.[76]

And so, around the same time that Leosthenes headed for Thermopylae, Antipater started marching his meagre-yet-modern army south to confront this menace. The Macedonian fleet accompanied him – only 110 triremes strong but nevertheless providing Antipater important logistical and naval support as he progressed south through Thessaly. Conflict was fast approaching.[77]

A new threat

Leosthenes knew that he had limited time to shore up defences around Thermopylae; every day that passed Antipater was closing in. Yet for Leosthenes and his mercenaries, battle would come sooner than expected. Trouble was stirring. Not to the north, but to the south.

Not all the Hellenic peoples immediately north of the Corinthian Gulf supported Leosthenes' calls for revolt. Some had benefited significantly from Macedonian hegemony – none more so than those who dwelled in the cities of Boeotia, the region directly west of Attica. When Alexander the Great had razed the prestigious *polis* of Thebes to the ground in 335 many Boeotian states benefited:

> *…he (Alexander) gave its land to the Boeotians who lived near by, and these Boeotians divided the farms of the hapless Thebans among themselves. The land they gained was very profitable for them…* – Diodorus 18.11.3–4

Leosthenes' quest for allies had fallen on deaf ears among the Boeotians; revolt was not in their interests, although neither was neutrality. Aligning with Antipater and the Macedonians, they mustered a significant force and prepared for war.

Leosthenes was rightly concerned by this threat to the rear. In the meantime he had learnt that Athenian battle preparations were finally complete. An impressive force had been mustered: 5,000 heavy-armed hoplite infantry, 500 cavalry and 2,000 mercenaries. Thanks to the wealth accumulated by Lycurgus and Harpalus' seized funds, the Athenians were able to cover the costs for outfitting this army. Onlookers gathered within Athens to view this well-equipped force of citizen soldiers as they prepared to march to Thermopylae. Among those watching was the veteran general Phocion.[78] When asked if he approved of this newly-raised Athenian force he replied:

> *Very well for the short course; but what I fear, is the long race. Since however late the war may last, the city has neither money, ships, nor soldiers, but these!* – Plutarch *Life of Phocion* 23.3[79]

Phocion's concern was warranted. The Athenians had put all available money and manpower into this mobilisation. There were no reserves they could call upon. A war with Macedon was a marathon, not a sprint. Would Athens be able to maintain its military strength over the long haul?

Leaving Phocion and the city of Athens behind them, the Athenian army set forth for Thermopylae. Military experience was limited, but it was not long before this newly-mustered force found itself thrown into battle. Standing in its way, between Athens and Thermopylae, was the large Boeotian army, supported by Macedonian soldiers who had been stationed in nearby Chalcis. They were determined to stop the Athenians from reaching Leosthenes and the war's expected front lines.[80]

Having heard word of this new Macedonian-Boeotian threat, Leosthenes faced a difficult decision. If left to combat the Boeotians alone, there was a high chance his Athenian allies would be overwhelmed – crippled before the first fight with Antipater even commenced. Do nothing and this war of 'liberation' might start off with a devastating setback. Yet to leave Thermopylae risked Antipater's arrival in the meantime, placing any weakened defence at the narrow pass in a very precarious position. Either decision could have severe consequences.

Still Leosthenes was a bold, exceptional general in a new age of warfare. He had learnt a lot from his time spent in Asia fighting either with or against

Leosthenes' Lightning March to Plataea. After reaching Plataea, Leosthenes' army joined up with the Athenians (bottom right), before overwhelming the Boeotian / Macedonian force.

Alexander the Great. Leosthenes therefore decided to take a leaf out of the legendary leader's tactics: a lightning strike was needed.

Along with his best men – his mercenaries – Leosthenes opted to leave Thermopylae and march to the aid of his Athenian allies. The 7,000 Aetolians would remain at Thermopylae in the meantime, well-equipped and capable of defending this narrow, fixed position until Leosthenes' return.[81]

Gathering his best men, Leosthenes headed south and reached Boeotia in record time. Circumnavigating the Boeotian army, they rendezvoused with their Athenian allies before any battle could be fought and dramatically shifted the balance of power. Leosthenes' arrival was critical. Unable to counter the now superior strength of their opponents Boeotian resistance quickly crumbled, culminating in a decisive defeat near Plataea. The Boeotian menace had been quelled.[82]

Leosthenes celebrated the first victory of the campaign. The dead were buried; a trophy was erected. Nevertheless, Leosthenes did not have long to bathe in his triumph. Every day his best force remained away from Thermopylae, Antipater and his army edged close to the Pass. With his allies in tow, Leosthenes signalled them to return at record pace.

Relief must have run through Leosthenes' veins when he returned to 'The Hot Gates' to see his defences still standing strong – the Macedonians nowhere in sight. His gamble had paid off. Now he and his force settled in to await Antipater.

Thessalian turncoats

Antipater's march through Thessaly had been making steady progress. The old viceroy was confident in his past military record and the quality of his army: he had the best infantry and siege equipment in the known world while a substantial navy protected his sea flank.

Despite these reassuring facts Antipater had lingering concerns about the upcoming face-off. His enemy would certainly outnumber him and occupied a strong defensive location – a challenging test for his Macedonians. Yet perhaps his greatest concern was his shortage of Macedonian cavalry, the main attacking arm for his army. What Antipater did have, however, was a substantial supply of elite allied horsemen: the Thessalians.

Described as 'the land of horses', the region of Thessaly is rich in equine history. For centuries this region had been home to the best cavalrymen in Europe. Equipped with the devastating 2-metre-long *xyston* lances and dressed in iconic purple cloaks that flew behind them as their horses galloped, the Thessalians were the equals of Alexander's Companions. They rightly sit among antiquity's most formidable cavalry forces. Antipater knew bolstering his mounted divisions with allied Thessalian squadrons was vital.[83]

Honouring their thirty-year-alliance with Macedonia, noble Thessalian cavalry flocked to join Antipater's army from across the region, including the Pharsalians – the best of the best. By the time Antipater had crossed the Sperchius River c.7 miles north of Thermopylae, these elite horsemen numbered some 2,000.[84]

Yet their loyalty to the Macedonians was tenuous and, in contrast, Leosthenes' influence far-reaching. Swept up by tales of liberation from the Macedonian yoke, Thessalian commitment to Antipater's cause dissolved.[85]

They rode off to Leosthenes, who posted them alongside the Athenians, and fought for Greek freedom.[86] – Diodorus 18.12.3

For Antipater, hearing that his greatest allies had deserted his cause was disastrous. For Leosthenes it was fantastic. The best cavalry in Greece were now fighting alongside his forces – something he was sure to take advantage of.

The Battle of Thermopylae

Leosthenes had spent significant time fortifying his position at Thermopylae, ready to fight a defensive battle, but the arrival of the Thessalians changed everything. Recognising that his army now greatly outnumbered Antipater's in both infantry and cavalry, combined with the fact that the Thessalians would prove almost useless in the close confines of the narrow pass, Leosthenes pursued a different kind of engagement. A pitched battle.

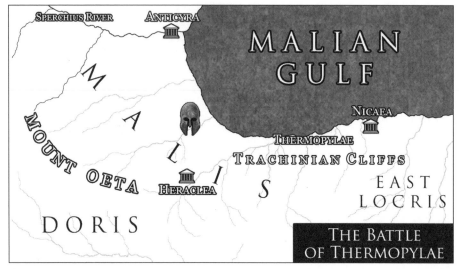

An approximate location for the battle between Antipater and Leosthenes in late 323 BC. The plain west of Thermopylae was home to Greek settlements such as Anticyra and Heraclea. Heraclea had stayed loyal to Macedon, almost certainly because there was a Macedonian garrison stationed within it.

To the immediate north of Thermopylae, on the western edge of the Malian Gulf, was a large plain. 157 years earlier King Xerxes' great army had encamped on this plain as they combated Leonidas' defences at the Hot Gates; in the future too, it would be the base for a huge Celtic horde as they similarly attempted to break through a Greek defence at the pass. Yet on this day in the autumn of 323, the plain would not be the location for a camp, but the first great battle of the post-Alexander era.[87]

Almost no detail survives of the battle that followed. The second century AD Macedonian author Polyaenus, writing almost 500 years later, provides one of our only insights. Greatly outnumbered and opposed by the only horsemen considered their equals in skill, Antipater knew that his limited Macedonian cavalry would struggle in the upcoming fight. It was a major issue but according to Polyaenus, Antipater had a cunning plan:

> *To impress the Thessalians with an opinion, that his cavalry was very numerous, Antipater advanced with a number of asses and mules; which he mounted with men, armed as troopers: but the first line of every troop he formed of his real cavalry. The enemy seeing so formidable an appearance, and supposing not only the front lines, but all the rest, to be cavalry, abandoned themselves to flight.* – Polyaenus 4.4.3

Deceived by Antipater's ploy the Thessalians supposedly fled, but such a reaction is hard to accept. Only recently these Thessalians had been part of Antipater's army. Surely they knew the truth behind Antipater's cavalry numbers? Surely they wouldn't fall for such a ruse? Fact or fiction, Antipater's ingenious scam did not alter the battle's outcome. In the clash that followed he and his men were bested and forced to retreat to the plain's northern reaches. Leosthenes had won the day. He was the man of the hour; he controlled the battlefield; he controlled the all-important war dead.[88]

Dire straits

Leosthenes and his Athenian-Aetolian allies may have won the day, but the battle was far from decisive. Although they had been forced to retreat, much of Antipater's army remained intact. Their position, however, was perilous. Finding themselves with Leosthenes' victorious army in front of them and a hostile Thessaly behind, retreating to the safety of Macedonia was not an option. In the meantime however, another enemy squadron had occupied the far bank of the Sperchius River, barring Antipater's immediate path north. Sandwiched between two hostile forces, Antipater's situation and that of Macedonian power in the Central Mediterranean, looked dire.[89]

By now almost all the cities of Thessaly had switched their allegiance to Leosthenes and the Athenians – prestigious *poleis* that included Pharsalus, Larissa and Pherae. A similar story occurred at Lamia. Initially the Lamians had stayed loyal to Antipater, their city's strategic position on the route between Macedonia and the Greek city-states south of the Sperchius River making it very likely that it had been the base of a substantial Macedonian

Situated to the immediate north of Thermopylae, the Sperchius River and the Malian Gulf, Lamia was a small city of sound strategic importance. It also boasted impressive defences, including strong walls.

garrison. By the time Antipater and Leosthenes came to blows on the plain near Thermopylae however, it appears that Lamia had followed in the footsteps of nearby Thessalian cities and switched allegiances.[90] It was a squadron of Lamian cavalry that Antipater and his defeated, deflated army now discovered patrolling the Sperchius' northern bank, blocking any crossing.[91]

Antipater was in dire straits. With his army caught between two enemy forces he knew Leosthenes' troops would soon be upon him. He had to cross the Sperchius.

Gathering his army, Antipater ordered his men to retreat a little distance south of the Sperchius and made camp for the night. The Lamians likewise retreated, returning to the comforts of their city until the next morning. They believed that Antipater and his army had decided to rest for the night. They were wrong. This was what Antipater wanted his enemy to think. It was merely a façade. Weapons remained ready. At the dead of night, Antipater advanced his entire army across the river unopposed. He had outwitted his opponents.

One can only imagine the horror that must have seized the citizens of Lamia when they discovered that Antipater's army had crossed the Sperchius. Even worse, this army was now heading their way, seemingly intent on storming the city if need be. Naturally the Lamians reconsidered their options. Once again they realigned their city's loyalty, opening the gates to the Macedonians and offering refuge. Antipater's forces filed into Lamia, taking up positions behind the city's strong walls. The Macedonians had a lifeline.[92]

Antipater's decisive thinking provided some respite, yet he knew it would only be a mere matter of time before he witnessed Leosthenes and his large army outside Lamia's walls; Leosthenes' arrival was imminent.

Realising he had little time Antipater set about improving Lamia's defences. State of the art bolt and arrow-firing artillery were amassed on the city's ramparts; soldiers stood guard day and night; ample weapons were furnished; food supplies were stocked up. As for the Macedonian navy, although this is only speculation, it appears that Antipater had already despatched it to the Hellespont under orders to command this vital waterway between Europe and Asia.[93]

Assaulting Lamia

Leosthenes and his army soon arrived outside Lamia's walls, fresh from burying the dead and erecting splendid victory monuments at the site of their success. But they were greeted with a troubling site. Their foe had significantly improved the city's defences, upgrading it into a formidable fortress. Storming it would not be easy.

Still Leosthenes remained undeterred. His victory against Antipater on the plain near Thermopylae had made him the most powerful man in the Central Mediterranean. Athenian confidence was high; the Macedonians may have found refuge, but they were now also confined within the small city. Trapped. Leosthenes knew victory was within sight; Antipater's actions had seemingly only delayed the inevitable.

In high spirits Leosthenes first had his men fortify their camp outside Lamia. A wooden palisade was erected, fronted by a deep trench. Once this was complete Leosthenes lined his soldiers up for battle between the camp and Lamia's walls, throwing down the gauntlet to Antipater's army to face them in battle on the plain outside Lamia. The Macedonians refused.

Denied a pitched battle, Leosthenes set about storming the city. Several assaults were made; several failures followed. Hardy hoplites found themselves transfixed by artillery bolts as waves of attackers attempted to breach the walls. Lamia's defences held strong.[94]

Initial assaults on Lamia made little progress, crushing Leosthenes' hopes of obtaining a swift success. Capturing this well-defended city would take time – time during which Leosthenes knew he would lose an ally. This was the Aetolians. It was around this time of year – the late autumn – that the Aetolian League's annual assembly took place. This was a very important event for the Aetolians – a cornerstone of their League's constitution. It was at this meeting, for instance that elections were held for various positions in the League, including who was to command the Aetolian army. Leosthenes must have known that it would only be a matter of time before the Aetolian commanders requested that they and their soldiers leave his army to settle this important national business and it proved so.[95] Following their failed assaults on Lamia, and Leosthenes' realisation that a longer-term strategy was needed, the Aetolians raised the issue of their annual assembly with Leosthenes and requested permission to return home temporarily. Leosthenes agreed.[96]

The Macedonians watched from Lamia's walls as 7,000 Aetolians departed the enemy camp and headed home. Although a welcome sight for the defenders, for Leosthenes it wasn't disastrous. His army remained sizeable, experienced and confident. He had more than enough manpower to see through the siege in the Aetolians' absence.

Leosthenes turned his attention to the new strategy. Stationing his army out of range of Antipater's artillery, he ordered his engineers to begin building further formidable defences. This time surrounding Lamia. A turf and timber rampart was to be constructed around the town, fronted by a deep, wide ditch. An extraordinary circumvallation, intended to cut Lamia off from supplies and outside assistance. Settling in for a siege, Leosthenes had made his decision. He would starve them out.[97]

The ambassador quest

In the meantime another conflict had been raging further south, on the diplomatic front. To the south west of Athens lay the Peloponnese, the peninsula that forms much of southern Greece. So far during the revolt no city-states from the Peloponnese had committed themselves to the revolt. The Athenians sought to change this and during the autumn of 323 teams of ambassadors headed to the Peloponnese, intent on securing the support of certain city-states. From city to city they would travel, using typical Athenian eloquence to try and convince their audiences to join the war on their side. But they were not alone. At the same time ambassadors from Macedon were also traversing the Peloponnese intent on opposing the Athenian delegations. It was their mission to stop certain city-states from joining the uprising. Among the Macedonian ambassadors were two Athenians who had decided to throw their lot in with Antipater: Pytheas and Callimedon, the latter nicknamed 'the spiny lobster' because of how much he loved that food.[98]

Macedonian and Athenian delegations toured the Peloponnese. Sometimes they would encounter each other at certain city-states. A war of words would ensue, as each side tried to convince their audience to support their proposal. Fortunately for the Athenians, they had a secret weapon. Demosthenes.

323 had so far proven an interesting year for Demosthenes. Although he had been exiled from Athens back in March, Demosthenes kept himself well informed about subsequent Athenian decisions: their reaction to Alexander the Great's death and their decision to revolt for instance. As soon as he had heard word of Leosthenes' success at Thermopylae, Demosthenes sent a letter to his former accuser Hypereides and the Athenian Assembly, praising their success and extolling them to keep going. With Alexander dead, Demosthenes' views had changed once more. He now fully supported the revolt and was keen to aid the Athenians in any way he could. So when he learnt that Athenian ambassadors were in the Peloponnese hoping to acquire more allies, Demosthenes saw his opportunity. He sailed over to the mainland from Aegina and hurried to offer his persuasive services to his city's representatives. Former enemies such as Hypereides and Dinarchus saw the value in having the experienced Demosthenes among their ambassadorial ranks. Putting aside past differences they toured the Peloponnese together, united in their aim to secure new allies. It was at Sicyon, an important city in the northern Peloponnese that was also the home of a Macedonian garrison, that Demosthenes gained his – and Athens' – first diplomatic victory in the Peloponnese. No doubt relaying news of recent Athenian successes, he convinced the Sicyonians to revolt. A certain Euphron oversaw the driving out of the Macedonian garrison from the city and in so doing confirmed Sicyon's new alliance with Athens.[99]

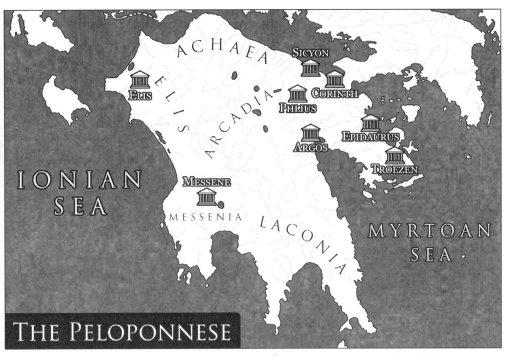

A map of the Peloponnese, including the city-states that we know either Athenian or Macedonian (sometimes both) delegations visited.

Sicyon proved a symbol of things to come for Demosthenes and the Athenian ambassadors. Over the next few months, they gained diplomatic success after success in the Peloponnese, the Athenians riding high on Leosthenes' recent victories and Demosthenes' brilliant way with words. The Macedonian ambassadors tried to counter, culminating in one noteworthy rhetorical clash between Pytheas and Demosthenes in Arcadia. Ultimately however, it was Demosthenes who emerged the victor. More city-states threw their lot in with the Athenians: Argos, Corinth and Troezen to name a few. The Athenian diplomatic mission had proven a great success – thanks in no small part to Demosthenes the exile.[100]

Euphoria in Athens

In Athens, reports of these military and diplomatic successes were flooding in thick and fast. Many were jubilant, excited after receiving word of so many successes in such a short space of time. Celebrations followed – festivals and public sacrifices to the gods in thanks for their continued good fortune. In this wave of euphoria, the Athenians also voted to recall their redeemed hero Demosthenes. He had certainly earned it.[101]

Athens was the scene of rejoicing and optimism, but not everyone shared such delight. Once again Phocion bucked the trend. He remained cautious; he was wary, knowing that the war was far from over. And his previous warnings remained relevant – if Leosthenes' army was destroyed Athens would be crippled. In the midst of these celebrations a comrade confronted Phocion, seeking to see whether the old general would admit that Leosthenes' stunning series of recent successes were worthy of his praise. Phocion replied:

'Yes most gladly, but also of the former counsel.' – Plutarch Life of Phocion 23.4

Phocion could not deny Leosthenes' impressive achievements, but lacking suitable reserves he feared these successes would not last forever. "When will the end of them come!" he supposedly exclaimed after hearing one report announcing more success from Leosthenes at Lamia. The longer the war lasted, the more Phocion feared an end to the good news was only a matter of when, not if. The more he feared long-term Macedonian success. Would his words prove prophetic? Time would tell.[102]

The Siege of Lamia

So far for the Athenians, so good. Back outside the walls of Lamia, Leosthenes' new siege strategy was working. Construction of the city-surrounding wall was well-underway and supplies inside Lamia were slowly starting to run low. Antipater knew that Leosthenes' siege strategy ultimately looked set to succeed. He had already tried to negotiate, hoping to gain favourable terms of surrender for him and his Macedonians. But Leosthenes had refused. Knowing full well how desperate his opposing number was getting, knowing how close he was to destroying Antipater's power, Leosthenes had haughtily replied that the victors would set the terms.[103] Only unconditional surrender would do.

Leosthenes knew he was close to gaining a victory that would immortalise him in Athenian folklore – putting him on par with other legendary leaders such as Pericles, Callimachus, Miltiades and Themistocles. All he had to do was persist a little longer.

The sortie

Although in dire straits, Antipater and his men refused to give up. Frequently small bands of soldiers sortied from the city to disrupt the siege works. In the late months of 323, some of Antipater's men made one such attack, targeting a section of the surrounding moat where Leosthenes' engineers were digging. With spear and shield the struggle was intense, but the Macedonian assault squad soon gained the upper hand.[104]

It was not long before news of the skirmish reached Leosthenes further along the siege line. Gathering a significant number of soldiers – a band of brothers – the Athenian commander hurried to relieve his men.

As they ran towards the scene of the skirmish, Leosthenes heedlessly hurried his companions across the ancient equivalent of 'no man's land' – the plain between Lamia and Leosthenes' besieging wall. The plain was within range of Antipater's artillery, positioned all along the city's ramparts. Seeing Leosthenes and his men emerge into the killing field, the Macedonian engineers loaded their artillery machines with bolts and stones and let loose. The chances of a successful hit were slim, but there was always the possibility of a lucky shot. The barrage began.

Under fire, the Athenian relief force hurried across the plain – Leosthenes at the helm. But then, disaster! As Leosthenes advanced a catapulted stone crashed into his ranks, striking the Athenian *strategos* on the side of his head and knocking him to the ground. Carried back to his camp, his life hung in the balance. Leosthenes had taken a needless risk; and it had not paid off.

Two days later the seemingly inevitable happened when Leosthenes breathed his last. The charismatic commander who many believed would lead Athens to victory, now lay lifeless outside Lamia. The Athenians lamented the luckless loss of Leosthenes – none more so than Hypereides, his champion in Athens. Leosthenes' death was a major blow, curbing the recent euphoric mood that had seized Athens, but the war was far from over. Would Leosthenes' death mark a turning point in the conflict? Was this the start of a turn in Athenian fortunes that Phocion had predicted? They would soon find out.[105]

Further Reading

Primary Sources
Dinarchus *Against Demosthenes*
Diodorus Siculus 18.8.2–18.13.
Hypereides *State Prosecution of Demosthenes*
Plutarch *Life of Demosthenes*
Plutarch *Life of Phocion*
Polyaenus 4.4 (Antipater).
Pseudo-Plutarch *Lives of the Attic Orators*

Secondary Sources
Bosworth, A. B. (1988), *Conquest and Empire: The Reign of Alexander the Great*, Cambridge, 204–228.
Bosworth, A. B. (2003), 'Why did Athens lose the Lamian War?', in O. Palagia and S. V. Tracy (eds.), *The Macedonians in Athens: 322–229 BC*, Oxford, 14–22.
Errington, R. M. (1975), 'Samos and the Lamian War', *Chiron* 5, 51–58.

Grainger, J.D. (1999), *The League of the Aitolians*, Leiden, 54–61.

Grainger, J.D. (2019), *Antipater's Dynasty*, Barnsley, 73–81.

Green, P. (2003), 'Occupation and co-existence: the impact of Macedon on Athens, 323–307', in O. Palagia and S. V. Tracy (eds.), *The Macedonians in Athens: 322–229 BC*, Oxford, 1–7.

Griffith, G. T. (1935), *The Mercenaries of the Hellenistic World*, Cambridge, 33–43.

Habicht, C. (1997), *Athens From Alexander to Antony*, Munich, 6–42.

Lawton, C. L. (2003), 'Athenian anti-Macedonian sentiment and democratic ideology in Attic document reliefs in the second half of the fourth century BC', in O. Palagia and S. V. Tracy (eds.), *The Macedonians in Athens: 322–229 BC*, Oxford, 117–127.

Mari, M. (2003), 'Macedonians and anti-Macedonians in early Hellenistic Athens: reflections on ἀσέβεια', in O. Palagia and S. V. Tracy (eds.), *The Macedonians in Athens: 322–229 BC*, Oxford, 82–92.

Worthington, I. (1986), 'The Chronology of the Harpalus Affair', *Symbolae Osloenses* 61 (1), 63–76.

Worthington, I. (1994), 'Alexander and Athens in 324/3 BC: On the Greek Attitude to the Macedonian Hegemony', *Mediterranean Archaeology* 7, 45–51.

Worthington, I. (2000), 'Demosthenes' (in)activity during the reign of Alexander the Great', in I. Worthington (ed.), *Demosthenes: Statesman and Orator*, Oxon, 90–113.

Chapter 3

The Thracian Test

Although Leosthenes – the Athenian Alexander – may have breathed his last, his city's prospects of victory remained high. Antipater's army, devoid of reinforcements, was besieged; Athens and her allies enjoyed a dominant position. Even better news was to follow.

As the forces in and around Lamia settled in for the winter siege, word soon spread regarding the rush of activity that had erupted to the northeast – on the great plain of central Thrace. There, traditional Athenian allies had taken to the field as they similarly sought to free themselves from Macedonian control. With Antipater holed up in Lamia, only one meagre force stood between these fearsome warriors and regaining their independence. But that army would not be so easy to overcome. Newly arrived from Asia, many of the soldiers were veterans of Alexander the Great's campaigns; their commander was famed as a fearless lion killer.

Until now this general's name has received little mention, but the task ahead offered him a baptism of fire into the world of statecraft. His name was Lysimachus.

Background

As with many other protagonists in this tumultuous period, Lysimachus boasted a prestigious background. Agathocles, his father, had been a high-standing member of the Thessalian nobility. In his prime Agathocles had ventured north to Macedonia and established himself at the royal court of Philip II, where he soon made his presence known. By 350 Agathocles had become a firm favourite of the king, having helped him extend Macedonian influence into the northern reaches of Thessaly. This relationship brought rewards. Partly in gratitude for his services and partly due to a need to replenish the Macedonian nobility with loyal followers, Philip provided Agathocles and his family estates in Pella. The generous gift of land instantly elevated the Thessalian's social standing, making him a member of the Macedonian elite social class – the *hetairoi* or 'Companions'. His family were sure to benefit.[1] Embracing their father's royal favour, Agathocles' young sons – among them

Lysimachus – were raised amongst Macedonian nobility at the royal court, the heart of Philip's ever-expanding Macedonian kingdom.

In 334 at least two sons of Agathocles had accompanied Alexander the Great into Asia as members of his elite cavalry wing and it was not long before the brothers started to enhance their family's reputation through a variety of noteworthy actions. Alcimachus, the eldest, was a prominent commander at the start of the Persian expedition, though all references to him abruptly vanish after 334. Philip, another brother, is remembered for one extraordinary exploit. While campaigning in modern-day Uzbekistan, Philip, at that time a young member of the king's elite infantry guard, although only on foot had been determined to keep pace with Alexander and a select band of horsemen as they pursued fleeing rebels. Many miles later their enemy resolved to fight and, in the ensuing skirmish, the exhausted Philip fought alongside the king in the thickest of the action. Only when victory was theirs did 'that vital spark which had kept him going in the heart of the fight desert him'. He collapsed and died from exhaustion moments later.[2]

Lysimachus proved no less extraordinary. During a royal hunt he came face to face with a lion and slew it single-handed – a feat Alexander had witnessed. The second eldest son of Agathocles did not come away from the encounter unscathed however – the lion had severely mauled his shoulder before Lysimachus dealt the killer blow. Nevertheless the event greatly enhanced Lysimachus' reputation and throughout the rest of his life, Lysimachus made sure this feat was never forgotten.[3]

Lysimachus' courage was unquestionable, developing a reputation during the course of Alexander's campaigns as one of the king's most fearless subordinates.[4] Yet this could not hide a more unfavourable trait: the man had a tendency for reckless action in the pursuit of personal glory. As a fighter he was a fearless asset. As a commander his rashness was a cause for concern, as Alexander appears to have realised.[5]

Although his impetuous nature seems to have caused Alexander to overlook him for senior commands, Lysimachus maintained a close relationship with the king. They had known each other since childhood, both having been raised at the royal court at similar times.[6] Combined with his father's high standing in the capital, these factors helped ensure Lysimachus enjoyed a rapid elevation into Alexander's inner circle of Companions. By 332 he was accompanying the king on lion hunts; by 328 (if not earlier), he had become one of Alexander's closest adjutants, as a member of his bodyguard. Lysimachus remained a member of this elite body, alongside the likes of Perdiccas, Ptolemy and Aristonous, for the rest of Alexander's life. When the Macedonian king lay dying in Babylon, Lysimachus was among those who surrounded his bedside.[7]

His close relationship with Alexander and his high standing within the army ensured Lysimachus was listened to during the week-long crisis that followed the king's death. Although we hear little about this role, his support for Perdiccas and the other senior *strategoi* is certain. But like Ptolemy and several other subordinates Lysimachus' loyalty was conditional. He expected a reward for his allegiance: a position of authority in the new regime worthy of one of Alexander the Great's top adjutants. Perdiccas did indeed give him a senior position, albeit one plagued with problems. Following Meleager's demise, the new regent named Lysimachus as the supreme military authority in one of the empire's most unstable regions: Thrace.

Thrace

Thrace. An ancient geographical area today split between Bulgaria, Romania and northwest Turkey. Divided among various tribes the peoples of Thrace were numerous and diverse but shared a reputation as some of the most feared

Map of ancient Thrace – showing the various tribes and their positions.

warriors in the known world. Some tribes championed their skill as hardened, highland swordsmen; others inhabited great plains mastering the art of mounted mobile skirmishing. Their large numbers and their 'devotion to Ares' ensured that the fear of unstoppable hordes of terrifying Thracians descending on the Aegean like 'a giant swarm of locusts' and wrecking unimaginable havoc on the heartlands of Hellenism forever lingered in Classical Greece.[8]

It proved a chimera. Despite a few infrequent cases of Thracian unity, by 323 this nightmare was but a frightening figment of imagination. It had never become reality. The land's plethora of petty princes proved a significant barrier to any attempt to attack an external enemy. Each clan cherished their strong sense of self-identity and were proud of their own heritage and history. Many hated their neighbours, all too happy to fight fellow clansmen who opposed their political goals. Tribal conflict was rife:

> *Were they only to share a single ruler or a common purpose, they would, in my opinion, be invincible, and put every other nation deep in their shadow. However, since these are eventualities that there is no question of bringing to fruition, the Thracians are perforce enfeebled.* – Herodotus 5.3

Their neighbours were sure to capitalise on this internal strife.

Invasion

In 513 Megabazus, a famous Persian general, had subdued much of southern Thrace for King Darius I. But Persian control of this northwest frontier quickly proved untenable as deep Thracian desires for independence resulted in large scale resistance. Ultimately, it culminated in a humiliating withdrawal in 479.[9]

Nearly 150 years later the land was once again subject to foreign invaders. Between 342 and 340, a significant part of the Thracian interior south of the Haemus Mountains fell to King Philip II's ever-expanding Macedonian Empire. After a long hard-fought campaign Philip had finally overcome King Cersebleptes, his defiant Odrysian foe, in a series of battles. He cemented his rule over the spear-won land through the founding of several new, bustling cities. One such city was the frontline fortress of Philippopolis, designed to affirm Macedonian authority over surrounding territory. Nevertheless, despite the construction of these bastions, resistance to Macedonian rule remained and Alexander the Great, Philip's son and successor, was forced to follow in his father's footsteps five years later. He further solidified Macedon's presence in Thrace, defeating the Triballi and campaigning past the Danube River.[10]

By 335 the many Thracian leaders within the Macedonian sphere of control had become nothing more than vassals, convenient figureheads for their tribe. To ensure their loyalty, Alexander made them swear an oath of allegiance and demanded they provide him with a substantial number of their best warriors to accompany him to Asia – partly for their undeniable skill, partly as hostages. Strong garrisons and new Macedonian settlements served to further secure his kingdom's control.[11]

Nevertheless, despite Alexander's pre-emptive measures, deeply ingrained Thracian desires to regain independence lingered.

Seuthes III was one Thracian leader who harboured such desire. He was a vassal king, the young ruler of the recently annexed Odrysian kingdom. Initially the Odrysians had complied with Alexander's demands: a large contingent of the tribe's best warriors, commanded by their prince, had accompanied the Macedonian king to Asia. Following Seuthes' accession to the kingship in c.330, however, plans of reviving Odrysian power came to the fore.[12]

The clan had a prestigious past. They were the greatest of all the Thracian tribes and had previously dominated large swathes of the region. In the latter half of the fifth century, Odrysian kings had controlled territory stretching the length of Thrace: from the Nestos River to the Black Sea (also known as the Hospitable Sea) and from the Danube to the Aegean. They had been able to gather armies of up to 150,000 men; their influence had reached as far as the fledgling Greco-Scythian Bosporan Kingdom in eastern Crimea. Their power had been legendary.[13]

But it was not long before Odrysian might came crashing down. The assassination of Cotys I, the kingdom's last great ruler, sent his domain spiralling into chaos. Internal strife, the old Thracian malady, reared its ugly head once more, as several powerful princes struggled for supreme authority. It was this infighting that paved the way for Philip II to march in and bend the Odrysians to his will.[14]

So it was that by 330 Seuthes governed a tribe that had become a shadow of its former self. From mighty power to annexed kingdom, the most prestigious of all Thracian tribes had been subdued.[15] Seuthes was haunted by the famous achievements of legendary predecessors such as Teres I, Sitalkes and Cotys. He felt it was his diehard duty to revive his kingdom, to regain Odrysian independence and in so doing restore its place amongst his fellow peoples. In 325 Seuthes was presented with a golden opportunity to do just that.[16]

The disaster

Four years earlier Antipater, Alexander's viceroy in Europe, had appointed a new commander to serve as occupied Thrace's new *strategos*, the region's chief military authority. His name was Zopyrion, presumably one of Antipater's senior subordinates. Keeping the peace was Zopyrion's main responsibility –

if need be with an iron fist. But merely maintaining order did not satisfy this ambitious general. As news filtered back to the west of the countless victories and great glory gained by Alexander and his comrades in Asia, Zopyrion craved similar success. Pushing aside his peacekeeping duties in favour of conquest he amassed a significant army – 30,000 men.[17] Mercenary Thracian warriors must have formed the mainstay of this force, supplemented by a small nucleus of Macedonians and Hellenic hoplites of varied experience.[18] Zopyrion had then marched his expedition north, across the Danube and beyond the empire's borders. They never returned.

As Zopyrion and his force encountered defiant resistance while laying siege to the rich city of Olbia at the mouth of the Hypanis River, disaster struck. A great storm destroyed Zopyrion's fleet – their vital supply lifeline. Isolated and unable to continue the siege the general attempted to march his men homeward to the borders of Thrace, hugging the coastline as best they could. It did not save them. Passing through hostile 'Getae' territory:

> He (Zopyrion) was wiped out with all his forces and paid the price for an impulsive attack on an unoffending people. – Justin 12.2.17

It was a catastrophic military disaster. A combination of poor weather and stubborn resistance had quickly doomed the expedition. His force annihilated – Zopyrion lay among the dead.[19]

The army's destruction sparked even greater consequences for Thrace. Macedonian control over large swathes of the region was left threadbare. Seuthes was sure to seize the opportunity. News of the expedition's demise was the trigger for revolt. He began amassing a powerful army, taking advantage of his tribe's great manpower reserves and the widespread animosity towards Macedonian overlordship. Now was the time to revive the past glory days of Odrysian might.[20]

Seuthes was emboldened in his revolt by the support he received from several neighbouring tribes, united in their desire to expel the Macedonian presence.[21] But he also had another, vital ally: Athens.

Throughout antiquity, the Odrysians and the Athenians experienced rocky relations: sometimes warring with one another, at other times striving for co-operation and political alliance. It was the latter, more harmonious relationship that Seuthes had revived. The Athenians had agreed to renew their old, historic ties with his tribe back in 330 and coinage minted over the next decade suggests these close relations were maintained. They were, after all, natural allies. Like Seuthes, many prominent Athenians sought independence from the Macedonians – hoping to revive their city-state's past prominence on the world stage. Co-operation between Seuthes and belligerent firebrands such as Hypereides seems likely.[22]

Seuthes must have been confident. He had considerable manpower resources and a strong, external ally in Athens. Between 325 and 323 his authority in the upper reaches of the fertile Tonzos River valley (today the Valley of the Roses) strengthened considerably, culminating in Seuthes proclaiming himself subordinate to no man. The Odrysian king knew his actions would bring consequences and he awaited the Macedonian response that was sure to come.[23]

The Empire strikes back

Lysimachus faced a daunting task. News of Seuthes' revolt would have been common knowledge by June 323, especially to those senior subordinates deciding the empire's fate half the world away in Babylon. Thrace was in turmoil; Perdiccas was sure to act. Control over the Empire's northern border in Europe had to be restored – not only to guard Alexander's homeland from the threat of raiding 'barbarians' in the north, but also to protect the Hellespont, the vital crossing-point for armies wishing to travel to and from Asia. Championing Lysimachus, Perdiccas exclaimed his need for a proven and fearless commander to take on the challenging task of overcoming Seuthes and restoring Macedon's uncontested control over the region.[24]

Lysimachus accepted the challenge:

> ...it was Lysimachus who was assigned the fiercest tribes on the assumption that he was the bravest of them all. – Justin 15.3.15

And yet...

Underlying political reasons surely also entered Perdiccas' mind when planning for Lysimachus' appointment. His authority was far from watertight. To help secure his position, Perdiccas aimed to reduce the power of other prominent figures elsewhere in the empire. One such man was the elderly viceroy Antipater, whose authority prior to 323 had stretched throughout Alexander's European empire, from the central Peloponnese to the Hellespont. The extent of Antipater's power worried Perdiccas. Already he had aimed to curb and fragment the viceroy's power by instructing the veteran Craterus to continue his journey west and share the governorship of Europe. But Lysimachus offered him a further means of reducing his rival's power. By appointing this prestigious bodyguard as Thrace's inaugural governor, Perdiccas had made Lysimachus Antipater's equal. The former's authority over restoring order on the northern frontier was clear to see. Losing control of Thrace and the

Hellespontine communities greatly weakened Antipater's sphere of influence over Alexander's European dominions, much to Perdiccas' delight.[25]

Lysimachus did not escape Perdiccas' political calculations however. Lysimachus was one of the highest subordinates in Babylon – famous for his fearlessness and his close relationship with Alexander. He was also highly ambitious. Perdiccas perceived this to be a threat to his own authority. Sending Lysimachus away to fight in the wild unconquered hinterland of Thrace seemed the perfect solution.

So why was Lysimachus chosen to deal with the Thracian revolt? Officially, it was due to the man's undeniable courage: a formidable and fearless fighter. Underlying political motives, however, were also at play.[26]

Lysimachus welcomed the military challenge Seuthes posed – keen to gain glory on the battlefield. Yet if he was to humble the Odrysian king, he needed an army, and a sizable one at that. Perdiccas was well aware of this. Before Lysimachus departed Babylon, Perdiccas had provided the new governor a professional force of battle-hardened mercenaries – a few thousand strong.[27]

At its heart were the heavy infantry, likely hailing from flourishing mercenary recruitment grounds such as Lydia, Caria, Lycia and Pamphylia,

Map of Lysimachus' territory on his arrival, and that of Seuthes. Much of the Thracian interior was controlled either by Seuthes or by hostile, independent tribes (the Bessi for instance). Philippopolis and the Haemus River valley does seem to have still been within Lysimachus' territory, but the lands north of this seem to have been in hostile hands. The former Macedonian 'penal colony' of Cabyle on the middle Tonzos seems to have been out of Lysimachus' sphere.

but trained to fight in the Macedonian manner.[28] Wielding their six-metre-long spears and fighting in dense phalanx formations, these pikemen were well-trained – vital to Lysimachus' chances of victory. Sufficient money to pay his mercenaries was also provided from the bountiful royal treasuries, giving Lysimachus the means to recruit more professional soldiers before his ultimate showdown with Seuthes.

His mission assigned and his army ready, at the height of 323 Lysimachus set forth for Thrace – never to cast his eyes over Babylon again.[29] More mercenaries were presumably enlisted *en route* and within a few months Lysimachus had crossed the Hellespont and arrived back on European soil for the first time in almost twelve years. Without delay he and his force headed into the Thracian interior – keen to quell Seuthes' insurrection at the earliest opportunity. Philippopolis may well have been their initial destination – Lysimachus could use this bastion on the Macedonian frontier as a base from where he could strike north into Seuthes' Odrysian heartlands.[30]

Late 323: Lysimachus invades

By the time Lysimachus arrived at the border of Seuthes' territory his army had swelled to some 6,000 men. 4,000 of these were infantry. Phalanx-forming heavy footmen comprised its core, supported by recently recruited Thracian auxiliaries and other unknown mercenaries.[31] The remaining 2,000 troops were cavalry.[32] Small but strong, this army was a professional force filled with veterans. At its head Lysimachus advanced deeper into central Thrace to quell the Odrysian unrest by the spear.

Seuthes accepted the challenge. In the meantime, he had assembled his own large army, awesome in scale due to his kingdom's vast reserves of manpower. When Lysimachus' scouts discovered Seuthes' encampment somewhere on the Thracian plain, the true extent of their opponents' numerical advantage and the daunting task the invaders faced, became clear. Standing in their way, ready to give battle, Seuthes stood ready with 28,000 warriors. He outnumbered his foe nearly 5:1.[33]

The quality of these warriors was clear to see; Seuthes had played to the military strengths of his kingdom, particularly in regard to his horsemen. The Odrysian elite enjoyed a rich equestrian heritage stretching back almost two centuries. Cavalry depictions are a common feature on their funerary friezes; horse skeletons have been uncovered in certain Thracian tumuli, buried alongside their owners for the afterlife. Seuthes had been sure to embrace his kingdom's strong cavalry draft and he had been able to muster some 8,000 horsemen – consisting overwhelmingly of Odrysians.[34]

Heavy cavalry presumably served as Seuthes' entourage, small in number but deadly in close combat. Armed with lances and long straight swords they were the Odrysian warlord's answer to the heavy-hitting shock cavalry of their Macedonian neighbours.[35] But although his heavily armoured entourage were a major asset Seuthes knew his greatest cavalry strength lay elsewhere: in his large number of light horsemen. Primarily equipped with two javelins and a small light shield (called a *pelta*), these swift skirmishers embodied the feared Thracian style of cavalry warfare. Initially they fought from a distance, throwing javelins down on their opponents with great power. Once they had expended their missiles they were no less deadly. Capable in melee, the Odrysians would then take out either a thrusting spear or sword and charge. Steady fighters both from range and in close-quarters, Seuthes' horde of light cavalry epitomised the Thracian style of fighting.[36]

Seuthes' Odrysian infantry were equally capable. Highly-mobile core elite footmen centred around his lightly armoured 'peltasts'. Armour was scant; for many a small shield served as their main material defence. Helmets and/or greaves were worn by those more fortunate. Their greatest defensive asset, however, was not a physical object. It was their swiftness of foot. Their agility.[37]

As with his cavalry, Seuthes' Odrysian peltasts fought both as skirmishers and as melee warriors. They too carried javelins, although on a much more numerous scale than their mounted counterparts.[38] Once they had expended their javelins, these peltasts would unsheathe their curved slashing swords and charge in to finish off a crippled foe.

Seuthes' Odrysians formed the mainstay of his 28,000-strong army, but the sheer size of this force suggests he had far more than just his kingdom's warriors within his ranks. Powerful, neighbouring clans, united in their desire to rid themselves of Macedonian interference, had sent bands of warriors to aid the revolt.[39]

One such tribe may well have been the Bessi. Inhabiting the rugged lands on the northern side of the Rhodope Mountains, these highland clansmen were renowned for the great size and strength of their infantry peltasts. Their skill as smiths was evident, epitomised by a new, terrifying weapon many Bessi warriors brought with them to battle.[40]

That weapon was the *rhomphaia*. Forged in the fires of Bessi blacksmiths since at least 350, the *rhomphaia* has become the iconic killing machine associated with ancient Thracian warfare. It consisted of a long iron blade – acutely-curved and finely-balanced. The blade's slight bend allowed the wielder to use the two-handed weapon in various ways. In compact areas and against cavalry, the warrior could use his *rhomphaia* as a thrusting weapon, lunging it into the flesh of horse and man alike and evoking the weapon's similarity to a sickle-like spear or pike. In more open scenarios, the warrior could exploit the *rhomphaia's* potential for powerful, downward slices, carving off limbs with relative ease. It was a truly terrifying weapon. Psychologically, the image of tall well-built Bessi warriors assembling on the plain, wielding their sharp *rhomphaia* blades, must have struck fear into many a heart within Lysimachus' ranks.[41]

Seuthes had used Thrace's military assets to his advantage. His mustering of powerful cavalry from his tribe, combined with his specialised peltast infantry – armed with various weapons stretching from long spears and javelins to *rhomphaias* and slashing swords – played to his peoples' strengths. As news of Lysimachus' arrival in Thrace undoubtedly reached him in late 323, the king had made sure he was primed and ready for battle.

Crush this threat and Seuthes could take the offensive, providing his Athenian allies welcome assistance. He could head south, capture and contest the vital Hellespont crossing. Or he could march his men southwest, following in the footsteps of Sitalkes and Cotys before him and lay waste Macedonia's heartlands. Hypereides and his Athenian allies would have been following events in Thrace closely, hoping to hear news of Seuthes' success.

The battle(s)

Lysimachus' aggressive stance provoked the intended reaction from Seuthes, drawing the larger Thracian force out from their camp for a decisive showdown on the open plain. If the Odrysian king had hoped to frighten his foe, it failed. Lysimachus remained unfazed – 'not frightened by the size of the enemy army.'[42] Despite being heavily outnumbered, fighting on this terrain was the best the general could ask for – the perfect topography for his core, mercenary phalanx and his heavy cavalry. Nevertheless, it was a high-risk strategy, characteristic of Lysimachus' reckless nature. If successful, the rewards would be great. But if he failed the consequences would be severe: Macedonian control over Thrace would crumble.

Seuthes, confident in the quantity and quality of his force, was happy to give Lysimachus the pitched battle he desired. We must also remember that Lysimachus had 'invaded' Odrysian home territory, so a feeling of duty to protect his subjects' land may also have encouraged Seuthes to accept Lysimachus' challenge of fighting in the open field.[43] Seuthes had the numbers, but Lysimachus had a battle of his own choosing. It proved critical.

Although the Odrysian king boasted the fiercest fighters in the land, there was one key unit he lacked: heavy infantry. Remember, his Thracian footmen championed mobility and agility, fighting more as individuals than cohesive units. They lacked large masses of warriors, heavily armed and trained to hold their own in dense units. Odrysian leaders in the past had fulfilled their army's heavy infantry requirement by hiring Hellenic hoplite mercenaries, fighting in tight, cohesive phalanxes at the core of the infantry line. But in 323 Seuthes had no such troops available, and he paid the price.[44]

The fight proved an arduous one. Javelins must have filled the sky as the Thracian and Macedonian styles of fighting clashed once more. Peltasts versus pikemen. Heavy cavalry versus harassing, skirmisher horsemen. *Rhomphaias* carving enemies in two. The dead and dying littered the battlefield. But the high quality of Lysimachus' mercenary heavy infantry, combined with the commander's clever use of tactics, must have eventually started to show. Despite suffering under the hail of missiles, the dense and disciplined phalanx proved more than a match for their Thracian counterparts on the plain. Light infantry presumably covered the phalanx's flanks, working in tandem with Lysimachus' cavalry to carve through the Odrysian light horsemen. Just over a century earlier, a great Odrysian army had met their match in mounted warfare whilst opposing heavy Macedonian cavalry:

> *Whenever they (the Macedonian cavalry) did attack, being excellent horsemen and armed with breastplates, no-one could stand up to them.* – Thucydides 2.100.5

It seems history was repeating itself in 323.[45]

After a long and bloody struggle, the fighting subsided and both sides retreated to their camps. Diodorus summarised the engagement:

> *Although he (Lysimachus) was numerically inferior, his men's martial skills were superior, and a hard-fought battle took place in which his losses were great, but nowhere near as great as those of the enemy. In the end, he returned to his camp the 'victor' of an inconclusive battle.* – Diodorus 18.14.3

Lysimachus' heavy infantry and cavalry had proven more than a match for their more numerous foe. But the battle proved far from decisive: many had perished on either side, Lysimachus' force having been whittled down by the great Thracian onslaught. The general's high-risk strategy had resulted in victory, but a Pyrrhic one.

Losses were high on either side, but neither Lysimachus nor Seuthes backed down. Following a brief period of preparation their armies clashed for a second time. Though no details survive of this follow up battle, it appears Lysimachus was all-but-defeated. What remained of his army was well and truly spent; he lacked the resources to complete the conquest of the Odrysian heartlands and eradicate a now, presumably more-cautious Seuthes. But similar war-weariness did not escape his opponent. The clashes had severely weakened Seuthes' power. Thousands of his warriors had fallen in the fighting, putting to rest his grand expansionist ambitions. Neither belligerents were hungry for further battle. It was time to lick wounds and negotiate peace.[46]

Seuthes and Lysimachus agreed to a meeting – the two former foes convening somewhere within Odrysian territory.[47] They soon found common ground; in their joint-desire to end hostilities with reputations intact, they signed an ancient 'entente' – a non-aggression pact between equals: Seuthes and Lysimachus would co-exist, ruling their own neighbouring domains at peace with one another. Seuthes earned official recognition as an independent leader over traditional Odrysian territory; Lysimachus remained the supreme authority over lands nearer the coasts.[48]

Seuthes and Lysimachus both benefitted from the treaty. Seuthes had revived his kingdom's independence; Lysimachus had subdued the great Thracian threat and could now turn his attention to consolidating his authority over his province. One power, however, was left disappointed. For Hypereides and his Athenians, news of the bloody battles and the subsequent non-aggression pact was a blow. No longer could they rely on Seuthes to descend on Macedonia from the north with a huge horde of warriors, wreaking havoc and aiding their revolt. They had to make do without a formidable ally.

Peace and prosperity

Despite Athenian disappointment, Seuthes triumphed the terms of the treaty. His defiant stand on the battlefield had allowed him to achieve major success at the negotiating table. His primary aim of reviving his kingdom and regaining Odrysian independence along the upper Tonzos River had succeeded. Militarily, his agreement to co-operate with Lysimachus helped secure his borders; economically, his kingdom had the potential to thrive with unfettered access to the lucrative Black Sea and Aegean markets.[49]

Seuthes made sure not to squander his new-found economic and political strength. Over the following years he prioritised modernising his kingdom, transforming it into an economic and cultural leading light within the Hellenistic world. It was an Odrysian cultural revolution, epitomised by one monumental project.

The king's agreement with Lysimachus proved a great coup for his reputation – he had officially revived Odrysian power in the region. To emphasise his achievement, he ordered the finishing of a grandiose new royal capital on the western bank of the Tonzos River.[50] Seuthes spent lavishly on this major project; wealth was poured into catalysing its completion. Zealous in his desire to emulate the cultural achievements of his southern neighbours, the king planned his new capital along Hellenistic lines. A sizable market-place (*agora*) and an altar to Dionysus, god of wine, dominated the city's centre; royal potteries and mints were constructed; strong walls surrounded the metropolis, pentagonal in its design; Greek became the official state language. In one further act to evoke even more similarity with his Hellenistic neighbours, Seuthes named his new royal seat after himself: Seuthopolis. It was the Odrysian Alexandria.[51]

Seuthes aimed Seuthopolis to be the pinnacle of his great Hellenisation project. He wanted to emphasise the modernisation of his Thracian kingdom – its economic might, its military strength and its cultural similarities with his Hellenistic neighbours. The move was practical: Seuthes' public adoration of the Hellenistic culture only aided his ability to co-exist with the likes of Lysimachus, emphasising his cultural alignment with his former foe.[52]

As the peace stabilised Seuthopolis' power continued to grow. Within a number of years, this Odrysian Alexandria had become a prosperous, urban centre – a central marketplace for merchants arriving from across the known world in their pursuit of profit. Trade flowed effortlessly up the Tonzos River into Seuthes' kingdom. Prosperity followed. Rich and powerful, Seuthes saw himself as subordinate to no man. The terms of the treaty had recognised his status as equal to Lysimachus and the other, dominant figures that now stretched the length of Alexander's empire. Finally, he could join the ranks of his famous Odrysian forebears as a mighty, independent monarch – all thanks to his successful resistance against Lysimachus in 323. He may not have won any defining victory, but he had benefited greatly from the war.[53]

As for Lysimachus, following his treaty with Seuthes, he turned his attention to statecraft. Political activity outside Thrace became of secondary importance. His Pyrrhic successes against Seuthes had ensured he lacked the necessary strength to march to Antipater's aid in Thessaly; meanwhile events in Asia were of little concern to him – at least for the short term. For now, he turned his attention to consolidating his rule and forging a strong, stable administration within this border province. And yet, the potential for future conflict was there for the military man. On the Black Sea's western edge, several prosperous city-states remained free from Macedonian control. Future opportunity to extend his dominion over these rich outposts lay open for the new governor.[54]

The great Thracian threat had been subdued – and brought further into the Hellenistic fold. For over ten years, Lysimachus and Seuthes would abide by the entente and co-exist. The land renowned for its peoples being 'devoted to Ares' and 'the most warlike' had returned to some state of order.[55]

The same could not be said elsewhere across the empire. War still raged in several theatres. Far-flung frontiers had proved especially susceptible to insurrection, no more so than in central Asia on the empire's north eastern fringes. There over 20,000 soldiers had risen in revolt, in their hopes to throw off undesired Macedonian overlordship. Would this uprising prove any more fortunate?

Further Reading

Primary Sources
Arrian *Events After Alexander* 1.10.
Diodorus 18.14.2–4.

Secondary Sources
Archibald, Z. H. (1998), *The Odrysian Kingdom of Thrace: Orpheus Unmasked*, Oxford, 215–316.
Delev, P. (2015), 'Thrace from the Assassination of Kotys I to Korupedium (360–281 BCE),' in J. Valeva et al. (eds.), *A Companion to Ancient Thrace*, Chichester, 48–58.
Dimitrov, D. P. and Cicikova, M. (1978), *The Thracian City of Seuthopolis*, Oxford.
Lund, H. S. (1992), *Lysimachus: A Study in Early Hellenistic Kingship*, Abingdon. 1–28.
Webber, C. (2011), *The Gods of Battle: The Thracians at War: 1500 BC–AD 150*, Barnsley.
Xydopoulos, I. K. (2010), 'The Odrysian Kingdom after Philip II: Greek- and Self-perception', *Eirene* 46, 213–222.

Chapter 4

The Bactrian Revolt

By December 323 the increasing fragility of Alexander's empire was becoming apparent. Reports of the king's death had sparked turmoil in Europe, where powerful armies challenged the authority of Antipater and Lysimachus. But the chaos was not just in the west. 3,000 miles away on the north-eastern fringes of the empire, another formidable force had arisen. Here veteran frontiersmen, desperate to return to their Hellenic homelands, seized the opportunity to revolt against their bonds of servitude. It would be a considerable challenge. To return home they had to travel the length of the empire, all the while battling any military forces that would await them. The scene was set for the next major confrontation of the post-Alexander period.

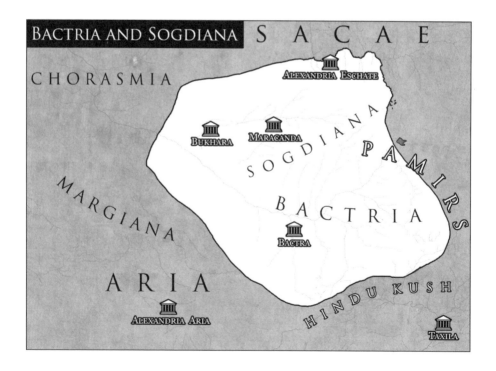

Background: The Land of a Thousand Cities

Bactria. Few areas of Hellenistic history evoke as much mystery and intrigue as the far-flung region of Bactria. Situated largely in modern-day Afghanistan, two towering mountain ranges dominate the land's geography. To the north, the Pamirs cover large swathes of the landscape; to the east and south the mighty, mineral rich Hindu Kush stands supreme.

Arising from the midst of the Hindu Kush was Bactria's other great natural feature: the mighty Oxus River. The Oxus and its many bountiful tributaries flowed through the heart of Bactria. Irrigated plains had been cultivated along these waterways since the Bronze Age, providing valuable farmland for the local people. Plentiful trees and vines supplied a rich variety of fruit; crops supplied grains such as wheat, barley and millet; pastures allowed for the breeding of livestock. It was these prosperous areas that were the bedrock for Bactria's native population, paving the way for the emergence of flourishing cities along the Oxus and its tributaries.

As Bactria's prosperity increased so too had its power. Producing strong and powerful horses famed for their endurance, Bactria's cavalry divisions became among the most feared in the known world, famously serving as elite horsemen in Achaemenid armies for over a century. From the plain near Plataea in 479 to Alexander the Great's decisive victory at Gaugamela 148 years later, Bactria's

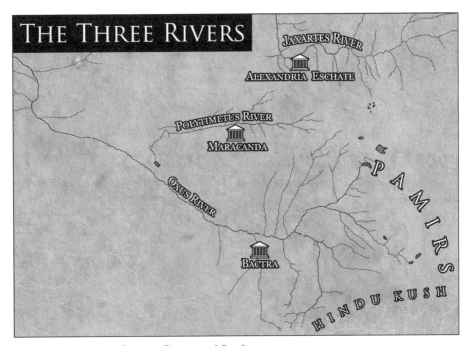

The three key rivers of ancient Bactria and Sogdia.

cavalry retained its elite reputation. Economically and militarily superb, it is no surprise that Persian monarchs heralded Bactria among their most valuable provinces.[1]

Bactria's power was clearly visible along the Oxus' banks, but away from the rivers and rich soils a very different landscape greeted travellers. Inhospitable deserts covered significant tracts of the hinterland. For any crossing these wastelands, knowing the right routes across was a matter of life and death. Water was scarce; the climate was unforgiving. Bactria's arid landscape, drier and hotter than anywhere in central Europe, proved one of its deadliest assets.[2]

A similar landscape defined Sogdia (Sogdiana), the region surrounding Bactria to the north and east. Like Bactria, the few rivers that flowed through the land provided the inhabitants with a vital lifeline for settlement and survival. At the heart of the region was the Polytimetus River (today the Zeravshan River), home to fertile, irrigated fields and the region's royal capital Maracanda (today's Samarkand).[3] So critical was the Polytimetus for sustaining life in Sogdia that the Greek name for it literally translates as 'very precious' while the Persians called it the 'spreader of gold'. On the region's northern edge was the similarly bountiful Jaxartes River (today the Syr Darya). Elsewhere however, wilderness and strategic rock fortresses were abundant.

For the ancient Greeks, Bactria and Sogdia were one of the farthest edges of the known world. Across the Jaxartes lay the land of horde and steppe; to the south and east were territories shrouded in myth and legend. The Bactrians and Sogdians were well-accustomed to their homeland's varied landscape, but it was an entirely different matter for the tens of thousands of European soldiers who arrived in this region in the mid-4th century.[4]

Alexander in Bactria

In the spring of 329 Alexander the Great and his all-conquering army had crossed the Hindu Kush and arrived in southern Bactria. They were in pursuit of Bessus, the notorious Bactrian regicide who continued to resist Alexander.[5]

Bessus had retreated to Bactria to recruit a new, powerful army, but his hopes of rallying significant support to his cause proved elusive. As Alexander had marched into the heart of the region, time and again cities willingly opened their doors to his army. Opposition was minimal.

Devoid of support and with Alexander in hot pursuit, Bessus and his withering supporters had fled north into Sogdia. This proved no friendlier. Resistance to Alexander was similarly non-existent and it was not long before the pretender was handed over for a brutal execution – betrayed by his last remaining comrades.[6]

Having subdued Bessus, Alexander had continued north. Crossing Sogdia he and his men reached the Jaxartes River without much difficulty, the local chieftains having submitted without a fight.[7] Naturally, Alexander's mind turned to consolidation.

Conscious of the ever-present threat of the nomadic eastern Scythians – or Sacae – to the north, he ordered the construction of a new Hellenic style military colony on the river's southern bank. He called it Alexandria Eschate – 'Alexandria the Furthest'.[8]

It was one of the most destabilising decisions of his life.

The Macedonian king had intended Alexandria Eschate to serve as a bulwark against the nomads beyond the river: a clear frontier marker for this far-flung corner of the empire. He had not reckoned upon the great anger it sparked among the recently contented Sogdians. For years Sogdians and Scythians had lived side-by-side; strong historical bonds existed between the two peoples. Alexander's creation of a 'non-fluid' border put those bonds in jeopardy.[9]

Pockets of rebellion erupted throughout Sogdia. Formerly allied chieftains turned against the king; marauding bands of Sogdian-Scythian cavalry harassed detachments throughout the province. Alexander's retribution was brutal, razing cities, conquering fortresses and inflicting massacres. Nevertheless, despite this reign of terror, the intensity of resistance only increased.

Time and time again the Macedonian king received news of enemy cavalry forces emerging from the desert and using their mobility and local knowledge to inflict devastating, lightning strikes on his forces. One disaster overshadowed all others.

In late 329 Alexander received word that the Sogdian warlord Spitamenes, a former ally, had renounced his loyalty and laid siege to Maracanda with a dangerous cavalry entourage. To counter the threat, Alexander dispatched some 2,000 troops with orders to relieve the city. Mercenary Hellenic hoplites formed the mainstay of the force, wielding their two-metre-long *doru* spears and large, circular *aspis* shields. In overall command Alexander appointed Pharnuches, his interpreter. Three high-ranking generals – Caranus, Andromachus and Menedemus – were ordered to serve as his military advisors.

After arriving at the scene, Pharnuches' force quickly chased away Spitamenes' cavalry from the walls of Maracanda and crossed the Polytimetus River in pursuit. What followed was disaster. A Scythian cavalry division reinforced the Sogdian army, and Spitamenes' superior knowledge of the surrounding countryside allowed him to lead his pursuers into a trap.

Confusion and indecision among the Macedonian officers culminated in disaster. As the disorderly column of hoplites plunged back into the Polytimetus River in their haste to escape, their enemies took out bows and javelins and rained a hail of death upon the slow moving and vulnerable – sitting ducks for Spitamenes' swift missile cavalry. Almost the entire unit perished – Caranus, Andromachus, Menedemus and Pharnuches among the dead. It was a massacre.[10]

When word of their demise reached Alexander's camp, fury had erupted among their comrades. Openly, they blamed the Macedonian officers for the deaths of their colleagues – it was their indecision that had catalysed the annihilation. The king was sure to take note.[11]

For two years Alexander remained in Bactria and Sogdia as he endeavoured to crush the revolt at huge cost to both his own and the army's well-being.[12] Eventually, however, the decisive blow was landed. Spitamenes was killed and Alexander attempted to heal the rifts with the Sogdian nobility, culminating in his marriage to the native noblewoman Roxana. Having restored a sense of stability, Alexander set forth across the Hindu Kush into India.

Those Left Behind

Alexander's pacification of Bactria-Sogdia had been limited, to say the least. Sogdian-Scythian warbands continued to control large swathes of the countryside, swarming around and wreaking havoc on the frontier garrisons. For the men Alexander left in the region, their duties remained fraught with risk.

Most of the soldiers Alexander left behind to maintain control of his north-easternmost province were his Hellenic hoplite mercenaries. They were formidable fighters, well-versed in the art of war and highly experienced, but despite their quality Alexander considered them unreliable. He did not trust them.

In 329 the king had received 8,000 Greek mercenaries as reinforcements sent from Antipater, his viceroy in Europe. Their allegiance to Alexander however, was dubious. Thousands had previously served Agis III, the Spartan king who had attempted to overthrow Macedonian hegemony in Europe a couple of years earlier. The revolt failed; as a consequence of being on the losing side, the mercenaries were forced to serve in their enemy's army.[13] Their love for Alexander was limited to say the least.

The loyalty of many other mercenaries was similarly suspect. Some had fought for Alexander since the start of his campaigns and were generally more loyal; others were not. Just as many of Antipater's reinforcements had previously served a Macedonian enemy in Agis, other Greek mercenaries already in the army had once fought for Persian gold against their new paymasters. Following Darius' defeats, Alexander had forced these men to swell his ranks as he continued eastwards – 'woe to the vanquished'.[14]

Relations between Alexander's Macedonians and a large section of these mercenaries were tense in late 329 and the ensuing disaster at the Polytimetus River had only increased the distrust between them. For Alexander, he needed to remove these destabilising soldiers from his ranks. But how? They were too dangerous to be returned to Europe to possibly serve in the armies of his enemies. They were unwanted in India. Ridding himself of them in this distant, volatile corner of his empire seemed a perfect solution.

Alexander left at least 13,000 mercenaries in this far-flung frontier region. Hundreds of miles from the nearest sea, suffering from an arid climate and surrounded by 'barbarians', to these Hellenic soldiers Bactria-Sogdia represented an alien and hostile landscape. What was more, the constant threat from marauding Sogdian/Scythian warbands haunted their patrols. Resentment was clear to see and this soon spilled over into insurrection.[15]

The first rising

In early 325 a rumour started to spread through Bactria-Sogdia. Alexander was dead, the king having succumbed to a fatal wound – inflicted while storming an Indian stronghold. His army was now stranded halfway down the Indus Valley – divided and doomed.

As the news filtered across the region, factions emerged among the mercenaries, split over how they should react. One group, spearheaded by a certain Athenodorus, championed insurrection. The king was dead. His army was stranded. It seemed the perfect opportunity for them to leave this most-hated land and return home.

They stormed the ill-defended citadel at Bactra, presumably murdered Amyntas, the Macedonian governor, and started rallying men to their cause. It was during that critical phase however, that more concrete news arrived from India: Alexander was very much alive.

Fearing reprisals from the Macedonian king, many mercenaries abandoned Athenodorus and his enterprise. For Athenodorus and his supporters, however, there was no going back. They had already crossed their Rubicon. Preparations continued, but the situation soon descended into turmoil.

Before Athenodorus could kickstart this return to the west, the leader was dead – murdered at a banquet on the orders of a rival mercenary leader called Biton. Further plotting and unrest followed. Ultimately Biton, having survived two dices with death, departed Bactria with 3,000 mercenaries on a homeward-bound journey to Europe. Their fate remains unclear: Curtius claimed they made it home; Diodorus stated that Biton and his comrades perished on Asian soil.[16]

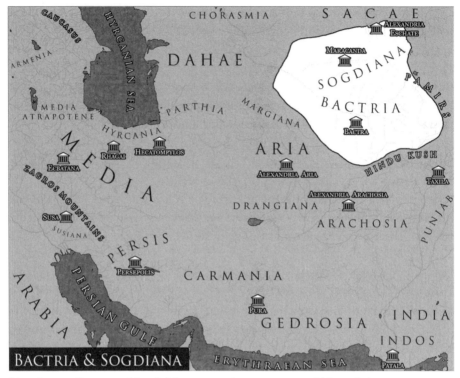

Map showing Bactria and Sogdia's location in the eastern part of Alexander's empire.

Regardless of its result, the revolt had highlighted the intense resentment felt among the Hellenic mercenaries settled in Bactria and Sogdia. The area teetered on the brink of anarchy.

The Bactrian Revolt

The fateful spark came in late 323, when confirmed reports of Alexander's sudden death in Babylon reached Bactria. This time it was no mere rumour. It was fact.

While the King was alive they put up with their situation out of fear. – Diodorus 18.7.1

But now Alexander was dead; now was their chance to use the ensuing chaos to their advantage.

What followed was a great surge of activity in Bactria-Sogdia.[17] All across the province soldiers abandoned their posts and assembled to muster a great mercenary host. Hellenic soldiers stationed across the east came together, united by their shared longing to return to Greece and leave this hated land behind. Frontier posts were emptied; a great army of hardened veterans had formed.

Very soon, the amount of mercenaries that had answered the rallying call numbered in the thousands. It was an awesome force that only emphasised the mass of disgruntled soldiers Alexander had dumped on his north-eastern frontier all those years before.

Overall command was assigned to Philon, a high-ranking mercenary captain originally from the fertile region of Aeniania – west of Thermopylae. Overseeing the assembly of this great mercenary host from frontier posts across the province was a noteworthy logistical achievement for the commander.[18] Nevertheless, preparations must have taken considerable time to complete. It was time that their enemies put to good use.

The region of Aenis / Aeniania, just west of Thermopylae. The home region of Philon and many other mercenaries stationed in Bactria.

The response

The unavoidable implications of thousands upon thousands of veteran soldiers abandoning their frontier posts and assembling to form a large host was not missed by those who had assumed the reins of power in Babylon. For Perdiccas and his supporters, it was unwelcome news.[19]

This threat from the east was considerable. Unlike in the west, where the challenge posed by Leosthenes and the Athenian-led confederation was countered by the likes of Antipater and a whole host of other famous generals close by, no substantial opposition stood in the way of Philon's force and the royal army at Babylon. Thousands of hardened mercenaries desperate to return home would soon be marching through the empire's Asian heartlands, ravaging the lands to sustain their army. Perdiccas had to act.

Act Perdiccas did. Immediately he and his adjutants agreed to dispatch a task force east to eradicate Philon and his force before they commenced their great *anabasis*. It would be no easy task. After all, the men they were facing were not ill-equipped levies; they were professional soldiers, survivors of one of the empire's most volatile frontiers.

Fortunately for Perdiccas, the regent had thousands of hardened warriors at his disposal. These included his 15,000 Macedonians, the scarred veterans who had won Alexander his empire by the tips of their *sarissa* pikes and *xyston* lances.[20] It was around these elite fighters that Perdiccas wished to form the task force's vital core. But such an assignment was highly unpopular.

Despite their loyalty to the king's official guardian, these veteran footmen had no desire to return to the hated far east: the land that had caused them so

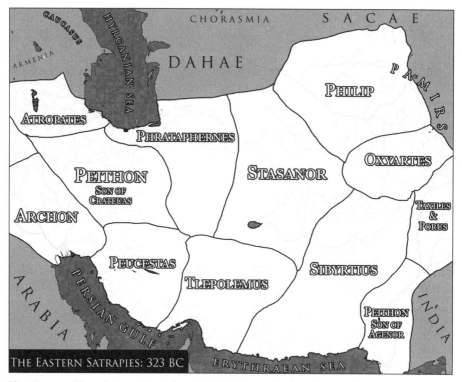

The Eastern (Upper) Satrapies in late 323. Babylonia: Archon. Persis: Peucestas. Carmania: Tlepolemus. Arachosia and Gedrosia: Sibyrtius. Indus Delta: Peithon Son of Agenor. Upper Reaches of the Indus: divided between the Kingdoms of Porus and Taxiles. The Hindu Kush: Oxyartes. Bactria and Sogdia: Philip. Aria and Drangiana: Stasanor. Parthia and Hyrcania: Phrataphernes. Greater Media: Peithon Son of Crateuas. Media Minor (Atropatene): Atropates.

much misery. In the end, some would have no choice: the lack of enthusiasm forced Perdiccas to make an unpopular decision. He needed a detachment for the expedition; he could not allow Philon's force to destabilise his authority any further. So the regent ordered that 3,800 Macedonians be chosen by lot to return to Bactria-Sogdia – 3,000 infantry and 800 cavalry.[21]

The 3,800 veterans would struggle to defeat Philon's force on their own, however. Substantial reinforcements were essential, but Perdiccas did not want to siphon off any more strength from the royal army.[22] Instead, Perdiccas turned to the eastern governors for military aid: to the likes of Peucestas in Persia, Sibyritus in Arachosia and his father-in-law Atropates in Media Minor. It was their duty to supply substantial reinforcements for the eastern expedition.[23]

So who was to command this task force? Perdiccas was out of the question: he needed to stay close at hand to events in the west. But the regent was not at a loss for loyal lieutenants. Proven commanders filled his council – Attalus, Seleucus, Alcetas and Aristonous had all remained by his side at Babylon. In the end, however, Perdiccas had settled on another.

His name was Peithon. Hailing from a noble Macedonian family, and a man with at least thirteen years of military experience to show, Peithon was no stranger to senior commands. Throughout Alexander the Great's campaigns he had served among the king's highest adjutants – as one of his 'bodyguards'. Despite this prominence, we hear little about his achievements during these campaigns. Presumably Peithon proved his martial prowess on the battlefield and his loyal service to Alexander was rewarded with prestigious honours.[24]

Peithon continued to serve as one of Alexander's advisers until the latter's death in June 323 and his senior position ensured his voice was significant when he and his fellow generals gathered to decide the fate of the empire. In the crisis that followed Alexander's death, he was one of the most outspoken opponents to Arrhidaeus' kingship. But a lack of diplomatic know-how, initially, had only heightened tensions between the generals and the rank and file. Early on during the crisis Peithon had openly ridiculed the soldiers' decision to choose such an incompetent figure as king.

> *This was when Alexander was most to be pitied, he said, for he had been cheated out of the enjoyment and support of such good citizens and soldiers, men who in thinking only of their king's glorious memory were blind to all other considerations.* – Curtius 10.7.4

Ridicule brought further rage; Peithon's verbal attack only deepened the rift between the two factions, and he had only managed to make the situation worse.

Still adamant in his opposition to Arrhidaeus' kingship, it was Peithon who had then proposed the ill-fated compromise: where Perdiccas and Leonnatus would share guardianship of Alexander's Asian empire until Roxana's child came of age. Once again, however, the refusal to even contemplate the soldier's regal choice of Arrhidaeus only inflamed Macedonian anger and culminated in bloodshed.

Despite his initially inflammatory actions, Peithon's support for Perdiccas throughout the crisis was rewarded. During the subsequent division of satrapies he had received as reward a large portion of Media, a wealthy eastern satrapy. It was Peithon who Perdiccas thus tasked with quashing the Bactrian revolt.

Aversion towards returning to the hated far-east may have seized the Macedonian soldiery, but for Peithon it was a different matter. He was delighted. The expedition offered him opportunity; it offered him the chance to cement his mark on this new regime and gain military glory on the world stage – the success his alone. Gladly he accepted the command Perdiccas had bestowed upon him and began preparations for assembling the expeditionary force.[25]

Without delay he and his reluctant nucleus of Macedonians commenced their eastward march, crossing the Zagros Mountains and arriving in the commander's home satrapy of Media.[26] Several thousand native auxiliaries – fine cavalrymen as well as infantry – swelled their ranks over the coming months, forming the mainstay of the allied army.[27] This was not all. The concurrent arrival of more contingents, sent by neighbouring governors who had answered the call for military assistance, further bolstered Peithon's force with levies and mercenaries alike.

The expedition sets off

By December 323 the expedition was ready. Peithon and his greatly enlarged army departed the bountiful plains of Media and set forth for Bactria. More allied detachments joined them on the march, sent by governors situated *en route* to the northeast frontier. By the time the expedition reached Bactria's borders Peithon's army numbered 21,800 men – 13,000 infantry and 8,800 cavalry.[28]

Perdiccas had placed a great deal of trust in Peithon. The latter's appointment as commander of the expedition had made him, in no uncertain terms, the most powerful figure in the eastern provinces. It was trust, our source suggests, that Perdiccas misplaced.

Now Peithon was a highly ambitious man, and he was delighted to accept command of the expedition because he intended to attach the Greeks to himself by treating them well. Then, once he had enlarged his army by taking them on as auxiliaries, he planned to go independent and rule over the Upper Satrapies.
– Diodorus 18.7.4

According to the above, Peithon had no intention of being Perdiccas' lackey; he wanted to carve out his own kingdom in the east. Some scepticism, however, should be attached to this claim. Diodorus, our sole source for this episode, based his account upon the writings of the historian Hieronymus. Although a contemporary of these events, Hieronymus had nothing but contempt for Peithon. They were bitter enemies.[29] It is very likely that Peithon's veiled treachery on this eastern expedition is a fabrication – designed to stain the general's name in the history books.[30]

Peithon's loyalty to Perdiccas in late 323 must have been fairly resolute. Why on earth would Perdiccas have entrusted such a vital mission to the general otherwise?[31] This is not to mention the soldiers themselves, warriors who were determined to make their stay in the hated far-east as short as possible. Despite Hieronymus' claim, Perdiccas' trust in Peithon seemed well-founded. The latter's ambitions were without question. Yet, for now at least, he believed his best chance at future power lay in crushing the revolt and returning to the west at the head of a victorious army.

A clash of veterans

Peithon and his hastily cobbled together army reached Bactria in the spring of 322 and it was not long before they encountered Philon. It must have been quite a sight to behold. Opposing Peithon's force on a plain somewhere in Bactria, thousands upon thousands of mercenaries stood ready, each housing a zealous desire to return home. In total, Philon had amassed a force of 23,000 men. Most of his warriors were infantry – of which presumably a substantial amount were heavy, spear-wielding hoplites. But he also had a considerable cavalry wing – 3,000 men in total.[32]

For Peithon and his men, the upcoming battle promised to be a tough engagement. Not only did Philon's force outnumber the bodyguard's army, but its experience was second to none. Peithon could take some comfort in the quality of his 3,800 Macedonians, but the rest of his troops' expertise is unclear. Philon's force, however, consisted almost entirely of experienced soldiers. Though many still fought in the rather archaic hoplite combat style, they had mastered the art and were survivors of a perilous frontier. If defeating Peithon's army was essential to continue their journey home, then defeat Peithon they would.

The two armies arranged themselves into their respective battle formations. On one side there was Philon and his hoplites, presumably reinforced by a substantial number of skirmishers. Opposing them was Peithon's Eurasian force. Preparations ended; Philon's wall of spears closed in on Peithon's army. Shouts erupted from either side. The battle had begun.[33]

And so, on a Bactrian battlefield in early 322, just as in mainland Europe, a large host of mercenary hoplites faced off against the Macedonian regime. Philon's army matched Peithon's in both quantity and quality, and for a considerable time the battle hung in the balance. But Peithon had prepared himself for such a situation. The decisive moment of battle had yet to occur.[34]

Suddenly, just as victory seemed within reach, Philon and his men watched on in horror as 3,000 allied soldiers proceeded to peel off from the battle line and retreat to a nearby hill. It was at that moment that Peithon's backroom dealing revealed itself.

The turncoat

Prior to the battle, Peithon had sent 'a certain Aenianian' to infiltrate Philon's camp. He was a spy, tasked to tempt defection within Philon's ranks. The vast wealth of the former Persian Empire ensured the Macedonian commander could promise rewards that would corrupt almost any individual. It proved so. The Aenianian spy's guarantees of unimaginable wealth and a comfortable return to the west had soon found a willing recipient among Philon's generals. His name was Letodorus, a senior adjutant who commanded a sizable regiment of 3,000 men. In a time where animosity between rival mercenary commanders was an all-too-regular occurrence, similar hostility may well have been brewing between Philon and Letodorus.[35] For the latter, Peithon's temptations proved irresistible.

And so, as Philon and his men appeared to be winning the fight, news reached them that Letodorus and his 3,000 troops had deserted. In an instant the pendulum of momentum shifted. The mercenaries were unsure why Letodorus' regiment had withdrawn. Had they been routed? And were they now about to be surrounded? As the uncertainty grew, panic spread through the ranks of Philon's force. Suddenly large segments of the army lost their nerve and fled the field. The battle was over.[36]

The side that had, until recently, looked likeliest to win, were scattered. Peithon and his army held the field – all thanks to Letodorus and his 3,000 turncoats. The Perdiccan army had triumphed, but the question of what was to be done with the routed remnants of the enemy force remained.[37] Thousands of mercenary hoplites had escaped the battlefield. Peithon knew he had to deal with them before a return to the west was feasible.

A bloody aftermath

Away from the battlefield, weary remains of Philon's frontiersmen slowly started to regain their composure and regroup. Demoralised and defeated, they must have evoked a sad and broken force; the soldiers were in no state to oppose Peithon a second time.[38] Nevertheless many readied their arms and armour once more. They thought they had no choice. It was then that a lone horseman came riding up to the makeshift camp.[39] The man was a messenger, sent by Peithon. Rather than fight a needless second engagement, the herald proclaimed Peithon's peaceful alternative:

Ordering them to lay down their arms and promising that they could return to their colonies with their safety guaranteed. – Diodorus 18.7.7

A wave of relief flowed through the camp. Casting aside their swords, spears and shields the mercenaries accepted Peithon's call for surrender. Their resolute commitment to leave this hated frontier had been shattered by Letodorus' brutal betrayal. Little spirit remained for fighting. Fear had gripped the army; morale was at rock bottom. Those that had managed to regroup were in disarray: exhausted and outnumbered.[40]

For these mercenaries, survival was more attractive than perishing in a forlorn fight that they had next to no chance of winning. Peithon had offered them a way out from needless slaughter. His weary opponents accepted, even if it meant remaining in their despised, far-eastern colonies. It was better than being dead.

Having thrown down their weapons and joined with Peithon's army, a public reconciliation followed between the two forces. Oaths of peace were exchanged, with Peithon and Philon (if he was still alive) presumably taking central roles. The mercenaries mingled with the Macedonians; harmony had returned. Or so they thought.[41]

Beneath the façade of fraternisation, the Macedonians remained ready. These mercenaries were the men who had forced them to return to this most hated province; these were the soldiers who had only recently willingly spilled Macedonian blood on the battlefield; these were the men who had shown so much resentment towards their Macedonian officers all those years before. Hands gripped sword hilts; Alexander's veterans awaited the order.

Suddenly the anticipated signal was given. The Macedonians unsheathed their swords, aimed their javelins and started slaughtering the unsuspecting mercenaries. What followed was a merciless massacre; none were spared. When the bloodbath finally subsided the death toll numbered in the thousands.[42]

The heinous act resembled a spontaneous butchery, sparked by the spilling over of boiled up frustration among the unruly Macedonians. In fact, the opposite was the case.

Before Peithon and the Macedonians had set off from Babylon for their eastern expedition, Perdiccas had issued them a brutal instruction:

He (Perdiccas) gave him (Peithon) express orders to kill all the rebels, once he had defeated them, and to share the spoils among his men. – Diodorus 18.7.5

Perdiccas, the most senior figure in the empire below the king, had sanctioned the slaughter. There would be no mercy for traitors.[43]

Despite Peithon's valiant attempt to avert this unnecessary mass slaughter, the veterans had taken the decision out of his hands.[44] Seeking the material rewards Perdiccas had promised them they brutally executed the regent's orders, reaping the spoils in the wake of the bloodshed as the humiliated Peithon bowed to their will and gave them permission to plunder the possessions of the dead mercenaries. The revolt had met with a ruthless end.

For those frontiersmen that had survived the slaughter – either those who had not revolted or who had not regrouped following the battle – Peithon permitted them to remain in the east. Hopes of ever returning to their homelands had evaporated. They were prisoners on this distant frontier. Nevertheless, these mercenaries and their families laid the foundations for a lasting Hellenic presence along the banks of the Oxus River, accepting their fate and taking advantage of the fertile land's many benefits. Overtime, more and more Hellenic colonists would settle here and within 120 years their descendants would form the nucleus of a powerful kingdom in central Asia.[45]

As for Philon, his name disappears from the history books. Almost certainly the Aenianian commander did not survive the encounter with Peithon's army, either perishing on the battlefield or in the treacherous massacre that followed. The ancient geographer Strabo offers a possible, although unlikely, alternative. In his writing he refers to an Aenianian settlement near the Hyrcanian (Caspian) Sea. Perhaps Philon and some of his mercenaries did manage to escape the clash and settle near this inland sea, but the evidence is far from certain.[46]

For Letodorus and his followers, however, their fate seems more fortunate. Their betrayal had turned the tide of the battle and earned Peithon his victory. Presumably the turncoats were richly rewarded.[47]

Victorious and booty-laden, Peithon and his Macedonians commenced their return march to the royal army. The first major challenge to Perdiccas' regime had been overcome. The revolt in the east was no more; but unrest in the west still raged.

Further Reading

Primary Source
Diodorus Siculus 18.4.8–18.7.9

Secondary Sources
Bosworth (2002), *The Legacy of Alexander: Politics, Warfare and Propaganda under the Successors*, Oxford, 61–2.
Holt, F. M. (1989), *Alexander the Great and Bactria*, Leiden.
Holt, F. M. (1999), *Thundering Zeus: The Making of Hellenistic Bactria*, Berkeley.
Iliakis, M. (2013), 'Greek Mercenary Revolts in Bactria: A Re-Appraisal', *Historia* 62 (2), 182–195.
Roisman, J. (2012), *Alexander's Veterans and the Early Wars of the Successors*, Austin, 82–86.

Chapter 5

The Spartan Adventurer

Spartan shields glimmered in the Libyan sunlight. Veteran soldiers stood ready. For the past 12 months these hardened hoplites had hired out their spears for an audacious enterprise – enticed across the Great Sea by promises of wealth and glory.

At their head was a Spartan *condottiere* – an adventurer. A general who had infamously thrown himself into the limelight following Alexander the Great's demise. Fickle fortune had dominated their venture so far – an unprecedented string of successes offset by several severe setbacks. Now this band of brigands hoped to turn the tide of their *Tyche* (fortune) once more. Together they stood on the battlefield, united in their desire to seize one of the greatest treasures in the known world: a divine city. Rich. Powerful. Beautiful. The jewel of Libya.

Background: Harpalus' flight

In late 324 a lone ship sailed away from Athens carrying the most wanted man in the Mediterranean. His name was Harpalus. Corrupt and crooked, the disgraced treasurer had once been at the forefront of Macedonian politics, a focal name within Alexander's empire. That time had passed.

Earlier in the year Harpalus had crossed his bridge of no return. The enormous wealth of Babylon and the central provinces had lured him into a decadent lifestyle. Luxury was endorsed; statecraft was side-lined. Today he is best remembered for fawning over prominent Athenian prostitutes – a story that has come to epitomise his negligence. Such dereliction of duty fostered its own consequences. Maladministration spread like wildfire across the empire's central provinces – temples and tombs were sacked, subjects mistreated. The chances of retribution seemed low; neither Harpalus nor his decadent partners in crime expected Alexander ever to return from fighting in the far east. But Alexander did return, and retribution was swift. Many of Harpalus' extravagant accomplices were charged with profligacy; all were swiftly executed.[1]

Harpalus saw the writing on the wall; the consequence of reckless extravagance during Alexander's absence in the east, he feared he would be next to receive a one way summons to his king's court. It was time to escape. In February 324, with hired muscle, a band of friends and a small fortune Harpalus headed west, culminating in his arrival at Athens in the summer. Thinking only of his safety the devious Macedonian had turned completely against his king and colluded openly with bellicose Athenians intent on revolt. His actions proved highly divisive. Though his rhetoric and bribes won him some significant supporters, many others opposed having the disgraced treasurer within their walls. Nor were the Macedonians going to stand idly by in the meantime. Three times they demanded the Athenians hand over Harpalus; three times Athens refused, although their resistance weakened. Imprisoned within the city, Harpalus' days looked numbered.[2]

Demosthenes and the Athenians faced a dilemma. They did not want to hand over Harpalus – a suppliant – to the Macedonians. Nor, however, did they want to provoke a futile war with the all-powerful Alexander for continuing to house Macedon's most wanted. Enemies were circling, urging Alexander to sail west and surround the city with thousands of soldiers and siege engines. Holding on to Harpalus kept the threat of war hovering.[3]

Harpalus' liability outweighed his financial benefits. His mere presence affected Athens' ability to negotiate matters of state. Already Demosthenes was trying to persuade the Macedonians to let Athens retain control over Samos, a colonial possession Alexander had recently ordered they return to the island's native inhabitants. Demosthenes and the Athenians were desperate to reverse this decision, but if they were to have any chance of convincing the Macedonian monarch to change his mind, ridding their city of Harpalus was essential. Securing Samos took precedence.

A solution was conjured up. As the days passed, Harpalus' custody grew more and more relaxed. Fewer and fewer guards were assigned to keep watch over him and before long all of Harpalus' armed captors had been relieved of their duties. Harpalus was free to flee – his prison having evaporated around him. Hurried down to the harbour he boarded a boat and sailed away into the Saronic Gulf. Macedon's most wanted was on the run once more.[4]

Having drifted out of the Gulf into the Aegean Sea, Harpalus and his crew sailed south, keeping close to the Peloponnesian coastline. His past submission had seen him sacrifice a small fortune, confiscated by the Athenians upon his arrest. But Harpalus had a fallback position. Before being admitted to Athens he had deposited much of his wealth at far-away Taenarum. Protected by his personal mercenary army – some 6,000 strong – neither the Athenians nor the Macedonians were able to seize this already-stolen Achaemenid treasure. It was to Taenarum that Harpalus sailed.

Harpalus' stay at the mercenary camp was brief. Having gathered both money and men, a great fleet was prepared. Soldiers boarded boats and the armada sailed away from the Greek mainland for the final time, across the Cretan Sea.[5]

Their first stop was Kydonia, a prominent coastal city-state in north-west Crete, where Harpalus and his friends considered their next move. Several options must have been touted. They could continue east to the strategically vital island of Rhodes, evict the Macedonian garrison from its namesake capital and turn it into an impregnable fortress. They could head west across the Ionian Sea, to aid the Italiote-Greek city-states against growing 'barbarian' incursions. Or they could sail south, across the width of the Mediterranean to the fertile lands of coastal Libya. For Harpalus, survivability and profit were key. Where was their best chance of fortune and victory? Where was the best chance of evading Alexander's grasp? Little did he know that this decision was to be taken out of his hands.

One man's demise, another's rise

In early 323 a companion approached Harpalus. His name was Thibron, a Spartan mercenary commander who had accompanied his paymaster since he fled Babylon. Harpalus considered Thibron a loyal ally. It was a grave mistake. Emboldened by his high-standing with the mercenaries, Harpalus' lacklustre leadership and his own ambitions, Thibron approached and then assassinated his unsuspecting leader. Harpalus, the most wanted man in the empire, was dead.[6]

Thibron acted fast. Quickly he proclaimed himself the new leader of the mercenary expedition, securing their loyalty through gifts and promises of future riches. Resistance was minimal; there was no love-lost for the infamous Harpalus. Thibron's calculated risk had paid off. The rewards came fast.

Within no time at all the Spartan had risen to a prominent position on the Mediterranean stage. Around 6,000 grizzled veterans stood ready to serve, expecting profitable conquest. Thibron knew exactly where to take them.[7]

A band of Hellenic statesmen had watched these dramatic events unfold before their eyes. But these prominent figures did not hold power in Kydonia. They were exiles. Suppliants. Banished from their place of birth. Far away from their home city they craved to reverse their current misfortune. They craved to return to their homeland with a formidable force. To expel their hated foes at the tip of a bloodied spear point. For that, however, they needed an army. They sought a general capable of restoring them to their homeland. They sought a liberator. They found Thibron.[8]

Where was home for these Hellenic exiles? It was not to the north, neither in Greece nor the Aegean. Nor was it to the east or west. It was to the south, in Africa.

THE SOUTH AEGEAN

Cyrene

In the mid-seventh century a group of émigrés primarily from the Aegean island of Thera had sailed south, lured by the prospect of a fresh start in a land renowned for its bountiful harvests and prosperity.[9] Their initial destination was an island off the Libyan coast, where they founded a trading station to take advantage of the constant commerce passing between east and west. For two years the island (modern day Geziret el Marakeb) remained their solitary settlement, until they finally crossed to the Libyan mainland and founded a colony on the continent at a place called Aziris.[10] For six years the Hellenic settlers in Aziris prospered, peacefully co-existing with the native Libyans and reaping the rewards their venture had brought them. In the seventh year, however, the colonists received a proposal that completely altered the path of ancient history:

> ...the Libyans begged them to abandon Aziris, declaring that they themselves would lead the way to a much better location – and this convinced the settlers.[11]
> – Herodotus 4.158

The Libyans kept their word and guided the newcomers west to their 'promised land'. Their destination did not disappoint. A striking plateau was shown to the settlers, situated eight miles from the sea. The elevated plain dominated the local landscape, surrounded by fertile lands and centred around a bountiful spring: the 'fountain (krene) of Apollo'. It was the perfect location for a city. In 631 the colonists settled for the final time; Cyrene was born.[12]

It was not long before further Hellenic colonies were founded on lucrative Libyan soil. Within decades of Cyrene's founding waves of colonists had departed the Aegean and sailed their ships south, attracted by promises of possessing arable land and encouraged by tales of wealth and opportunity. Within fifty years of Cyrene's founding, a sizable Hellenic presence existed within the region – dubbed Cyrenaica by ancient Greek sources after its most famous city.

For the native Libyans, this rapid influx of Greek colonists was difficult to tolerate. As the cities expanded, Hellenic settlers started encroaching on native Libyan lands and appropriating it for themselves. Relations soured and it was not long before hostilities erupted. In c.570 a Libyan king appealed for aid from the Egyptian Pharaoh, Apries. Apries acknowledged the appeal, gathered a large army and headed west. Disaster ensued. In the following clash – the first ever between Greek and Egyptian armies – Apries' force was all-but annihilated by the Cyrenean phalanx. The Greeks were there to stay.[13]

'A country of many flocks and all kinds of fruits'[14]

The successful defence catalysed Cyrene's development and before long the city had become a thriving, autonomous urban centre on the southern border of the Greek World. Its lands were among the most fertile and most productive in the Mediterranean; Cyrenean farmers embraced bountiful eight-month-long harvests. Flourishing trade naturally followed. Cargo ships filled with Cyrenean grain sailed far and wide, finding willing buyers across the Mediterranean.[15]

When dreaded, catastrophic crop failures caused city-states to desperately cast their eyes further afield for aid, they looked to Cyrene. The Cyreneans were only too happy to oblige, providing shiploads of home-grown grain and earning the eternal gratitude of many city-states for rescuing them from the brink of famine.[16] Cyrenean coffers consequently swelled, but it was not just grain that the Libyan city became famous for exporting. There was also silphium.

Silphium was an extraordinary commodity. Coming from Cyrenaica, this plant was considered extremely valuable. Elites sought it as a culinary spice; healers used the herb in their medicinal methods. Silphium soon became a widespread symbol of status, leading the Cyreneans to later depict the luxury item on their coinage. Meanwhile Cyrenean horses were similarly highly sought after, renowned for their strength and skill at pulling chariots.[17]

'A most bright eye to strangers'[18]

For merchants, Cyrene became a vital crossroads both on land and at sea. Apollonia, Cyrene's port, was a stop-off point for traders sailing alongside the Mediterranean's southern coastline between east and west. On land, Cyrene became a focal destination for Libyan caravan routes, the end point from where African traders could sell their exotic goods – ivory, dyes and skins – to the Hellenic merchants seeking these high-value items.

For pilgrims too, visiting Cyrene was equally vital. The divine city was situated on the pilgrimage path for those making the arduous but well-trodden journey to the sanctuary of Zeus Ammon at Siwa.[19]

By the end of the fourth century, Cyrene's wealth was legendary – a beautiful city adorned with monumental marble temples, thick stone walls, richly-

The Temple of Zeus at Cyrene. It was larger than the Temple of Zeus at Olympia, the latter being one of the Seven Wonders of the Ancient World.

decorated racecourses and a thriving cosmopolitan market-place. Away from the marketplaces academia also flourished; the city boasted one of the most famous schools of philosophy in the Mediterranean. All this helped to establish Cyrene as one of the largest and most prosperous cities in the Mediterranean – the epitome of Hellenic colonial achievement.

Yet no kingdom enjoys endless immunity from instability. No golden age can last forever. In the mid-320s a vicious civil war erupted within the city, as oligarchs and democrats struggled for supremacy. In the end the oligarchs emerged victorious; they chased what remained of the democrats out of the city and banished them from their homeland. Exiled, some of these fugitives fled north across the Mediterranean to Kydonia on Crete. It was they who turned to Thibron, seeking a swift return to Cyrene's shores.[20]

Thibron required little convincing. The possibility of controlling Cyrene was too tantalising a prize to refuse. Nevertheless, the Spartan made sure to control his ambitions in front of the exiles. He declared himself their saviour, their champion, the man who would restore them to Cyrene. By the spear if necessary. In reality however, Thibron's ambitions stretched much further. His expedition would not simply be a noble crusade for the benefit of others. Cyrene's vast riches would be his prize.[21]

The expedition begins

At the height of 323 Thibron's army set sail for Cyrenaica. The exiles guided Thibron and his army to a secure landing zone. Once assembled upon *terra firma* the soldiers wasted no time and started marching towards Apollonia, intending to cut off Cyrenean communications to their port before heading inland. The Cyreneans, however, had no intention of letting this happen without a fight. Having learnt that their exiled enemies had returned to Libyan shores with force, they amassed a sizable army and marched to meet the mercenaries on the open field. *En route* to Apollonia, Thibron found his path blocked by this enemy host. A mix of cavalry and infantry opposed his men, but the Spartan's attention must have been drawn to the most iconic unit his enemy fielded.[22]

Chariots had long been closely associated with Cyrene. Described as 'a city of fine chariots' by the poet Pindar, racing these vehicles was the traditional sport for the city's nobility:

> *Instead of the short-finned dolphins*
> *They shall have swift horses, and reins for oars:*
> *They shall drive the stormfoot chariots.* – Pindar *Pythian IV* 12–13

Chariot races were a keystone feature of the *polis'* heritage, but militarily too they had long-served an important role.

This way of warfare was iconic of an archaic age. Images of Assyrian chariot archers skirmishing enemies from a distance or Greek heroes being escorted up to the walls of Troy may well come to mind. For the Cyreneans, however, chariotry was not an antiquated method of fighting. They had mastered the science; they had learnt to use these chariots with deadly effect.

Stationed behind the front line the chariots functioned as fast-moving troop transports. Four of the city's famous horses pulled a semi-protected cabin, capable of carrying three passengers. At the forefront was the driver, expert at guiding his four-horse-team across the battlefield. Supporting him were two infantry soldiers – the real teeth of the team – wielding spear, bow or javelin. After battle commenced these chariot teams would ride up and down behind the army's front line, close enough to view the action but far enough away to ensure the vehicles did not become bogged down in a deadly melee. For a time, they remained at a distance. That was, however, until the line began to falter. As soon as news reached the chariots that a part of the formation was crumbling, the horses would race across the field, urged on by their charioteers. Once they had reached their destination, the infantrymen dismounted and plugged the gap in the line. Two men on their own would do little to alleviate a faltering line, but these chariots served in large squadrons. If they worked together, these chariot teams formed one of antiquity's most ingenious, mobile reinforcement units. Once the threat on one side of the line was repulsed, the soldiers would remount the chariot and quickly be taken to another part of the battle. Though these weapons of war may have looked out of place on a Hellenistic battlefield their function ensured they were far from obsolete.[23]

The Cyreneans fielded the best force their city had to offer to oppose Thibron. Nevertheless, despite larger numbers and their iconic chariots, the experience of the Spartan's hoplite mercenaries proved telling. Using their *doru* spears to knock aside those of their adversaries with ease, time and time again the veterans landed killing blows; the Cyrenean part-time infantry proved incapable of putting up an effective resistance; it was a slaughter. Cyreneans fell left, right and centre, unable to halt the mercenary onslaught. Soon the battle's outcome was beyond doubt. What remained of the Cyrenean army fled back to the safety of their city's defences, abandoning their port to Thibron's victorious army. Having buried the dead, Thibron proceeded to Apollonia, seizing the wealthy maritime trade centre and dividing the spoils among his men. This was merely a taster of things to come. Cyrene, the jewel of Libya, was within reach.

Thibron's siege of the city did not last long. Seeing no hope in further resistance the terrified Cyreneans agreed to Thibron's demands. To pacify the plunderers, they would tribute 500 talents of silver – over five million pounds today.[24] The democrats were restored, but they were merely puppets. Thibron's military might ensured that he was Cyrene's ruler in all but name. The man who less than a year before had been a mere fugitive now controlled one of the greatest cities in the known world.[25]

Next steps

Thibron had achieved his goal yet the adventurer had always wanted more than simply subduing Cyrene. The city's vast tribute would fund further expeditions; it would allow him to start extending his power along the Mediterranean's southern coastline. Cyrene was the first step in a much larger Libyan imperial dream.

As silver-filled wagons bearing the Cyrenean tribute began to arrive at Thibron's camp near the city the Spartan started preparing his men for the next campaign of conquest. He showered riches and rewards among his band of brigands, spurring their eagerness to take to the field once more and seize further plunder by the tips of their spears. Thibron knew that his mercenaries formed the nucleus of his newfound military might – the veterans who had won him Cyrene. They knew it too and their commander took precious care to safeguard their loyalty.[26]

Nevertheless, Thibron needed more soldiers; he needed allies to aid his invaluable mercenaries in the upcoming campaign. Alongside the obligatory tribute he had also demanded the Cyreneans provide him military assistance.

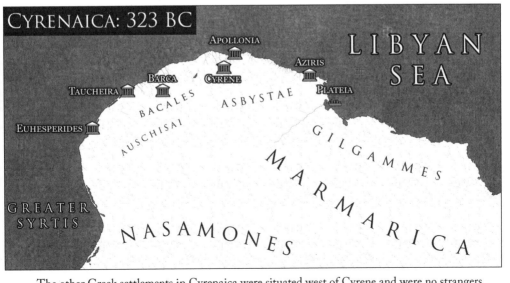

The other Greek settlements in Cyrenaica were situated west of Cyrene and were no strangers to their southern Libyan neighbours, especially the southernmost city-state Euhesperides.

They would supply infantry and cavalry but most importantly, they had to provide him with half of their chariot squadrons – perhaps some fifty vehicles. Thibron must have noted their potential as rapid reinforcement carriers in the previous battle. One must never underestimate the importance of logistics and an effective command structure.[27]

The Spartan *condottiere's* campaign plans were drawn up. He would lead his army west, crossing Cyrenaica to the western edge of a great gulf of water that the Greeks referred to as 'Greater Syrtis' (the Gulf of Syrtis). From there they would march south, shadowed by the navy and subduing the seaside settlements one by one. It would be no easy task. Much of this land was dominated by the Nasamones, a powerful Libyan tribe that shared a long and contentious history with Cyrene and its fellow Greco-Libyan cities. So to aid him in this campaign Thibron sought alliances with the other Greek city-states in Cyrenaica: Barca, Taucheira and Euhesperides.[28]

When Thibron's emissaries arrived, championing the Spartan's plan to subdue the tribes situated across their frontier, the city-states needed little convincing. With money and men, they agreed to follow their new ally to war.[29]

Thibron commanded a powerful position. Through a mix of military might and shrewd diplomacy, he had united the Hellenic cities in Cyrenaica under his banner; every passing day his army was getting stronger. New coinage started being struck, bearing Thibron's name alongside the head of a young Heracles. The Spartan adventurer dared to dream of forging a Greco-Libyan Empire.[30]

The Cretan

Thibron had taken the time to strengthen the allegiance of his soldiers, garnering support as he generously shared out the spoils they had stolen at spear point. But this distribution of plunder did not please everyone. One man was outraged with his reward: Mnasicles, an experienced mercenary commander from the island of Crete.[31]

Like his Spartan overlord, this Cretan was ambitious, a 'hot-headed troublemaker' who provided Thibron with just as many problems as his military capability provided benefits. Championing his mastery of war Mnasicles had expected his general to richly reward him once Cyrene had succumbed – he had probably played a vital role in winning the previous battle. Whatever his expectations he was to be greatly disappointed as Thibron rewarded Mnasicles with less spoils than the mercenary captain had expected. It proved a big mistake. Mnasicles was outraged, angered by what he saw as an unfair division of spear-won spoils. In a fit of reckless rage he vowed vengeance on the Spartan, mounting his horse and covertly deserting the camp, making all haste for Cyrene. Could a personal disliking of Thibron have also contributed to this extreme reaction? Almost certainly. But as soon as Mnasicles rode out of the camp there was no turning back.[32]

Mnasicles made haste for Cyrene and was welcomed within the city's walls. Many citizens remained disillusioned with their Spartan conqueror; they mourned the many who had perished at his army's hand on the battlefield not long before. It was this resentment that Mnasicles planned to exploit. Very quickly he commenced his troublemaking. Wherever he could, he took measures to smear Thibron's name within the city. He emphasised the Spartan's cruelty, his dishonesty. A commander infected with vice whose continued demands would leave the city in the depths of servitude. How could they trust such a ruthless leader who would stop at nothing to forge the empire he so desired? How could they trust the man who had murdered Harpalus, his friend and employer, purely for personal gain? The man was a dishonest tyrant, Mnasicles proclaimed, who they must overthrow at all cost.

Using such strong-worded rhetoric Mnasicles hoped to convince the Cyreneans to break with Thibron and pick up the spear of defiance a second time. It worked. Riled by Mnasicles' vexatious words, the Cyreneans vowed to oppose the marauding army once more and fight for their freedom. Even the democrats, recently restored and indebted to Thibron for their return, seem to have been convinced.[33]

Shattered plans

As Thibron continued preparations for his great western campaign, Cyrene's hostile change of heart was confirmed. Wagons filled with silver stopped arriving at the camp. The tribute from Cyrene ceased – only twelve per cent of it having been paid. No longer would the city help fund the Spartan's imperial ambitions – neither with money nor with military aid. They had reneged on their commitments. In an instant Thibron's thought-through plans came crashing down. The Spartan was outraged, as were his men. In their eyes the Cyreneans had committed a heinous betrayal, breaking the previously agreed pact and shattering the fragile unity Thibron had briefly forged across Cyrenaica.

Thibron vowed vengeance. Any unfortunate Cyreneans currently residing in Apollonia were arrested in an act of immediate retaliation. He did not stop there. Gathering his forces, he marched his men inland without delay to bring the Cyreneans' bid for freedom to a swift conclusion.

Thibron had little intention of sitting in for a long, drawn-out siege. His men had proven their superiority over their Cyrenean foe on the open field.

Now they could repeat their previous heroics, storming the battlements and exacting extreme measures to ensure these agreement-renegers did not revolt again. The assault commenced.

What followed was disaster. The impetuous assault proved woefully ill-prepared; Cyrene's walls held strong. Thibron's desire for a swift resolution to the revolt had resulted in spectacular failure. In fact, his army's disastrous attempt to assault the fortified plateau had made the situation worse. Cyrene became a beacon of resistance.[34]

As Thibron retreated to the port, news reached him from western Cyrenaica of further betrayal. The citizens of Taucheira, a colony of Cyrene, had torn up their alliance with Thibron and sided with the mother city. It was a big blow, further fracturing Cyrenaican loyalties. Putting his plans for further conquest on hold, Thibron regrouped his army at Apollonia and convened with his adjutants to consider their next move.

The Cyreneans would soon force their hand. Buoyed by their first major military success they decided it was time for them to take the fight to Thibron. It was time to go on the offensive. The generals assembled their army once more, replenishing its ranks as best they could.

They devised a plan. Thibron's men still commanded large swathes of Cyrenaica. Though Taucheira had joined the Cyrenean fightback, Barca and Euhesperides had stayed loyal to the Spartan. Rarely in ancient Greek history were neighbouring city-states on good terms with one another, and it was these Thibron-supporting allied *poleis* that the Cyreneans set their sights against.

As Thibron and his advisers contemplated their next strategy, half of Cyrene's army – still many thousands strong – hurried out of the city and headed west. Reaching enemy territory, first Barca and then Euhesperides, Cyrenean soldiers commenced their devastating raiding campaign. The ill-defended countryside burned. Crops were razed; rural communities were pillaged; soon the cities' surrounding farmland resembled desolate wasteland. It was a ruthless strategy, but it caused the predicted reaction.[35]

Emissaries from Barca and Euhesperides made all haste for Apollonia and Thibron's camp, bringing word of the devastating onslaught on their lands. Crops burnt. Villages destroyed. They demanded aid.

Thibron could do little but comply. If he did not, he would lose his last allies in the region and the vital resources they provided his army – particularly grain. Assembling his troops, the Spartan marched his men out of their camp and headed west towards Barca and Euhesperides, leaving behind a token garrison in Apollonia. With the full-might of his mercenary army he aimed to unite with his allies, cut off the Cyrenean raiders, force them to fight and gain another crushing victory.

Thibron seems to have been convinced that the entire Cyrenean army had marched to ravage his allies' farmland. Indeed it is easy to imagine the emissaries from Barca and Euhesperides exaggerating the size of the Cyrenean contingent threatening their lands to ensure the Spartan's entire force came to the rescue. Thibron was gravely mistaken.[36]

Cretan versus Spartan

Reports confirming Thibron's westerly march were quickly relayed to those within Cyrene. At first the Cyrenean high command was unsure how to react, but it was Mnasicles who quickly realised that their enemy had presented them with an unmissable opportunity. Apollonia, Cyrene's gateway to the Mediterranean, was vulnerable. Thibron had been successfully lured away along with almost all his mercenaries. Now was the time to recapture the port. The Cyreneans agreed.

The small force Thibron had ordered to remain at Apollonia was not expecting trouble. Future fighting appeared destined to occur further west. Their job was simply to guard the baggage, tend the wounded and manage supplies. No-one portended an imminent enemy assault. Horror must have gripped them as, one day, they were risen from slumber to see hundreds of Cyrenean soldiers descending on the port – Mnasicles leading the way. The fight that followed was a foregone conclusion. Any resistance was quickly crushed and the Cyreneans restored their control over Apollonia.[37]

For Mnasicles the Cyrenean plan had proved a resounding success. The port was theirs once more, as was the great abundance of wealth Thibron had previously stolen from them.

He (Mnasicles) gave the traders back what remained of their cargoes and put the port under close guard. – Diodorus 18.20.5

The tables of fortune had turned. Mnasicles had completely outmanoeuvred his Spartan foe.

As news of Apollonia's recapture reached Thibron and his men, its repercussions hit home like a hammer blow: all the hard-earned riches they had left behind their enemy had seized. The ill-fortune of Thibron's western expedition only compounded their demoralising situation. Little progress had been made. The Spartan had failed to bring the Cyrenean raiding expedition to the pitched battle he so desired.[38] Thibron and his army were in dire straits, but the Spartan persisted.

Continuing west, Thibron's force set their vengeful sights on Taucheira. Unleashing all their might upon the city their siege was swift. It was not long before they overwhelmed any defences, stormed the settlement and terrorised its inhabitants.[39]

Cyrenaica was firmly divided. To the west Thibron's army held control; in the east Cyrene remained a revived bastion of resistance.

Nevertheless Mnasicles' successful seizure of Apollonia continued to have serious knock-on effects for Thibron's forces, particularly his fleet.

> *Since they had no access to the port (Apollonia) and were short of food, the crews of his ships were in the habit of going out every day into the countryside and foraging for their food.*[40] Diodorus 18.20.7

It was not long before Thibron's sailors were openly encroaching on the countryside of neighbouring Libyan tribes – perhaps the Bacales or Auchisai. The Libyans were enraged. Gathering their guerrillas, a large band of their tribesmen lay in ambush for the foraging parties. As soon as their unsuspecting foe arrived, they unleashed hell on the surprised sailors. Isolated and unprepared, a slaughter ensued. Death or capture was the result for many, though a few did manage to flee back to the safety of their ships. In their haste to escape the survivors set sail, intending to head to the safety of either Euhesperides or Taucheira. It was not to be. By then it was the winter months of 323/322 – a time when stormy seas were common. As the ships set sail,

> *A violent wind arose and most of the ships were swallowed up by the sea. Of the few survivors, some were driven ashore on Cyprus and others on Egypt.* – Diodorus 18.20.7

Thibron had lost all of his fleet. It was the latest in what was becoming a long strand of military disasters. The days when he and his men had been the supreme power over all Cyrenaica must have seemed a distant memory. His insatiable desire for military conquest, always a high-stakes game, had done more harm than good.

Thibron had lost Cyrene. He had lost Apollonia. He had lost his spear-won plunder. And now he had lost his fleet. Still the Spartan did not give up. Though disheartened, his men remained loyal – perhaps resigned to the fact that their best chance of survival in this distant land was by remaining within Thibron's service. Together Thibron and his mercenaries were more than a match for most adversaries but if they were to reverse their misfortunes, they needed more men. They needed more veteran soldiers.

Reinforcements (322)

As winter ended Thibron initiated his fresh recruitment drive. The most capable and persuasive recruiters were selected from among his adjutants and sent across the Great Sea, their task to enlist more mercenaries. Taenarum, that famous mercenary haven situated on the southern tip of the Peloponnese, was their destination.[41]

Taenarum had transformed since Harpalus and Thibron had sailed away more than a year earlier. No longer was it brimming with nearly 10,000 soldiers. Thousands had left, recruited by the charismatic Leosthenes to fight for Athenian independence in the Lamian War. Still, Leosthenes had not emptied the camp completely of combatants. Over 2,500 hardened hoplites remained, seeking employment.[42]

Having arrived at the mercenary haven, Thibron's agents pitched their offer to its occupants. The wealth of Cyrenaica was emphasised to strengthen the appeal of Thibron's cause. It worked. Within little time, Thibron's friends had managed to recruit many mercenaries, lured by the opportunity of a short-term, lucrative venture overseas. Without delay, Thibron's reinforcements boarded boats and set sail for Cyrenaica. Taenarum had been emptied.[43]

It was late spring by the time Thibron's soldiers spotted these ships on the horizon. Their arrival could not have been more timely. As Thibron's friends disembarked and marched their fresh recruits into camp, relieved soldiers greeted them, recovering from another more recent disaster.

Encouraged by their recent successes, Mnasicles and the Cyreneans had launched a fresh offensive against their adversary, marching west and confronting Thibron in a battle of their choosing. This time there was to be no repeat of the Spartan's previous heroics. Overwhelmed, the adventurer's brow-beaten army had been routed; dead hoplites scattered the field, having paid the ultimate price of their profession. The defeat was the Spartan's latest setback, but it was not decisive. Thibron had survived the battle, as had many of his mercenaries. Together they were still a capable fighting force, but to lose the martial quality their fallen comrades had possessed would have been a bitter blow. No matter how small their number these were losses Thibron could ill-afford. Each mercenary's skill and expertise was vital. Whereas the Cyreneans could quickly bolster their forces with raw recruits and Libyan allies, Thibron could not easily replenish his mercenary nucleus.[44]

The defeat had sent Thibron to the brink of despair. His enemy, riding high on recent successes, tasted victory; the Spartan considered abandoning any attempt to recapture Cyrene. It was then, as he pondered whether to fight on any longer, that Thibron's friends had returned bringing more than 2,500 professional reinforcements. This changed everything. Once again Thibron's feelings dramatically transformed: from despair to determination, from forlorn hope to renewed confidence. Once more the adventurer gathered his men. Once more cheers erupted as he announced that they would resume the war with renewed vigour and conquer the Cyreneans. Significantly reinforced, the recently defeated army took the offensive yet again.[45]

The final clash

The expedition headed east. Thousands of soldiers marched – an awesome spectacle for any onlooker. At the heart of the army remained the mercenary spear-wielding heavy infantry, many of whom had served with their seasoned general since the start. They had witnessed the successes. They had witnessed the setbacks. Still they remained committed to the adventurer's cause, their eyes firmly fixed on obtaining lucrative plunder. Alongside the veterans, an array of other units marched: light infantry, cavalry and a draft of citizen hoplites – provided by those Greek city-states in western Cyrenaica that still rested their hopes on the Spartan's success. A versatile mix of units, the adventurer had cobbled together a capable army several thousand strong. He knew his foe would outnumber him, but as previous experience had shown numbers only counted for so much when facing a force of superior fighting ability. In a time where rash provocations by overconfident commanders were becoming a mainstay, Thibron had thrown down the gauntlet to his Cyrenean foe – to face him on the open field one final time.[46]

They accepted the challenge. In the meantime, the city had been a hive of activity. News of the Spartan's strengthening had been swift in reaching the Cyreneans. Recognising the increased power of their adversary, they had reacted accordingly: using their great wealth to recruit a sizable army of citizen soldiers, Libyans from neighbouring tribes such as the Asbystae, Gilgammes and Bacales and, perhaps, even some Carthaginians. By the time Thibron had taken the offensive, the Cyrenean army was ready for a final, decisive face-off.

...they prepared to settle things once and for all. – Diodorus 18.21.4

Spartan shields glimmered in the Libyan sunlight. Veteran soldiers stood ready to confront their Cyrenean foe. Once again, the size of the enemy force must have astonished Thibron and his men. Hoping to end this *condottiere* menace once and for all, the Cyreneans had assembled one of the largest armies in their city's history. 30,000 soldiers had been mustered, called to arms to oppose the Spartan and his mercenaries. Once again, the infantry nucleus consisted of citizen hoplites, part-time soldiers equipped with spears and shields and trained to fight in dense phalanx units. Screening the heavy infantry were the lighter footmen – presumably provided by their local Libyan allies. A Greco-Libyan cavalry force may well have covered its flanks, ready to pursue fleeing troops in wake of the upcoming phalanx versus phalanx clash. Finally, there were the famous four-horse chariots, ready and waiting behind the front line to provide rapid relief to wherever Cyrenean courage wavered.[47]

Thibron's troops were vastly outnumbered. The Cyreneans had thrown everything into confronting their foe in one, final battle. Both sides intended the clash to be decisive. Both sides staked all on victory.

Under the sweltering Libyan sun, probably on a plain in western Cyrenaica not far from the coast, the two forces finally clashed. One can imagine javelins hailing through the air. Shield walls colliding with one another, fighting for more ground. Chariots racing up and down behind the lines, shouting encouragement to their allies and obscenities at their foe.

Thibron's smaller but more experienced force soon started to win the all-important infantry fight, using their skill with spear and shield to block, parry and strike with deadly efficiency. Steadily Cyrenean soldiers fell back, many succumbing to spear thrusts from their foe. Among the dead were the Cyrenean generals, who it seems had decided to fight alongside their soldiers. It was an extremely powerful, charismatic style of leadership; it was also extremely risky and this gamble did not pay off. As the commanders fell to the floor one by one the Cyrenean chain of command came crashing down. Barely trained and losing ground, the resolve of the Greco-Libyan force evaporated. The citizen phalanx was irreversibly punctured; Cyrenean casualties began to mount rapidly and as soon as the soldiers saw their shield wall disintegrate, all thought of further fighting evaporated. They fled. The battle was over.

Thibron had done it. What may well have been the largest army the Cyreneans had ever fielded in their history had transformed into a shattered leaderless rabble.

He was delighted, believing that the nearby cities would fall to him in short order. – Diodorus 18.21.4–5

Thibron had won the decisive victory he so craved. He had turned the tide once more, reversing previous misfortunes. Now all he and his men had to do was conquer the enemy bastions and Cyrene would finally be his.

You can imagine the despair that seized the Cyreneans as the defeated, leaderless remnants of their *grande armée* came trickling back into the city, relaying news of the catastrophic disaster. Once more their resurgent foe was coming to conquer their city. The chances of a vengeful Thibron showing leniency to those in power were slim and no-one was more aware of this than Mnasicles, the cunning Cretan. He had been the mastermind behind past Cyrenean successes; he had proved Thibron's greatest foe. Through either absence or fortune he had not lost his life in the previous battle. He vowed to fight on.[48]

Resistance continues

Knowing that only a slow, painful death awaited him if he fell into his former commander's hands Mnasicles acted, convincing the Cyreneans to continue resisting from behind their strong walls. The Cyreneans complied, gathering supplies for a siege and electing Mnasicles to their new council of generals. They readied the defences for the blockade that was sure to come.

Thibron's plan of attack was twofold. Placing his army between Cyrene and Apollonia, he targeted the two objectives simultaneously. Some of his men laid siege to Apollonia, aided by whatever remained of the fleet; others marched inland, launching daily assaults on Cyrene's walls and hammering home to the besieged some terrible facts: Thibron's men controlled the countryside. Thibron's men had deprived them of access to the port.[49]

Days. Weeks. The siege dragged on. An isolated island surrounded by a sea of enemies, food supplies in Cyrene dwindled. Fresh assaults kept coming with every passing day; resources became more and more strained. Resentment grew among the population. For their current misfortune they pinned the blame on those in power – to Mnasicles and his fellow oligarchs. Political enemies sensed opportunity to exploit this crisis and it was not long before resentment boiled over into revolution. Political strife – *stasis* – erupted within Cyrene's besieged walls. The democratic party riled the citizens up against the oligarchs and evicted them from the city.

Stranded in political no-man's land, the outcast oligarchs faced a difficult choice. Submitting to Thibron seemed their best chance of survival, hoping their pitiful state would allow them to gain their foe's forgiveness and favour. Many took this course of action and were welcomed into Thibron's camp. Others, however, did not. For those exiles, Mnasicles among them, the idea of laying themselves at Thibron's mercy was a risk they did not dare. Fortunately, they had another option.[50]

Eluding Thibron's patrols, Mnasicles and his companions fled toward the coast, where they boarded a boat and sailed east. Their destination was Egypt. They had heard that a new governor had recently arrived in the province – a proven general and former friend of Alexander the Great. Mnasicles and his comrades hoped he would be their saviour.[51]

Ptolemy

Ptolemy was careful. He had taken his time to arrive in Egypt following the preceding, near-anarchical events in Babylon, keen to ensure that Perdiccas did not renege on the agreed Settlement – the new division of power. But as soon

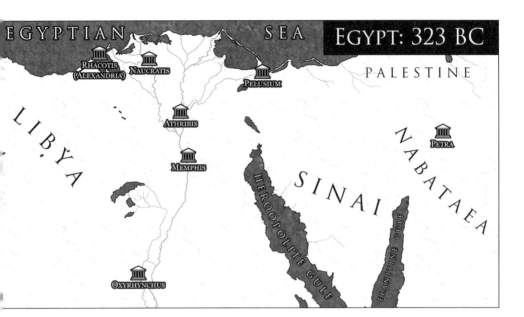

as he and his companions had crossed the Nile in early 322 the new governor quickly set about consolidating his position. Egypt was his – a reluctant reward Perdiccas had provided him for his invaluable support during Meleager's past insurrection. The province's wealth, its topography and its peripheral position within the empire provided the new governor opportunity. Egypt was the ideal power base – a starting region for future empire.[52]

Immediately Ptolemy sought to solidify his rule. Within weeks of establishing himself at Memphis, Egypt's traditional capital, the governor had committed his first decisive deed.

Cleomenes of Naucratis had controlled Egypt's great wealth for almost a decade, since Alexander the Great had instated him in 331. The Greek had gained a notorious reputation – living a decadent lifestyle, encouraging corrupt tax-collecting and publicly showing a blatant disregard for local Egyptian customs. His subjects loathed him but Alexander had loved him. His obscure birth and public shows of loyalty ensured the Greek had avoided Alexander's infamous attention in later life.[53] Cleomenes continued to thrive at the expense of his subjects. That was, however, until Ptolemy arrived. Thanks to the Babylon Settlement, Cleomenes found himself demoted to Ptolemy's deputy. For a man who had grown used to wielding unprecedented power and wealth obeying a new provincial overlord must have been a difficult command to follow and Cleomenes was sure to show his dissatisfaction. Tensions soon sprang up between Ptolemy and his disillusioned deputy. The new governor took swift action.

Cleomenes' disillusion worried Ptolemy. Having an insubordinate deputy at the heart of his regime could inflict great damage on any of his future plans. The man was a potential mole, reporting back to Perdiccas every plan and ambitious idea being touted within Ptolemy's provincial court. At a time when he was so focused on cementing his authority in the province, Ptolemy could ill afford a disloyal Cleomenes undermining his every move. He had to rid himself of his deputy, permanently. So he did. Within months of Ptolemy's arrival in Egypt, Cleomenes' body lay cold and lifeless. Unceremoniously murdered on Ptolemy's orders. Across the region Egyptians rejoiced as news of Cleomenes' demise spread. Finally, they were free from the grasp of this decadent, corrupt official who had inflicted so much misery upon them. In their eyes, Ptolemy was a hero.[54]

For Ptolemy the cold-blooded killing brought instant material rewards. Unfettered control over the province's vast treasury – 8,000 talents – was now his. Cleomenes had amassed the fortune through infamous tax collecting. His demise saw Ptolemy inherit this wealth – free to use it as he wished.[55]

Killing Cleomenes set an instant tone for Ptolemy's governorship. On the one hand, he had further consolidated his prime position within Egypt. On the other hand, it added further strain to already-stretched relations with the most powerful man in the empire. Ptolemy knew this act would greatly irritate Perdiccas – the regent had made it explicitly clear in their agreement that Ptolemy could be governor of Egypt so long as Cleomenes remained his chief adjutant. Within a year of the two striking this agreement, however, Ptolemy had ripped it up in the most brutal, irreversible fashion. And who could blame him? With Meleager now nothing more than a rapidly-decaying memory, both Perdiccas and Ptolemy knew that a new source of significant danger for each of them stemmed from the other's insatiable ambitions. In the latter's eyes, conflict with Perdiccas seemed merely a matter of 'when' not 'if'. He had to act quickly; he had to secure his region; he had to turn it into a bastion of strength. His far-reaching imperial ambitions depended on it.[56]

With Cleomenes' death Ptolemy strengthened an already-strong starting position. The province was at peace; no powerful native princes contested his rule – a luxury for the time! A vast treasury lay at his disposal, as did a sizable garrison force – 4,000 soldiers and a fleet of thirty triremes.[57] Ptolemy, however, needed more manpower if he was to one day defy the might of Perdiccas. Straight away he embraced Egypt's overflowing riches to attract mercenaries from far and wide to swell his ranks. The allure of wealth and seniority in Ptolemy's new province proved highly effective. Within no time at all, the governor had considerably bolstered his forces.[58]

Ptolemy had strengthened his position on land. Newly recruited soldiers received orders to occupy the forts dotted alongside the western bank of the Nile, guarding Egypt's eastern gateway from any approaching army.[59] Yet Ptolemy's northern boundary proved less secure. Bordering the Mediterranean's southern shore ensured the threat of seaborne invasions – those that circumnavigated his Nile barrier – remained. The governor's navy was miniscule and lacking in powerful quadriremes and quinqueremes, the strong hard-hitting battleships of the age.

So to strengthen his position at sea he had looked across the sea to an island famed for its seafaring prowess: Cyprus. Emissaries were dispatched to the many maritime monarchs that dominated the island. Forming friendships with these powers was Ptolemy's aim – the first vital step toward securing the aid of their modernised navies in any future war. It worked. Several Cypriot kings proved well-inclined to Ptolemy's amiable attitude. The most notable was Nicocreon, King of Salamis and the most powerful monarch on the island. It was the start of a remarkable working relationship between Egypt's new governor and Cyprus' greatest king. Ptolemy had gained his first diplomatic success.[60]

Within months of his arrival in Egypt, Ptolemy had worked tirelessly to strengthen his position. He had done away with his disillusioned deputy; he had strengthened his power on land and at sea. Slowly but surely, he was transforming Egypt into a defensive bastion.

Ptolemy had no intention of stopping. The governor was determined to keep strengthening, to keep extending his influence. That opportunity now presented itself.

The Cyrenean call for aid

Mnasicles and the oligarchs disembarked onto Egyptian soil. Immediately they made for Ptolemy and, reaching the new governor, informed him of the tumultuous events in the west: of Thibron's arrival, the back-and-forth campaign that followed, his final decisive victory and its consequences. They looked to Ptolemy as their saviour. They pleaded with him to march to their aid. Send an army west, liberate Cyrene from their foes and restore a sense of peace and stability to their beloved city.[61]

Ptolemy needed little convincing. The opportunity to further strengthen his power had arrived at his provincial court. Very quickly he acknowledged the oligarchs' call for aid. He would gather a strong task force; he would have it sail west, confront Thibron and liberate Cyrenaica from these brigands. In reality, however, his motives ran far deeper. Controlling prosperous Cyrene and its neighbours was his main incentive. Restoring the exiles was simply a façade – a convenient pretext under which he could conceal his own ambitions.

Similarly self-serving motives had influenced Thibron's decision to aid the exiled Cyrenean democrats over a year earlier; now it was the turn of the city's fugitive oligarchs to be exploited by an external ally.

Ptolemy's military forces began to bustle with activity. Near the Mediterranean coast, the expeditionary army gathered during the summer of 322. Macedonians and mercenaries prepared to board ships and sail west to Cyrenaica. Ptolemy had invested in the enterprise's mobilization but he would play no active part in the campaign. He was needed in Egypt – to govern the province. In his stead, supreme command of the Cyrenean campaign was assigned to one of the governor's most trusted subordinates: Ophellas.[62] A veteran of Alexander the Great's expedition, Ophellas had accompanied Ptolemy to Egypt in the wake of Alexander's death. An experienced commander, loyal and dependable, the man was the perfect choice.

Reaction

It was not long before rumours started reaching those in and around Cyrene about developments to the east. A small armada had been sighted sailing west from Egypt and transporting a large army. It was a troubling whisper, swiftly followed by more distressing confirmation that the fleet had arrived in eastern Cyrenaica and disembarked its army. Its intention was clear: a fresh enemy was marching to destroy Thibron and restore oligarchic rule to Cyrene.

History was repeating itself for Thibron. Once again, when seemingly in a position of great strength, unforeseen developments had greatly disrupted his strategy. The siege had been going well. Cyrene's fall seemed imminent. Yet the arrival of this new major threat forced him to drastically alter his plans. The size and skill of Ophellas' approaching army caused fear to spread through senior figures in Thibron's army. Coming against them were veterans of Alexander the Great's conquests, many of whom had served in at least two of the conqueror's famous pitched battles. Leading them, too, was no raw general but a man who had ventured to the edges of the known world – a battle-hardened, confident commander. Panic gripped the oligarchs who had chosen to throw themselves in with Thibron. No longer did they favour their patron's fortunes in the war. With no love lost for the commander, one night these men unanimously agreed to flee the camp and reconvene with their fugitive friends accompanying Ophellas. Covertly, under cover of darkness, they aimed to switch sides. It was not to be. As the oligarchs put their escape plan into action the Spartan's soldiers spotted them and gave chase. The escapees were soon overwhelmed, cut down to a man by their enraged pursuers.[63]

An enemy's enemy…

The arrival of Ophellas had cost Thibron his Cyrenean exiles, but the loss of such disloyal allies was far from disastrous. In fact, it offered him opportunity. Cyrene's democrat generals were in dire straits – terrified by the arrival of this new expeditionary force championing the cause of those who they had so recently expelled. They sought a strong ally, someone to stand with them against their most hated rivals. At the same time, they discovered that Thibron had put to death the Cyrenean oligarchs within his ranks. He had executed many of their political enemies. The democrats sensed opportunity. Putting aside past differences they reached out to the Spartan offering terms: let them unite against the greater threat.

Thibron saw the logic. Meeting with the democrats, former friends-turned-foes, the two sides agreed terms in the face of this immediate danger. What remained of the war-weary Cyrenean army marched outside the city's walls and united with their former enemy.[64]

It was not long before Ophellas' expedition – full of fresh, professional warriors – arrived near the city. Thibron's conglomerate force stood ready to oppose them. The Spartan's mercenaries boasted a glowing military record – the victors of several stunning successes that only confirmed their capability for combat on the open field. But this would be no rerun of previous engagements. In the ensuing battle the superior quality of Ophellas' force became clear, his infantry carving through Thibron's mercenaries and the supporting Cyreneans. The result was decisive – a disaster for Thibron.

After over a year of campaigning – of retreats and resurgences – for Thibron this was the end. There would be no recovery from this setback. As his army melted away the adventurer fled west with whatever troops remained. Abandoned, defeated and with little stomach for further fighting, it was not long before the Cyreneans sued for peace – the city once again at the mercy of a foreign commander. Ophellas did not stop there. With Cyrene subdued he rapidly went in pursuit of Thibron capturing his strongholds one-by-one and instating loyal subordinates in each. Within no time at all Ptolemy's influence stretched the length of Cyrenaica. Thibron found himself in a hopeless situation. Devoid of allies and labelled the most wanted man in the region the Spartan was forced to flee deeper and deeper into Libya. This did not save him:

> He was brought in by Libyan horse-herders and taken before Epicydes of Olynthus at Taucheira, which is the city that Ophellas had saved... – Arrian *Events After Alexander* 9.17

Retribution – the Taucheiran citizens demanded it for the past misery they had suffered at Thibron's hands. Ophellas obliged. Epicydes handed the Spartan over to the Taucheirans for torture. Beaten and bruised, a broken Thibron was then marched east to Apollonia, the place where this one-time mercenary leader had planned a great Libyan venture many months before. Times had changed. There would be no miraculous reversal of fortune for the Spartan that day. A shadow of his former self, Thibron was paraded through the port and crucified.[65]

> Thibron, son of Tantalus, a man who was softly out-talented of his talents. – Athenaeus *Deiphnosophistae* VI. 230–231

Thibron was dead. In one decisive campaign, Ophellas had completed what Thibron had so spectacularly failed to do. He had subdued Cyrenaica.

Ptolemy in charge

News of Ophellas' stunning success soon reached Ptolemy further east. Nevertheless, the situation was far from perfect. Discontent was still rife within Cyrene's walls, many of its war-weary citizens not wanting to trade one conqueror for another. So when Ptolemy did finally visit Cyrene, in either 321 or 320, he presented himself as a mediator, a friend of the city visiting merely to restore order on Cyrene's behalf. Embracing this pretext, he imposed a moderate oligarchy on the wealthy metropolis. 10,000 property owners would form the nucleus of the new constitution, with the exiles who had escaped to Egypt taking the prime positions. Nevertheless, their true power was limited. Officially this small elite group of power holders would rule but Ptolemy's overarching authority was clear to see. He would hold the highest position in this novel constitution. He would choose the officials; he would be a general for life; his coinage would be minted in the city. Ptolemy had made himself ruler in all but name.[66]

Ptolemy had secured his influence over a war-weary Cyrenaica. Now he had to maintain it – it was only a matter of time before disillusionment with the new constitution would rear its ugly head once more. To keep order he imposed a strong garrison in the region under the command of Ophellas. The commander would serve as the region's chief authority, enforcing Ptolemy's will with military muscle. The cities of Cyrenaica had simply swapped one overlord for another. Resentment would slowly build, but that is for another story.[67]

Despite being a mere spectator for most of the anarchy that had gripped Cyrenaica, Ptolemy had landed the decisive blow. The remarkable story of Thibron – the damaging intrigues, the decisive successes, the catastrophic failures – had ended pitifully. Today his tale has become side-lined to a few, insignificant lines in the history books. But no longer. How different his story might have looked if Mnasicles had not betrayed him that day in 323.

Ptolemy's opportunistic ambition was becoming clear. With every passing month his position in Egypt was getting stronger – his power more formidable. He had taken advantage of the turmoil in Cyrenaica to extend his influence and access the lucrative resources the region offered. Such a self-interested, unauthorised act was sure to further increase the ire of Perdiccas, as Ptolemy knew full well. Submitting to Perdiccas' authority was not in his interests. Laying the foundations for a 'Ptolemaic' empire in all but name certainly was. The scene was being set for a climactic showdown that continued to edge ever nearer.

Further reading

Primary Sources
Arrian, *Events After Alexander* 9.16–9.19.
Diodorus Siculus 18.19.1–18.21.8.
Parian Marble B(10) and B(11).

Secondary Sources
Austin, M. (2006), *The Hellenistic World from Alexander to the Roman Conquest: A Selection of Ancient Sources in Translation*, New York, 69–70.
Bosworth, A. B. (1988), *Conquest and Empire: The Reign of Alexander the Great*, Cambridge, 191–2.
Newell, E.T. (1938), *Miscellanea Numismatica: Cyrene to India*, New York, 3–11.
Stucchi, S., Robinson, E. G. D., and Descoeudres, J. (1989), 'Problems Concerning the Coming of the Greeks to Cyrenaica and the Relations with their Neighbours,' *Mediterranean Archaeology* 2, 73–84.
Worthington, I. (2016), *Ptolemy I: King and Pharaoh of Egypt*, New York, 89–93.

Chapter 6

The Lamian War: Part Two

Although Leosthenes' demise was no doubt welcomed by Antipater and his Macedonians holed up in Lamia, their situation remained bleak. The siege continued; supplies within Lamia were coming under increasing strain.

The besieged held out for relief, but would any come? Antipater had heard nothing from his Macedonian brethren across the Aegean in Asia. It seemed as if he was on his own.

Outside of Lamia meanwhile, across the plain on the far side of the siege lines, Leosthenes' sudden death had dealt a massive blow to the Athenians and their allies, destabilising their chain of command. Fortunately for them however, they did not lack experienced commanders. Following Leosthenes' death, they quickly elected two new generals to continue the war.

The first was Antiphilus, an Athenian who we know little about prior to this appointment. When Leosthenes and his army had headed north to confront Antipater, it appears Antiphilus had remained in Athens. He had neither the political standing to match the likes of Phocion and Hypereides, nor the charisma and reputation to rival the legendary Leosthenes. What Antiphilus did have however, was experience commanding infantry.[1]

It was the relatively obscure but experienced Antiphilus that the Athenians looked to when news of Leosthenes' sudden downfall reached them and they soon ordered him to ride north and take command of the siege works. Antiphilus would struggle to match the 'energy or prestige' of his predecessor, but what he did have was an outstanding military mind and personal courage. Antiphilus aimed to make use of all these qualities.[2]

And then there was Menon, the Thessalian. Hailing from the prestigious city of Pharsalus, Menon was the chief commander of the Thessalian horsemen in the confederate army. He boasted a military career brimming with experience. The Pharsalians, after all, were regarded as some of the finest riders in the world – the best of the best among the Thessalian cavalry.[3]

Menon was a prominent figure. Indeed, his family was so prestigious that Menon's daughter had even married a powerful, neighbouring king. A charismatic and capable commander, the besieging generals made a wise choice when they appointed Menon *strategos*-in-chief alongside Antiphilus.[4]

Menon and Antiphilus' appointments injected fresh life into the confederate army, the former commanding the cavalry, the latter instructing the infantry. The Siege of Lamia continued.

The home front

Lamia was not the only location for fighting on the Greek mainland at this time. In Athens, citizens were once again at loggerheads with Phocion, their war-weary, veteran Athenian statesman.

After Leosthenes and his army had defeated the Boeotians at Plataea a few months earlier, many Athenians cried out for a 'revenge strike' on their subdued neighbours. They demanded retaliation, a raid into the region to punish past Boeotian hostility.[5]

Phocion was less convinced. He could see that this demand was fuelled more by emotion than by strategic thinking. Nevertheless, the revenge attack was approved and the Athenians prepared to assemble another army. They selected Phocion to lead it, but Phocion, disillusioned with the strategy, formulated a plan to deter the Athenians from carrying through this strike:

> ...*he commanded the crier to make proclamation, that all the Athenians under sixty should instantly provide themselves with five days' provision, and follow him from the assembly.* – Plutarch *Life of Phocion* 24.3

The Athenians were aghast. Complaints about the enlistment soon became widespread – 60 was too old to wield spear and shield and serve in the ranks of a phalanx. Phocion's response was swift and brutal:

> ...*he demanded wherein he injured them, 'For I,' says he, 'am now fourscore, and am ready to lead you.'* – Plutarch, *Life of Phocion* 24.3

The message was clear: 'If I, an 80-year-old man, can do it, so can you.' Very quickly, as it became clear that Phocion was not going to back down, Athenian appetite for a raiding mission declined. Phocion's words had quelled the Athenian desire for a Boeotian foray. Conflict, however, was merely delayed. Phocion and the Athenians would be back on the battlefield soon enough.

The amphibious invasion of Attica

When the Athenians declared war on Macedonia, they had not restricted military operations solely to mainland Greece. Across the Euboean Gulf, the Athenians had also landed another expeditionary force on the island of Euboea. Their task had been to capture the town of Styra, a prominent *polis* in the south of the island and a Macedonian ally. Carystus – Euboea's southernmost city, ally of the Athenians and hated neighbours of Styra – had likely demanded the strike as the condition for them joining the alliance.[6]

Styra soon succumbed to the Athenians. The city was sacked and for a time seems to have remained in Athenian control. But the Macedonians remained

Euboea, Boeotia and Attica. The Euboean Gulf was the stretch of water that separated mainland Greece from Euboea.

dominant throughout much of Euboea, thanks to their garrison at the strategically vital town of Chalcis. What was more, Athenian naval control over the Euboean Gulf was far from secure. This was something the Macedonians decided to take advantage of.[7]

Not long after the death of Leosthenes and the appointments of Antiphilus and Menon, a mixed Macedonian mercenary force sailed from Euboea, along its namesake gulf, and disembarked at Rhamnus on Attica's north-eastern coastline. Their mission: to ravage Athens' home region. Micion, an otherwise unheard-of commander, led the raid and duly carried through his orders with brutal efficiency.[8]

As word of Micion's pillaging spread, anger and grief seized Athenian hearts. They were determined to expel this enemy warband from their home region. Once again, they selected Phocion as commander and mustered whatever military forces they could. Phocion would play no clever rhetorical tricks this time, not when Athens itself was under threat. With the veteran statesman at its head, the Athenian army marched to meet Micion and his raiders.

What followed was Phocion's shining military achievement of the war. Despite commanding an army that presumably lacked in experience (Leosthenes' mercenaries and the bulk of the Athenian army were outside Lamia), he won a decisive victory, routing the enemy and killing Micion in the process. The Macedonian threat to Attica had been quelled…for now.[9]

Antipater remains defiant

To the north meanwhile, within the walls of Lamia, things were getting desperate for Antipater. If no help came, if no external force arrived to relieve him and his men soon, then unconditional surrender appeared only a matter of time. Already, many months earlier, he had sent calls for aid to notable Macedonian commanders across the Aegean Sea in Asia Minor. Yet time passed and still he received no responses.[10]

Antipater refused to give up. Sallies continued, with the Macedonians even managing to successfully tear down at least part of the Athenian siege rampart. Through this gap, Antipater dispatched messengers to powerful allies, in a fresh request for assistance.[11]

Antipater's initial hope was Hecataeus, the tyrant of Cardia, a Macedonian-aligned city-state overlooking the European side of the Hellespont. Cardia did not have sufficient manpower to relieve the Siege of Lamia on its own, yet this was not the reason why Antipater had reached out to Hecataeus first and foremost. Hecataeus was a staunch supporter of Antipater and Antipater hoped that this tyrant would act as his envoy in his time of need.

Hecataeus did not disappoint, agreeing to aid Antipater in this desperate situation. From his home city he made the short journey across the Hellespont to Asia Minor, where he soon reached the camp of the intended liberator of Lamia.[12]

The liberator

His name was Leonnatus, a veteran of Alexander the Great's campaigns and a celebrity of the time. For eight years he had served as one of Alexander's closest adjutants, fighting with his king in the thickest of the action on several occasions. His heroic actions had reached a highpoint in 325 when Leonnatus, Alexander and two other soldiers had become isolated from the rest of the Macedonian army whilst assaulting an Indian stronghold. Stranded and facing countless enemies, there they fended off wave after wave of Indian attackers. Leonnatus' courage, charisma and his proven ability to command ensured he remained a firm favourite of Alexander for the rest of his reign.[13]

When Alexander died in June 323, Leonnatus' reputation was legendary. Combined with his seniority among the generals, these factors ensured Leonnatus initially received the prestigious position of 'guardian of the empire' – a position shared with three others. Yet the subsequent strife that seized Babylon turned this on its head. Leonnatus had his position taken away and he was instead assigned as satrap (governor) of Hellespontine Phyrgia. Although a vitally-strategic region – commanding the gateway to Europe from Asia – for a celebrity commander like Leonnatus, this marked a sudden fall from grace. He had briefly tasted a top position in this new post-Alexander regime, only for internal turmoil to quickly snatch it from his grasp.[14]

Despite feeling aggrieved at his loss, at face value at least Leonnatus remained loyal to Perdiccas and the new regime. In 323 Perdiccas had tasked him with campaigning in Cappadocia to aid Eumenes, the new satrap of the region, establish control over this troublesome province and to eradicate the threat from Ariarathes, a Persian warlord who dominated the region. More on him later.

Leonnatus obeyed. Together with Eumenes, a long-time friend of his, he had marched from Babylon to Hellespontine Phrygia at the head of a small mercenary army and quickly started preparing for the campaign.[15]

Preparations continued into the late months of 323. Plans were drawn up, men were mustered, mercenaries were hired. Yet it was then, in early 322, that Hecataeus arrived at Leonnatus' camp bringing news of Antipater's dire situation.

This was not the first request for aid Leonnatus had received from Antipater. A few months earlier Alexander's former bodyguard had been the object of Antipater's primary plea for assistance. But Leonnatus had ignored the request. Even Antipater's offering of one of his daughters in marriage to sweeten the deal had not convinced the dashing general. Perdiccas had tasked him with aiding Eumenes in Cappadocia, and it seemed he aimed to fulfil that mission.[16]

When Hecataeus arrived in Leonnatus' camp in early 322 however, circumstances had changed. Antipater's position had become perilous; Macedonian hegemony over Greece was in jeopardy. If Leonnatus did not liberate Lamia, the western conquests of Philip II and Alexander the Great could easily collapse like a pack of playing cards. The situation was grave.

This was not all. Leonnatus had also received another incentive to abandon his Asian plans and cross over to Europe. And this was a much stronger one.

Not long before Hecataeus had arrived at Leonnatus' base the Macedonian general had received several other envoys from Olympias and Cleopatra, the mother and sister of Alexander the Great who had, until then, been residing in Epirus. In her letters Cleopatra had invited Leonnatus to Pella and offered him her hand in marriage, a political move undoubtedly orchestrated with the aid of her mother.[17]

Olympias and Cleopatra's hatred of Antipater was well-known. Not only did this marriage to Leonnatus give the two royal women a strong ally against Antipater, but it also offered Leonnatus the chance to marry into Alexander the Great's family and to stake a strong claim for the Macedonian throne. For Leonnatus and his insatiable ambition this was an offer he could not turn down. Finally, he had an opportunity to obtain a prize more worthy of his standing.[18]

Leonnatus' mind was set. His next war would not be in Asia, but in Europe. But how could he break the news to his ally Eumenes, who had been planning the Cappadocian campaign with him for the past four to six months? Considering him a worthy ally, Leonnatus decided to confide in Eumenes and share his plans.[19]

How close he was to convincing Eumenes to join him we shall never know, but Eumenes' personal hostility towards both Hecataeus and Antipater ensured he did not feel protected enough to venture with Leonnatus on his planned European campaign. And when Leonnatus subsequently confided to him that rescuing Antipater was merely a pretext for heading west, and that his main intention was to marry Cleopatra, Eumenes realised the real motive for his comrade's new venture: an audacious play for the Macedonian throne.

Eumenes told his former friend he needed time to consider the proposal. In fact, he had already made up his mind. One morning Leonnatus discovered Eumenes and his small army gone, nowhere in sight. His ally had fled; Eumenes had opted to remain loyal to Perdiccas and headed east to inform the regent in Babylon of Leonnatus' intended power play.[20]

Leonnatus had lost a valuable ally, but his plans remained the same. Committed to his changed course of action, in early spring 322, he and his mercenary army prepared to cross the Hellespont, a one-mile-wide stretch of water that divided Europe from Asia (today we know it as the Dardanelles).[21]

The Athenians, however, were determined to challenge this crossing. They were no doubt aware of the presence of powerful, famous Macedonian warlords like Leonnatus in Asia Minor. Preventing their crossings into Europe was a wise, strategic move if they were to stand the best chance of victory. So when word of Leonnatus' impending arrival on European soil reached them, the Athenians had dispatched a significant portion of their fleet to blockade the Hellespont and take control of the crossing. With the Athenian navy controlling the strait, Leonnatus would be forced to find an alternative, more dangerous crossing point.[22]

When Leonnatus arrived at the Asian side of the Hellespont, possibly near Abydos, a fleet of ships came into view. Yet rather than holding aloft the banner of Athens, these vessels promoted the Macedonian sun – Antipater's pre-emptive thinking had ensured his fleet guarded the Hellespont. If there was any engagement between Athenian and Macedonian ships in the Hellespont at the time of Leonnatus' crossing – of which no details survive – it was the Macedonians who emerged victorious. Unhindered, Antipater's fleet escorted the army across the Hellespont and Leonnatus set foot on European soil for the first time in twelve years.[23]

Wasting no time, Leonnatus headed west towards Pella, where you can imagine his return being heralded with jubilant cries. One of Alexander's most famous companions had returned home, carrying arms of astounding beauty, riding a strong, Nisaean horse clad in gold and resembling the late Alexander in his appearance. There Leonnatus presumably also reunited with Cleopatra, his royal wife to be who had recently returned from Epirus.[24]

Their marriage would have to wait, however. From Pella, Leonnatus started to assemble all the Macedonian forces he could muster. The army that had crossed over with him from Asia consisted almost completely of mercenary and Oriental troops, a mix of cavalry and infantry. Macedonia however was not overflowing in available manpower at the time; Antipater had barely been able to scrape together 12,000 troops for his march south just six or seven months earlier. Leonnatus needed men. But from where?

Fortunately for him the Macedonian recruitment pool seemed to have somewhat replenished since the viceroy's departure some six months earlier (it seems Sippias had governed Macedonia efficiently in Antipater's absence). But the quality of these Macedonians was dubious – raw recruits enlisted in a time of crisis. Nevertheless, they provided Leonnatus with a solid core of heavy infantry, able to form the powerful Macedonian phalanx. By the end of his recruitment drive, Leonnatus had raised an army of over 20,000.[25]

Cavalry conundrum

Similar to Antipater however, Leonnatus had only a very limited amount of cavalry. Just 1,500 horsemen in total, many of whom presumably hailed from regions east of the Hellespont such as Persia, Cappadocia and Paphlagonia.[26] Heavy cavalry, especially, seems to have been in short supply.

Despite being relatively few in number, Leonnatus' cavalry had a fearsome reputation, none more so than the commander's very own 300-strong *agema* squadron. Consisting of the best of the best, this squadron was a mixture of Macedonian and Oriental cavalrymen well-versed in the art of war. They were a splendid sight, adorned with gold-studded bridles and armour that gleamed in the sunlight. These were the soldiers who Leonnatus cherished most of all, his elite corps.[27]

And so Leonnatus and his army marched south, to liberate Lamia and crush the Athenian-led confederate force. What followed was a lightning march through a largely hostile Thessaly.[28] Below is a reconstruction of his campaign, based on the argument of Slawomir Sprawski, which I find convincing.

It is likely Leonnatus' initial destination was Pelinna, a friendly city surrounded by a sea of enemy strongholds. Nevertheless, Leonnatus and his army reached it without much difficulty. From Pelinna, Leonnatus and his army headed southeast, down the Enipeus River valley. Progress proved quick and it was not long before they neared the hostile city of Pharsalus.

Only then, it seems, did forces loyal to those besieging Lamia discover that a new Macedonian force had arrived on the scene and was storming south at record speed. Messengers hurried south with haste, traversing the 60km or so to bring word to those besieging Lamia that Leonnatus would soon be upon them.

Leonnatus' lightning march, a tricky tactic he had presumably perfected after witnessing Alexander the Great perform several similarly successful exploits years earlier, had allowed him to traverse large swathes of Thessaly before the enemy even knew of his arrival. He had no intention of slowing down.

Already, Leonnatus and his army were approaching the more rugged terrain around Mount Othrys, taking the road towards Thaumakoi and Lake Xynias that would ultimately lead them to Lamia.[29]

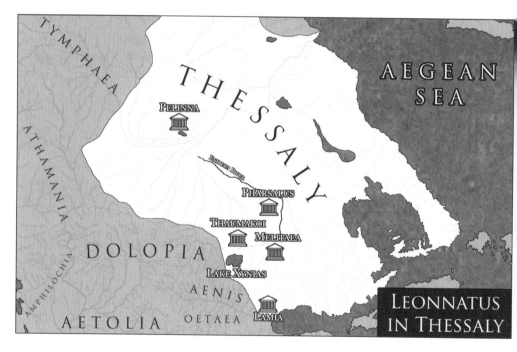

For Antiphilus and Menon, news of Leonnatus' impending arrival was unwelcome. Do nothing and this Macedonian relief force could reach Lamia within a couple of days. This was the worst case scenario. If Leonnatus was allowed to reach Lamia, then the besiegers would become the besieged. They would be the ones that would be trapped, sandwiched between Leonnatus on the one hand and the army of Antipater on the other, sallying out from behind Lamia's walls. Antiphilus and Menon had to react, and quickly.

React they did. One morning, the camp became a hive of activity. Fires were lit; smoke started rising into the air, no doubt spotted by the Macedonian defenders looking out from Lamia's walls. The besiegers were burning their camp. At the same time, perhaps behind the natural cover this smoke screen provided them, Antiphilus and Menon prepared to move their army out. All non-military personnel – camp followers, supply animals etc – would head for the nearby safe haven of Melitaea. The rest of the army meanwhile, marching light, would head north to confront Leonnatus and stop his army in its tracks that same day. And so, as the smoke from the smouldering camp died down, Antipater and his defenders looked out to see their enemy no longer blocking their escape. The half-year-long siege of Lamia was over.[30]

For Antiphilus, Menon and their confederate army, there was no turning back. All thoughts were now focused on confronting, and defeating, the approaching Leonnatus as soon as possible. Quickly the army headed north, just as Leonnatus and his relief force continued their own march south. Battle was close at hand.

Leading the way for Antiphilus and his forces were Menon and his 2,000 crack Thessalian cavalrymen. They were the vanguard, right at the front of the column. In what must have been the late afternoon, the same day that they had left Lamia behind them, Menon's contingent emerged onto the plateau near Lake Xynias, just south of Thaumakoi. There, a little to the north, was Leonnatus' army.[31]

Leonnatus sensed an opportunity. Seeing Menon and his Thessalians form up on the plain ahead of the rest of the enemy force, this was the perfect chance to initiate a cavalry clash. Battle was offered, and accepted.

For both Leonnatus and Menon, meeting on this battlefield was the ideal situation. Both were primarily cavalry commanders; both led their own squadrons from the front; both believed they commanded the best cavalry divisions in the known world. Menon had an advantage. He outnumbered his foe, having 2,000 horsemen compared to Leonnatus' 1,500. Nevertheless, Leonnatus' confidence in his ability and the quality of his men – particularly his personal *agema* – ensured the battle was far from a forgone conclusion.[32]

Battle lines had been drawn up. Menon and Leonnatus' elite cavalry forces had positioned themselves far ahead of the rest of their respective armies. Leonnatus' first foray into battle since Alexander's death was about to occur.

The Battle by Lake Xynias

A thundering of hooves must have echoed around the plain, before the sound of spears piercing flesh and shouts of pain and anger filled the air as the two cavalry forces clashed. *Xyston* lance versus *xyston* lance, the best cavalrymen in Greece now fought for dominance – Leonnatus and Menon in the thickest of the action.

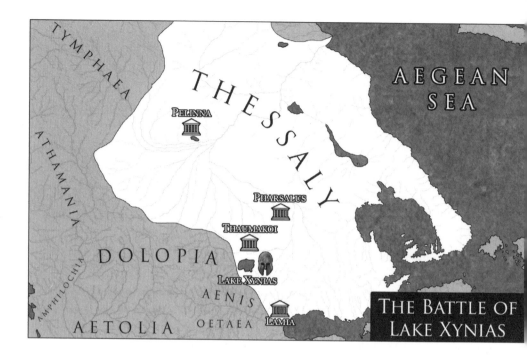

The cavalry battle was long and bitter. One can hardly imagine the confusion it entailed – the Thessalians' iconic purple cloaks soon becoming smeared with blood. Yet eventually a breakthrough was made. Being seemingly equal in quality, quantity now became a key factor in deciding the battle's course.

Suffering from the significant strength of their enemies, Leonnatus' squadron began to give ground. The Thessalians pressed and pressed, the Macedonian-Oriental contingent retreated and retreated. Soon Leonnatus' troopers left the flat, stable footing, as Menon and his Thessalians carefully forced them back onto the wetland by the lakeshore. The rough terrain proved a death trap. Hindered by the swamp, Leonnatus' corps struggled to manoeuvre and were slowly cut down.[33]

The general himself would not escape this fate. While fighting bravely to the end in the thickest of the action, epitomising Alexander the Great in his charismatic leadership and bravery, Thessalian lances found their mark, severely wounding the Macedonian general.

Leonnatus' elite cavalry wing collapsed. Having rescued their dying general, what remained of Leonnatus' cavalry fled to their camp to try and save their commander. But before they could arrive Leonnatus was already dead. He was the first of the generals who outlived Alexander the Great to meet his end on the battlefield. He would not be the last.[34]

Menon had decisively won the battle for cavalry supremacy and, although a large portion of Leonnatus' army remained intact, the infantry knew they could not succeed without supporting horsemen. Seeing the nearby hills, their commanders decided upon an ordered retreat. The victorious Thessalians followed close behind.

Lowering their long *sarissae* in dense phalanx formations, the infantry presented a wall of iron to Menon and his pursuing horsemen. Having obtained the high ground, devoid of cavalry support, their commanders knew that their best hope was a defensive stand. This proved right. Menon's Thessalians were unable to break the Macedonian line and signalled the retreat.[35]

With the death of Leonnatus and the defeat of his cavalry, the battle had reached its end. Menon and Antiphilus celebrated their army's success. A trophy was set up on the battlefield; the dead were buried with proper honours. With these hallmarks of ancient Greek military success fulfilled, Antiphilus and Menon led their forces away from the battlefield, presumably heading east to link up with their baggage train at Melitaea. They were the victors of the day no doubt, but the decisiveness of the clash was far less clear.[36] The majority of Leonnatus' army had survived the battle, shaken by the recent loss of their legendary commander but still a very able threat. And they did not remain grounded for long.

The next day, after Antiphilus and Menon's army had left the battlefield, Antipater and his own army reached the plain, having only recently left Lamia. They arrived too late for Leonnatus' last battle, but this worked to Antipater's advantage. Antiphilus, Menon and their forces had retired to Melitaea. Free from attack, Antipater was able to join his forces with what remained of Leonnatus', positioned on the nearby hills.[37]

With this sizable army Antipater withdrew further north into Thessaly. It was not long before their enemy caught up with them, tracking their every move. Antipater made sure his men kept to rough terrain where the Macedonian army had proven they could hold their own. If they were to survive, avoiding the region's extensive flat plains, the ideal hunting ground for Menon and his unmatched horsemen, was essential.[38]

Antipater's days of crisis in Lamia were at an end – for that he had Leonnatus to thank. It was Leonnatus who had forced the besiegers to lift the siege and abandon many months of effort to confront his unwelcome arrival. It was his army that Antipater now had among his own ranks. Leonnatus may have perished, but his actions would help decide not only the fate of the War, but also the future of Greece for decades to come.

The war continues

As Antipater retreated so Antiphilus and Menon followed close by, tracking their foe's movements and seeking any occasion where they could use their crack cavalry to inflict heavy losses on their foe. Yet Antipater's military planning prevented any opportunity. The war on land had reached a stalemate.[39]

Meanwhile in Athens, news of the confederacy's victories on land had sparked great rejoicing. But there was also sorrow. The luckless loss of Leosthenes all those months before had hit the Athenians hard, particularly Hypereides. During the annual funeral oration, dedicated to those who had given their lives for the Athenian cause that year, the prominent statesman was sure to single out the charismatic, young Athenian *strategos*:

> *He realized that our city stood in need of a commander, and Greece herself of a city able to assume the leadership, and he gave himself to his country and the city to the Greeks, in the cause of freedom…For on the foundations laid by Leosthenes the subsequent success of his survivors rests.* – Hypereides *Funeral Oration* 6.10–14

The Athenians mourned their dead. How many more names would be added to that list before the war could end? Time would soon tell.

A new threat

So far the Athenian-led confederacy had won all of their engagements on *terra firma*, but the war was far from over. A new Macedonian threat was fast approaching – an armada by sea, a new army by land. Antiphilus may have never lost a battle, but the chances of losing the war still remained high.

Leonnatus had not been the only prominent Macedonian general to whom Antipater had sent a plea for aid those many months before. The viceroy had also reached out to another well-known general situated further to the east – who similarly possessed a sizable army. His name was Craterus, one of the most senior, most reliable and most capable of the late Alexander's commanders.[40]

Craterus' reputation among the Macedonians was legendary, especially among the foot soldiers. He had served with many of them since the start of Alexander the Great's Asian expedition, together journeying to the distant reaches of the known world. This – combined with his charismatic 'leading from the front' leadership style – ensured he had earned the highest level of respect and loyalty from his men. He was one of the most formidable characters of the time.[41]

In 324 Alexander the Great had despatched Craterus with a large portion of the Macedonian veterans west with orders to take these formidable, yet also highly troublesome, fighters home to Macedonia. Alexander had also designated Craterus as Antipater's replacement, as the king's new viceroy in Europe. Alexander's faith in Antipater had been waning for some time, culminating in his decision to have Craterus replace him.[42]

Map of Asia Minor, highlighting the region of Cilicia.

Craterus' end goal was Macedonia. Yet he did not return to his homeland straightaway. On his journey west Craterus and his men had entered Cilicia, a province rife with instability.[43]

It had been while Craterus remained in Cilicia that several notable events occurred. First of all – not long after settling with his army – Craterus heard word of Alexander the Great's plans to construct a new Macedonian fleet in the eastern Mediterranean, manned by skilled sailors recruited from Cyprus and the maritime cities along the Phoenician coastline: Byblos, Sidon and Tyre for instance. The construction was to be based in Cilician harbours, funded by the abundant, former Persian treasury at Cyinda. It is possible Craterus offered to supervise the fleet's construction with Alexander's blessing.[44]

But Craterus' orders were soon thrown into confusion. In June 323 the devastating news had reached him: Alexander the Great was dead and considerable uncertainty had seized large swathes of the empire. Backed by the world's greatest warriors Craterus had pondered his next move. Perhaps he had sensed opportunity for his own power play if he returned to Babylon? Or perhaps he was simply waiting for more clarity from the new regime? Whatever the reason, Craterus opted to stand firm in Cilicia with his veterans, advertising his expected authority in the new regime by dressing in splendid clothing fit for a king.[45]

Key maritime cities of Phoenicia (highlighted), as well as Salamis, Tarsus and Rhodes. Cynda was likely situated just west of Tarsus.

A few months later, at the end of 323, Craterus received another messenger – this time from Antipater, seeking aid against the Athenian menace. The plea convinced Craterus to continue his journey westwards the following spring, although two other figures seem to have also greatly influenced this decision.[46]

The first was Phila, the daughter of Antipater who was then residing in Cilicia. She was the widow of Balacrus, the previous governor of Cilicia who had perished in 324. Having remained in Cilicia following her husband's death, it is not difficult to imagine Phila's path crossing with Craterus' during his prolonged stay in the region. When word reached them in late 323 of Antipater's troublesome situation in Europe, Phila may very well have urged Craterus to march to the aid of her father.[47]

Phila, however, was not the only figure who helped convince Craterus. In April or May 322, news reached Craterus from further east. Perdiccas was marching west, towards Cilicia, with over 50,000 soldiers for a large-scale campaign in Cappadocia. In such uncertain times, this news must have been highly concerning for Craterus. Keen to avoid a face-to-face meeting with the unpredictable Perdiccas, this likely catalysed Craterus' decision to head for Europe. More on this later.[48]

Marching west

Craterus' mind was set. In the spring of 322 the legendary Macedonian general prepared his men for their resumed march westwards – towards the Hellespont.[49]

By this time the new fleet was ready. Numbering some 240 ships it presumably consisted overwhelmingly of quadriremes (fours) and quinqueremes (fives), two ship designs that would revolutionise the art of naval warfare for centuries.[50]

These ships brought to the fore a new kind of maritime warfare where size, power and resistance was key – very different to the days of old when swift, small Athenian triremes (threes) ruled the waves. Their designation of multiple oarsmen to one large oar not only gave them greater power, but also allowed less reliance on skilled rowers – only one sailor in each grouping needed to have experience. What was more, their heavy build and strong bow meant they could survive frontal ramming attacks from their smaller trireme cousins virtually unscathed, while their more powerful ram ensured their foe would almost always come off worse for wear in such an encounter.[51]

A larger and wider deck also proved highly beneficial. The increased space allowed many, if not all, of these ships to be fitted out with small *petroboloi* (rock-throwing catapults) on their bows, dramatically increasing the range and effectiveness of their firepower. Together with the increased number of archers that dotted the decks of each vessel, quadriremes and quinqueremes were well-fitted for fending off enemy ships that got too close.[52]

Fitting out such a modernised fleet was undoubtedly very expensive. But backed by the seemingly unlimited Persian wealth at Cyinda, money was not an issue for the Macedonians. To man this new fleet they recruited the best of the best: experienced Phoenician and Cypriot sailors well-accustomed to staffing these powerful vessels since the mid-fourth century. Expert helmsmen commanded the sailors, each having a shrewd knowledge of where and when their ships could deliver the greatest damage to their enemy.[53]

It was a powerful armada, the most modern fleet of its age. If any naval force could effectively challenge Athens for control in the Aegean Sea, this was it.

In command of the fleet Craterus placed Cleitus 'the White', another veteran commander of Alexander the Great's campaigns who had accompanied Craterus back west. Known for his love of splendour, his flagship was presumably one of the largest and most formidable of the quinqueremes in the squadron.[54]

And so, as Craterus' army prepared to march west, Cleitus set sail with this new navy to restore Macedonian thalassocracy in the Aegean.

Reaction

The Athenians soon discovered that Craterus was on the move. Some of the world's greatest soldiers and a huge Macedonian fleet commanded by two expert generals were closing in. Hastily Athenian generals gathered to discuss how they could best counter this new threat and quickly agreed on a course of action.

Just as in Leonnatus' campaign a couple of months earlier, the evident crossing point for any army wishing to cross from Asia to Europe was the Hellespont. Once before the Athenian fleet had attempted to use their ships to prevent a Macedonian army sailing across the strait; once before they had failed. Nevertheless, again the Athenians realised that their best hopes centred around preventing Craterus' passage into Europe. They had a plan, but achieving it would not be easy.

The Athenian fleet would be sizably outnumbered if they allowed Cleitus the White's new navy to unite with Antipater's remaining ships at the Hellespont. But if they could prevent this rendezvous, then the Athenian fleet's odds of success would dramatically increase. They therefore decided on intercepting Cleitus' fleet before it could reach the Hellespont.[55]

And so in early June 322, enlisting all available manpower, Euetion, the Athenian admiral, manned 170 ships and sailed out to confront Cleitus' larger armada in the Aegean. Traditional triremes formed the mainstay of Euetion's fleet, supported by perhaps as many as forty-nine of the larger and more powerful quadriremes.[56] It was a risky strategy, but if they could defeat Cleitus, the chances of victory in their war against Macedonia would significantly improve.[57]

On 26 or 27 June the opposing fleets came into view near Amorgos, an island equidistant between Athens and Rhodes in the middle of the Aegean Sea.[58]

The Battle of Amorgos

The feared Athenian navy had played a daring move offering battle against Cleitus in their hopes for a victory heroic enough to rival their finest hour at Salamis 158 years earlier. Yet it was not fool proof. Nearly 100 years earlier Hermocrates, a renowned Syracusan general, had remarked of the Athenians,

What daring people like the Athenians find most awkward is to be confronted by equal daring on the other side. – Thucydides 7.21.3

Cleitus, confident in his armada's exceptional quality, must have thought likewise.

The Battle of Amorgos: 26/27 June 322 BC. Amorgos was situated in the Central Aegean.

No detailed account survives of how the ensuing battle off Amorgos progressed, but it was Cleitus and the Macedonians who emerged the victors.[59]

After the Macedonians had wrecked several Athenian ships, presumably at little cost to their own, Euetion commanded what remained of his fleet to disengage and withdraw to the safety of Piraeus. The Macedonians had won the day.[60]

Cleitus was sure to celebrate his victory in a splendorous manner. Equipping himself with a trident, he proclaimed himself Poseidon, God of the Sea and the true master of the waves. His celebrations may have been far-fetched, but no-one could deny the strategic importance of the success. Numerically the Athenian fleet was not too worse for wear – many of its vessels had successfully fled the field. Strategically however, it was a hammer blow. Cleitus' route to the Hellespont lay clear; his aim to unite with Antipater's armada was all-but-assured, paving the way for Craterus' route to Europe.[61]

Stratocles' folly

Athenian reaction to their strategically crushing defeat at Amorgos was, initially, one of jubilant celebration. A bizarre reaction no doubt, created because of a statesman called Stratocles. Before news of the disaster had reached Athens, Stratocles had proclaimed quite the opposite outcome to the people:

that Euetion had gained a great victory on par with their finest hour at Salamis and that the Athenians were masters of the sea once more.[62]

For two days the Athenians rejoiced, believing their bold plan had paid off. So when the actual Athenian fleet, damaged and demoralised, arrived in Piraeus and the real result started to spread around the city Athenian celebrations crumbled. Joy was replaced with dismay, hope with grief and anger. Soon they confronted Stratocles, asking why he had orchestrated the spreading of such serious 'fake news'. The statesman merely replied:

> What harm have I done you, pray, if for two days ye have been happy? – Plutarch *Life of Demetrius* 11.3

Hellespont take two

As Athens and its remaining allies started coming to terms with their contrasting fortunes in the war – victories on land, defeats at sea – news reached them that the forces of Cleitus and Craterus were now nearing the Hellespont. Soon another mighty enemy army would be descending on Thessaly.

The Athenian commanders were running out of options and now decided on a desperate strategy. Having manned as many seaworthy triremes and quadriremes as they could muster, in July 322 – barely weeks after the Amorgos disaster – the fleet sailed out from Piraeus into the Aegean once more. Their target this time was the Hellespont, hoping to pull off some miracle by using the narrow topography of the straits to their advantage against the significantly larger, more modernized and stronger fleet of Antipater and Cleitus. It did not work.[63]

The ensuing battle – which inscriptional evidence suggests may have occurred near Abydos – proved catastrophic for the Athenians. The Macedonian fleet stayed strong; their control of the Hellespont remained unchanged and Cleitus gained his second victory within the space of a month.[64]

Once more the Athenian fleet fled. They had lost their chance to revive their past naval hegemony at Amorgos; the following defeat at the Hellespont simply hammered home this fact.

Craterus' homecoming

Arriving at the Hellespont to see the Macedonian fleet ready to transport him and his army, Craterus crossed into Europe with relative ease. Just as it had been for Leonnatus a few months earlier, it was the first time Craterus had set foot on that continent in twelve years.

Cardia, Southern Thrace, Macedonia and Thessaly – quickly Craterus marched his army through all as he hastily made his way towards Antipater, who was still in northern Thessaly with the remains of his and Leonnatus' army on strong, defensive vantage points. Antiphilus and Menon's opposing force remained close by, shadowing their foe's movements and waiting for any opportunity.

When Craterus' awesome army came into view Macedonian hearts must have lifted. 6,000 Macedonian veterans, 4,000 recently enlisted Asian mercenaries and 1,500 horsemen marched into Antipater's camp behind Craterus, battle ready and eager to achieve victory for either Macedonian pride or Macedonian gold. This was not all. Within Craterus' ranks were also 1,000 Persian marksmen – slingers and archers who were renowned as some of the best light infantry in the world. In total Craterus and Antipater's newly-combined army numbered nearly 50,000 men.[65]

The balance of power had dramatically shifted. As Antiphilus, Menon and their men saw their enemy's ranks swell in number, they could not help but contrast it with their own army's depleted numbers:

...a lot of their men had returned home to take care of domestic business, since their earlier successes had led them to belittle the enemy's abilities.' – Diodorus 18.17.1[66]

Most notable among these absentees were the 7,000 Aetolians, who had left Leosthenes' army as they laid siege to Lamia all those months before.

Outnumbered and facing soldiers of the highest military repute, it was now Antiphilus' army that went onto the defensive. But there was still hope. If their allies returned, then the odds against the Athenian-led coalition would dramatically decrease. There was also Menon and his Thessalians, the veterans of two victorious clashes who prided themselves as the best and most feared cavalry force west of the Hellespont. It was the Thessalians, Antiphilus knew, who were his best chance of pulling off a brilliant victory.

Having united their forces, and seeing their foe retreat to a defensive position, once more Antipater went on the offensive, this time with the invaluable Craterus as his second. They had encamped on a hill beside the Peneus River, north of the city of Crannon in central Thessaly. Now, however, they advanced. They descended from their fortified position down onto the plain where only days earlier, Antiphilus' army had been confidently challenging their foe to battle. Now it was Antipater's turn to throw down the gauntlet to his foe.

For several days, the Macedonians marched up to the Greek camp to offer battle on the plain. For several days Antiphilus and Menon refused. They prayed that their allies would return to aid them in their struggle. It was not to be; no relief column came into sight. Every day they waited Antipater's army tightened the noose, attacking foraging parties and slowly depriving their enemy of supplies.

Finally, in early August 322, Antiphilus and Menon realised they could delay no longer. With their army they marched down onto the plain close to Crannon and deployed their forces for battle.[67]

Antiphilus knew he was greatly outnumbered, so he decided on a highly innovative plan. In a one-on-one fight he knew his outnumbered hoplite infantry would melt before Craterus' hardened Macedonian veterans – their *sarissae* carving through all before it.

The cavalry battle, however, was a different matter. Time and time again the Thessalians had proven that, even when outnumbered, they could hold the line and slowly beat back their foe.[68] He therefore placed Menon and his 3,500 cavalry directly in front of the hoplite line, seemingly inviting Antipater's approaching cavalry to fight them in a duel for supremacy. Antiphilus placed great faith in their ability.[69]

Antipater and Craterus accepted the cavalry fight. Their own 5,000 cavalry, which presumably they had initially placed on either wing as was custom, charged their counterparts from both sides. Menon's cavalry contingents counter-charged and once again thousands of horsemen were engaged in an almighty cavalry clash. The Battle of Crannon was underway.

The Battle of Crannon

One can imagine dust quickly filling the air – raised from the hooves of the horses engaged in this epic, many thousand strong cavalry clash at the height of a hot and dry Thessalian summer.[70] It lasted a long time. Antiphilus' hopes seemingly rested on Menon's success and his faith in his Thessalians proved worthwhile. Gradually the Macedonian cavalry gave ground; gradually they pulled back to the wings. The Thessalians followed close behind. It proved a fatal error.[71]

Were the Macedonian cavalry really being pushed back? Or had Antipater and Craterus ordered them to slowly give ground to deliberately lure out the Thessalians? The truth is unclear and, if indeed it were the latter, nerves of steel and cool heads in such an anarchical cavalry struggle would have been essential. Nevertheless, the Thessalian pursuit cleared the central plain of combatants. Antipater saw his chance.[72]

As the dust cloud started to settle, bugles sounded and the Macedonian battle cry echoed across the plain. From out of the dust thousands of spear points emerged, pointing towards Antiphilus and his hoplites. Arrows, slingshot and javelins likely also flew through the air, supporting the phalangites as they marched forward. Relentlessly the advance continued towards the hoplites – who now found themselves isolated and devoid of cavalry support. Outnumbered and outclassed, what followed was a slaughter as the Macedonian infantry smashed into their foe. Unable to combat the *sarissa* phalanx, rows of hoplites were cut down as they put up a desperate defence.[73]

The decisive blow had been struck. Antiphilus knew his side had lost the battle. Now it was about saving as many of his soldiers as possible. He ordered his footmen to retreat from the plain, towards the hills. The Macedonians followed close behind.

Reforming on the slope of the hill, Antiphilus now adopted a tactic he had witnessed from his enemy months earlier during his victory against Leonnatus. Just as Leonnatus' stranded infantry had done, Antiphilus ordered his men to reform on the hill and use the terrain to help beat back their pursuers. Once again it worked. Unable to fight effectively on rough ground – one of the Macedonian phalanx's greatest weaknesses – the attackers retreated to the plain.

Down on the central plain meanwhile Menon and his Thessalians had continued to show their prowess, maintaining the upper hand against their Macedonian counterparts. As soon as they discovered that Antiphilus' men had retreated however, they too decided to withdraw.[74]

The Battle of Crannon was over. Numerically the battle's result did not appear a decisive defeat for Antiphilus and Menon – only 500 of their soldiers had perished in the fight compared to just 130 Macedonians. Mentally however, it was another hammer blow. It had shattered the confederate army's aura of invincibility, especially that of Menon's elite Thessalians.[75]

The cause withers

As news of Antipater's victory spread, support for the Athenian cause crumbled. Calls for negotiations with the Macedonians were touted and pursued. But Antipater and Craterus turned a deaf ear to the demands, making clear that they would deal with each city individually.

Slowly the Macedonians turned the screw, city by city. Detachments were sent to intimidate nearby settlements. It worked. Quickly the city-states of Thessaly folded in the face of these significant Macedonian forces, agreeing peace terms and abandoning the Athenian-led confederacy. Crannon, Larissa, Pharsalus, Pherae – all prestigious cities that came to terms with the Macedonians following Antipater's victory.[76]

As Thessaly folded, so too did the region's elite horsemen, returning to their cities after discovering that they had agreed peace terms. As for the military mastermind Menon, involuntary exile for him and his close comrades almost certainly followed. Still the commander's hostility to Macedonia remained. He would contest Macedonian hegemony on the battlefield once again. But that is for a later chapter.[77]

With all that remained of the Athenian army, Antiphilus retreated to Attica to await Antipater's arrival. Past strategic advantages had evaporated; the mercenary forces dissolved; total defeat appeared imminent. Nevertheless, supported by the Aetolians to the west, the Athenians continued the war. Both remained highly hostile to the thought of Macedonian hegemony returning; both grasped to the ever-withering hope of regaining lost liberty.[78]

The Echinades

By then a portion of Cleitus' Macedonian fleet had arrived outside Piraeus, blockading the entrance to the harbour and barring any vessels carrying supplies. A dreadful food shortage loomed, but the Athenians rested their hopes on one last hoorah.[79]

Following their setbacks at Amorgos and the Hellespont, it appears what remained of the Athenian armada had headed west, past Athens, around the Peloponnese to the Ionian Sea and the borders of Aetolia and Acarnania. It is likely Euetion – or whoever was leading the Athenian fleet – had hoped to receive naval reinforcements from the Aetolians, perhaps on condition that they aid the Aetolians against their troublesome Acarnanian neighbours.

There, with whatever ships the Aetolians could muster in support, the last bastion of Athenian-Aetolian maritime strength remained. But not for long. Cleitus and a large proportion of his fleet had quickly followed in pursuit, determined to eradicate this last naval threat and take control of the northwest maritime passage to southern Italy. Alongside the Hellespont, this was another route along which Athens received large shipments of grain.[80]

In early September 323 the two navies clashed in what would be the war's final engagement near the Echinades Islands, situated off the coast of the war-torn border city of Oeniadae. A swift, devastating Macedonian victory followed. Many Athenian ships were destroyed and Cleitus won his third victory. The last bulwark of Athenian naval resistance had been wiped out.[81]

Surrender

When news of their last fleet's decisive defeat off the Aetolian coast reached Athens in mid-September 322, resistance swiftly ended. Their navy was gone; their army was demoralised and outnumbered; their people were starving. Antipater's army stood supreme in nearby Boeotia; meanwhile Macedonian fleets controlled Athens' two main supply routes, tightening the Macedonian noose around Athens' neck.

Acknowledging defeat the Athenians despatched delegates to treat with Antipater at the Cadmeia, overlooking the ruins of Thebes, to negotiate terms of surrender. Among the delegates was Phocion, whose previous claim that Athens would struggle to defeat Macedonia in a prolonged war had seemingly turned true. There was also Demades, another prominent Athenian statesman who had similarly come to terms with the imminent Macedonian hegemony that his city's surrender paved the way for.[82]

In Phocion and Demades resided, the Athenians believed, their best chance of a favourable peace. But Antipater quickly dashed these hopes. Although the viceroy acquiesced to Phocion's plea that the Macedonian army not march into Attica proper, that was the furthest Antipater's generosity stretched. The words of Leosthenes all those months before when he – besieged and starving inside Lamia – had sought a negotiated peace, remained fresh in Antipater's mind:

> *Leave them (the terms) to the conquerors.* – Plutarch, *Life of Phocion* 26.4

The Athenians had demanded unconditional surrender when Antipater had been at his weakest. Now he would do the same. In no position to negotiate with the viceroy, Demades, Phocion and the rest of the delegation agreed to the city's total surrender. Their revolt – today known as the Lamian War – had ended in failure.[83]

With Athens at his mercy Antipater put forward the terms of Athens' surrender to Phocion and Demades. The root of the rebellion had stemmed from powerful, bellicose demagogues using their skill with speech to play on deep-felt Athenian desires to restore lost liberty, especially among the Athenian masses. Antipater aimed to eradicate that threat. He ordered the Athenians to dissolve their existing democratic government and, almost certainly with Phocion and Demades' assistance, drafted a new constitution.[84]

This new polity was a moderate oligarchy. Those Athenian citizens who possessed property worth 2,000 drachmae or more continued to enjoy the benefits Athenian citizenship offered. Those who did not, lost everything. Voting rights, eligibility for public office, social privileges – the less wealthy Athenians lost all these key aspects of their city's citizenship.

No matter if they were anti-Macedonian or not, anyone who fell into this lower-bracket, Antipater automatically had labelled as 'disruptive' and 'hawkish'. In his eyes these people were the undesirables. They were the people who had been most receptive to Hypereides' calls for war and bloodshed. These were the people who generally despised Macedonian hegemony the most.[85]

According to Plutarch, Antipater's new Athenian constitution disenfranchised 12,000 Athenians. Diodorus meanwhile claims it was even higher – some 22,000. Those who retained their citizenship numbered just 9,000.[86]

A fresh start

Antipater did not leave the thousands of newly disenfranchised Athenian 'troublemakers' completely bereft of options. He offered them a chance to start anew: land, civic structure, citizenship. But not in Athens.

Twenty years earlier Antipater had been involved in King Philip II's campaigns against tribes in Thrace, a region consisting of several highly-hostile peoples that caused continuous problems for the Macedonians. Maintaining control over the land proved difficult. But Philip had a solution.[87]

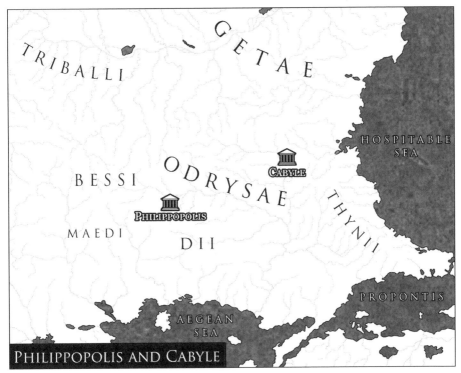

Philippopolis and Cabyle, two of Philip II's foundations in Thrace, populated by 'the most villainous people' of his kingdom.

He relocated parts of his kingdom's population to new foundations on his Thracian borders, where they settled new cities to help maintain control. These frontier *poleis* had an evident strategic purpose, but they also had a socio-political one. The colonists of these new foundations were not normal settlers seeking a fresh start in a highly unstable environment. They were 'the most villainous people of Philip's kingdom', undesirables sent by the king to remove any potential troublemakers from the heart of his empire. They were expendable colonists, sent to settle in dangerous, far-flung penal cities.[88]

Antipater had witnessed, and likely helped create, this policy for ridding Macedonia of troublesome parts of the population back in c.341, and nearly twenty years later it provided him the perfect precedent on how he could deal with the newly disenfranchised Athenians. To all these citizens he offered the chance to start anew: to board boats, sail north to Thrace and settle in the interior of one of the empire's most unstable provinces. Safety was far from guaranteed. Lysimachus' recent clashes with Seuthes had shown Antipater that this border region was in desperate need of stability. Nevertheless, despite the dangers, it appears a good proportion of the disenfranchised Athenians did accept the offer. It was better than nothing.[89]

Antipater's radical actions had transformed Athens and its constitution, but the old viceroy did not stop there. Not only did the Athenians also lose control of their outpost at Oropus, but Antipater also addressed the conundrum of Samos, one of the last bastions linking Athens back to its former 'glory days' of colonial power and a key cause in the outbreak of the past war. Would Antipater allow it to remain in Athenian control? Or would he fulfil Alexander's wishes to return it to the Samians? In the end he did neither. Antipater deferred the decision to Perdiccas in Asia. He likely knew the answer was almost certainly not going to come back in Athenian favour, but that was a decision for Perdiccas.

The garrison

Antipater's victory was total, but he could ill-afford to allow the Athenians to be left to their own devices. A symbol of Macedonian hegemony had to loom large over the city – a physical presence to watch over, deter and remind Athens of its subjugation and recent defeat. To that end he prepared a garrison to remain within Athens under the command of Menyllus, a fair-minded Macedonian general and a friend of Phocion.[90]

In mid-September 322 Menyllus and the new garrison took up their new post at Munichya, the Athenian citadel situated at Piraeus. Antipater had timed the move to perfection, ensuring that it had a very emphatic impact on the Athenians. Not only did this date coincide with the important, and sacred, Athenian celebration of the Eleusinian Mysteries, but it also coincided with the anniversary of their greatest naval victory: the Battle of Salamis in 480.[91]

Salamis had signalled the start of Athens' golden age as a significant sea power. For Antipater to place a garrison in the city – the ultimate sign of lost liberty – either near or on the anniversary of this naval battle, was particularly emphatic. It hammered home a depressing fact: Athens' reign as a dominant maritime power was well and truly over.

Thus Antipater created the new Athenian constitution. His long-awaited return to Macedonia – Craterus and the army in tow – was tantalisingly close. Yet there was one final issue that he wished to see resolved before he could depart.

The hunt

Several of Antipater's greatest enemies still evaded his grasp, and so he ensured that one of the new oligarchic constitution's first actions was to pass through death sentences on Athens' former wartime leaders – Hypereides and Demosthenes most notably. Under Antipater's orders Demades put forward the motion, the oligarchic assembly swiftly ratified it and Athens' former favourites became fugitives.[92]

Demosthenes and Hypereides had not been idle while this course of events unfolded however. Prior to Antipater's arrival in Attica both had fled with their supporters, away from Athens across the Saronic Gulf. Antipater was determined to prevent their escape. The hunt was on.[93]

Antipater tasked a certain Archias to oversee the hunt. Originally from the Italiote-Greek city of Thurii, Archias was a renowned tragic actor – a celebrity of the time. But he was also a bounty hunter, commanding a hardened band of Thracian mercenaries well-suited for doing Antipater's 'dirty work.' Archias and his Thracians followed on the heels of Hypereides and Demosthenes and soon discovered the former, seeking sanctuary in Aegina.[94]

Hypereides' fate was sealed. Archias' men took the vociferous anti-Macedonian ringleader to Antipater, then residing at Cleonae, where these two most hated enemies came face to face with one another for perhaps the first, but certainly the final, time. Antipater swiftly ordered his nemesis' execution, along with two other leading anti-Macedonian orators similarly seized by Archias at Aegina. Yet Antipater made sure Hypereides' fate was especially cruel. His oratory had played a key role in increasing Athenian desires for revolt and heartening hopes of victory. Consistently his speeches had attacked Antipater and the Macedonians as the true enemy. In vengeance for all his wicked words, Antipater first had Hypereides' tongue cut out. Only then did he have his men carry through the execution.[96]

Demosthenes did not last much longer. Within weeks of capturing Hypereides, Archias had tracked Demosthenes down to a temple of Poseidon on the island of Calauria.

Initially Archias attempted to persuade Demosthenes: return with him to Antipater, plead his case and make peace with the victor. But Demosthenes refused. He knew a cruel fate almost certainly awaited him if he willingly became Antipater's prisoner.

Eastern Greece 322 BC. Though we know of two places called Cleonae, it seems Antipater was based at the Cleonae in Argolis (Cleonae in Phocis was a ruin at this time). Antipater was probably dealing with city-states in the northern Peloponnese that had sided with the Athenians, exacting retribution on leading figures who had advocated war with Macedon. One such figure was Euphron of Sicyon, who we know perished around this time, possibly at the hands of one of Antipater's bounty hunters.[95]

In a final act of defiance, Demosthenes, one of antiquity's most eloquent orators, decided to end his life by his own choosing, taking poison while still within the sanctuary. Two accounts on how he administered the fatal dose survive. One claims he had stored the poison within his writing reed and covertly administered it when he bit into it. The other claims he had kept the poison in a hollow ring.[97]

On 12 October 322 the poison claimed its intended victim and Demosthenes breathed his last. In time the Athenians would honour him as one of their most gifted public figures – a man to admire and emulate for his rhetorical skill and strength of heart:

> *'Had you for Greece been strong, as wise you were,*
> *The Macedonian had not conquered her.'*
>   – Plutarch *Life of Demosthenes* 30.5

For future orators the quality of the works and speeches Demosthenes left behind would become a major source of inspiration – to none more so than Cicero, Rome's answer to Demosthenes. Although his life was filled with troubles and turmoil resisting the rise of Macedonia, after his death he became the epitome of Athenian virtue. Despite his political prominence during the revolt, no similar stardom endured for Hypereides. It was Demosthenes who history would remember as Athens' greatest orator of the fourth century.[98]

Athens' defeat in the Lamian War resulted in significant changes for the city: a new constitution, a purge of the troublemakers and the instalment of a permanent Macedonian military presence overlooking the city. Their year-long war with Macedonia had aimed to throw off the shackles of Macedonian hegemony. In fact, their ultimate defeat had only bound the fetters tighter. This confrontation marked the first major conflict of the new post-Alexander age. Yet already other smaller military actions had erupted throughout the length and breadth of the empire. Pandora's box was slowly beginning to open.

Further reading

Primary Sources
Arrian *Events After Alexander* 9.13–9.15
Diodorus Siculus 18.13.1–18.18.9
Hypereides, *Funeral Oration*
Plutarch *Life of Demosthenes*
Plutarch *Life of Phocion*
Plutarch *Comparison of Demosthenes and Cicero*

Secondary Sources

Ashton, N. G. (1977), 'The Naumachia Near Amorgos in 322 B.C', *The Annual of the British School at Athens* 72, 1–11.

Baynham, E. (2003), 'Antipater and Athens', in O. Palagia and S. V. Tracy (eds.), *The Macedonians in Athens: 322–229 BC*, Oxford, 23–29.

Bosworth, A. B. (2003), 'Why did Athens lose the Lamian War?', in O. Palagia and S. V. Tracy (eds.), *The Macedonians in Athens: 322–229 BC*, Oxford, 14–22.

Heckel, W. (2016), *Alexander's Marshals: A Study of the Makedonian Aristocracy and the Politics of Military Leadership*, Oxon, 298–304.

Morrison, J. S. (1987), 'Athenian Sea-Power in 323/2 BC: Dream and Reality', *The Journal of Hellenic Studies* 107, 88–97.

Grainger, J.D. (2019), *Antipater's Dynasty*, Barnsley, 80–92.

Green, P. (2003), 'Occupation and co-existence: the impact of Macedon on Athens, 323–307', in O. Palagia and S. V. Tracy (eds.), *The Macedonians in Athens: 322–229 BC*, Oxford, 1–7.

Sprawski, S. (2008), 'Leonnatus' Campaign of 322 BC', *Electrum* 14, 9–31.

Wrightson, G. (2014), 'The Naval Battles of 323 BCE' in H. Hauben and A. Meeus (eds.), *The Age of the Successors and the Creation of the Hellenistic Kingdoms (323–276 BC)*, Leuven, 517–535.

Chapter 7

The Rise of Perdiccas

Dissident governors and a war-torn kingdom. Already by early 322, barely six months since Alexander the Great's death, Perdiccas' supreme position was weakening. Acquiescence to his directives was minimal – ignored and cast aside. Subordinates sought to strengthen their positions through conquest and victory.[1]

But Perdiccas was far from a spent force. Boasting control over both the world's most powerful army and the empire's royal figurehead, he had the tools to transform the situation. He needed to utilise them effectively if he were to reverse the rot currently gnawing away at his authority. No longer could he remain a mere bystander in Babylon. It was time to take the offensive.

Enter Eumenes

Alexander the Great's empire had fallen into the hands of his most senior aides and generals – their triumph over Meleager in Babylon had seen to that. Nevertheless, within a year of this success the consequences of such divided authority had started to show, from Lysimachus' aggressive clashes against Seuthes in Thrace to Ptolemy's provocative strengthening of his position in Egypt. The postings several key figures received that summer's day in Babylon had determined their following actions. All were intent on making the most of a newfound opportunity – each possessing 'great powers of body and mind alike'. Eumenes was no different.[2]

This extraordinary bureaucrat had been another of Alexander the Great's closest aides, yet he possessed several traits that helped him stand apart from most of these 'brilliant men'. His background for instance was unique. Unlike many of the period's most prominent figures Eumenes was not a Macedonian by birth. His home city was the prestigious *polis* of Cardia, an Ionian colony that dominated the Gallipoli Peninsula. He cherished a noble background, nevertheless. Hieronymus, his father, had served as a leading figure in the city-state at the height of the fourth century, crossing paths with the imperialist King Philip II and establishing close ties of friendship with the Macedonian monarch. It was this friendship that greatly influenced Eumenes' career.[3]

By 342 Eumenes – then aged 19 – had fallen on difficult times. His father had died; his enemy had taken control of Cardia and banished him from the city. An exiled Eumenes had fled to Philip seeking sanctuary and the king welcomed him with open arms. Recognising the Cardian's talents, Philip even appointed him his personal secretary – a prime bureaucratic role within the kingdom for young Eumenes. As Philip's personal secretary Eumenes oversaw all communications between king and kingdom. It was a critical, 'behind the scenes' administrative role and Eumenes thrived in it. Patronage followed. Before long Philip had rewarded his talented secretary with estates in Macedonia, incorporating him into the kingdom's nobility. Eumenes was an exile no longer.[4]

Eumenes was clever. He was cunning. At a time when court intrigue was rife, he managed to walk the political tightrope. He maintained the confidence of several key figures: Philip II, his estranged wife Olympias and their son Alexander. In this unstable world Eumenes learnt how to earn people's trust and respect – convincing them not only that he was on their side, but also that he did not pose a threat. It was an invaluable skill, a careful balancing act that allowed him to retain his powerful administrative position for almost two decades.[5]

In return Eumenes provided his royal overlords unquestioned loyalty. Following Alexander the Great's accession he had accompanied the king on his conquests, staying by the young ruler's side at the heart of his 'mobile' empire for the entirety of Alexander's thirteen-year-reign. He served as a chief administrator, managing imperial affairs. He was bilingual; he maintained a daily record of events; he oversaw all royal correspondence. Alexander may have won territories by the spear. Eumenes maintained them with the stylus.[6]

However, Eumenes was unusual. He was unusual not because of his Cardian origins – several figures among Alexander's inner-circle boasted non-Macedonian roots – but because he was not primarily a military figure.[7] Contrary to the likes of Perdiccas, Leonnatus and Lysimachus, Eumenes did not carry extensive war wounds – visible proof of past service in the thick of battle. He did have a degree of military talent – Eumenes had shown a clear capability at commanding cavalry companies during the latter years of Alexander's reign. Nevertheless, his martial experience was limited. What Eumenes did have was unmatched administrative skill and unquestioned loyalty – two traits that ensured he retained Alexander's favour until the king's dying day.[8]

Eumenes' battle record paled in comparison to the scarred, veteran commanders that gathered alongside him the day after Alexander's death, to decide what must happen to the Empire.[9] But this belied his importance.

Eumenes' invaluable service to Alexander ensured his senior status in the regime outlived the conqueror. He used this to his advantage, playing a key role in quelling the turmoil that quickly gripped Babylon. It was Eumenes who had helped convince Meleager's soldiers to negotiate. Partly in recognition of this vital mediatory role in alleviating the crisis, Perdiccas provided Eumenes with a share of the spoils in the subsequent division of empire.[10]

This prize, however, came with a sting in its tail:

> ... *to Eumenes Cappadocia, Paphlagonia, and the land along the Euxine Sea as far as the Greek city of Trapezus* – Arrian *Events After Alexander* 1.5

Eumenes was rewarded with governorship over Cappadocia and Paphlagonia in eastern Asia Minor.

At first glance this may have seemed a powerful posting. Protected by the sea to its north and mountains to its south, Paphlagonia had proven potential to form the nucleus of a strong nation. Cappadocia meanwhile was large, boasting a varied landscape that stretched from treeless plains to mineral-rich mountains and volcanic 'red earth'. It occupied a dominant position overlooking 'the isthmus' of Asia Minor. What was more, several prosperous Greek colonies dotted the province's coastline: Sinope, Amisus and Trapezus for instance. Strategically and economically the territories had great potential. The only problem was possessing them.[11]

Macedonian control was non-existent. The regions were a 'Wild West' of the empire, all but untouched during Alexander's campaigns. If Eumenes was to govern, he first had to conquer.

This would be no easy task. Though they had initially acquiesced the Paphlagonians had emphatically thrown off the Macedonian yoke as soon as Alexander had departed nearby lands, renouncing their allegiance and fending off a retaliatory attack. Although Paphlagonian power had since disintegrated, a hostile reception was still guaranteed.[12] Nevertheless subduing the Paphlagonians was not Eumenes' main concern – they were a side-show to the far greater force the Cardian had to face. To the east in Cappadocia a powerful Persian warlord loomed large: Ariarathes.

Ariarathes

Since the start of the fourth century the chiefs of northern Cappadocia had enjoyed a high-degree of autonomy from their Persian overlords, ruling as independent monarchs in all but name. The many tribal societies that inhabited the region bowed to their will and provided a useful source of manpower. It was this strong position that Ariarathes inherited when Ariamnes, his father and predecessor, passed away in c.350.[13]

Family was everything for Ariarathes. Early in his reign he had sent Olophernes, his beloved younger brother, to accompany the Persian King Artaxerxes III on his Egyptian expedition with a crack Cappadocian contingent. It proved the making of Olophernes; the prince returned to Ariarathes a decorated war hero. Rather than envy his popular brother Ariarathes welcomed him home with honour. Together they went on to govern their native land for more than a decade until Olophernes' death in c.330. Family was right at the heart of Ariarathes' rulership and it remained so for the rest of his reign.[14]

Alexander the Great's arrival had transformed the political make-up of Asia Minor. As the Macedonian king proceeded east several prominent Persian governors experienced rapid demise, either meeting their ends on the battlefield or being forced out of office by the invading army. For Ariarathes, however, Alexander's arrival proved less seismic. Rather than oppose the defiant Cappadocian chief on the open field Alexander had bypassed Ariarathes and his strong army, as he hastened east in pursuit of the Persian King Darius III.[15]

Ariarathes embraced his continued independence. He was already in his early 70s by the time Alexander departed Asia Minor, but this did not stop him taking advantage of the instability that the Macedonian conquest left behind. In late 333 Alexander had gained his first great victory against King Darius III, at the Battle of Issus. Although a decisive success the Persian army was not annihilated. Thousands of soldiers – Oriental cavalry, infantry and Hellenic mercenaries – had fled the field, many sharing a deep hatred of Alexander. Some had hurried east, Darius among them. Others had journeyed south, meeting a horrible end in Egypt.

Others still had escaped north, across the Taurus Mountains to the lower regions of Cappadocia. This remnant of Darius' great army was significant. Among its ranks were several Persian commanders, united in their aim to strike into the heart of newly-won Macedonian territory and sever a vital artery between Alexander and his western conquests. Yet Ariarathes proved less accommodating than the Persians had hoped and it appears he did not commit his men *en masse* to their cause. The ruler had his own aggressive plans.[16]

As the Persian rebels commenced their counter-attack, marching west, Ariarathes and his men annexed southern Cappadocia and Cataonia. In one swift move the warlord had doubled the size of his territory. The neighbouring Macedonian governors could do little in retaliation – Ariarathes could call upon tens of thousands of troops, too strong an enemy host for Alexander's provincial leaders to counter on their own. Choosing to concede the territory to the Cappadocian, the two sides agreed a pact: Ariarathes and the Macedonians would co-exist – the former ruling the entirety of Cappadocia, the latter governing lands to its west and south.[17]

Through shrewd diplomatic skill and a decisive show of force, by 330 Ariarathes had overseen the dramatic expansion of his realm. From Sinope to Trapezus along the Black Sea shoreline as far south as the Taurus Mountains, this elderly ruler reigned supreme. There he remained for the next seven years, consolidating his strength.

With his nominal Persian overlords gone and being free from Macedonian rule, the road lay open for this chieftain to become king. Ariarathes seized the opportunity and assumed the royal diadem. He was now Ariarathes I, king of the Cappadocians.[18]

By 323 Ariarathes' position in eastern Asia Minor was formidable. Having access to huge manpower reserves, both mercenary and levy, bountiful wealth and a royal title, he was a major force in Western Asia. If Eumenes was to remove him, it would have to be at the head of a formidable and elite army.

Ariarathes' territory in 323, having taken control of southern Cappadocia (Cappadocia Proper) and Cataonia.

Preparation

Eumenes was all-too-aware of Ariarathes' powerful situation. He held little appetite for embarking on such a high-risk endeavour. Perdiccas, however, persisted. He was well aware of Ariarathes' strength; he knew he had to provide substantial support if Eumenes was to crush Cappadocia's king and take control.[19]

Provide aid Perdiccas did. Before Eumenes departed Babylon the allies met to plan the upcoming Cappadocian campaign. The first issue they had to address was its leadership. Who would command this expedition? Although Eumenes had proven his capability to command cavalry, overseeing a large army in pitched battle against Ariarathes was another matter. This required a renowned general to lead the expedition, a general who was experienced but also expendable to Perdiccas. The legendary Leonnatus, Alexander's trusted adjutant and the newly-instated governor of Hellespontine Phyrgia, was selected.

Perdiccas provided Leonnatus with troop contingents from the royal army. Several thousand soldiers – mercenaries and Asian recruits – were assigned to Leonnatus' command for the upcoming campaign.[20] These soldiers would not be enough to defeat the might of Ariarathes on their own however, and Perdiccas knew it. So he also provided his two commanders with more than 5,000 talents from the royal treasury. The sum was a small fortune, donated so that Eumenes and Leonnatus could bolster their ranks with thousands of the battle-hardened mercenaries that were then situated across western Asia searching for employment. With money and men, Perdiccas had fitted out the expedition as best he could. It was now the task of Leonnatus and Eumenes to see it through.[21]

In the late summer of 323 these two companions, accompanied by their small army, quit Babylon and set forth for Anatolia. At the same time couriers left the capital, carrying Perdiccas' orders for a Macedonian statesman that dominated large swathes of western Asia. Leonnatus was to lead the expedition, but this other famous military figure was expected to share the burden of command. That figure was Antigonus.[22]

Antigonus

Grizzled. One-eyed. A veteran of battles that spanned three decades, by the time of Alexander the Great's death, Antigonus boasted a reputation few could rival. Born into a noble Macedonian family in c.382, Antigonus had grown up mastering the skills so often associated with the leading figures of this age. He could ride. He could fight. But he was also well-versed in rhetoric and literature. Traits shared with the fearless Homeric warriors of old were encouraged among Macedon's male elite. Antigonus was no different.[23]

It was during Philip II's reign that Antigonus had risen to prominence, playing a key role in helping Philip transform his kingdom into the dominant force on the Greek mainland. He was a vital adjutant; he played his part in several campaigns, for which he paid a heavy price.

In the midst of one such campaign Antigonus had suffered a terrible wound. An enemy projectile pierced one of his eyes, striking down this towering figure. He survived, but the injury left a permanent scar. For the rest of his life he would be called Antigonus *Monopthalmus* – Antigonus 'the one-eyed'.[24]

By the time Philip died in 336 Antigonus was a formidable warrior, bearing his distinctive battle wound. His loyalty and experience proved invaluable to a newly-proclaimed King Alexander. Not only did this earn him a place on the young monarch's council, but Antigonus also received a significant command at the start of Alexander's Asian campaign: *strategos* over 7,000 allied hoplites. Alexander placed great faith in Antigonus' ability to lead. To inspire.[25]

Nevertheless, despite his glowing military record, Antigonus did not accompany Alexander for long. A year into the campaign the king appointed his one-eyed veteran as the new governor of Phrygia.[26]

ANTIGONUS' SATRAPY: 333 BC

Establishing his new base of operations at the regional capital of Celaenae, it was Antigonus' job to bring stability to Phrygia. To protect the vital, overland supply route to Alexander's army – his 'lifeline to Europe'.[27] Immediately he started enlisting native soldiers, levies, from across the land to bolster his military strength. These men, Antigonus knew, would form the basis of his power.[28]

Antigonus' rapid recruitment drive proved wise. Only a year after taking up his position he had found himself faced with the greatest challenge of his career so far: the Persian counter-attack. Thousands of Persians, Cappadocians and Paphlagonians invaded Antigonus' lands, determined to retake Asia Minor for Darius and sever Alexander's supply route. Antigonus' combined army of mercenaries and Phrygian levies faced a difficult contest, but it was one they simply had to win. Win they did. In three separate battles they decisively defeated the Persian resurgence. It was Antigonus' finest hour.[29]

Antigonus had quelled the Persian storm and he wasted no time in eradicating its hostile remnants by invading neighbouring Lycaonia and assuming control over much of the region. The one-eyed veteran's victories dramatically increased his standing in Asia Minor. Whereas other governors met with either defeat or death he enjoyed success and increased power. A couple of years after acquiring Lycaonia, the rich mercenary recruitment regions of Lycia and Pamphylia were also assigned to Antigonus' authority. Meanwhile close allies commanded prominent positions in the provinces to his west. Within five years of assuming control over Phrygia, Antigonus had become the undisputed chief governor in Asia Minor.[30]

Crossing paths with Ariarathes, Asia Minor's other powerful ruler, was inevitable for Antigonus. Nevertheless, relations were more amiable than expected and it appears these two Anatolian hegemons agreed some sort of

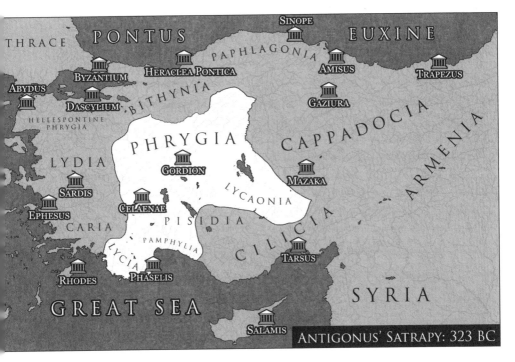

non-aggression pact – an understanding where both could co-exist. It proved a success. For the remainder of Alexander's reign – c.330 – 323 – each ruler kept to their own affairs and their own territories; Antigonus had secured his eastern border.[31]

Boasting a powerful army, a large territory, riches and a working arrangement with Ariarathes, by mid-323 there was a sense of strength and stability throughout Antigonus' domain. This was all about to change.

The choice

It was not long before couriers reached Celaenae, informing Antigonus of Alexander's death and the subsequent turmoil over the division of power. A letter from Perdiccas followed, requesting – on behalf of King Philip Arrhidaeus III – that Antigonus support Eumenes and Leonnatus' upcoming expedition against Ariarathes. In no uncertain terms Perdiccas had commanded Antigonus not only to supply his men, but also to offer his own military services for this major campaign against his powerful Cappadocian neighbour. The question was: would Antigonus comply?

The answer soon became apparent. As Eumenes and Leonnatus crossed Antigonus' lands, no assistance from the one-eyed governor greeted them. The message was clear: Antigonus would not comply with Perdiccas' orders.[32] He ignored the regent's command. But why?

Power. Antigonus was a highly ambitious man. For the past six years, he had been the dominant Macedonian official in Asia Minor. His agreement with Ariarathes was working. And now Perdiccas, a man over twenty years his junior, was demanding he establish Eumenes in a position that would not only nullify his past diplomatic successes, but would also counter his own authority. By installing Eumenes in Cappadocia, Perdiccas hoped to curb Antigonus' control over Asia Minor and the wily veteran knew it. He had no intention of helping this come about. In time this inaction would bring consequences.[33]

Antigonus' no-show was a huge blow for Eumenes and Leonnatus. Before it even commenced, the expedition had been dealt a severe setback. Leonnatus' loyalty to seeing it through wavered, but nevertheless preparations continued. Over the winter, troops continued to be levied. Mercenaries continued to be hired *en masse*. By the time spring neared Eumenes and Leonnatus had amassed a significant force. Perhaps the Cappadocian campaign would succeed after all?

It was not to be. At the beginning of 322, Eumenes' final hopes came crashing down. Envoys from across the Hellespont arrived at Leonnatus' base, offering its commander rich rewards if he marched his mercenary army west rather than east. The allure of a royal marriage, a claim to the kingdom and military success quickly convinced Leonnatus that his best chance of fame and glory lay in Europe rather than in the highly unattractive Anatolian hinterland. He opted to abandon Perdiccas' orders; the Cappadocian campaign was no more.

Leonnatus wanted Eumenes to join him, but Eumenes was far from convinced. Wary of Leonnatus' ambitions and far-flung hopes of kingship, one night he fled the general's camp with 500 followers and 5,000 talents. Together they hurried east, to inform Perdiccas how personal ambitions had caused the campaign's collapse before it even commenced. Leonnatus refrained from pursuit. Marching east was no longer in his interests. His mercenary army was destined for the west. Glory awaited. Or so he thought.[34]

Mustering the royal army

Babylon beckoned for Eumenes once more. By the time he and his small band had returned to the Mesopotamian metropolis, it was already March. No sooner had he arrived than Eumenes informed Perdiccas of Leonnatus' regal ambitions. Perdiccas was impressed. Despite Leonnatus' tempting offer Eumenes had proven his loyalty, making the c.2,000 mile march back to Babylon in quick time.[35] He had shown his allegiance in striking fashion. As fitting reward – at a time where trusted allies were at a premium – Perdiccas promoted Eumenes to his advisory council.[36] Nevertheless neither could deny that this prize masked a major setback. Their planned Cappadocian campaign had resulted in disaster. Antigonus had proven insubordinate; Leonnatus had been turned with an offer too irresistible for his lofty ambitions. Most importantly Ariarathes remained free, and stronger than ever.

Ariarathes, this octogenarian monarch, knew he would soon have a fight on his hands. The Macedonians had been recruiting mercenaries in the thousands and Antigonus may have even subtly warned Ariarathes to prepare his kingdom for impending invasion. Prepare he did. The Cappadocian king used the time wisely, mustering a mighty force from across his territory. Paphlagonians, Cappadocians and mercenaries filled its ranks – funded by the wealth Ariarathes had amassed as an independent monarch. It was a show of force that neither Perdiccas, nor Eumenes, nor the other generals in Babylon missed. If they were to overthrow Ariarathes they required a large, experienced force – the greatest in the empire. The royal army.

Perdiccas was keen. He wanted to march west, and not just to eradicate Ariarathes. Craterus, the much-loved veteran commander, was still residing in Cilicia with his 10,000 veteran Macedonians. Perdiccas' previous attempts to force them westwards had failed miserably – another humiliating example of insubordination towards him from an older commander. Contact between

Craterus and Perdiccas had continued, but still the former put off the latter's demands that he set off west. Instead he had done quite the opposite: despite Perdiccas having officially annulled Alexander's last wishes, Craterus had continued to oversee the building of a huge, modernised fleet in Cilician harbours. Craterus' continued obstinancy must have frustrated Perdiccas, but he now had a solution. Now he had the perfect pretext with which to march west with the royal army. A Cappadocian campaign would provide the perfect pretext to coerce Craterus westwards.[37]

Perdiccas had other aims too. He wanted to shore up his support with his soldiers – the key to his power. If he was to one day further his imperial ambitions, ensuring their unwavering loyalty was paramount. And what better way to strengthen their support than by declaring a campaign to eradicate booty-laden Asian usurpers and rebel warlords. Promising vast plunder in the process of forcibly removing all those who still resisted their authority, Perdiccas secured the support of Alexander's Macedonian veterans – the nucleus of the royal army. The Cappadocian campaign was revived.[38]

In either April or May 322, Eumenes quit Babylon and headed west for the second time within twelve months – his aim once again to secure Cappadocia by the spear. This time things were different. In place of the lone Leonnatus, Eumenes had a whole host of famous generals accompanying him; rather than a small mercenary army, he had the greatest concentration of military might in the known world.[39]

It was a huge force of more than 50,000 men, filled with soldiers wearing striking sets of armour that gleamed in the sun. At its core remained the veteran Macedonian infantry – the men who had brought Babylon to the brink of civil war only a year earlier. Alongside them were the much more numerous mercenary and Asian battalions trained for various styles of warfare: from *sarissa* phalanx companies to units of elite archers, slingers and spearmen. The cavalry was no less formidable. *Hipparchies* of Macedonian and Oriental heavy-hitting horsemen formed Perdiccas' elite squadrons, supported by horse archers and other light cavalrymen. Finally there were the elephants, the feet of which had brutally crushed Meleager's comrades the preceding summer.[40]

Famous figures were plentiful. Leading *strategoi* such as Seleucus, Attalus, Alcetas and Aristonous. There was also Neoptolemus, a man of royal Molossian blood who commanded the king's elite infantry guard. Ensuring the royal army lived up to its name the monarch himself – Philip Arrhidaeus III – was also present. So too was Roxana, Alexander the Great's Sogdian widow. For Perdiccas it was vital that these royal figures – symbols of his legitimacy as regent – remained by his side. The Macedonian royal court was mobile once more. In its midst was an infant. A boy. Barely six months old, he was the baby of Roxana: Alexander, the namesake son of the revered conqueror born in the aftermath of the Babylon Crisis. So far Perdiccas had refrained from proclaiming the child king alongside Arrhidaeus. Infancy was, after all, a perilous time. Nevertheless officially announcing Alexander the Great's sole, legitimate son as monarch was in the regent's mind. He awaited the right opportunity.[41]

Into Armenia Perdiccas and the royal army marched, planning to circumnavigate Cilicia and descend upon Cappadocia from the east. The route offered Perdiccas several benefits but most importantly it avoided an uneasy confrontation. Craterus' reaction to Perdiccas arriving in Cilicia with an army was uncertain. Would the two figures come to blows? If so, would Perdiccas' Macedonians really fight against their beloved infantry commander? Uncertainty was abundant. Perdiccas wanted to coerce Craterus west; he also wanted to avoid the chance of conflict at all costs.[42]

The plan worked. As soon as Craterus heard word that Perdiccas was approaching Anatolia, the veteran general acted. Readying both the army and navy, he and more than 12,500 men started heading west. So Craterus finally set forth, marching to Antipater's aid against the Athenian-led coalition opposing him in Thessaly. For Perdiccas his plan to coerce Craterus from Cilicia had succeeded. All eyes now focused on Cappadocia and the upcoming clash.[43]

Campaigning in Cappadocia

By the time Perdiccas and his great host invaded Ariarathes' domain it was c.July 322. The Cappadocian was waiting for them. He had used his time wisely, having amassed a huge army with which to oppose the invaders. 30,000 soldiers formed his infantry force, consisting of light-armed Cappadocians and veteran mercenaries. Ariarathes' greatest asset, however, was his cavalry.[44]

Horses were central to ancient Cappadocian culture. The many tribes that inhabited the region's treeless-but-fertile plains enjoyed an excellent landscape for pastoral faming. Horses, mules, sheep and cattle were all raised by Cappadocian communities. Naturally many of their men were raised to fight from horseback – lightly-armed, presumably with javelins. No strangers to Persian service these Cappadocian horsemen formed the keystone of the region's military strength. Ariarathes was sure to embrace this resource. By the time he took the field against Perdiccas, his cavalry wing numbered 10,500.[45] It was these horsemen that Ariarathes knew would be key if he were to achieve victory.

The Cappadocian king's force was an impressive sight – 40,500 men strong. It was one of the largest armies in the Near East, second only in size to Perdiccas' royal host marching against them. In total, over 100,000 combatants had been mobilised for this campaign.

The scene was set for one of the largest military engagements of the age. For Perdiccas, the decisive moment of his high-risk, aggressive strategy had arrived. He had not tasted any major military action since the death of Alexander the Great. Now he aimed to achieve his own heroic victory against a formidable Iranian opponent – his own Gaugamela.

The battle proved hard-fought. On paper the invaluable skill of the veteran Macedonian and Asian battalions provided Perdiccas' phalanx a clear edge in the infantry fight. Nevertheless, the battle's outcome depended on the cavalry clash that must have ensued between Ariarathes' Cappadocians and Perdiccas' Greco-Asian squadrons. Perdiccas' *hipparchies* prevailed, but it proved indecisive. Ariarathes successfully managed to retreat and regroup most of his army. A second battle was required; this time victory was total. Encouraged by their past success, Perdiccas' forces were triumphant. Ariarathes' Cappadocians broke and ran; without cavalry support the infantry melted away. Thousands surrendered. Others fled the field, desperate to escape slaughter. Ariarathes' host had offered stubborn resistance, but in the end they had proven no match for the invaders on the open field. 4,000 of their soldiers, mainly horsemen, lay dead on the battlefields; Perdiccas marched a further 5,000 into captivity.[46]

Ariarathes would not escape a second time. Either during or immediately after the final battle, Perdiccas' men captured the octogenarian. The king and almost all of his family were placed in captivity. Perdiccas had them at his mercy.

Once before Perdiccas had inflicted a gruesome death on those who dared oppose him. Now, riding high with the unquestioned support of his successful soldiers, again Perdiccas chose to send a strong, gruesome message to potential enemies. An 82-year-old Ariarathes, along with his family, was sentenced to death – a painful and long-winded killing. Men, women and children – together Cappadocian royalty were tortured before experiencing their end either by hanging, crucifixion or impalement.[47]

Ariarathes was no more, but his legacy lived on. Though most of his family perished alongside the king that summer's day, one man survived. Ariarathes' adopted, namesake son – who may well have been a leading commander during the previous battle – had escaped capture. With a small band of followers this Ariarathes had fled east, to Armenia. There he remained, gathering remnants of his adopted father's defeated army and vowing one day to return and reclaim the kingdom. For now however, he remained in western Armenia, threatening Macedonian communications between east and west. For Perdiccas the survival of the younger Ariarathes posed a sizable threat. Without delay he despatched

Neoptolemus with a small army of Macedonians to march east and eradicate the last remnants of resistance – a mopping up operation.[48]

Perdiccas had prevailed; his men had crushed the great Persian warlord. Lesser Cappadocian chieftains now submitted to Perdiccas and received his pardon. For the first time in its history, the whole of Cappadocia had come under Macedonian sway. Finally, Eumenes could assume his intended role as governor.[49]

Consolidation

Eumenes wasted no time consolidating his new command:

> *He accordingly proceeded to dispose of the chief cities among his own friends, and made captains of garrisons, judges, receivers, and other officers, of such as he thought fit.* – Plutarch *Life of Eumenes* 3.7

Perdiccas was happy to support these appointments. As Eumenes boasted decades of experience managing the day-to-day affairs of empire, he could hardly doubt his ally's administrative skill.[50]

Perdiccas reaped the rewards success on the battlefield had brought him. The army cheered his name – honouring he who had guided them to a victory the scale of which they had not seen since the days of Alexander. Perdiccas, riding high on this rejuvenated wave of support, was sure to take advantage. Having conferred with his council, the regent assembled his men for an important announcement.

One figure currently ruled as king: the simple-minded Arrhidaeus. This was all about to change.[51]

Addressing his victorious army, Perdiccas announced that it was time to enact the final decision agreed at Babylon a year earlier. It was time to crown Alexander the Great's infant namesake son as monarch in his own right, alongside Philip Arrhidaeus III.

Perdiccas had seized the moment. Alexander was still a baby – less than a year old. But for Perdiccas the young prince's pedigree made him an invaluable pawn. If the army accepted his proclamation and named him the new king's protector, then his power and authority would be stronger than ever – the official guardian of not one, but *two* monarchs. Much depended on the military's response. Would they recognise the young Alexander as their king? More importantly, would they recognise Perdiccas as the baby boy's rightful protector?[52]

Perdiccas need not have worried. With no hostile governors in sight and surrounded by faithful adjutants, there was no repeat of the turmoil his proposals had helped provoke the previous summer. The army approved his proclamation, emphatically so. They hailed the child King Alexander IV. Most importantly they acknowledged Perdiccas' position as Alexander's official protector – sole guardian of the boy king. Perdiccas had attained the legitimacy he so desired. In no uncertain terms the army had reinforced their approval of Perdiccas as the empire's chief authority – ruling the kingdom on behalf of two incapable, royal figureheads. Alexander and Arrhidaeus may have been kings, but Perdiccas held true power.[53]

Perdiccas' position had never been stronger – legitimate guardian of two kings, supreme commander of the empire's mightiest military force and ever-growing popularity among his men. At first glance it was the soldiers who had elected him to this heightened position of power, but Perdiccas had pulled the strings. It was he who had cleverly orchestrated the whole scenario – just as he had done in Babylon when exposing Meleager. His imperial ambitions were progressing, his increased power cemented through a legitimised regal proclamation, fashioned in the aftermath of a famous victory. From possessing a rather perilous position in the empire – distant and ignored – in one sharp campaign Perdiccas had risen to a place of unprecedented power.

Winter quarters

It was well into autumn by the time Eumenes had consolidated his control over Cappadocia. With the army no longer required in the region, Perdiccas had plans for further military conquest. These designs would have to wait however: the campaigning season was coming to an end. So he gathered his men and headed south, across the Taurus Mountains to the lush, fertile lands of Cilicia. Enjoying a restored sense of order thanks to the recent peacekeeping presence of Craterus, the region was a perfect place for Perdiccas to establish the army's winter quarters.[54]

Cilicia's ideal topography was not the region's sole allure. Present within was the royal treasury at Cyinda, providing Perdiccas further funds with which to cover the costs of past and future military endeavours. Just as important for the regent, however, were the men whom Craterus had left to guard the supply. These were the Silver Shields, the former infantry guards of Alexander the Great, the elite of the elite among the Macedonian footmen. For these 3,000 soldiers, their desires to return to Macedonia appear to have evaporated.[55] Fifteen years of hard campaigning in Asia had left them changed men, their way of life now firmly centred around the army. Many had taken Asian wives, raised children and seized great amounts of plunder; all enjoyed membership of the empire's most elite regiment. Their loyalty to the Argead line remained steadfast and Perdiccas hoped to re-enlist these veterans into the royal army.

The Silver Shields required little convincing. Perdiccas, a military hero and the official protector of Alexander the Great's family, soon won their allegiance. It was a huge coup for Perdiccas and further good news was to follow.[56]

It must have been around this time that a second Macedonian army arrived in Cilicia, laden with loot. Numbering several thousand this expeditionary force had marched over 1,500 miles, since mercilessly crushing the Greek uprising in far-flung Bactria. At its head was Peithon.[57]

Having arrived at Perdiccas' camp, the popular Peithon confirmed his achievements to the regent: the fight with Philon's veterans, the suborning of Letodorus, the mercenary rout and the infamous 'reconciliation' that had followed. Peithon's expedition had secured the east.

Perdiccas welcomed Alexander's former bodyguard back into the fray, installing him amongst the higher echelons of his commanders. The man's return was the latest in a series of fortuitous events for Perdiccas since arriving in Cilicia. His army had strengthened significantly – bolstered with reinforcements that were not fresh-faced levies, but thousands of veteran Macedonians.

New problems

As the winter progressed, news of activity all across the empire no doubt reached Perdiccas at his headquarters. By then he would have received reports of Ptolemy's newfound control over Cyrenaica, causing serious concern. Word from Europe also arrived: of Athens' final capitulation, of Antipater's imposed settlement on the vanquished and of Lysimachus' entente with Seuthes in Thrace. One report, however, required Perdiccas' immediate attention more so than the rest.

Reports had reached him from the northeast. Neoptolemus, the grizzled infantry commander currently campaigning in western Armenia, was in trouble. His mopping up operation was proving more difficult than expected. Remnants of the defeated Cappadocian army – the younger Ariarathes included – were proving tough to eradicate. Crack horsemen were using their speed and skill at skirmishing to inflict effective strikes against Neoptolemus and his Macedonian footmen. Devoid of Armenian allies, the Molossian general lacked sufficient cavalry to counter the threat; he had struggled to make any progress.[58]

Thus, when word reached Perdiccas of Neoptolemus' situation, the regent acted. He decided against siphoning off further troops from the royal army and sending them to Armenia. He had a better idea.

Eumenes had accompanied Perdiccas to Cilicia. Though he was now governor of Cappadocia, Eumenes had also retained his senior status among Perdiccas' advisors. He was desperate to maintain his influence at the heart of the empire – accompanying the kings and the regent whenever he could. But Perdiccas had other plans for his loyal ally. Relaying word of Neoptolemus' dismal situation just across Cappadocia's eastern border, he ordered Eumenes to raise an army and march to the Molossian's relief. Eumenes obeyed, leaving Cilicia and crossing the Taurus Mountains in the winter of early 321.[59]

Perdiccas and his generals now turned their attention west. Ariarathes had been crushed, but that Persian warlord was not the only hostile force they needed to quell. Dissident Anatolian tribes still needed to face justice.

The Isauri

Almost directly west, across the Mountains, was eastern Pisidia. The region's geography was large and varied: stretching from fertile plains and river valleys to the rugged foothills below the Taurus' western fringes. Like Cappadocia, Alexander the Great had all but bypassed this area as he progressed eastwards and the local tribes retained a clear sense of independence – independence they were loath to give up. This was especially true of the 'Cetae', or Isauri, a

Southeast Asia Minor. The Isauri were located west of Cilicia, across the Taurus Mountains.

highland people that resided in the foothills of the Taurus Mountains. Divided among various tribes led by petty chieftains, each clan cherished their own self-identity. Nevertheless, an overriding sense of shared 'Cetae' ancestry remained; they were not afraid to unite in the face of a common, external enemy.[60]

A fierce 'warrior culture' existed among these tribes; from a young age they were taught to ambush and plunder. The mountain terrain of the Cetae's homeland was ideal for skirmishing – the perfect landscape within which to practice, and master, hit-and-run raiding tactics. Greedy bands of Isauri raiders descending from the foothills raped and pillaged, becoming the bane of settled communities in wealthier, neighbouring regions such as Pamphylia. They were fierce fighters, who happily antagonised and opposed stronger, external powers in their search for booty. They attacked without fear of retribution – confident in the natural strength their rugged home region offered if any adversary foolishly decided to follow. They would attack any who dared venture near their homeland with military force, as the Macedonians found out.[61]

In late 333 Alexander the Great defeated Darius at the Battle of Issus and secured his control over much of Cilicia. He left the land not long after, intent on securing the Levantine ports and starving the Persian navy of its harbours. Nevertheless, Alexander was not oblivious to the instability he left behind. Remnants of Darius' army were congregating in Cappadocia for a counter-attack; meanwhile the Isaurian brigand threat loomed large, stronger than ever.[62] To help pacify these problems and maintain Macedonian authority in the region, Alexander had entrusted Cilicia to a stalwart adjutant. His name was Balacrus, one of the most experienced commanders in the army and a noble of high status. He was a war hero. A legend among the Macedonian forces. The perfect choice for so vital a task as consolidating Cilicia and pacifying its neighbouring lands.[63]

Initially Balacrus and his men met with success, helping the likes of Antigonus vanquish Persian attempts to wrestle away Macedonian authority in Asia Minor. But the victories did not last. In 324, perhaps in an attempt to quell the Isauri threat, Balacrus had headed towards their homeland with force. They never returned. Balacrus and his men were ambushed *en route*. Isaurian brigands, aided by fighters from the nearby city of Laranda, annihilated the army; Balacrus was killed.[64]

It was a terrible incident. One of the most senior and well-respected nobles in the kingdom had been unceremoniously slaughtered at the hands of 'barbarian' bandits. Outrage must have erupted among the Macedonians when the news reached them. It was a tragedy that 'cried out for vengeance.'[65]

Vengeance proved a long time coming – three years passed and still the Isaurians remained unpunished. Yet Perdiccas did not forget. While they were resting in Cilicia, Perdiccas and his commanders finalised their plans for the spring and announced their intentions to the army. Their campaign to remove those who resisted Macedonian power would continue; they were going to invade eastern Pisidia and bring the full might of the royal army down on the Isaurians and Larandians – no quarter given. The aim was punitive: it was time to avenge Balacrus and bring these brigand attacks to a halt.

Spring 321 – the reckoning

Winter ended and the royal army mustered for the new campaign. They aimed first to attack Laranda, before heading west and sending a strong message to the Isauri by striking at their homeland's central bastion. The natural path would lead them up the Calycadmus River valley, a route which took them almost to the walls of their first target.[66]

Laranda boasted a strategic position. Situated on the southern edge of the Lycaonian Plain, it overlooked two routes through the Taurus Mountains to the Mediterranean. Despite the fearful odds stacked against them, the Larandians were loath to accept Macedonian authority. They opted to fight, much to Perdiccas' delight. Whatever had prompted their warriors to engage in that infamous ambush, the Larandians would now suffer the consequences.[67]

Their resistance did not last long. Within a day of the royal army arriving outside the city's walls, Laranda had capitulated. Citizen defenders attempted to resist Perdiccas' veteran forces as they assaulted the settlement, but it proved hopeless. The Macedonians – experts of many a siege – proved their mettle,

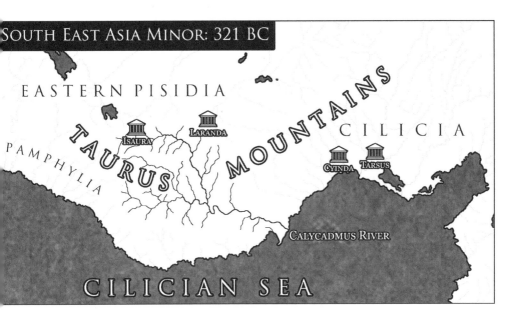

SOUTH EAST ASIA MINOR: 321 BC

EASTERN PISIDIA

TAURUS MOUNTAINS

CILICIA

PAMPHYLIA

ISAURA

LARANDA

CYINDA   TARSUS

CALYCADMUS RIVER

CILICIAN SEA

further affirming their status as the world's most formidable force. Ladder teams scaled the walls; resistance was cut down.[68] The Larandian defence was broken and a slaughter ensued. All men of military age were massacred; women, children and the senile were sold into slavery. It was brutal punishment – something that was becoming all too common in Perdiccas' actions towards defeated foes. The town was left a ruin, its meaning clear. This was the fate for any who dared practice brigandage against the new regime.[69]

Isaura

Leaving Laranda behind, a smouldering wasteland, Perdiccas marched his army southwest towards the highland homeland of the Isauri. As the land became more and more mountainous it is likely Perdiccas decided to divide his army, following in Alexander the Great's footsteps by gathering together an elite corps, consisting of Macedonians and an array of crack light infantry.[70]

With this special force Perdiccas pressed ahead into the rugged heartlands of the Isauri. His target was Isaura, the tribe's dominant hill fort. Isaura was large, strengthened by natural geography and thick walls. Artillery machines stretched the length of the barricade, able to shoot bolts and boulders down on any attacker who dared assault their defences. The Isaurians had made sure their central bastion was well-prepared to withstand a siege. Their warriors were equally ready. These men were renowned raiders, perhaps the most feared brigands in the whole of Anatolia. Most, if not all, were hardened, montane herdsmen – bred for waging guerrilla warfare in a rugged landscape. Their infamous reputation for plunder had provided cities such as Isaura plentiful wealth. Within the city's walls was a horde of stolen riches – infamous fruits of past pillaging. The Isaurian warriors had fought to obtain these possessions. They would fight to retain them.[71]

Perdiccas faced a tough challenge. War was a mainstay for these mountain people. The Isaurian defenders would rather die than submit; they would rather perish than hand over their hard-earned spoils. They would defend the hillfort to their last, no doubt emboldened yet further in the knowledge that only a miserable fate awaited any who survived a Macedonian victory. With an undying determination to resist this foreign intrusion, hundreds of brave defenders made ready for the siege.

Having arrived outside the hill fort's walls, Perdiccas prepared his men for an immediate assault. The regent hoped to repeat their successful storming of Laranda, swiftly seizing the stronghold just as his mentor Alexander had done on several occasions. Perdiccas had no intention of a prolonged siege; speed was of the essence. The plan was soon drawn up. Just as at Laranda Perdiccas' veteran Macedonians would lead the way, scaling the walls with ladders, disabling the artillery, capturing the ramparts and storming the city. The plan was set.

If Perdiccas had anticipated a repeat of his past lightning success at Laranda, he was very much mistaken. As the Macedonians advanced, artillery opened fire from Isaura's walls, shooting stones and bolts down into enemy ranks. Casualties were severe. Nevertheless, the attackers weathered this hailstorm of projectiles and reached the walls. Ladders were put in place and up the infantry went. Before long the ramparts had become the scene of fierce fighting as the Isaurian defenders desperately opposed the Macedonian veterans. For the mountain warriors, everything depended on a successful defence. Losing their liberty was not an option – victory or death. This stark acceptance provided many with almost superhuman courage:

> ...*they had steeled themselves mentally to endure the ordeal with desperate courage, and were giving their lives willingly in defence of freedom.* – Diodorus 18.22.3

They were not afraid to die.

To the death

The heroic defence proved too much for the Macedonians. Unable to break through they retreated back to their base. The Isaurians had won the day.

The second day's events were similar. Once again Perdiccas' men launched an assault, attacking in relays; once again the critical fighting occurred at the city's ramparts; once again the attackers were ultimately beaten back.[72] But their actions were not in vain.

By the start of the third day, Isaurian resistance was withering. Slowly the Macedonians were whittling down their foe's strength. Perdiccas – himself wounded – persisted in the assault; victory was close.[73] For the third successive day the regent's men scaled the walls and battled the defenders for the ramparts. This time it proved more successful. Although the attackers once again failed to force a breakthrough, for the Isaurians this victory proved Pyrrhic. By the time the sun set, many of their comrades had fallen. No longer did they have the manpower to resist the next assault.[74]

Day turned to night. The Isaurians convened to discuss their next move. Their defence was faltering; it was almost certain that the attackers would overrun the ramparts and sweep into the stronghold at daybreak. When that happened, what could they and their families expect but pain? Their history, the punitive reason behind Perdiccas' expedition and the recent razing of Laranda showed them that a dismal fate awaited any who fell into enemy hands alive. They would rather die.

The Isaurians therefore agreed on one final act of defiance:

> They shut their children, womenfolk, and parents inside their houses and set fire to them, making fire the instrument of their communal death and burial. – Diodorus 18.22.4

It was truly horrible. To a man the defenders decided to burn their families alive, rather than see them fall into Perdiccas' blood-ridden hands. As the night progressed the act was carried out. It was not long before the besiegers witnessed flames rising high from within Isaura's walls – illuminating the night sky. The accompanying sounds too terrible to imagine.

Amazement seized Perdiccas and his men. Risen from slumber quickly the regent acted, ordering soldiers to encircle the city and force their way in wherever they could. Yet once again the attackers were met with fierce resistance, as the last remnants of the Isaurian defence fought them back from the walls – aided by the unmatched spirit of knowing that this would be their final stand. Having expected his foe would try and escape this burning fortress, Perdiccas was perplexed.

> ...he was left wondering why men who had consigned their houses and everything else to the flames were still determinedly defending the walls. – Diodorus 18.22.6

But defending the walls they were, and successfully. In one last, titanic effort the thin Isaurian line repelled their foe. An astonished Perdiccas retreated his men from the walls to watch the spectacle from a distance – the city burning in front of their eyes. There would be no further fighting that night.[75]

By sunrise the flames had died down. Perdiccas' forces marched towards the smouldering town for another assault. This time, however, they encountered no resistance. Quickly they occupied the walls and the men marched into what remained of the bastion. Still there was no resistance, only burning buildings and communal groups of charred bodies. If it had not already, the horrible truth must have then dawned on them.

Having given their all in that last defence the night before, the few Isaurian warriors that remained had withdrawn and thrown themselves into their burning houses to be cremated alongside their families. The aftermath was a terrible sight to behold, but the veteran Macedonians were no strangers to seeing fallen enemies reduced to such horrific states. All they cared for was plunder. Not wanting to disappoint, Perdiccas permitted the pillaging and his men started hunting for booty amongst the ruins. Flames were extinguished, with the Macedonians finding rich rewards. Alongside burned bodies, within the houses they discovered Isaura's legendary wealth: molten gold, silver and other possessions. Despite the Isaurians' best efforts to deprive their foe of war-spoils, much of it remained intact and was seized by the victors.[76]

Victory

Isaura had fallen. Perdiccas' punitive expedition had been a resounding success. With Laranda and Isaura no more than ruins he could proclaim himself the man who had avenged Balacrus' death – strengthening his support among the Macedonians yet further. Departing Isaura laden with loot and witness to a remarkable tale, he led his army away from the rugged region. He would never return. Isauri herdsmen still dominated the countryside and Perdiccas had no desire to throw away more Macedonian lives on a costly guerrilla campaign, against a people who would rather die than submit to a foreign power. It was not worth the effort. He had won his war of retribution; swiftly he departed the Isauri homeland, reconvening with the rest of the royal army and establishing their base of operations in more fertile Pisidian lowlands.[77]

The expedition was at an end. Military success had seen Perdiccas' power grow even stronger. Official protector of both kings and popular with the soldiers, the man was at the peak of his power. Every passing day his regal ambitions were becoming more and more conceivable. He had every intention of pursuing them. At the same time Perdiccas had scores to settle. Ptolemy, Antipater and Antigonus all required his attention. As did another figure. A warrior princess, poised to enter the political fray. A Macedonian amazon.

Further Reading

Primary Sources
Diodorus Siculus 18.16.1–3 and 18.22–18.22
Plutarch *Life of Eumenes*

Secondary Sources
Anson, E. M. (1988), 'Antigonus, the Satrap of Phrygia', *Historia* 37 (4), 471–77.
Anson, E. M. (1990), 'Neoptolemus and Armenia', *Ancient History Bulletin* 4, 125–128.
Anson, E. (2015), *Eumenes of Cardia*, Leiden, 79–93.
Billows, R. A. (1990), *Antigonos the One-Eyed and the Creation of the Hellenistic State*, London, 3–58.
Bosworth, A. B. (1993), 'Perdiccas and the Kings', *The Classical Quarterly* 43 (2), 420–427.
Bosworth, A. B. (2002), *The Legacy of Alexander: Politics, Warfare, and Propaganda under the Successors*, New York, 9–11 & 60–61.
Jones, A. H. M. (1937), *Cities of the Eastern Roman Provinces*, New York.
Lenski, N. (1999), 'Assimilation and Revolt in the Territory of Isauria, from the 1st Century BC to the 6th Century AD', *Journal of the Economic and Social History of the Orient* 42 (4), 413–465.
Panichi, S. (2005), 'Cappadocia Through Strabo's Eyes', in D. Dueck, H. Lindsay and S. Pothecary (eds.), *Strabo's Cultural Geography: The Making of a Kolossourgia*, 200–215.

Chapter 8

Consolidation

Perdiccas' power had never been stronger. Through military victories and shrewd political plays, he had risen from aloof regent to dominant warlord. General of the empire's most powerful army, having unfettered access to the royal treasuries – an ancient billionaire – and the official guardian of two monarchs. Yet for Perdiccas, his struggle was far from over. Prominence provided him opportunity, but it also provoked his rivals to dig vicious political pitfalls that he had to avoid at all costs. He was walking a political tightrope – as hostile, ambitious figures searched for vulnerable chinks in the regent's armour, hoping to deliver a critical blow to his authority. Perdiccas had to tread carefully. So far he had made remarkable political progress in the Macedonian Game of Thrones. Now he had to maintain it.

Dealing with dissidence

Having reduced the stronghold of Isaura to a crumbling ruin, in the late spring of 321 Perdiccas and the victorious royal army descended into the lowland plains of Pisidia. There they established camp, well-situated for Perdiccas and his adjutants to tackle their next, major task. Turning their attention away from attacking powerful Iranian kings and punitive campaigns against the highland tribes of Pisidia, they focused on a more 'internal' problem – a dissident governor who had refused to obey official orders. This was the veteran statesman Antigonus.[1]

Perdiccas had to tread carefully. The previous year he had instructed Antigonus to aid Eumenes and Leonnatus in their planned invasion of Cappadocia. Antigonus had refused to obey, his inaction catalysing the campaign's collapse before it even commenced. The charges against Antigonus were severe – verging on treason. Such an unreliable governor was unfit to manage one of the most important provinces in the empire. Nevertheless, Perdiccas was loath to immediately march his army into Antigonus' domain and remove the governor by force, possibly provoking a military showdown. Not only had Antigonus built up a formidable powerbase in Asia Minor but Perdiccas did not want his enemies to paint him as the instigator of civil war –

Pisidia in the spring of 321. Perdiccas and the royal army encamped somewhere between Isaura, now little more than a ruin, and Antigonus' capital at Celaenae.

as an impetuous aggressor. It was imperative that Antigonus face punishment for his past misdemeanours, but his accusers had to be careful.[2]

Perdiccas and his supporters had a solution. Just as they had done with Craterus the previous year, they would coerce Antigonus to flee through a show of force. Antigonus could not ignore the military might Perdiccas had at his disposal. Positioned just across Phrygia's southern border, these soldiers were worryingly close. The strategy was agreed and Perdiccas summoned Antigonus to the camp to face charges of insubordination.[3]

Perdiccas was in no rush to receive a response. He wanted to give Antigonus time. Time to flee, knowing that travelling to the royal camp would almost certainly be a one-way trip and that a blunt refusal would provide Perdiccas a suitable pretext to march in and justifiably remove him by force. Suitable replacements for Antigonus' position waited in the wings. Alcetas, Perdiccas' younger brother and lieutenant, would seem an ideal candidate.[4]

The summon was sent. Perdiccas and his adjutants awaited Antigonus' reaction, as the one-eyed governor pondered his options.

Word from Armenia

While these events were unfolding a cavalry contingent had arrived at the camp. It was Eumenes, Perdiccas' trusted ally and the governor of newly subdued Cappadocia. Eumenes had returned from Armenia, bearing welcome news. He had resolved the dire situation facing the Macedonian expedition in the region.[5]

Prior to Eumenes' arrival Neoptolemus, the commander of the expedition, had struggled. Pursuing the remnants of Ariarathes' Cappadocian army he and his infantrymen had endeavoured to combat the enemy cavalry without significant squadrons of their own.[6] Their forces were inadequate. Progress proved painstakingly slow, almost non-existent. Unable to effectively combat their enemy, Neoptolemus' Macedonians had grown disillusioned on the Armenian frontier. This disillusion soon transformed into outright disobedience, as Eumenes discovered upon his arrival:

> *The Macedonian foot, whom he found insolent and self-willed...* – Plutarch *Life of Eumenes* 4.2

Eumenes had been ordered to resolve the situation, and resolve it he had. Recognising the expedition's critical need for cavalry he had overseen a remarkable and rapid recruitment campaign through the winter of 322/321:

> *...he contrived to raise an army of horse, excusing from tax and contribution all those of the country (Cappadocia) that were able to serve on horseback, and buying up a number of horses, which he distributed among such of his own men as he most confided in, stimulating the courage of his new soldiers by gifts and honours, and inuring their bodies to service, by frequent marching and exercising...*[7] – Plutarch *Life of Eumenes* 4.2–3

6,300 of the Near East's most renowned horsemen – mainly Cappadocians – served Eumenes' command. With them he had returned to Armenia, stunning the Macedonian infantrymen and giving them renewed hope to see through their mission. Though undoubtedly envious of Eumenes' overwhelmingly successful preparations, with his army's deficiency in cavalry resolved the proud Neoptolemus proceeded to police the border region.

Eumenes did not linger with the expedition long. Wanting to keep close to Perdiccas, the kings and the centre of power, he had quickly sought a return to the royal army. For the time being he left his Cappadocians in the hands of either Neoptolemus or one of his loyal adjutants, while he and a small entourage departed for central Anatolia in the spring of 321.[8]

Perhaps the most famous depiction of Alexander the Great that survives, shown in the Alexander Mosaic from Pompeii.

The deathbed of Alexander the Great, from Codex 51 of the Hellenic Institute. Perdiccas is shown in the centre, receiving the signet ring of Alexander the Great as told in the work of Quintus Curtius Rufus.

Bust of Ptolemy, currently in the Louvre Museum.

Mounted Macedonian depicted on the right of one of the long side carvings of the Alexander Sarcophagus. The figure is sometimes identified as Perdiccas, but there is no substantial evidence affirming that it is. (*Adobe Stock*)

Third century medallion depicting Olympias, the mother of Alexander the Great. Though Olympias does not feature much in the literature recording the events between 323 and 320 BC, she strived to align herself and her daughter Cleopatra with powerful figures such as Leonnatus and Perdiccas.

Bust of Demosthenes, the Athenian statesman who was hunted down at the end of the Lamian War by Antipater's agent Archias.

Bust of Hypereides, an anti-Macedonian Athenian figurehead during the Lamian War.

Bronze head of Seuthes III, discovered in the Tomb of Seuthes near Kazanluk. Ruler of the Odrysian Kingdom in central Thrace, it was Seuthes who opposed Lysimachus in either late 323 or early 322 BC.

Gold coin of King Philip Arrhidaeus III, struck at Babylon when the city was governed either by Archon, Docimus or Seleucus. (*Classical Numismatic Group, Inc./CC*)

Detail from the so-called Alexander Sarcophagus, originally from Sidon and now on display at the Istanbul Archaeology Museum. The scene depicts a Macedonian cavalryman (right), a Persian infantryman (bottom centre), a Persian archer (top centre) and a Macedonian infantryman (left), probably a hypaspist. All such units fought in multiple early Hellenistic armies between 323 and 320 BC. (*Adobe Stock*)

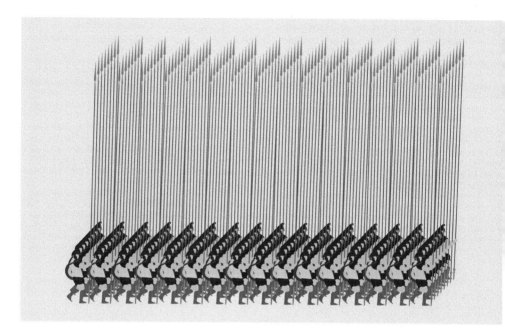

Artistic reconstructions of a Macedonian phalanx, eight men across and sixteen men deep. Most, if not all, of the Macedonian heavy infantry serving in the armies of the Successors were equipped in this manner. We also hear of non-Macedonian contingents fighting in this manner, perhaps most famously the 30,000 strong *epigoni*, that presumably served in the royal army of Perdiccas. (*Images courtesy of Kings and Generals YouTube Channel*)

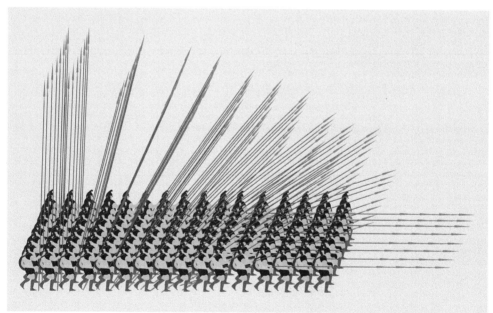

Artistic reconstructions of Silver Shield infantrymen, veteran Macedonain footmen of Alexander the Great's campaigns. The left figure depicts a Silver Shield phalangite (pikeman), while the right figure depicts a Macedonian equipped for siege combat (perhaps a hypaspist). It was probably Silver Shield infantrymen equipped with swords, spears and shields that assaulted the walls of Isaura and the Camel Fort for Perdiccas. (© *Johnny Shumate*)

Artistic reconstruction of a late fourth century BC hoplite. Equipped primarily with a c.2 metre long *doru* spear and a large round shield. These hoplites would have formed the mainstay of the Athenian army that fought the Macedonians during the Lamian War. (© *Johnny Shumate*)

Artistic reconstruction of light Asian cavalry. Presumably equipped primarily with javelins, but also swords and axes, you can imagine cavalrymen like these fighting in the armies of Eumenes, Ariarathes, Perdiccas and Antipater between 323 and 320 BC. The Cappadocians of Eumenes likely fought in this manner. (© *Johnny Shumate*)

Artistic reconstruction of the duel between Eumenes and Neoptolemus. Vividly described both in Plutarch's *Life of Eumenes* and in Diodorus Siculus, this duel occurred during a much larger clash between the forces of Eumenes and Craterus, fought in Phrygia in around mid/late May 320 BC. (© *Johnny Shumate*)

Artistic reconstruction of Macedonian Companion Cavalry, the elite heavy-hitting cavalry for Alexander the Great during his most famous clashes against the Persians. We hear of several generals such as Leonnatus, Craterus, Neoptolemus and Eumenes having retinues of elite horsemen with them in battle. Usually these retinues were a mixture of Macedonian and Asian cavalry. (© *Johnny Shumate*)

The site of Cyrene today. (*UNESCO, Creative Commons 3.0*)

Cape Tainaron today. The southernmost point of the Peloponnese, in the late fourth century BC this Cape was home to a large mercenary haven. From here, mercenaries were hired by both Leosthenes and Thibron to fight against the Macedonians and Cyreneans respectively. (*G Da (CC BY-SA 3.0)*)

The rugged landscape above Mersin in southeast Turkey, among the Taurus Mountains. It was rough terrain like this that Perdiccas and his army would have had to march through to reach the Isaurian stronghold of Isaura in Eastern Pisidia. (*Image courtesy of Dr Nicholas Rauh*)

The empty sarcophagus of Nectanebo II, now in the British Museum. Lying empty at Memphis in 321 BC, it is possible that Ptolemy placed Alexander the Great's body in this coffin once the body reached Egypt. Alexander the Great's body may also have been transported to Alexandria in this sarcophagus, in the early third century BC. (*Image Courtesy of Dr Chris Naunton*)

Reports of Eumenes' success were quick to reach Perdiccas when the Cardian arrived at the royal camp. Despite his limited martial experience, the man's ability to rapidly recruit elite cavalry had proven excellent; his loyalty remained steadfast. For Perdiccas having dependable subordinates during these troublesome times was vital and Eumenes' successes only served to solidify the former's trust in the latter. Eumenes' opinions carried greater weight than ever in the regent's council – something the Cardian would soon use to his advantage.[9]

Atalante

Eumenes' return to the royal camp benefitted Perdiccas' plans, as did the arrival of another figure. A prominent Macedonian noblewoman. Her name was Atalante, the sister of Perdiccas. Two years earlier, at the height of the Babylon Crisis in June 323, Perdiccas had promised his absent sister Atalante in marriage to the veteran infantry commander Attalus.

The agreement was political; Perdiccas had used his sister to secure the loyalty of Attalus, his family and – most importantly – his soldiers. Now, two years on, this arrangement was to finally be concluded. Summoned from Macedonia, Atalante had journeyed to the royal camp in Pisidia, where her marriage to Attalus was quickly sealed.[10]

Attalus' loyalty to the Perdiccan regime strengthened; Perdiccas now had two siblings by his side – Alcetas and Atalante.

A marriage proposition

Atalante and Eumenes were not the only major figures to arrive at Perdiccas' camp in the late spring of 321. At around roughly the same time that Eumenes reached the base from the east, another small entourage had arrived from the west, bearing news from Europe. Among these horsemen was the famous Archias, the ancient 'bounty hunter' who had so ruthlessly stalked the sentenced Athenian statesmen – Hypereides, Demosthenes and their followers – the previous autumn.[11]

Having been retained in Antipater's service, Archias was once again seeing through a special mission for the Macedonian viceroy – escorting two of his adult children to the royal camp. The first was Iollas, his youngest son and then aged c.20. Iollas had arrived to seal another major, diplomatic arrangement that would significantly strengthen ties between Antipater's family and Perdiccas: a marriage alliance.[12]

Marriage alliances had long been used in Macedonian politics to help secure a family's prominence within the kingdom – Attalus' marriage to Atalante for instance. Antipater was no stranger to the concept. The elderly viceroy had at least four daughters – diplomatic pawns intended to seal a series of strong alliances with several *strategoi* who had risen to serious positions of power in the wake of Alexander the Great's death. Arriving at the royal camp alongside Iollas and Archias was one such daughter. Her name was Nicaea, the object of this proposed alliance between the two most powerful men in the empire.[13]

A spokesman, presumably either Iollas or Archias, announced Antipater's proposal that Perdiccas marry Nicaea and unite their houses. Perdiccas pondered the decision; the proposal was nothing new. Nearly two years earlier at the very start of his tenure as regent it was Perdiccas who had first suggested this political marriage, hoping that an alliance with Antipater would help secure his new position. Yet Antipater had dithered in his reply. The eruption of the Lamian War had undoubtedly diverted his attention to the more pressing matter of preventing the downfall of Macedonian supremacy in the Aegean, but even this had not stopped him from negotiating marriage alliances with several other generals. Perdiccas' fragile position far away in Babylon had likely concerned the elderly Antipater. The regency appeared to lack authority. Perdiccas' orders were being openly ignored by figures across the empire, governors were pursuing their own interests, insurrection was rife and the regent himself appeared to be somewhat aloof from proceedings in the all-important Mediterranean.[14]

Almost two years on and everything had changed. No longer was Perdiccas this aloof regent. He now had several victories to his name – the crushing of Ariarathes, the destruction of Isaura, the coercion of Craterus, the isolation of Antigonus and the proclamation of King Alexander IV, not to mention Peithon's annihilation of the Greek rebels in distant Bactria. Perdiccas was dominant; he held true power at the heart of the empire. Antipater knew he should not delay any longer.[15]

And so, almost two years since Perdiccas had first proposed the match between himself and Nicaea, it appeared that this powerful marriage alliance was to finally take place and further cement the power of both families in the new regime. But there was a problem. Perdiccas' supreme position ensured that he was no longer at a loss for notable Macedonian brides. Nicaea was the daughter of the most powerful Macedonian in Europe – few could match either the prestige or the political muscle she could provide her husband.

But there was one woman who could.

The princess

That woman was Cleopatra, the sister of Alexander the Great. At around the same time that Nicaea and her escort arrived at the camp, Perdiccas received news that this royal princess had also recently landed in Asia, similarly seeking his hand in marriage.[16]

Cleopatra was no fool. She knew that if she was to guarantee her safety and standing in this unstable post-Alexander age, attaching herself to one of the empire's most powerful generals was essential. Already, through the machinations of her cunning mother Olympias, she had sought the hand of the legendary Leonnatus, only for him to subsequently perish in a headstrong cavalry clash against Menon and his Thessalians the previous year. Marriage to one of Antipater's many sons was out of the question – deep felt animosity existed between the viceroy and Alexander's immediate family. Yet by the beginning of 321, there appeared one clear candidate.[17]

Perdiccas seemed the perfect marriage choice for Cleopatra. He had the army, the money, the fame, the legitimacy and, most importantly, the ambition to marry into the Macedonian royal family. The wedding would provide Perdiccas a direct link to Alexander the Great and the ability to further pursue his imperial desires.[18]

What was more, for Olympias and Cleopatra, the match would damage their enemy Antipater, scuppering his marriage plans once more. Prizing Perdiccas away from sealing close ties with Antipater would secure themselves a formidable ally in the former and further alienate the latter. The question was, would Perdiccas decide to follow this risky path? Would he shun Nicaea and be complicit in this royal power play?[19]

Who to wed?

Perdiccas found himself forced to make a seismic choice. Nicaea or Cleopatra? He convened his council of most trusted advisors to inform them of the two concurrent marriage proposals he had received. Which should he accept?

The council was split. Alcetas and his faction formed one party advocating that his older brother marry Nicaea, at least for the time being. The regent was currently in an incredibly strong position, Alcetas reassured him. Not only did he have full control over the kings, but his recent successes had greatly strengthened the army's confidence in him. And this was not to mention the huge wealth Perdiccas had at his fingertips, both spear-won plunder and the many treasuries that had fuelled the Persian Empire. Perdiccas' position had never been stronger; the power he had as regent was unprecedented in the whole of Macedonia's history. But now was not the time to strive for the kingship, at least not yet.[20]

Although it seems Alcetas ultimately did envisage his brother marrying Cleopatra, he believed Perdiccas was not quite ready to cross this bridge of no return. Until he was, they needed to avoid humiliating the powerful and proud Antipater at all costs. They needed to keep the most powerful Macedonian in Europe satisfied, oblivious to the grand Perdiccan imperial scheme until it was too late. Marrying Nicaea would serve as a useful façade, behind which Perdiccas, Alcetas and their allies could continue covertly preparing their family's royal future. Marry Nicaea now, Alcetas advised. Keep Antipater propitiated. But reassure Cleopatra that the marriage was only temporary. Keep the princess on side. Keep her close, in Asia, until the time was right.[21]

Alcetas urged Perdiccas to wed Nicaea as soon as possible, but still the regent pondered. Another of his trusted confidantes had offered him the opposite advice.

Eumenes objected. Vehemently he advocated that Perdiccas seize the moment and marry Cleopatra. Yet such a strong stance evidently had personal motives. Eumenes was no friend of Antipater. The latter's support for Hecataeus, the tyrant who had forced Eumenes to flee from his home city of Cardia all those years before, had caused a deep divide between the two. The thought of Perdiccas and Antipater forming an alliance that could potentially curb his position of increased influence must have alarmed him. Eumenes therefore advised conflict with Antipater. Strike the first blow and marry Cleopatra.[22]

Eumenes' argument was dangerous. Discarding Nicaea and marrying Cleopatra would almost certainly set in motion a concerted effort by Antipater, Craterus, Ptolemy and their allies to depose Perdiccas – civil war would erupt. Nevertheless, Eumenes remained adamantly in favour of Cleopatra. Perdiccas would have royal legitimacy and support. His enemies would not.

The decision

Perdiccas wavered between the two options, but in the end Alcetas' proposal for patience prevailed. In the late spring of 321 he married Nicaea. The matter seemed settled. Alcetas' argument had won through. Eumenes had failed to convince Perdiccas, although he remained with the army. Still, nothing was certain in this highly turbulent time. No-one could have expected the major political storm that Perdiccas and Alcetas were about to weather.[23]

Troubling news reached the royal camp not long after Perdiccas' marriage to Nicaea. *Another* princess had arrived in Anatolia, on a high-risk political venture, also seeking marriage. This time, however, Perdiccas was not the object of the power play. This princess had no intention of achieving her goal solely through rhetoric. An army accompanied her; she would support her cause with the spear if need be.

Chapter 9

The Macedonian Amazon

Cynane and Allies	Perdiccas and Allies
Cynane	Perdiccas
Adea	Antipater
	Alcetas
	Cleopatra
	Olympias

Cynane. Her fame was legendary. A queen slayer. A warrior princess. An 'Amazon' – heroic, defiant and determined to fulfil her political goals. Now she saw an opportunity – one that was fraught with risk, but which offered rich rewards if successful. Cast aside for too long, no longer would she accept a life of relative royal obscurity for her and her immediate family. It was time for Cynane to re-enter the political fray.

Who was Cynane?

Cynane was the half-sister of Alexander the Great. Like Alexander, she was the child of Philip II and a foreign princess. Rather than the famed Olympias however, Cynane's mother had been Audata, a relative of the veteran Dardanian chieftain Bardylis, whose Illyrian raiders had been the bane of Macedonia for much of the early fourth century until his eventual death and defeat at Philip's hands in 358. Audata's subsequent marriage to Philip was political. Uniting their houses, it sealed an 'honourable peace' between the Macedonian and Dardanian kingdoms, ending hostilities between the two age-old enemies. At least temporarily.[1]

Audata had needed to adapt to this new life among Macedonian royalty. Residing at Philip's court she changed her name to Eurydice, a 'proper' Argead name. Still, her Illyrian roots remained. Within a few years of their marriage, Audata bore Philip a child. A daughter called Cynane, the one and only recorded offspring of their union. Instead of her native Dardania, Audata raised Cynane in Macedonia, at the heart of Philip's ever-expanding empire. Nevertheless, this did not prevent Audata from raising Cynane in her own

Dardania was situated to the north of Macedonia. It was the centre of a powerful kingdom during the first half of the 4th century.

image. The arts of war were critical components of an Illyrian noblewoman's education. In their youth they learned to ride, they learned to fight and to command on the battlefield. Rather than stay away from weapons and military action, from a young age they fought and hunted alongside the men. They were raised to be warrior queens and warrior princesses. Cynane was no different. Through her youth she was raised in this Illyrian fashion, experiencing an upbringing very different to that of most Macedonian noblewomen. A 'legend' was born. While still a teenager she had accompanied her father on one of his Illyrian campaigns, not just as a soldier but as a commanding figurehead.[2]

According to Polyaenus, she excelled in her first taste of combat:

In an engagement with the Illyrians, she with her own hand slew Caria their queen; and with great slaughter defeated the Illyrian army. – Polyaenus 8.60

It was an impressive feat for the Macedonians to tell tales about. Cynane the queen slayer. Stories spread about her as a fearless fighter, affirmed by analysis of battle scars on the young princess's cremated remains. She may have received a severe wound to her shin during the fighting, leaving her with a limp for the rest of her life.[3]

By the early 330s, Cynane's martial feats had reached legendary status across the kingdom. She evoked a Macedonian Amazon – this fearless, exotic warrior woman. Philip was only too happy to enhance this appearance, honouring his daughter with a gilded Scythian bow and quiver – 'quintessential marks of an Amazon in the making' as David Grant points out.[4] Nevertheless, a beneficial marriage for his daughter was also of prime concern for Philip. The Argeads and their followers preferred a tight-knit royal bloodline and so in c.336 Philip orchestrated Cynane's union with Amyntas, the king's nephew. The marriage was short-lived. Philip died not long after the wedding – assassinated at another daughter's marriage ceremony. Within a year of that Amyntas was also dead – murdered by Philip's son and successor Alexander, who perceived his cousin as a major threat to his throne and a figurehead for his enemies to champion. Barely 20 years old Cynane found herself a widow. What was more she now had a daughter of her own: Adea, the product of her short-lived marriage with Amyntas.[5]

Alexander's murder of Amyntas greatly affected Cynane, who showed little desire to marry again. Alexander however, had other plans for his half-sister. He saw her as a useful pawn – a tool to use in his diplomatic dealings. In 335, within months of Amyntas' murder, he offered Cynane's hand in marriage to his loyal ally Langarus, the king of the Agrianes, to strengthen ties between the two domains. Cynane had no choice but to comply. Langarus headed to Pella to receive his bride, but he never reached his destination. *En route* the king suddenly fell ill and died; the political marriage failed to come to fruition.[6]

Alexander had embarked on his intrepid Persian campaign shortly after, making no further marriage plans for Cynane (that we know of). For the rest of her half-brother's reign she remained in Macedonia, raising her daughter as Audata had raised her – instructing her in 'the science of war'. Cynane remained distant from the vitriolic political battles raging between Alexander's official European viceroy Antipater and his mother Olympias. But the Macedonian Amazon would not stay in the shadows forever.[7]

Re-emergence

News of Alexander the Great's death sent shockwaves throughout Macedonia and its neighbouring lands. The Athenians had launched their great revolt under Leosthenes' leadership; meanwhile Seuthes' control in the Thracian interior continued to strengthen. In this highly turbulent time, as renowned leaders crossed into Europe at the head of sizable armies, political schemes were being orchestrated left, right and centre. Large-scale, decisive battles were being fought on land and at sea. Still Cynane and her daughter remained 'inactive' in Macedonia, skipped over in the history books. Cynane was clever. She was no stranger to the ruthless machinations aligned with Macedonian politics. She bided her time and planned to use her lineage and legendary reputation to her advantage. All she needed was an opportunity.

In early 321, that opportunity presented itself to Cynane. Perdiccas was settling in Asia Minor with the royal army, having announced his arrival by crushing Ariarathes and subsequently cementing his control over the kings. With the emergence of this new force in the Eastern Mediterranean, Cynane realised the potential for a power play. Once again it revolved around marriage to a prominent figure – a key tactic for high-ranking noblewomen seeking influence and security during this unstable period.[8]

Yet Cynane's marriage play had some unique twists. She could hardly rival the prestige and royal benefits Cleopatra could offer Perdiccas. Cleopatra was, after all, Alexander the Great's full sister. So Cynane didn't try. Marrying Perdiccas, and competing directly against her stepmother Olympias and the powerful Antipater, was not her intention. Such a plan would be foolish and almost certainly doomed to failure. Instead, she found a clever alternative.

Rather than offering herself as the proposed bride, Cynane championed her daughter Adea – now c.14 years old. Rather than target Perdiccas as her daughter's prospective husband, Cynane set her sights on the one adult figure who, in theory but not in practice, reigned supreme over the army and the empire: none other than the simple-minded King Philip Arrhidaeus III. The monarch was of age, unwedded and incapable of ruling alone. If Cynane could obtain enough support from the Macedonian soldiers for the marriage, Perdiccas and his faction would have no choice but to allow Adea and her to assume the respective roles of queen and queen mother. Cynane's grip on the bloody business of Macedonian politics was solid. She understood the realities of being a princess in this age. She knew that she could expect a favourable reaction from the Macedonian troops, given their support for a close-knit royal Argead house; she knew that Perdiccas would do all he could to prevent her achieving her goal and contesting his control; she knew that the best chance of securing her family's importance was by becoming a significant voice of influence from the shadows, whispering thoughts into the king's ears.[9]

Cynane was no stranger to holding influence over men in powerful positions. Fourteen years earlier, she may have encouraged her husband Amyntas and his supporters to strike a claim for the Macedonian throne – an idea that resulted in Amyntas' swift murder on Alexander's orders. She followed several precedents of women using their prominent positions to fulfil their own aims. Olympias was one such woman, a queen who Cynane now aimed to outmanoeuvre in the Macedonian Game of Thrones. But for Cynane – and indeed for many of these women – it was not just about power. It was about survival. It was about making her move before she was forced to, before Cynane was once again used as a political pawn and before another powerful figure tried to use her royal blood to increase his own standing in this post-Alexander age. Cynane was determined to secure the future of her immediate family. If that meant going up against some of the most powerful figures in the empire, so be it. The venture was risky. The cost of inaction – of waiting in obscurity until another ambitious figure inevitably forced her back into the deadly political sphere – was worse. The time for sitting on the side lines was over.[10]

In the winter of 322/321 Cynane put her plan into action. Using her own funds, she amassed a small entourage – mostly of mercenaries. With her daughter and private army in tow, the Macedonian Amazon proclaimed her intentions and set forth for Asia.[11]

The Strymon River was on Macedonia's eastern border.

Word spread quickly and it was not long before Cynane and her force found themselves confronted by an opposing army. At the Strymon River, on the eastern border of Macedonia, soldiers blockaded their path to the Hellespont with orders to force Cynane back without bloodshed. At their head was Antipater. He had heard of Cynane's intentions and was determined to stop the princess's power play before it was too late. Cynane's plan, if successful, would directly affect Perdiccas' control over King Philip Arrhidaeus and the army. It would affect Perdiccas' power in the empire, and therefore, the political strength of the marriage he believed Iollas and Archias were finalising between his daughter Nicaea and the regent. Antipater had no intention of allowing Cynane's plan to ruin this, but at the same time he knew that physically fighting her force was out of the question. She was royalty. Despite all attempts to convince Cynane to remain in Macedonia, the warrior princess refused to back down. Her mind was set. Undeterred she gathered her troops and together they forced their way past Antipater's men. The guards gave way. Antipater's attempt to keep Cynane in Macedonia failed. Messengers hurried to Asia bearing news that another unexpected princess was about to arrive, and this one was bringing an army.[12]

It was spring by the time Cynane reached the Hellespont. Following in her half-brother's footsteps all those years before, she crossed with her entourage and stepped ashore onto Asian soil. Determined to fulfil her goal but no doubt knowing that further challenges awaited, she headed south.

The reaction

Perdiccas was troubled. News of Cynane's arrival in Asia, and her intentions, were deeply concerning. Her plan directly threatened his power; it threatened his interests. He could not allow her to reach the royal army and fulfil her marital objective. He did not want a teenage queen and a scheming, strong-willed queen mother eroding the strength of his position as regent, vying with him for control over King Philip Arrhidaeus and the soldiers. Through military successes and shrewd political announcements, the man had worked hard over the past year to gain unprecedented power and advance his own ambitions. Cynane threatened to wreck this. Like Antipater, Perdiccas was determined to stop Cynane in her tracks. Yet ultimately Antipater had failed – unable to persuade the princess to abandon her enterprise. Cynane was now Perdiccas' problem and, in his eyes, failure was not an option. He had to take Cynane down. But how?[13]

Perdiccas gathered his council of closest confidantes to address Cynane's recent arrival in Asia. Support to stop Cynane reverberated around the meeting, presumably echoed most vociferously by Alcetas. He had, after all, been the leading advocate of Perdiccas marrying Nicaea and it was his family's power that Cynane's intentions threatened. Alcetas was determined more than most to ensure Cynane did not reach the camp.

The two brothers and their allies soon decided upon a course of action. Perhaps due to his personal loyalty to Perdiccas, and because the regent did not have any other adjutant with such determination to ensure this royal princess never reached Pisidia, Alcetas was placed in charge of the mission. He received a sizable detachment of Macedonians, with whom he would march west, confront Cynane and coerce her home with an awesome show of force. Perdiccas and Alcetas hoped that this would be enough to convince Cynane to turn around and abandon her plan.[14]

Confrontation

In the early summer of 321 Alcetas commenced his march west, aiming to intercept Cynane as she made her way ever closer to the royal camp. Already messengers must have been dispatched to Cynane, carrying royal letters advising that she should not pursue her aims any further. All had failed; Cynane and her entourage continued south. The critical confrontation was coming.

Somewhere in western Anatolia, perhaps near Ephesus, the two armies came to a head. Cynane and her small entourage found their progress contested. Alcetas' veterans lined the way, *sarissae* and shields in hand, arrayed for battle in their phalanx battalions. Alcetas aimed to send Cynane the strongest message: turn around or face annihilation.[15]

Cynane, however, was not one for threats. Her strong character, combined with her acute knowledge of the Macedonian soldiery, convinced her that Alcetas' show of force was not nearly as strong as he thought. She called his bluff.

Mounting her horse, the princess advanced ahead of her army, aiming to awe the opposing veterans with her striking appearance. Picture the scene. Cynane, adorned in her ceremonial arms and armour. Specially designed gilded bronze greaves covered her lower legs and shinbones; her golden Scythian bow and quiver visible by her side.[16]

The Macedonians were awestruck. Cynane riding towards them in gilded armour would have resembled the stories, the legends, they had heard about this semi-Illyrian half-sister of Alexander the Great. The question of why they were daring to oppose this renowned Macedonian Amazon must have crossed their minds.[17]

As his solders gazed in wonder at the sight of Cynane, Alcetas advanced to meet the princess. Between the two forces the leaders convened – Alcetas demanding that Cynane abandon her enterprise and presumably offering her assurances of safety. But Cynane refused to back down. Openly she berated Alcetas for daring to block her way with armed force, for daring to defy a suitable royal marriage. She was determined to see her daughter assume the queenship. Past success in the face of armed opposition may have also emboldened her. Already she had successfully forced her way past Antipater and his guards. Would Alcetas resort to bloodshed? Most importantly would his Macedonian veterans really be willing to fight off their beloved warrior princess? Or would they back down, clearing a path for Cynane to reach the camp and becoming champions of her cause.

Alcetas' attempts to appease his foe failed. Cynane's mind was set.

...resolved upon a glorious death, rather than, stripped of her dominions, accept a private life, unworthy of the daughter of Philip. – Polyaenus 8.60

But there would be no battle; there would be no 'glorious death' that Cynane perceived herself finding in the midst of the clash. Before she could return to her army the warrior princess fell to the ground – dead. In full view of his own army, an exasperated Alcetas had given in to rage and slain Cynane. Attempts to coerce her return to Europe had failed. Rather than risk battle, an enraged Alcetas had resorted to the most extreme measure to ensure Alexander the Great's half-sister never made it to the royal camp alive. Cynane had been murdered.[18]

Alcetas had likely considered killing Cynane a last resort, but this did nothing to hide the stupidity of his action. Overconfident in the loyalty of his Macedonian veterans, the general may have expected a degree of sadness from his soldiers at Cynane's death but nothing further. He was very much mistaken.

A foolish decision

As the Macedonian veterans watched Cynane fall lifeless to the ground, outrage erupted. They were furious, triggered into an almost-anarchical state that Alcetas had not witnessed since the dark days of Babylon immediately after Alexander the Great's death. Their duty was to protect the royal Argead house, not to destroy it. And yet their commander, for no justifiable reason in the soldiers' eyes, had just openly assassinated the half-sister of Alexander the Great. Already many had felt anxious that they were having to oppose this Macedonian princess in battle order. Her cold-blooded murder at Alcetas' hand was the trigger that transformed this uneasiness into unprecedented outrage.[19]

The foolishness of his action slowly dawned on Alcetas. Unwilling to follow their commander's lead any longer, his soldiers took matters into their own hands. Crossing the field, they mingled with Cynane's entourage, seeking her daughter Adea to ensure she was protected from Alcetas' murderous intentions. Cynane may have died, but the Macedonians were set on seeing that her mission was carried through. They demanded that Alcetas take Adea to the royal camp; they demanded that her marriage to King Philip Arrhidaeus III take place. Alcetas' murder had made Cynane a martyr.[20]

Alcetas could do little but relent. The soldiers had emphatically shown him that their loyalty was not absolute – Cynane's murder was a step too far. For the commander it was now a question of damage limitation. He had to appease the indignant veterans. Reluctantly he complied with their demands: they would escort the young Adea to Pisidia and advocate the marriage of

Adea and Arrhidaeus. There was also the question of Cynane's decaying remains. Considering the importance of burial for them, the soldiers would have demanded an immediate funeral for their deceased princess. Cynane's body was cremated, with Adea subsequently taking her mother's remains and possessions with her to Pisidia. Cynane would never reach the royal camp alive, but she would reach it dead.[21]

Perdiccas had no choice but to consent to the Macedonians' demands once they returned to the royal camp. The marriage between Adea and Arrhidaeus would go ahead. The outcome that Perdiccas had strived to avoid came to pass, albeit with the notable exception of Cynane. Had the regent countenanced the murder of the princess if all else failed? Or was it an ill-tempered 'red mist' action by his younger brother? The truth was likely somewhere in-between.

Murdering royal princesses was not below Perdiccas' thinking. Two years before, during the early months of his tenure as regent, he had supported the killing of two Persian princesses by Alexander the Great's Sogdian widow Roxana. One of these princesses was Stateira, another wife of Alexander who may have been pregnant at the time. Plutarch records the story:

> *Roxana, who was now with child, and upon that account much honoured by the Macedonians, being jealous of Stateira, sent for her by a counterfeit letter, as if Alexander had been still alive; and when she had her in her power, killed her and her sister, and threw their bodies into a well, which they filled up with earth, not without the privity and assistance of Perdiccas...* – Plutarch *Life of Alexander* 77.6

The murders were political. Neither Perdiccas nor Roxana wanted any potential challenger to the latter's unborn child. Perdiccas was therefore certainly not averse to advocating the murder of royal women if they threatened to get in the way of his imperial ambitions.[22]

But Alcetas' killing of Cynane was different. Rather than a discreet assassination, his actions had taken place in front of an entire army; rather than a Persian princess largely unknown and uncared for by the Macedonian soldiery, Cynane was a legendary figure – unique in her martial prowess. Overconfident in his soldiers' loyalty, Perdiccas may well have countenanced a discreet killing of Cynane if all-else failed, but Alcetas' public execution was foolish. Now Perdiccas was met by an unplacatable host of Macedonian veterans, outraged over recent events and increasingly anxious that the royal marriage take place as soon as possible. Desperate to appease his soldiers as soon as possible, Perdiccas swiftly approved the marriage and gave orders to make preparations for the royal wedding.[23]

The marriage went ahead without any problems. Following in her grandmother Audata's footsteps, Adea married a Macedonian king and embraced the proper Argead name of Eurydice – further strengthening her support among the soldiers. Cynane's power play had succeeded, albeit at the cost of her own life. Her spirited, teenage daughter was a new figurehead for the royal army, implanted in a position that gave her clear control over her simple husband. Cynane had secured relative safety for her daughter.[24]

Trouble ahead

Though the Macedonian Amazon was no more, her legacy haunted Perdiccas' authority. Word about Cynane's murder and the soldiers' sudden insubordination would soon spread – welcome events which Perdiccas' enemies could use to land crushing damnations against the regent and his suitability for high office. What was more Adea's new position as queen compromised Perdiccas' sole control over the king. Though she showed no signs of dissent yet, if she was anything like her stubborn mother this would certainly not last long. Perdiccas needed Philip Arrhidaeus' full support if he were to conduct any future operations. Adea threatened this, but more importantly her presence threatened the loyalty of the Macedonian soldiers. If the queen decided to use her voice to instigate opposition to the regent within the ranks, there could be trouble.[25]

Perdiccas had to tread carefully. His brother's blunder dealing with Cynane had destabilised his authority. But he too was to blame. By countenancing the murder of Cynane if all else failed, Perdiccas and Alcetas had overplayed their hand, believing their support among the Macedonian veterans was all-but absolute. A string of past successes had left them overconfident in the extent of their control. Cynane had seen them pay the price.[26]

As for Alcetas, Perdiccas' brother received no known further punishment. His standing among the Macedonians no doubt suffered, but bending him to their will was humiliation enough.

The Cynane fiasco had put a dampener on Perdiccas' string of recent successes – the 'alliance' with Antipater, the subjection of Antigonus, the military victories. Still there was some good news. As events between Alcetas and Cynane had unfolded, Perdiccas' grand imperial scheme was progressing. Cleopatra, Alexander the Great's sister, had decided to remain at Sardis in western Asia, convinced by Perdiccas' covert communications that his alliance with Antipater was merely temporary – a façade to keep the viceroy unaware of his true intentions. Cleopatra would patiently wait for Perdiccas to discard Nicaea and marry her as soon as the regent was ready to cross his Rubicon.

Nevertheless during this scheme's crucial preparation stage, when Perdiccas *needed* to keep his enemies as oblivious as possible to his plan for the kingship, the cold-blooded murder of Cynane could not help but arouse alarm. Such a public and infamous execution of the princess begged the question why? What had motivated Alcetas to take this drastic step? Suspicion of Perdiccas was mounting. One man was determined to exploit it.

Further Reading

Primary Sources
Arrian *Events After Alexander* 9.20–9.24
Polyaenus 8.60 (Cynane)

Secondary Sources
Carney, E. (1988), 'The Sisters of Alexander the Great: Royal Relics', *Historia* 37 (4), 385–404.
Grant, D. (2019), *Unearthing the Family of Alexander the Great: The Remarkable Discovery of the Royal Tombs of Macedon*, Barnsley.
Macurdy, G. H. (1927), 'Queen Eurydice and the Evidence for Woman Power in Early Macedonia', *The American Journal of Philology* 48 (3), 201–214.
Roisman, J. (2012), *Alexander's Veterans and the Early Wars of the Successors*, Austin, 90–92.

Chapter 10

Antigonus' Flight

Antigonus was quick to receive word of events in western Asia Minor. Alcetas' cold-blooded killing of Cynane was extraordinary; the famous Amazonian half-sister of Alexander the Great had been slain – assassinated in plain sight so that she could not disrupt the new political order. For Antigonus, the imperial ambitions of Perdiccas and Alcetas had never been more starkly visible. No matter how drastic the measure, the two brothers were determined to retain their family's monopoly over the kings and the army. Meleager, Stateira, Ariarathes, the Isaurians and now Cynane – all who had threatened this had encountered a gruesome end. And more would follow.

Antigonus knew he was to be next. Since the spring of 321 Perdiccas had sent several official summonses to the one-eyed governor, demanding he ride to the royal camp and contest the charges set against him. Antigonus delayed his arrival, as Perdiccas turned his attention to the flurry of noblewomen that had then arrived in Pisidia over the summer to fulfil various diplomatic agreements.

For Antigonus, respite was welcome. The veteran statesman knew that past charges of insubordination were irrefutable – it would not be difficult for Perdiccas' 'lackey' Eumenes to lay the failure of his initial Cappadocian campaign upon Antigonus and his refusal to provide aid. Mercy was not a trait Perdiccas was renowned for when dealing with those who had defied his wishes. Antigonus was no fool. If he were to ride to the royal camp and partake in this 'sham trial', he knew he would not leave alive. The governor faced a dire situation; Perdiccas' carefully constructed noose was tightening. Nevertheless, throughout the summer, Antigonus had put on a brave face – defiantly declaring that he would contest the charges and oppose Perdiccas within the regent's lair.[1]

As Antigonus suspected, Perdiccas wanted him gone. Permanently. Already smears against Antigonus had been spread among the army's ranks – verbal attacks deriding his past insubordination. Now, in the wake of the Cynane fiasco, Perdiccas upped his efforts to displace Antigonus once and for all. Come to the royal camp or be deemed a traitor and face invasion.[2]

Making his move

Bravado was no longer an option for Antigonus. But the governor had used his time wisely. Behind the façade of defiantly protesting his innocence and adamantly announcing that he intended to face down these ridiculous charges, the governor had been finalising plans to flee. By the late autumn of 321 these were ready.

Gathering his small entourage of friends and family, Antigonus fled his satrapal capital at Celaenae and hurried west to the coastline of Asia Minor. Athenian ships awaited his arrival. Officially, they had sailed across the Aegean with orders to transport their fellow countrymen home from the island of Samos, following Athens' forfeiting of this imperial colony at the end of the Lamian War. They held little love for Perdiccas – the man who had ultimately decided to drive the Athenians off the island. Antigonus and his small band found refuge on their ships. They had found a means of passage to Europe.[3]

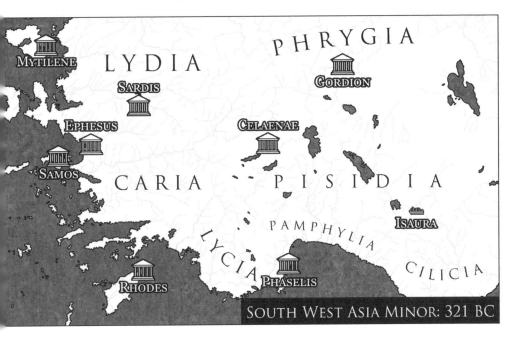

Perdiccas must have expected the news of Antigonus' flight. This had been his aim. He had wanted to coerce Antigonus into fleeing, and he had succeeded. Once again, through a powerful show of force he had successfully displaced a major political opponent without a single sword being unsheathed. The vital satrapy of Phrygia was now in his control. In the wake of Alcetas' catastrophic killing of Cynane, Antigonus' bloodless flight was welcome news. The policy had proven successful, or so it seemed.[4]

Antigonus vowed vengeance on Perdiccas. Prior to leaving Asian shores, he had gathered intelligence and information – assets with which he could damage Perdiccas' power. Alcetas' murderous dealing of Cynane was golden, only affirming Perdiccas' imperial ambitions. Yet this alone was not enough; the one-eyed general sought knowledge that could further damage Perdiccas. He found it.

A royal rumour

Antigonus had friends in powerful places in western Asia. Menander and Asander, the governors of Lydia and Caria respectively, had long been on cordial terms with the late ruler of Phrygia. Neither felt much loyalty to Perdiccas. It was not difficult for Antigonus to obtain their covert pledges of support if he were to one day return to Anatolia. For the fugitive Antigonus, they were welcome allies on Asia's westernmost seaboard. Menander, however, provided Antigonus with much more than the supply of possible future support. He provided invaluable information.[5]

The arrival of Alexander the Great's sister Cleopatra in Asia was no secret. At the height of 321 she had arrived to compete with Nicaea for Perdiccas' hand in marriage. As we noted previously, after due deliberation Perdiccas had chosen to marry the latter, sealing a long-sought after alliance with Antipater. Things, however, were not quite as they seemed. Rather than return to Macedonia in the wake of her rejection, Cleopatra had settled at Sardis, the capital of Lydia. But why? Rumours abounded among those close to Alexander the Great's sister. Whispers surfaced to amplify the rumour that communications between Perdiccas and Cleopatra had continued: that Perdiccas had requested she delay any departure. That he did intend to discard Nicaea and marry her in due course.[6]

When Antigonus arrived in Lydia, nothing was confirmed. The whispers were merely rumours, but their strength had increased. Talk had spread, with reports of continued communication between Perdiccas and Cleopatra reaching Menander. With no reason to conceal Perdiccas' personal ambitions, Menander leaked the rumours to Antigonus. For the latter, this was the information he had been seeking. It was potentially explosive. If true, not only did the rumours further confirm Perdiccas' quest for the kingship, but they also revealed the regent's perfidious plan to publicly demean his new ally Antipater. Shunning Nicaea would humiliate the powerful viceroy.[7]

Perdiccas was no stranger to reneging on his word if it meant fulfilling a carefully-constructed scheme – Meleager's orchestrated downfall was testimony to that. Now Antigonus had acquired some extraordinary intelligence – albeit rumour – that he could use to further his aim of seeing Perdiccas experience a dramatic and bloody fall from grace. Boarding the Athenian ships, he and his companions sailed away to Europe. For personal gain, he aimed to inform Antipater of these developments. If he were to reach the viceroy, however, Antigonus' destination would not be Macedonia. Instead, it would be one of the most hostile battlegrounds in the whole of Greece: Aetolia.[8]

Chapter 11

The Aetolian War

Aetolian Allies	The Macedonians
Menon of Pharsalus	Antipater
	Craterus
	Polycles
	Polyperchon
	Phila
	Antigonus

There had been little respite for Antipater since the subjugation of Athens the previous autumn. Demosthenes and Hypereides were dead; the Lamian War had ended. But several key political issues remained outstanding – none more so than Antipater's desire to cement his family's standing in this new post-Alexander world.

A powerful union

As soon as Athenian resistance crumbled Antipater had returned to Macedonia, intent on shoring up his position on the world stage. He intended to use his daughters as political pawns – to seal powerful marriage alliances between Antipater and other dominant figures in the empire. Antipater had sent one such daughter, Nicaea, to Perdiccas in the hope of forging a formidable union and securing his family's influence at the heart of the new regime. Closer to home, however, he hoped to bind another dominant figure to his family.

Craterus, saviour of the Lamian War and a figure possessing 'the pride of a king', had returned to Macedonia with Antipater and the army.[1] Archaic orders from Babylon, in the wake of Alexander the Great's death, had instructed the general to assume joint rule of the European territories alongside Antipater. Yet Craterus never carried through this command. Rather than fulfil these orders upon his merging forces with Antipater in the face of Antiphilus' Athenian army, Craterus defied them. The two titans reached an agreement. The returning hero withdrew any claim to co-rule Europe; Craterus acknowledged Antipater as superior. Nevertheless, gaining Craterus' concession at this critical time had come at a price for Antipater. And now, with the Athenian crisis having abated, he sought to fulfil his end of the deal. Once again, Antipater's offer centred around a marriage alliance. He was not at a loss for eligible daughters. For Craterus, however, there was one clear choice.[2]

Phila, one of Antipater's eldest daughters, was well-acquainted with Craterus. Their paths had almost certainly crossed during Craterus' prolonged stay in Cilicia. The widow of Balacrus, the region's governor that had perished at Isaurian hands, she had returned to Macedonia with Craterus and his army. She was a remarkable woman, renowned for her virtue and sage advice. Phila may well have caught Craterus' eye. It was something that Antipater was sure to utilise for political gain. Upon their return to Macedonia, the wedding took place in an elaborate ceremony: the most righteous woman of Macedon marrying 'the paragon of military virtue'. It was a powerful union. Gifts and honours were lavished upon them, Craterus receiving excessive attention from his jubilant new father-in-law. Merry-making gripped the Macedonian soldiers as they were similarly showered with praise – the heroes of the Lamian War.[3]

For Antipater, he had good reason to be cheerful. The marriage and its celebrations abounded in benefits. Not only did it increase his standing among the soldiers, but it sealed the strongest bond between him and the legendary Craterus. Alexander the Great's most renowned adjutant – the world's most famous commander – was now his closest ally.[4]

A return to Asia

As the celebratory atmosphere died down, Antipater, Craterus and their adjutants had gathered to consider their next moves. Once more military preparations were on the agenda. Antipater had not been able to win Craterus' support solely through allowing him the venerable Phila's hand in marriage. Craterus sought a legacy that would match his formidable reputation. He sought his own power. He sought a prominent position in the empire alongside the likes of Antipater and Perdiccas. Antipater was fully cognisant that his ally's king-like character demanded that he ultimately assume a position of high authority, rather than remain the viceroy's deputy. Craterus was, after all, the general who had briefly received the regency in the days after Alexander's death. So Antipater had added another incentive to seal Craterus' loyalty. In return for Craterus acknowledging Antipater's supremacy in Europe, the latter promised him his support for an imperial venture. Not in Europe, but in Asia. He would sponsor Craterus' return to Asia and the division of the empire east of the Aegean between his two sons-in-law.[5]

Antipater envisaged an unstoppable triumvirate. Craterus, Perdiccas and himself – all united through marriage – would supervise the length of Alexander's kingdom on behalf of the kings. Antipater in Europe, Craterus and Perdiccas in Asia. The fine detail of the agreement still required work – Perdiccas had to be involved. But a rough outline was there that suited Antipater's interests and convinced Craterus to prepare for a powerful position in the east. Once before Antipater had formed the fulcrum in a powerful triumvirate between leading Macedonians, culminating in the kingdom reaching the greatest heights it had ever witnessed in its history. Now he hoped to repeat this between himself and two highly ambitious sons-in-law.[6]

Consensus was reached. Preparations were made for Craterus' glorious return to Asia. His departure, however, would have to wait. Delay was essential. Before initiating these plans, Antipater required Craterus' expertise one final time. A strong remnant of resistance to Macedonian rule on the Greek mainland remained and had to be brought to heel. One beacon of rebellion still had to be extinguished. Permanently.

The last enemy

Aetolian defiance towards Macedonian authority had reached its peak. Inhabiting the rugged lands northwest of the Corinthian Gulf these people had a history for being unruly – opposing the wishes of Antipater and Alexander before him. During the Lamian War 7,000 of their warriors – all in their prime – had marched to swell Leosthenes' ranks at Thermopylae, playing a key role in the Athenian's subsequent humbling of Antipater's forces. It was a humiliation Antipater was loath to forget. Now, with the Athenians reduced to puppet status and Craterus by his side, the viceroy could focus his attention upon the Aetolians – the only people who had fought the Macedonians in the Lamian War, but never submitted. Antipater sought to change that.[7]

Punishing the Aetolians for their past hostility was but one of several charges the viceroy brought against his enemy. Having retained their antagonism to Macedon in the wake of Athens' capitulation, despite their isolation, the region had advertised itself as a safe haven for Antipater's exiles. A refuge for the enemies of Macedon – for newly-made exiles. Among these fugitives (it seems) was none other than Menon of Pharsalus, the dashing Thessalian cavalry commander who had driven the vainglorious Leonnatus to his doom and caused his mounted Macedonian counterparts so much trouble in the past war. The Aetolians posed a very real threat to Antipater's control in Greece – their strength epitomised through their powerful constitution.[8]

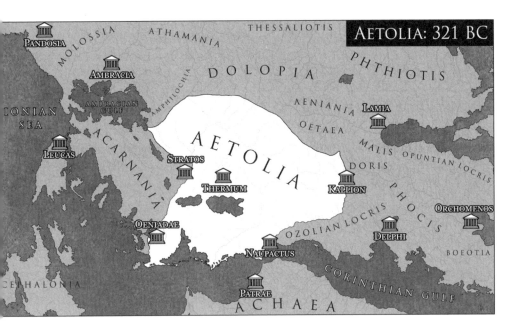

This was the Aetolian League, a region-wide union of Aetolian communities centred around a working government. Recognised throughout the land as the official authority, oligarchic magistrates oversaw almost all matters of state. Assemblies convened twice a year, designed as meetings where representatives could debate pressing military matters. Nevertheless it was the oligarchs who held true power, invested with the authority to issue region-wide instructions that they expected their subjects to obey. Tried and tested as a system the Aetolian League had proven its power. Orders to mobilise could result in musters of over 10,000 men; subjects from all over Aetolia willingly obeyed official directives issued by the governing body.[9]

The League's strength was in no small amount due to Antipater's own past actions. In 331 he had allowed the Aetolians to restore the League following their neutrality during King Agis III's Spartan revolt. Fast forward ten years however, with the downfall of both Athens and Sparta, the League's power shone out like a spotlight.[10] It was the Aetolian League that now posed the most significant political challenge to Macedonian authority among nearby city-states. Their assistance to Athens during the Lamian War made Antipater determined to dissolve this League and cripple Aetolian power. Forever. Any attempts to persuade the Aetolians to submit and sacrifice their precious League had failed. If he were to break this powerful governing body, he would have to do so through martial means – through invasion. A campaign of blood and terror.[11]

Preparation

Craterus would command the invasion. Who better to crush this sole bastion of defiance than the seasoned general who had successfully stormed the near impregnable rock fortresses on the edges of the known world? Putting aside his plans for a return to Asia, Craterus gathered his subordinates and prepared for invasion. Defeating the Aetolians in their rugged homeland would be no easy feat, as Craterus and Antipater knew full well. Surplus manpower was essential. 32,500 soldiers would comprise the Macedonian force – 30,000 infantry and 2,500 horsemen. Engineers were present among its ranks, tasked with the construction and operating of various siege machines. As for Alexander's veteran infantrymen – the senior soldiers that had returned to Europe with Craterus – it seems they were not required. The land's most formidable fighters would remain in Macedonia.[12]

By the summer of 321 preparations were complete. The army had assembled; supply stations had been set up along the line of march. Without delay the march to the borders of Aetolia commenced – Craterus and Antipater leaving their Macedonian homeland at the head of an army once more.

The Aetolians were ready to receive the attack with arms and armour. Rumours of the impending invasion had reached them long before Antipater and Craterus had completed preparations. Reports of the huge force coming towards them must have given even the most warlike of Aetolian magistrates cause for grave concern. Yet the price of submission had proven too steep – the return of Oeniadae to their hated Acarnanian neighbours and, most unacceptable of all, the dissolution of their constitution. They would not submit.[13]

Summoning their own soldiers, the Aetolians dared to resist the legendary Craterus and his 30,000-strong force. From far and wide across Aetolia their brethren answered the call to arms, gathering their weapons and convening to combat the all-but-inevitable invasion. 10,000 warriors awaited orders – all hardened men in the prime of physical condition, loyal to Aetolia and its League.[14]

As these Aetolian warriors answered the summons, the generals gathered to dictate strategy for the coming invasion. They recognised their weaknesses; Craterus far-outnumbered their soldiers in manpower – over three to one. No matter how fierce and determined their soldiers were, the chances of them being able to carve open the feared Macedonian phalanx in pitched battle were low. The Athenian infantry's capitulation at Crannon was proven testament to that. In addition, a distinct lack of an Aetolian cavalry arm meant that destruction was even more likely. Even Aetolia's greatest warriors would have little chance against the Macedonian masters of open warfare. Their best bet would be to try to negate their enemy's advantage – to fight the invaders on terms more favourable to the Aetolians.

A defensive strategy was drawn up. Orders were sent out across the region for all Aetolians – men and women, the old and the young – to gather supplies and possessions and head for the highlands. Well-fortified bastions on the apex of these mountains would serve as their new homes for the duration of the war. Settlements lacking in sufficient defensive armaments – walls, artillery, supplies – they willingly abandoned; well-fortified cities were greatly strengthened with garrisons numbering in the thousands. Artillery crews presumably manned the walls to add extra menace to the defences. History offered the Aetolians valuable precedents of how numbers counted for little when assaulting a suitably-strengthened stronghold – especially when these fortresses were located on mountainsides. Antipater himself had successfully resisted the much larger Athenian-Aetolian army from within the strong walls of Lamia barely two years earlier. Having learnt lessons from this past failure, the Aetolian generals aimed to use their enemy's strategy against him.[15]

The Aetolian plan centred around refusing the Macedonians the style of warfare they desired most: a pitched battle on flat ground. Instead, the League would welcome them with brutal guerrilla warfare. Although several thousand Aetolian warriors seem to have been highly capable serving as heavily-armed hoplites, this strategic highland retreat demanded that most, if not all, put down their *doru* spears and fight primarily as light infantry. Mobility and skirmishing was preferred, as the Aetolians prepared to defend their powerful mountain retreats. Enemies would be picked off – the warriors using their knowledge of their homeland's terrain to conduct effective ambushes and launch hit and run tactics against their foe.[16]

The well-fortified cities would form the nuclei of their strength, occupying dominant positions that looked out over the local landscape. It was a sound strategy, officially agreed by the League's military hierarchy and effectively put into effect throughout the land. The soldiers took up their positions in and around the mountain bastions; non-combatants and reserves gathered supplies and headed to the hill forts. It was a nation on the move, loyally following the League's designated plan to resist the invaders. Much depended on their success – the preservation of their way of life, their League, their homeland. They prayed that lengthy highland resistance would deliver them from the Macedonian invasion.

For Antipater and Craterus, they were about to embark on a type of warfare very different to the pitched battles they had fought on the rolling plains of central Thessaly to decide the Lamian War. And they knew it. Over 30,000 soldiers followed them to Aetolia. But would that be enough?

The invasion of Aetolia

Summer had already arrived by the time Antipater and Craterus' army reached the borders of Aetolia – the local population having already gathered the harvest and headed to the hills. Sparsely populated lowlands greeted the invaders. Abandoned Aetolian cities were occupied without a fight – useful supply bases for the army as Craterus ordered them inland, towards the hill forts.[17]

Now the real fighting began. Aetolian skirmishers ambushed Macedonian units as they approached the central bastions. Confident in their ability, Craterus had his men make several attempts to dislodge the enemy from their positions of strength. All failed miserably. The Macedonians struggled to make progress over the broken ground under a hail of projectiles, both thrown and shot from places of great natural strength. Confident in their defences and resolute in their defiance, the skills of the Aetolian warriors came to the fore – contrasted by the seeming ineptitude of Craterus' attacking forces. Impatience mounted among Macedonian ranks. The idea that they, the heirs of the most feared fighting force in the world, were being bested by a people they derided as no better than barbarian hill folk must have been riling. Still the Aetolians held their enemy at bay. Any desperate attempts to break through by reckless individuals fuelled with the Macedonian military *élan*, keen for glory under the watchful gaze of Alexander's greatest adjutant, met only with a tragic end. Macedonian casualties began to mount. Despite showing no lack of determination, a characteristic of their nation's martial prowess, they failed to make any significant progress against their foe.[18]

Frustration continued to increase among the Macedonians. They were angry at the unorthodox Aetolian way of fighting – disheartened by this successful defiance of Macedonian military hegemony. The Aetolian avoidance of pitched battle in favour of this defensive highland strategy was having the intended effect on their enemy's morale, withering it away slowly but surely. Patrols and supply routes through the region's rugged hinterland must have been targeted – small bands of Aetolian warriors using their knowledge of the terrain to inflict devastating ambushes on these enemy units. Craterus' soldiers were suffering, struggling to combat an enemy that had no intent of fighting them man to man.[19]

Craterus had to change tack. He had no choice. Winter was nearing; despite months of effort, still his men had failed to make any significant inroads against their foe. Strengthened in the knowledge that all they held dear was at stake if their defence faltered, Craterus' foe remained resolute in their resistance to the invaders and continued to carry out their well-thought-out strategy with near impunity. Craterus, however, would not give up. His stellar reputation demanded that he conjure a reaction in the same vein of genius as Alexander the Great had overcome his greatest challenges in the far east. If he was to prove himself a worthy successor to the conqueror, then finding a way to overcome the Aetolians was essential.

Determined to reverse his army's fortunes Craterus conjured up a new carefully planned strategy, designed specifically to counter the Aetolian tactics.

The coming of winter

Winter's harsh climate descended on the Aetolian highlands. Throughout the late summer and the autumn, the League's forces had held out against the Macedonians from the safety of their mountain strongholds. Now, however, they had to deal with months of freezing cold. Craterus sensed an opportunity.

Though initially well-prepared, Craterus knew that Aetolian supplies could not last much longer. Thousands of Aetolians – men, women and children – had taken up residence in these fortresses. All required food and warm clothing – substantial resupplies of which they could only gather from the land below.

Withdrawing his men from the immediate vicinity, Craterus ordered them to commence a winter-long blockade of the strongholds. Putting into practice the lessons he had learnt from years of experience in the east, Craterus had his men construct shelters to protect them against the elements. Soldiers guarded all routes to and from the Aetolian hill forts. It was a brutal blockade, forcing the hated Aetolians and their families to try and hold out in the face of dwindling supplies and severe cold.[20]

Crucially Craterus targeted his foe's morale. As the Aetolian soldiers and their families suffered within their snow-covered strongholds reports must have reached them emphasising the contrast in conditions among their besiegers below. Well-supplied and protected from the elements, a deflated feeling must have gripped even the stoutest of Aetolian hearts as they discovered that their enemy were not suffering similar hardships. Still the Aetolians refused to give up. Hardened highlanders probably continued to carry out irritant raids on Macedonian supply lines. Nevertheless, no one could deny that Craterus' plan was working.[21]

Antipater and Craterus' decision to conduct the siege through the winter only confirmed their determination to see the war through to a definite conclusion. The Aetolians remained defiant in their resistance, but with every passing day an unfavourable end to the war was becoming more and more likely. Food was running out. The Aetolians knew any chance of a peaceful solution without having to first fight a decisive military engagement had evaporated. Two options faced the Aetolian generals:

> *They had to either come down from the mountains and fight an army that outnumbered them by far and was commanded by notable generals, or stay where they were and die of hunger and cold.* – Diodorus 18.25.2

Both options presented slim chances of victory. Desperation was mounting among Aetolian high command. Despite their continued attempts to frustrate the blockade, Antipater and Craterus were turning the screw. Victory seemed certain; only a miracle could preserve the Aetolians and their way of life.

It was then, during the Aetolians' darkest hour, that heralds arrived outside their defences. The envoys carried messages from Antipater and Craterus. What they announced must have astounded the exhausted Aetolians:

> *…as though one of the gods had taken pity on them for their courage.* – Diodorus 18.25.2

Their enemy were offering peace. And a favourable peace at that. But why?

News from abroad

Antigonus had ridden hard for Aetolia. Having arrived at Athens in late 321 the one-eyed general had wasted no time in heading for Aetolia and the headquarters of Antipater. Cordial relations existed between the two senior statesmen, but the former certainly did not reside among the latter's closest confidantes. It was the first time Antigonus and Antipater had seen each other in some fifteen years. Yet Antigonus' mediocre standing belied the importance of his information.[22]

Addressing an audience that included both Antipater and Craterus, Antigonus informed them about recent events across the Aegean in Asia Minor. Dramatic emphasis encapsulated Antigonus' audience as the one-eyed fugitive retold a highly exaggerated version of Cynane's death. How Perdiccas had ordered Alcetas to confront her with armed force and the latter's subsequent unceremonious slaughter of the princess in plain view. For Craterus and Antipater the news was cause for concern. Perdiccas' move to confront Cynane with a show of force Antipater could understand – after all he had done exactly the same against the warrior princess as she had attempted to leave Macedonia, not wanting her mission to jeopardise the strength of the triumvirate he was envisioning between Perdiccas, Craterus and himself. But the brutal, merciless action – so colourfully described by Antigonus – that Perdiccas and Alcetas had decided upon to prevent Cynane's arrival at the camp was deeply troubling. Despite his attempt to coerce the princess to remain in Macedonia, Antipater had not dared kill Cynane. She was a renowned warrior princess, adored by the soldiers; she was the 'Amazonian' half-sister of Alexander the Great. Alcetas had shown no similar restraint. For clear, personal reasons the general had not hesitated in killing Cynane when all else had failed. It evoked a need for supreme control; extreme action was not beyond Perdiccas and Alcetas' doing if it helped them retain power. Even if that meant murdering royalty.[23]

Antipater and Craterus' plan for a powerful triumvirate was now less certain. If murdering a princess was not beyond Perdiccas and Alcetas' means to maintain their family's control over the kings, what likelihood was there that they would willingly sacrifice this dominant position and reach a power-sharing agreement? Could Craterus expect a similarly gruesome fate to Cynane when he returned to Asia?

Antigonus' report of Cynane's death was certainly concerning for Antipater and Craterus – no doubt causing the latter two to question their grand strategy of a working union with Perdiccas. But Antigonus' report did not end there.[24]

Sensing growing concern, the colourful storyteller revealed the most important nugget of intelligence he had acquired before departing Ionian shores. Rumours of Perdiccas' continued dealings with Cleopatra in Sardis were relayed to Antipater. That Perdiccas aimed to marry the princess, discard Nicaea and humiliate Antipater when the time was right. Menander, the source of the information, gave enough credence to the rumoured intrigues of Perdiccas to incite alarm within Antipater. In other circumstances the viceroy may well have brushed off Antigonus' story as an unproven smear – a desperate attempt by a man who had fallen from grace seeking to regain lost power by inciting suspicion among allies. Yet the source of Antigonus' information proved convincing; Antipater could not ignore it. Further fuel was added to the already-smouldering fire that Perdiccas could not be trusted. The man was clearly advancing his own imperial ambitions and was willing to embrace all manner of shocking methods to get there: murder and reneging most notably.[25]

A change of plans

Antipater and Craterus' suspicions of Perdiccas had reached an all-time high; Antigonus' report had achieved its intended mayhem. Without delay, the veteran statesman Antipater summoned his commanders to an emergency council to decide their next moves.

Generals gathered for the impromptu council, as their men continued the Aetolian blockade. Antigonus' shocking reports of events across the Aegean in

Asia were relayed to them. But how should they respond? Slowly but surely the Aetolian blockade was working. Breaking it off when they were so close to a successful conclusion would, in most circumstances, be an act of sheer madness.

Yet these were certainly not 'normal' times.

Strong accusations abounded that Perdiccas sought the royal purple. Antipater and Craterus, the leaders the generals looked up to, were staring at humiliation. Loyal to their commanders, the officers provided Antipater and Craterus unanimous advice: cut off the Aetolian campaign and make ready for war with Perdiccas without delay.[26]

Further detail was quickly added to this new plan of action. Having completed their preparations Antipater and Craterus would take the offensive, crossing the Hellespont with an army and throwing the gauntlet down at Perdiccas' feet for a showdown in Anatolia. Antigonus would lead the vanguard. Having cemented strong ties in southwestern Asia Minor, he would sail across the Aegean with a small advance force and secure a bridgehead for the invaders along the coastline. Together, at the head of a large army, Antipater, Craterus and Antigonus would then march inland to confront Perdiccas and remove him from power by force.

Alliances with similarly disgruntled figures were essential. Fortunately, Antipater was not at a loss for powerful friends. Perdiccas' relations with several governors 'nominally' under his authority were strained. None more so than Ptolemy, the opportunistic governor of Egypt. Ptolemy's relations with Perdiccas were dismal – the former having already sparked the latter's ire through a plethora of unauthorised, provocative actions: the murder of Cleomenes, the building up of his own private army and his conquest of Cyrene at Thibron's expense. Contrary to Perdiccas, healthy relations existed between Ptolemy and Antipater. Both had maintained friendly ties and Antipater now saw this governor as an invaluable ally in any war with Perdiccas – a man who could distract the regent and force him to fight a two-front war.[27]

By the time the council of officers departed the meeting, an outlined plan for a possible war with Perdiccas had been drawn up. Antipater's triumvirate idea was cast aside. Should they succeed, they would divide the empire among the victors – Craterus ruling supreme in Asia, Antipater in Europe.[28]

Orders were sent to the soldiers to break off the winter blockade. Macedonian emissaries ascended into the highlands to announce to the Aetolians their lucky escape from annihilation and Antipater's proposal for a truce.

The Aetolians could not believe their fortune. They had been staring into the jaws of defeat, but now the mistrust and rivalry of Macedonian politics had thrown them a lifeline. Dismayed but resigned to follow orders, the Macedonian soldiers started dismantling the blockade as Aetolian officials headed to conclude an agreement with Antipater. The two sides quickly approved a treaty – a temporary truce rather than a long-term peace. Though Perdiccas' actions had forced Antipater to conclude the campaign before his desired conclusion, the viceroy intended this merely to be temporary. Sooner or later, he was determined to eradicate the Aetolian menace. Laying the groundwork for a future second invasion, he ensured a strong garrison was maintained around the strategically-important city of Amphissa in neighbouring Locris – tasked with keeping a watchful eye over the Aetolians as Antipater headed to Asia. Polycles, a trusted subordinate, received this command.[29]

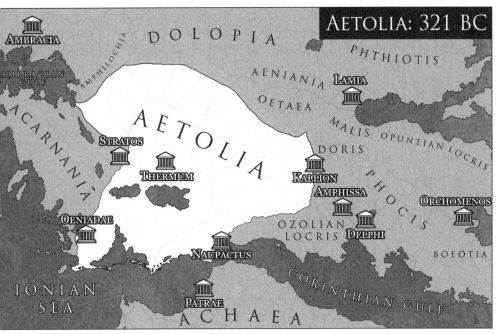

Amphissa was situated directly to the east of Aetolia and commanded a very strategic position.

Though Antipater reassured himself that the terms of the treaty were only temporary, it could not cover up a degree of Aetolian success. Their much-cherished Aetolian League remained intact; their forces had suffered no calamitous defeat. They were stronger than ever. Events elsewhere had saved them, but to the Aetolians this mattered little. Against all the odds they had successfully resisted invasion from the world superpower. Where the likes of historic city-states such as Athens and Sparta had failed, the lesser-known Aetolians had succeeded. Macedonian hatred towards them for their public defiance and unconventional style of warfare, they knew, ran deep. They had no intention of waiting patiently for a second invasion in the meantime. Antipater's departure to fight a war elsewhere offered opportunity. The Aetolian menace would return.[30]

And with that, Antipater's army headed home to Macedonia. Along their route was Delphi, the religious heart of Hellenism and 'the navel of the Ancient World'. For centuries, this was where prominent figures had made monumental offerings to promote their name far and wide across the Greek World. Craterus proved no different. For the veteran general, this leading panhellenic sanctuary was the perfect place to advertise his credentials as a worthy 'successor' to Alexander the Great. To proclaim himself a pious and virtuous figure who was worthy of high office in this new age.[31] Wanting to emphasise his close relationship with the deceased Alexander, sometime since his return to Europe Craterus had commissioned the crafting of bronze sculptures dedicated to Apollo, Delphi's patron deity. These sculptures would portray an event of Homeric heroism: a lion hunt in Syria,

> ...consisting of the lion and the dogs, of the King (Alexander) engaged with the lion, and Craterus coming in to his assistance. – Plutarch, Life of Alexander 40.5

Lysippus, a famous Sicyonian sculptor, was tasked with turning this envisioned piece of powerful propaganda into reality.[32]

(Another) war on the horizon

By the beginning of 320 Antipater, Craterus and their army had returned to Macedonia. Antigonus was no longer with them. He had returned to Athens with a band of 3,000 mercenaries to prepare for a vanguard expedition to Asia Minor. The success of his European venture had proven phenomenal. He had arrived on mainland Greece a fugitive; he would leave as the commander of a small army, fuelled by a zealous desire to destroy Perdiccas' regime.[33]

To the north in Macedonia, Antipater and Craterus made their own preparations for invasion. Craterus' grizzled veterans were summoned for their return to Asia – their unmatched experience at war proving invaluable. Mercenaries and younger Macedonians would provide the rest of the force. But what about Europe? Who would rule as interim viceroy of these western territories in Antipater's stead while he was in Asia?

Polyperchon was the clear choice. Another veteran of Alexander the Great's campaigns, he had returned to the west as Craterus' second in command one and a half years earlier. A battle-hardened, senior commander, a shrewd negotiator and a staunch supporter of the decision for war with Perdiccas, Polyperchon's record highlighted invaluable experience and loyalty to their cause. As Craterus and Antipater headed east, it would be his job to maintain order in the west. It would prove no easy task.[34]

The army assembled. Antipater and Craterus addressed the soldiers concerning their situation. A strong feeling of resentment towards the Aetolians and how they had escaped Macedonian vengeance must have resonated. Capitalising on this anti-Aetolian sentiment, Antipater took great pains to reassure his men that he had every intention to exact brutal retribution on those hated hill folk. A second campaign of conquest was emphasised, with no objective but to eliminate the Aetolian menace permanently. Any foe who did not fall in battle, they would deport to the farthest and most extreme deserts of Asia. Men, women and children would be destined to live a life of hardship in an alien land. An official decree was drawn up, publicly reaffirming this brutal commitment. One can imagine cheers rippling through the Macedonian ranks, reassured that their hated foe's 'freedom' was only temporary: terrible vengeance was coming.[35]

Attention now turned to the matter at hand: the invasion of Asia. Accusations against Perdiccas were easy to announce to the soldiers. The murder of Cynane, the strong rumours surrounding the regent's intended marriage to Cleopatra and his intent to humiliate Antipater and Craterus. Antipater and his supporters presumably used all these arguments to deride Perdiccas as an enemy of the kingdom, as a man who sought to displace Alexander the Great's bloodline and seize the imperial throne. The soldiers could do little else but agree. Their seniors had already led them across their Rubicon – united in their approval for armed conflict. The assembly merely 'rubber stamped' their motions.[36]

A year had passed since Craterus and Antipater had started preparations for the former's glorious return to Asia. In that time much had changed.

Antipater's hopes for a new triumvirate between himself, Craterus and Perdiccas had crumbled – Antigonus' connivance having fermented serious suspicion within the old viceroy. Craterus would still be returning to Asia; an army would still accompany him. But now, Antipater would be joining him and together these two titans of the time would be returning as invaders. Instigators of

> the greatest armed conflict between Macedonians in more than a generation. –
> Joseph Roisman *Alexander's Veterans*, 118[37]

Civil war beckoned.

Further Reading

Primary Source
Diodorus Siculus 18.23.3–18.25.6

Secondary Source
Grainger, J.D. (1999), *The League of the Aitolians*, Leiden, 61–64.
Mendels, D. (1984), 'Aetolia 331–301: Frustration, Political Power and Survival', *Historia* 33 (2), 129–180.
Roisman, J. (2012), *Alexander's Veterans and the Early Wars of the Successors*, Austin, 113–118.

Chapter 12

The Greatest Heist in History

Perdiccas' Allies	Ptolemy's Allies
Cleopatra	Arrhidaeus (the general)
King Philip Arrhidaeus III	Archon
Attalus	Laomedon
Polemon	Antipater
Alcetas	Craterus
Peithon	
Seleucus	
Eumenes	
Gorgias	
Pharnabazus	
Phoenix of Tenedos	
Neoptolemus	
Cleitus the White	
Aristonous	
Antigenes	

Antipater was on the warpath. It would not be long before his army headed for the Hellespont and turned the threat of civil war into reality. For the Perdiccan regime, it was cause for concern. But confronting this threat was not their sole priority. Unbeknown to Antipater, Perdiccas had faced an ever-greater problem.

News of warlike preparations in Macedonia were not the most disturbing reports Perdiccas received that winter. To the southeast, a rogue governor threatened his grand plans with one of the greatest heists in history. The culprit? None other than Perdiccas' arch nemesis Ptolemy. Animosity between the two had been building ever since Alexander the Great's dying days in Babylon. Now tensions were about to boil over into direct confrontation, as each pursued their own ambitions at the expense of the other. Perdiccas versus Ptolemy, over powerful regent versus defiant governor. The two entwined in a bitter contest for control of a mobile mausoleum and its precious cargo: the divine corpse of a conqueror. Both desired this talismanic symbol; neither wanted such a powerful, political tool to fall into the hands of their enemy; both would risk much to acquire it. The stage was set for a grand climax – a confrontation that Ptolemy was set to provoke.

Babylon: spring 321

For two years Alexander the Great's corpse had resided in Babylon – the aromatised and embalmed body of the dead conqueror lying in state somewhere within the Asian metropolis. Perdiccas, Ptolemy, Leonnatus and the rest of the army's most senior figures had agreed upon this at the Babylon Settlement.[1]

It was, however, merely to be a temporary measure. Babylon would not be Alexander's final resting place. Nevertheless, if the generals were to move the dead conqueror's body elsewhere, they required a vehicle. A funeral carriage, within which they could place the embalmed corpse and escort it to its next destination. This, however, could not be any funeral carriage. It was to house the greatest commander the world had yet seen. The man who had been declared the son of Zeus and Lord of Asia.[2] The king who had inspired his men to countless military successes and led them as far as the Indus Valley. Whatever vehicle carried his corpse demanded magnificence beyond measure. His newfound divinity, his military might, the empire he left behind – a suitable carriage needed to emphasise all if it were to convey the corpse of this conqueror.

Perdiccas spared no expense funding the project. The royal treasuries financed the hiring of the finest artists, smiths and craftsmen from across the empire: Asian and Hellenic. Leading smiths, sculptors, painters and carpenters convened in the capital. For the next two years they worked tirelessly within the royal workshops to construct a funeral carriage unlike anything the world had witnessed before.[3]

Arrhidaeus oversaw the project. Not to be confused with Alexander the Great's simple half-brother, this Arrhidaeus was an otherwise-unknown Macedonian officer present in Babylon at the time of Alexander's death. For almost two years he stayed in the city, guarding the construction works with a contingent of soldiers as it slowly started to take shape.

Finally, in the spring of 321, Alexander's funeral carriage was ready.

A mobile mausoleum

As the carriage was led out from the royal workshops, wonder gripped all those in Babylon who cast eyes upon it. It was unlike anything they had seen before. Its design was monumental, financed by former Achaemenid wealth that spared no expense:

> ...it was the most expensive such vehicle that has ever been made, costing many talents to build, and was famous also for the exceptional artistry that went into it... – Diodorus 18.26.2

Everywhere an onlooker gazed, the carriage emphasised Alexander's glory. A remarkable description survives in Diodorus Siculus' history:

> They started by making a casket of hammered gold, the right size to accommodate the body, and they filled the inside of it with aromatics which had the property of both imparting a sweet smell to the corpse and preserving it. On top of the casket was laid a lid of gold, which was a perfect fit and covered the upper rim of the chest. Over the casket was draped a magnificent piece of purple cloth, embroidered with gold, beside which they placed the dead man's weapons. Their intention was that the overall appearance should reflect what he had accomplished in his lifetime.
>
> Next, they brought up the carriage that was to transport this casket. It was topped by a golden vault, the surface of which was studded with precious stones, and which was eight cubits wide and twelve cubits long. Under the roof, running along the whole length of each side, was a rectangular golden beam, on which were carved the heads of goat-stags. From the beams hung golden rings, with diameters of two palms, and through them was threaded a brightly and variously coloured festoon, of the kind that might be used in a parade, that hung down from the rings.
>
> On the ends of the beams were network fringes furnished with bells that were large enough to ensure that the sound would be heard from a long way off as the carriage approached. On each corner of the roof, where the sides met, there was a golden Victory bearing a trophy. The colonnade on which the vault rested was of gold, with Ionic capitals. Set back from the colonnade was a golden net, made of strands twined as thick as a finger on which were fixed four painted panels at the same height as one another, with each panel occupying an entire side.
>
> The first of the panels had a chariot in relief, in which Alexander was sitting, holding a magnificent sceptre in his hands and escorted by two units of the Household Guard, one consisting of Macedonians and the other of Persian Apple-bearers, with their shield-bearers in front of them. The second panel showed the elephants that used to follow the Household Guard, accoutred for war and with mahouts mounted in front and Macedonians, armed in their usual fashion, behind. The third had cavalry squadrons made to look as though they were engaging in combat, and the fourth had ships in battle formation. – Diodorus 18.26.3–27.1

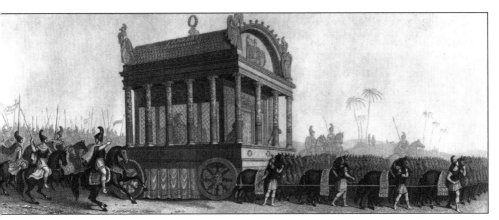

An artistic depiction of Alexander the Great's funeral carriage.

Below the panels, two life-size golden lions guarded the netted entrance to the central chamber. They resembled pharaonic 'guardian statues', protecting the sarcophagus and looking far beyond the mortal world.

Finally, at the roof's central and highest point, a clear Babylonian influence was visible. A stylised royal palm, a tree that only grew in Babylon, towered above the carriage into the open air.[4] Once again this decoration was tipped with precious metal, being crowned with a large golden olive wreath,

> *...which shone with a bright and scintillating light when struck by the sun's rays, so that from a long way off it looked like a flash of lightning.* – Diodorus 18.27.2

The carriage's exterior evoked a miniature, Hellenic temple – the art and architecture designed to emphasise Alexander's 'life after death.' How Alexander had followed in the footsteps of his divine ancestor Heracles to take his seat alongside the Olympian gods.[5]

The question of the carriage's mobility had also been addressed. The best wheelwrights from across the continent had assembled in Babylon to apply their skills to the base of this monumental design. They did not disappoint.

Richly decorated Persian wheel axles were visible at the carriage's base, specially designed to provide the best suspension available as the cart made its journey west. Road menders and engineers would accompany it, on hand for the almost-inevitable repairs that would be required *en route*. Even the animals were spared no expense. To pull this wheeled carriage were sixty-four of the fittest mules, each beast of burden decorated with gold and precious stones. A bell was fitted around each mule's neck, its sound announcing the cart's arrival outside various towns.[6]

The carriage amazed all those who laid eyes upon it. It emphasised wealth. Gold was everywhere – from the strong mules to Alexander's semi-concealed sarcophagus. It emphasised military might – from the painted panels to the armed escort and their shining, ornate armour. It emphasised divinity – from the Ionic colonnade to the golden veil and its nearby guardian statues. And it emphasised an empire that encompassed any Greco-Asian divide. Persian, Hellenic and Egyptian elements combined to create this iconic catafalque – filtered to reflect artistic brilliance from across the empire.[7]

Perdiccas had invested heavily in Alexander's funeral carriage. Nevertheless, it was what this vehicle housed within that was most valuable. Great men can be just as valuable dead as they were alive. The divine Alexander's body quickly became a powerful relic, enhancing the reputation of whoever possessed it at the dawn of this new era. Perdiccas knew this full well. His lavish spending on the funeral carriage and his control over the body increased his legitimacy as regent. His possession of the corpse – 'the heritage of the empire' – was a talisman of authority. It confirmed Perdiccas as the dead conqueror's successor in managing affairs of his already-ailing empire, something the regent was determined to retain at all costs.[8]

Another reconstruction of Alexander the Great's funeral carriage, based on Diodorus' description. Created by the German Archaeological Institute in the late 1800s. (*Alamy*)

Departure from Babylon

Alexander's final journey commenced in around September 321.[9] At the head of a sizable escort, Arrhidaeus guided the elaborate carriage out of Babylon to begin its westward journey. Among those watching on as the great procession departed was Archon, the Macedonian governor of Babylon. Though he had forged close ties with Arrhidaeus and been privy to discussions over the carriage's construction, it was his duty to remain in Babylon. Under his watch Babylon had transformed dramatically. For the past three years this Asian metropolis had formed a centrepiece of the empire. It had witnessed the death of the king, it had housed the world's most powerful fighting force and it had provided a safe haven for the construction of the greatest funeral carriage the world had ever seen.

Yet as Arrhidaeus and the carriage disappeared over the horizon, Babylon's imperial importance faded. Archon could not complain. In control of insurmountable Achaemenid wealth and in possession of decent military resources, he could enjoy a favourable posting outside the Macedonian political spotlight. For now….

On the road

Progress was slow; road menders and craftsmen regularly attended to the carriage as Arrhidaeus and the escort edged westward. Houses along their route emptied before their eyes, as people flooded into the streets to view the cortège as it passed by. Crowds greeted their arrival at the entrance of every town – the many bells on the mules and the carriage alerting the residents far in advance that this amazing spectacle was approaching. From end-to-end locals guided Arrhidaeus and the catafalque through their hometown, eager to gaze upon this unique temple on wheels, hoping to glimpse the outline of the legendary conqueror's sarcophagus behind its golden veil, before the procession passed through and the chiming of bells faded into the distance once more.[10]

But where was the cart travelling to? What was its destination? Two years earlier, at the Babylon Settlement in the aftermath of Alexander's death, the generals had agreed to comply with the dead king's wishes that he be buried at the Siwa Oasis in Libya, home to the Oracle of Ammon. Fresh from murdering Meleager but still not strong enough to promote his own preferred idea, Perdiccas had accepted the resolution. He hoped to appease Ptolemy, who was no doubt eager to have Alexander buried near the borders of Egypt. But Perdiccas only intended this concession to be temporary – a delaying tactic that would provide him breathing space to solidify his own, senior position. With

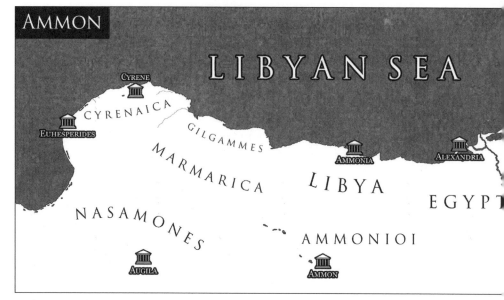

Ammon and its namesake oracle was situated at the Siwa Oasis, in the Libyan desert. This was where Alexander the Great had supposedly expressed a wish to be buried.

Meleager's demise, Perdiccas recognised that Ptolemy posed another challenge to his authority. He was proved right.[11]

Two years later and tensions between Perdiccas and Ptolemy had neared breaking point. Future hostilities between the two looked likely. Ptolemy was building up his military strength; Perdiccas had already started contemplating future plans to forcibly depose this troublesome governor. For Perdiccas, however, marching against Ptolemy was not his priority. The destination of Alexander's funeral carriage was uppermost in his mind. Reneging on his promise at Babylon two years earlier, Perdiccas had no intention of having the body buried at Siwa; he would not allow items as valuable as either the golden carriage or its precious, semi-divine cargo to fall into Ptolemy's hands. Instead Perdiccas planned to use these powerful objects for his own benefit. Naturally.[12]

A change of destination

In early 321, perhaps after receiving reports from Babylon that its construction was nearing completion, Perdiccas had sent fresh instructions concerning the funeral carriage's final destination. The lush oasis of Siwa was no longer to be Alexander's final resting place. Macedonia was.[13]

For Perdiccas, this was all part of his grand imperial plan. Once Arrhidaeus and the carriage reached the royal camp in Pisidia, situated *en route* between

Babylon and Macedonia, Perdiccas would personally escort them – alongside the royal army and the puppet kings – back across the Hellespont to Macedonia. This was the trigger for Perdiccas to initiate his carefully constructed power play. As soon as Alexander's body lay safely in his grasp, he would shun his recent bride Nicaea, and the alliance with Antipater that she personified, would be discarded. Princess Cleopatra waited in the wings, having remained in Sardis.[14]

Only months before, Perdiccas' imperial ambitions had alienated some of the Macedonian veterans when Alcetas slaughtered Cynane. But once these soldiers laid their eyes on the carriage and saw first-hand the amount of time, money and effort Perdiccas had invested into creating such a magnificent object that honoured their beloved Alexander, the regent must have expected that any lingering dissent would evaporate. The carriage would serve as a powerful tool for Perdiccas, its monumental design healing his family's authority over the army in wake of the Cynane fiasco.[15]

Once he had acquired the carriage, Perdiccas would be unstoppable. Married to Cleopatra, greeted by Alexander's mother Olympias, in possession of Alexander's body and his magnificent funeral carriage, commander-in-chief of the royal army and official guardian of the two kings, no-one would be able to contest his authority upon his return to Macedonia. Perdiccas would be the shining light of the Argead cause, bringing Alexander's body back to the traditional royal burial place and having close official ties with the revered leader's sister, mother, half-brother, wife and infant child. Unable to compete with his power, any challenge from Antipater and Craterus would swiftly dissolve. Perdiccas would be invincible.[16]

This was Perdiccas' plan. It was certainly bold, but once he had the body he could see through the subsequent steps that he had already prepared. First however, he needed the body.

By the time Arrhidaeus and the catafalque departed Babylon, the general had received fresh orders from Perdiccas, instructing him to lead the carriage to Pisidia without delay. As soon as the entourage reached Perdiccas, the regent could initiate the next steps of his master plan that would make him the undisputed, dominant power in the empire. But Ptolemy knew this too.[17]

The plot

Just as Perdiccas was determined to see Alexander's body secured safely in his hands, Ptolemy was equally resolved to see that it didn't. Like Perdiccas, and presumably having already guessed that the regent would renege on his past promise and contest the corpse's heading to Libya, Ptolemy had conjured up his own plan for the body. Throughout 321 the governor of Egypt had maintained close communications with senior officials in Babylon: Archon and Arrhidaeus most notably. Together with Laomedon, Ptolemy's friend and the neighbouring governor of Syria, these four officials had colluded, conjuring up a plot to ensure that the body stayed out of Perdiccas' hands. A heist![18]

Spearheading the plot, Ptolemy convinced Arrhidaeus and Archon to ignore the regent's updated orders. In doing so they would pull the keystone out of Perdiccas' imperial scheme, forestalling the regent's grand intentions under the pretext of fulfilling Alexander's final wishes.[19]

By the time Arrhidaeus departed Babylon in September 321 the four figures had finalised the plot. Initially Arrhidaeus would head northwest, crossing the Euphrates and arriving in northern Syria. He would then initiate the heist. Rather than continue west he would head south, marching via Laomedon's satrapal headquarters at Damascus and continuing from there on to Egypt.[20]

Ptolemy had raised the stakes. To oppose Perdiccas' frighteningly ambitious scheme, the governor had conjured up his boldest and most provocative plan yet. He knew that this attempt to seize the funeral carriage and prevent Alexander's talismanic corpse falling into Perdiccas' hands was a huge risk, no doubt bringing the full ire of the regent down upon him. But Ptolemy had little choice. He knew he was already set on a collision course with Perdiccas – one that had been growing ever closer since June 323. For him it was now or never. He had to act before Perdiccas became too powerful – something that seemed all but certain if Alexander's funeral carriage reached the regent in Asia Minor. Seizing the carriage would almost certainly provoke war, but it would be a war that Ptolemy was already anticipating. Better he that landed the first strike.

And so in late 321 Arrhidaeus put the plan in motion. Having arrived in northern Syria, the general turned his entourage south and headed toward Egypt. The theft was afoot.

The chase

The secrecy surrounding the plot provided Arrhidaeus a notable head start, but even so it was not long before messengers reached the royal camp and informed Perdiccas of the funeral cart's unexpected southward turn towards Egypt. Horror seized the regent. The very thought that such a vital and powerful tool as Alexander's corpse could fall into the hands of his most hated foe and wreck his own great plans must have chilled him to the bone. Suspecting pre-arranged collusion between Ptolemy and Arrhidaeus, Perdiccas acted with haste. He assembled a special task force – lightly armed and designed for relentless pursuit. It was to this special contingent that Perdiccas assigned the

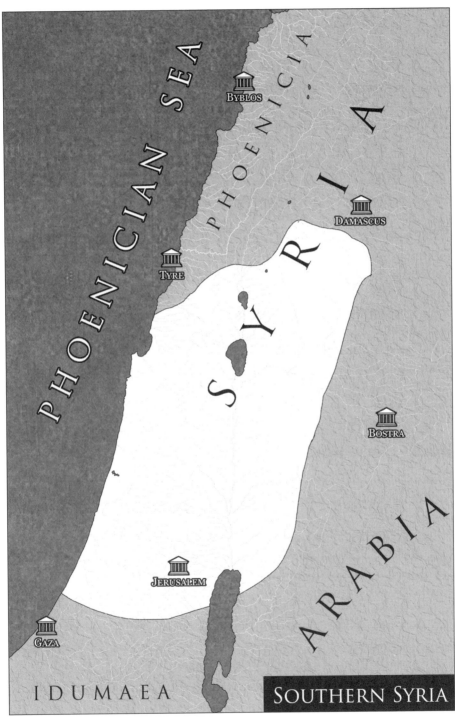

A map of southern Syria, highlighting the general vicinity where Attalus and Polemon must have caught up with the funeral carriage.

vital task of retrieving the funeral carriage, reaching and re-routing it to Asia Minor by force if all else failed.[21]

Attalus received command of the mission. Boasting a wealth of military experience and having recently become the regent's half-brother through his marriage to Atalante, Perdiccas placed great faith in the ability of this general. Polemon, Attalus' youngest brother, would also accompany the task force. Though unable to equal the vast experience of command Attalus had acquired under Alexander the Great, the youthful Polemon would serve and observe alongside his older brother as they strived to accomplish the vital mission.

The task force assembled; orders were issued. Attalus and Polemon led their soldiers out of the royal camp and headed at full speed for Syria. The chase was on.

The retrieval force made good progress, crossing the Taurus Mountains and traversing much of ancient Syria. Past Damascus they hurried and it was not long before their pursuit provided dividends. In late 321, somewhere in southern Syria, they finally caught sight of Alexander's conspicuous funeral cart. They had reached the carriage; now they had to retrieve it. But they were in for a shock.

As Attalus, Polemon and their force approached the funeral carriage, hundreds of mercenary heavy infantrymen opposed them. This was certainly not the escort Arrhidaeus had departed Babylon with. Where had these reinforcements come from?

Protecting his winnings

Ptolemy had anticipated the move. He knew that Perdiccas would try to retrieve the cart by all means necessary. He knew that Arrhidaeus and the cortège required military assistance if they were to reach Egypt and repel the regent's retrieval force. So provide assistance he did. Having gathered an army of mercenaries, Ptolemy had headed to Syria to meet the cortège *en route* to Egypt. He portrayed this martial advance simply 'as a way of honouring Alexander', as a fitting greeting for such an extraordinary king and conqueror. In fact, Ptolemy's army had arrived for a far more practical purpose. It had arrived to defend his winnings. To hold off any enemy attempts to retrieve the cortège.[22]

Rows of soldiers positioned themselves between Arrhidaeus' funeral convoy and Attalus' force. For the latter, this posed a serious and unforeseen problem. His men had been kitted out for speed and pursuit. They had expected to face opposition from Arrhidaeus' escort alone, having enough strength to overwhelm that military force. But Ptolemy's contingent of heavily armed veteran footmen were another matter. The urgent need for speed in catching up with the carriage meant that Attalus' army lacked their own heavy infantry; they lacked a force capable of tackling Ptolemy's mercenaries head on. If they were to attempt to wrestle control of the carriage from Arrhidaeus' hands with direct military force, the chances of victory were far from certain. For Attalus and Polemon, the sons of Andromenes, it was time to recalculate. Rather than confront the reinforced carriage escort head on, they would hinder it. They would play to their light-armed contingent's strengths.

As the escort slowly made its way south Attalus and Polemon attempted to slow its progress – delaying tactics perhaps. Laomedon, the local governor, provided no support. In on the plot, he may well have aided the carriage's progress as it had passed through Damascus, providing supplies and accompanying the convoy southwest towards Egypt. Nevertheless, despite all their efforts, in the end Attalus and Polemon's mission was a failure. Commanding a force ill-suited to take on the escort, they watched on as Ptolemy, Arrhidaeus, their soldiers and other accompanying figures guided the cart closer and closer to Egypt. Resigned to defeat, the two brothers hastily headed north to report their failure to Perdiccas.[23]

Free from Polemon and Attalus' surveillance, the rest of Ptolemy's homeward march went smoothly. Through Gaza and Palestine they marched, keeping close to the sea until they reached Pelusium and the eastern most branch of the Nile Delta.[24] From there they headed inland to Memphis. Guided into the city, there Alexander's body was interred in the winter of 321/320.

At that time, a royal Egyptian sarcophagus lay empty. Nectanebo II, the last Egyptian pharaoh, had fled his kingdom to Ethiopia when the Persians had conquered Egypt for the final time in 343. He never returned, dying in exile. His royal coffin, however, lay vacant in Memphis. Not one to miss an opportunity Ptolemy may well have had Alexander's embalmed body placed within the pharaoh's empty sarcophagus, emphasising a clear link between the Egyptian kings of old and the dead conqueror. For now,

The sarcophagus of Nectanebo II, now on display at the British Museum.
(*Author photograph*)

however, the governor had greater issues at stake. The theft had succeeded; the repercussions would be enormous. Conflict with Perdiccas had been coming – this provocation merely catalysed it. Strengthening his eastern border, mercenaries and garrison troops were assigned to man the various forts that dotted Egypt's eastern approaches. Ptolemy prepared to defend his winnings with spear and shield. Invasion was coming.[25]

Ptolemy was right to predict invasion. One can only imagine Perdiccas' anger when he discovered that his rival had outfoxed his attempt to retrieve the body. His grand plan lay in ruins. If he were to march to Macedonia, having both the elaborate carriage and Alexander's body were essential. Though carefully conceived, Perdiccas had poorly executed the preparations for his grand plan. Why had a force not greeted the carriage as it reached Syria's eastern borders? Why had he taken Archon and Arrhidaeus' loyalty for granted? Hindsight truly is a wonderful thing.[26]

The council

Perdiccas now found himself in a position he had hoped to avoid at all costs. Still, the regent was a man of action. If Ptolemy wanted war, Perdiccas would give him one. He would bring the might of the royal army down upon the dissident governor, retrieve the body and resume his progress towards the imperial throne. He summoned a council of war. Almost all of Perdiccas' senior generals were present: Antigenes, Aristonous, Attalus, Eumenes, Peithon and Seleucus for instance. They listened as their leader laid bare the situation: how Ptolemy had once again defied the regime's wishes and seized the funeral cart. Their advice was unanimous. Aligning with Perdiccas' preferred course of action, they recommended immediate war. Such a provocative and outright rebellious act could not go unpunished; it demanded the strongest response.[27] With most of the royal army they resolved to march on Memphis. They would retrieve the body. They would crush Ptolemy, overwhelming his army and removing the governor from the scene for good:

> They thought it would be best to forestall the possibility of any interference from him (Ptolemy) when they went on the offensive against Macedon. – Diodorus 18.25.6

But what about the threat from the west? By the time the council convened reports had reached Perdiccas and his adjutants, bearing word of worrying developments from Europe. Antipater's abrupt halt to the Aetolian campaign and the military preparations currently underway in Macedonia was no secret.

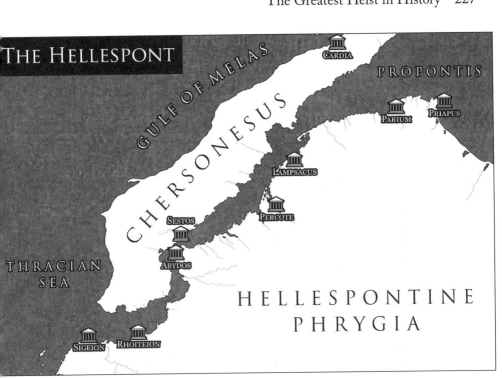

The Hellespont. It was a key crossing point for armies throughout antiquity.

It was troubling news. Though still far from certain, if Perdiccas marched on Egypt his regime faced the threat of invasion from the west: a two-front war.

So Perdiccas and his adjutants made preparations to counter any invasion from the west, as the bulk of their best army were away fighting in Egypt. A defensive strategy was drawn up: hold their European enemy at bay long enough for Perdiccas to eliminate Ptolemy and retrieve Alexander's body. Triumphant, the royal army could then return to Asia Minor and bend Antipater and Craterus to their will.

A solid plan, but if it was to succeed Perdiccas and his adjutants needed a location where numbers counted for little. A location where a smaller force had every chance of holding its own against a greater enemy host for months. Fortunately, they had such a position: the Hellespont, the gateway to Europe from Asia Minor and vice versa.

If Perdiccas' forces could control this narrow strip of water, then the chances of their enemy launching a successful amphibious invasion were slim. Maritime forces would be critical to this defence. Fortunately for the regent, he had a fleet ready and available. Not just any fleet either. Flushed with recent victories and the dominant armada in the eastern Mediterranean, it was well-suited for the task.

Strength at sea

Cleitus the White was a formidable figure. Since his string of naval successes in the Lamian War one and a half years earlier, he had returned to western Asia Minor with the greatest concentration of maritime power in the Aegean (perhaps as many as 350 ships). Cleitus had remained in western Asia Minor, cementing powerful connections within prestigious cities such as Ephesus and receiving honours in return. Yet in the early months of 320 Cleitus would return to the waters once more. At Perdiccas' council, the admiral received orders to sail a large portion of his fleet north to the Hellespont.[28]

Establishing his base at portside cities along the Asian shoreline of the Hellespont, Cleitus would guard the crossing, keeping a watchful eye out for any attempt of amphibious invasion. Ready to sail out and intercept any attack. Cleitus' past relations with Craterus must have been a cause for concern at the council – the admiral had accompanied the general to Cilicia almost four years earlier; he had co-ordinated his naval efforts with the famous commander and Antipater during the Lamian War. Nevertheless, Cleitus retained his charge; his recent shows of support for Perdiccas' regime seem to have earned the admiral the regent's trust.[29]

Who to command?

The course of action was agreed. Cleitus and his navy would sail to and guard the Hellespont. For maximum effect a land force would work in tandem with the maritime defence, designed to eradicate any remnants of Antipater's invasion force that survived the perilous water crossing.[30] This army formed the second half of Perdiccas' Hellespont strategy. But who would command it? The regent required his best adjutants – Seleucus, Aristonous, Antigenes, Peithon – for his march to Egypt. Nevertheless, Perdiccas was not lacking in capable subordinates. Three generals stood out as potential leaders for the northern defence. His younger brother Alcetas, the Molossian prince Neoptolemus and Eumenes. All carried capable military records – Neoptolemus in particular had gained great fame for his heroic actions during Alexander the Great's campaigns. Yet of the three, Perdiccas could not deny that two had reputations mired with recent failings.[31]

Alcetas' cold-blooded slaughter of Cynane was still fresh in the mind of Perdiccas and the Macedonian soldiers. If this event, so colourfully described by Antigonus, had helped sow distrust in Antipater's mind towards Perdiccas' regime, what was there to stop Antipater and Craterus weaponizing it themselves? Vivid descriptions of Cynane's murder, spread by his foe, could severely undermine Alcetas' authority among his men. He embodied everything that Antipater and Craterus had championed their invasion to be fighting against: the imperial ambitions of Perdiccas' family and the threat they posed to Alexander's relatives. Justified or no, Alcetas had taken the full brunt of the blame for the Cynane fiasco; Perdiccas could not nominate him to lead the defence of Asia Minor.[32]

Neoptolemus was the other mired with recent misfortune. In the wake of King Ariarathes' demise in Cappadocia, the Molossian's mop up operation in Armenia had seemed straightforward. It proved anything but. Following months of chaotic setbacks, in no small part due to his own lack of cavalry, the general had only started to make progress after Perdiccas had been forced to intervene. For Perdiccas, Neoptolemus' initial failings in Armenia must have also crossed his mind when deciding who was to lead the defence of the Hellespont.

That left Eumenes. The 'saviour' of Neoptolemus and his infantry in Armenia and the political opponent of Alcetas within Perdiccas' council. Yet Eumenes, unlike the other two, was boosted by his recent military achievements. Some 6,000 Cappadocian cavalry served his command, loyal to their Cardian patron above all others. For Perdiccas, having this fine force of horsemen at his disposal was invaluable. Not only was the cavalry's mobility well-suited to work in tandem with Cleitus' fleet at the Hellespont, but they had already proven their military ability aiding Neoptolemus in western Armenia. They embodied Eumenes' recent martial achievements: their rapid mobilisation, their loyalty and their expertise. Unlike Alcetas and Neoptolemus, Eumenes had proven himself an adept cavalry commander – something Perdiccas valued in the general who was to patrol and defend the Hellespont's Asian shoreline.[33]

Perdiccas made his decision. Eumenes received command of the Asia Minor defence – Perdiccas' general in the north. A plethora of experienced and able adjutants would assist him in this task. These included Gorgias, a veteran of Alexander's campaigns, and Phoenix of Tenedos, perhaps Eumenes' most trusted adjutant. But there was also Pharnabazus, a former Persian satrap (governor) turned loyal subordinate. He was also Eumenes' brother-in-law.[34]

Alongside these notable commanders, Eumenes also received 'enough men' to defend the Hellespont. Mercenaries and relatively untrained local recruits formed the mainstay of the force. Cavalry was lacking, but Perdiccas knew his Cardian commander would quickly resolve this shortage. Resolve it Eumenes did. Messengers hurried to Cappadocia, carrying orders for his renowned horsemen to mobilise and make haste for the Hellespont.[35]

But what of Alcetas and Neoptolemus? Though neither had been selected for the high command, both generals still commanded sizable contingents – thousands strong. Perdiccas knew this full well. Though he did not expect them to accompany Eumenes' lighter force to the Hellespont, these generals received orders to cooperate with the Cardian if the defence faltered.[36]

This subordinate role was no doubt difficult for Alcetas to swallow. Eumenes, his political opponent, had been chosen in his stead. Alcetas' murder of Cynane – an action his elder brother almost certainly approved – had come back to haunt him. Despite any protests he may have voiced, he could not change Perdiccas' mind. Neoptolemus, still stationed further east, was not present to voice his own opinion. Perdiccas had made his decision. The plan for countering Antipater and Craterus was approved.

The powerful Hellespont defence was intended to delay any intended invasion by Antipater and Craterus. But Perdiccas did not stop there. He sought allies to distract and hinder Antipater closer to home. And there was one power that immediately stood out.

My enemy's enemy is my friend

This was, of course, the Aetolians. In no small part thanks to Perdiccas' actions across the Aegean, these people had been saved from almost certain defeat. Its League had maintained its military strength and Antipater's public declaration to one day return and uproot the Aetolian way of life meant that these people had little desire to abide by any truce for long. Perdiccas sensed an opportunity. A Perdiccan-Aetolian alliance against Antipater had potential to greatly damage his enemy. Antipater would have to contend with hostile forces to the east and to the west, a two-front war. Orders were issued for Perdiccas' agents to open negotiations with the Aetolians. Ships laden with gold sailed west, hoping to help convince the Aetolians to agree to an alliance against Antipater. If they succeeded it could prove decisive.[37]

With that, Perdiccas and his generals finalised their strategy against Antipater and Craterus. They would stall their advance at the Hellespont – Cleitus' fleet and Eumenes' territorial army working in tandem to prevent any possibility of a successful amphibious invasion. Alcetas and Neoptolemus would provide support inland, reacting to any unforeseen problems that might arise during the defence. Meanwhile in Europe, the Aetolians would provide Antipater with a headache, forcing the elderly viceroy to fight his own two-front war. The strategy's purpose was delay. Perdiccas wanted to hold off the European threat long enough for himself to march south and crush Ptolemy once and for all.

Egyptian offensive

The generals turned their attention to the main event: the invasion of Egypt. Ptolemy's dissident actions did not make it difficult for Perdiccas and his adjutants to draw up a list of damning accusations against the governor. In front of the troops they charged Ptolemy with ambitions to seize the throne. The murder of Cleomenes, the unauthorised acquisition of opulent Cyrenaica, the recruiting of his own mercenary army, his stealing of the funeral cart, his recommendation back in Babylon to abandon the Argead monarchy altogether – all these actions must have been voiced as evidence for Ptolemy's insolence towards the regime.[38]

Perdiccas wanted Ptolemy out of the way. Once the latter was eliminated and the body of Alexander retrieved the former could march on Macedonia and put his grand scheme back on track, marrying Cleopatra upon his victorious return to western Asia Minor.

Despite all the official reasons for war, Perdiccas had two main aims. Eliminate Ptolemy. Retrieve Alexander's body. Just as with Antipater in Macedonia, the soldiers approved the planned invasion. Faced with a united command that had already agreed upon the strategy, they could do little else. Besides, the idea that they were venturing on a righteous 'crusade' to retrieve their dead king's divine body from a thief, and return it to their homeland, must have appealed.[39]

The bulk of the royal army readied themselves for this campaign. Perdiccas would command, accompanied by the royal family and his key subordinates: Seleucus, Antigenes, Peithon and Aristonous. Attalus, however, would not be joining them. At least not initially. As Perdiccas prepared to set off east his brother-in-law had headed west, to Cleitus' fleet stationed off Asia Minor's western shoreline. Attalus was to command the navy that would accompany the royal army to Egypt. He was to acquire these vessels from Cleitus' grand armada, siphoning off a significant portion of its powerful warships and sailing them around Asia Minor's southern coastline to Cilicia, where he would rendezvous with Perdiccas and the army.[40]

Once more Attalus was leaving his newlywed Atalante, his brother-in-law having issued him with another important command. Atalante, however, would remain with the army, accompanying her eldest brother to Egypt. Perhaps Perdiccas feared leaving Atalante in Pisidia? Perhaps he wanted to keep her close to strengthen Attalus' loyalty? Or perhaps the likelihood that Atalante was then several months pregnant may also have been a factor. Whatever the reasons, Atalante was to accompany her brother to Egypt – her fate tied to the fortunes of her sibling.[41]

No turning back

In February 320 the Perdiccan forces parted ways. The stage was set for a civil war that would rage all across the Eastern Mediterranean: from Thessaly to Cyprus; from the waters of the Hellespont to those of the Nile and the Euphrates. The connivance of Antigonus and the provocations of Ptolemy had caused any possibility of co-existence between Craterus, Antipater and Perdiccas to collapse. The three titans were now set on war.

And yet Perdiccas must also share the blame. His grand imperial dreams, encouraged by the likes of Alcetas and Eumenes, had ensured that confrontation always appeared a matter of when, not if.[42] Antigonus and Ptolemy had merely catalysed it.

So it was that Macedonia, her leaders split between warring factions, armed herself to stab her own vitals, turning her sword from war against a foe to shed the blood of countrymen, and ready, like the insane, to lacerate her own hands and limbs. – Justin 13.6.17

The First War of the Successors had begun.

Further Reading

Primary Sources
Arrian *Events After Alexander* 9.25 & 10A.1, R24.1.
Diodorus Siculus 18.26–18.28

Secondary Sources
Anson, E. (2015), *Eumenes of Cardia*, Leiden, 101–111.
Erskine, A. (2002), 'Life after Death: Alexandria and the Body of Alexander', *Greece and Rome* 49 (2), 163–179.
Miller, S. G. (1986), 'Alexander's Funeral Cart', *Ancient Macedonia* 4, 401–412.
Saunders, N. J. (2006), *Alexander's Tomb: The Two Thousand Year Obsession to Find the Lost Conqueror*, New York, 33–48.

Chapter 13

The Fight for Asia Minor

Perdiccas' Allies	Antipater's Allies
Eumenes	Craterus
Cleopatra	Antigonus
Menander	Lysimachus
Asander	Autodicus
Cleitus the White	Nicaea
Alcetas	Dionysius of Heraclea
Neoptolemus	
Hieronymus	

Eumenes headed north. Thousands of local and mercenary footmen followed his lead, as did a handful of skirmisher cavalry. The force was largely made up of infantry. Horsemen were lacking, but this did not remain so for long.

As Eumenes progressed through Phrygia, the Cardian's cavalry wing transformed from a near non-entity to a standout, elite contingent. Almost 5,000 Cappadocian cavalry reinforced his ranks.[1] Once again these horsemen had reacted quickly to Eumenes' summons, and hurried westward to convene with him *en route* to the Hellespont. For a proven cavalry commander like Eumenes they were a welcome addition, as were the fresh Phrygian infantry recruits that we may presume he continued to enlist on the march. As Eumenes progressed through western Anatolia, his ranks swelled sizably.[2]

The army continued to head north towards the Hellespont, but for a time Eumenes would not be accompanying them. He had urgent state business elsewhere. Somewhere on the way, perhaps around Synnada, Eumenes had changed course, diverging westward with a small bodyguard. His destination: Sardis.[3]

The princess in the city

It had been roughly eight months since Cleopatra had arrived in this prestigious Lydian city. There she had remained, having received regular reassurances from

Perdiccas that he intended to discard Nicaea and marry her in due course. The time for delay was over. Although Ptolemy's hijacking of Alexander the Great's funeral carriage had completely derailed Perdiccas' grand imperial scheme, the regent had decided that now was the time to repudiate Nicaea and push on with his pursuit of Cleopatra. Swiftly, he finally opened official marriage negotiations between himself and Cleopatra. Eumenes was instructed to secure the arrangement.[4]

With lavish gifts for the princess in hand, Eumenes and his entourage arrived at Sardis. Menander, the local Macedonian official, may well have greeted his arrival, perhaps even pledging Eumenes military assistance in the upcoming war. Nevertheless, for Eumenes this was of secondary importance. Without delay he hurried to meet Cleopatra, conveying the gifts he carried from Perdiccas and announcing the regent's wishes to open marriage negotiations. For Cleopatra this was welcome news. She accepted the gifts and agreed to remain in Sardis to await Perdiccas' glorious return from Egypt – reassured by Eumenes that the regent's victory in the war was all but guaranteed. In no uncertain terms the Macedonian princess was convinced to entwine her fortunes with Perdiccas' success.[5]

It was then, as negotiations continued, that Cleopatra received news that shattered the aura of confidence surrounding the Perdiccan defence plan in Asia Minor. An invasion!

Antigonus had returned. Ahead of Antipater and Craterus' main approach, the one-eyed veteran had been tasked with establishing a significant spearhead of friendly territory along Asia Minor's western shoreline. 3,000 mercenaries had accompanied him on this mission, escorted across the Aegean by ten Athenian warships. They were the advance force. It was Antigonus' task to secure western Asia Minor for Antipater's cause before the viceroy even left Europe.[6]

Antigonus had prepared for his return. Not only had he secured maritime aid from Athens, the city with the best naval tradition in the Aegean, but he had also ensured that his landing would receive a welcome reception. Prior to leaving Asia Minor the previous autumn, Antigonus had maintained close ties with Asander and Menander, leading authorities in Caria and Lydia respectively. Now the experienced warrior aimed to take advantage of these connections.[7]

Communications with Asander were established. Antigonus urged him to switch sides, to abandon Perdiccas. The governor required little convincing. Upon landing in Caria unopposed, Antigonus' ranks were swelled by Asander's military forces. Together they commenced their march along Asia Minor's western shoreline.[8]

Antigonus next turned his attention to Menander. Covert messages were sent to the general at Sardis, similarly encouraging him to abandon Perdiccas and support the invasion. Fortune was on Antigonus' side. Menander's relations with Perdiccas were poor. In fact, relations were more than poor: they were dismal. The official was angry with Perdiccas for his recent actions. Sometime in the past few months he had demoted Menander. Once governor of wealthy Lydia, Perdiccas had removed him from this administrative role, letting him retain authority solely over the region's military forces. For Menander, a former companion of Alexander the Great who had governed affluent Lydia for more than ten years, the demotion was humiliating. What made it more unbearable was the figure who Perdiccas selected to replace him: none other than Cleopatra. Though western Asia Minor's history provided several precedents, appointing a woman as governor was deeply unusual. Nevertheless, Cleopatra was an extraordinary figure. For years she had governed the rising kingdom of Molossia and its allied Epirote neighbours following the death of her first husband on campaign in southern Italy. No-one could deny that she had experience in statecraft. But neither could anyone, Menander especially, fail to see the evident political motives that accompanied the appointment. By naming Cleopatra governor, Perdiccas had hoped to further reassure the princess that he had every intention of marrying her: that he took her proposal seriously; that he was not delaying indefinitely. It was a powerful bribe: give Cleopatra a senior position in the empire to help convince her to remain in Asia Minor and stay on his side. Evidently, it worked.[9]

Perdiccas and Eumenes had held little regard for Menander's feelings following his demotion. For this ambitious and seasoned statesman, it was a terrible affront. Menander was angry. Despite maintaining the façade of obedient lieutenant, he held little love for either Perdiccas or his imperial desires. So when he heard word that Antigonus had returned and was seeking his assistance, Menander quickly decided to defect. With haste he left Sardis, riding south to convene with Antigonus, Asander and their advance force.[10]

Antigonus welcomed his old friend with open arms. Without delay Menander provided his new ally a fresh eyewitness report about the situation in Sardis: how Eumenes was openly conveying marriage gifts to Cleopatra. For Antigonus, Menander's report confirmed the whispers that same commander had revealed to him when he left Anatolian shores six months earlier. It confirmed the rumours that Perdiccas did indeed intend to wed Cleopatra and tie himself through blood to the royal family. It confirmed that Antigonus had been right to report these credible rumours to Antipater and Craterus in Aetolia. The report was welcome, but of more immediate importance to Antigonus was the other information Menander provided. Eumenes was in

Sardis. Antigonus sensed an opportunity. If he could capture Perdiccas' leading general in Asia Minor without a fight right there and then, not only would it greatly aid Antipater's invasion but it would be a huge coup for Antigonus' personal reputation. He would be the warlord who captured their enemy's supreme commander. Without delay he made plans to seize Eumenes before the latter could escape Sardis. Speed was of the essence.[11]

The trap

The province of Caria in southwest Asia Minor.

Without delay, Antigonus put his proposed ambush into motion. He sent 2,000 infantry and a small contingent of cavalry northeast, under the command of Menander. Their destination was the road directly east of Sardis, the highway which linked that city with Greater Phrygia. Reaching this road relatively quickly and as covertly as possible, there these soldiers took up positions and awaited an unsuspecting Eumenes to fall into their trap. The ambush was set.[12]

At the same time, to give the illusion that he and his army were actually marching up the coast further west, Antigonus led the rest of his army north into Ionia. Ephesus and the surrounding cities swiftly switched to Antigonus' side, welcoming the veteran statesman back to Asia Minor. With the Ionian coastline secured, Antigonus next readied his men to march northeast, inland towards Sardis itself, hoping to drive Eumenes out of the city and into his ambush.[13]

With Antigonus to the west and the ambush to the east, hostile forces opposed Eumenes and his companions on two fronts. Fortunately for Eumenes however, Antigonus' plan had lacked the necessary secrecy. Embracing the far-reaching contacts, spies and informants she had at her disposal across Lydia now that she was the region's governor, Cleopatra uncovered Antigonus' plan. She discovered that Menander's detachment was waiting in ambush due east of Sardis. Throwing her lot in with Eumenes and Perdiccas, Cleopatra relayed this information to Eumenes, who wasted little time. Hieronymus, a member of the entourage that had accompanied Eumenes to Sardis, recalled what happened next.[14]

That afternoon, Eumenes gathered Hieronymus and the rest of his men, ordering them to make ready to leave as soon as possible. Preparations were kept discreet:

> ...summoning them (the troops) with neither trumpets nor any of the standard signals troops waited for, as they were fully prepared to march quickly. – Arrian Events After Alexander R25.6

As soon as all was ready, Eumenes and his men left the city. Their expected route was east, following the road towards Phrygia before turning north and reuniting with the main army en route to the Hellespont. Determined to avoid Antigonus' ambush, however, Eumenes did the unexpected. Marching light, he and his men headed west. For roughly twenty miles they headed along the road towards Magnesia, before turning right and hurrying along a different route inland. The road where Antigonus' forces lay in ambush was given a wide berth. Eumenes had circumnavigated the trap.[15]

Reaching relative safety Eumenes, Hieronymus and the rest of the entourage continued north to reconvene with the main army. They had escaped. Although Antigonus' unexpected advance had caused chaos, Eumenes saw the bigger picture. Antipater and Craterus' impending invasion still posed the greatest threat. He had to be ready for it.

Once again Cleopatra was alone at Sardis. The former governor, she was now little more than a prisoner – under watch from forces loyal to Antigonus and Menander's cause. For her, much depended on Eumenes and Perdiccas reversing this predicament. She hoped to await news of their success.

The ambush had failed, but the road to Sardis was now open to Antigonus. That night he marched his men inland from Ephesus, crossing over the River Cayster west of Mount Tmolus. He reached Sardis, and Cleopatra, not long after – Eumenes having evaded his grasp.[16]

If Antigonus stopped to meet Cleopatra in Sardis, he did not linger there for long. Quickly he and his soldiers returned to the main bulk of his force nearer the coast and proceeded to win the allegiance of several notable city-states. Very soon much of Asia Minor's Ionian and Carian coastline triumphed the cause of Antipater and Craterus.

A successful Antigonus sailed north to the Hellespont. He had paved the way for Antipater and Craterus as best he could. He had encouraged defections and weakened Eumenes' defence. Any hope of continued success depended upon the main invasion force. Even with the defections of Asander, Menander and the city-states, Antigonus still lacked the forces to contest Eumenes in open battle. Inland too the sizable host of Alcetas was also lurking – more than a match for Antigonus' mercenary army. If the campaign was to progress beyond a beachhead, much depended on Antipater and Craterus crossing the Hellespont and joining forces.[17]

That was easier said than done.

March to the Hellespont

Perdiccas' Allies	Antipater's Allies
Eumenes	Craterus
Cleopatra	Antigonus
Cleitus the White	Lysimachus
Alcetas	Autodicus
Neoptolemus	Nicaea
Hieronymus	Menander
	Asander
	Dionysius of Heraclea

It was the start of spring by the time Eumenes and his army established themselves along the Hellespont's Asian shoreline. Antigonus' intervention in the west had proven a nuisance, but Eumenes likewise realised that his foe's irritant actions would count for little if Antipater and Craterus could not join him in Asia. Eumenes still held the cards. Cleitus and his fleet of powerful warships awaited Eumenes and his army's arrival at the Hellespont – no doubt a welcome sight. With the navy patrolling this vital strait the chances of Antipater mounting a successful amphibious invasion looked nigh impossible. Cleitus ruled the waves. Eumenes and the admiral divided their forces among the shoreline settlements, awaiting an attack.[18]

Antipater and Craterus' preparations in Macedonia had taken time, Antipater perhaps clinging to the possibility that Perdiccas would sue for peace when he heard that his grand scheme had been discovered. If so, he soon received news that confirmed the opposite. Reports from Antigonus about his successes since landing in Asia came streaming into Antipater's headquarters. The defections of Asander, Menander and the Ionian Greek city-states were all relayed to emphasise the vanguard's glorious success in disrupting Eumenes' defence. As too was a report detailing how Eumenes had narrowly escaped Antigonus' grasp at Sardis. But it was the purpose of Eumenes' visit to Sardis that affected Antipater the most. Eumenes' public dealings with Cleopatra confirmed the rumours Antigonus had relayed to him back in Aetolia. It confirmed Perdiccas' overwhelming ambition. His public courting of Cleopatra was concrete evidence that the regent was pursuing the Macedonian kingship. It confirmed that Perdiccas had no intention to avert war, but rather to emerge the victor of it.[19]

For Antipater this was the final straw. If his desire to march to war had at all wavered over the winter, Antigonus' report stiffened his resolve. Now more than ever, Antipater was determined to oversee the campaign and remove Perdiccas from power by all means necessary. With Craterus and some 30,000 soldiers in tow, he hastened forth for the Hellespont.[20]

The journey was uneventful. Antipater had ensured logistical support by securing aid from a useful ally: Lysimachus.

Since his entente with Seuthes, the fearless Lysimachus had turned to consolidating his control over much of the region. Yet at the same time he had maintained a close relationship with Antipater, his neighbour.[21] No doubt Alexander's former bodyguard was aware of the large military preparations that had occurred across his western border over the previous winter; no doubt he had kept regular tabs on its progress and its intended purpose. Maintaining friendship with his neighbours, Lysimachus threw his lot in with Antipater and Craterus' cause. His aid was limited, albeit vital. Though he had little interest in accompanying them to Asian shores, we can presume Lysimachus offered Antipater and his army welcome support as they progressed through the southern reaches of Thrace *en route* to the Hellespont: access to provisions and expert local guidance through his lands seem likely.[22]

Thanks in no small part to Lysimachus' logistical aid, Antipater's journey to the Hellespont went smoothly. But providing military assistance proved a different matter. Still reeling from his Pyrrhic conflicts with Seuthes, Lysimachus could ill afford to provide Antipater and Craterus additional manpower for the campaign ahead. Nevertheless at least one representative did decide to join Antipater's ranks. His name was Autodicus, the youngest brother of Lysimachus and at that time in his early 20s. Perhaps as an act of good faith between Lysimachus and Antipater, combined with Autodicus' ambition to make a name for himself that could rival his older brother and live up to the distinguished reputation of his family, the young man assumed a prominent position at the heart of Antipater's army. Next stop: the Hellespont.[23]

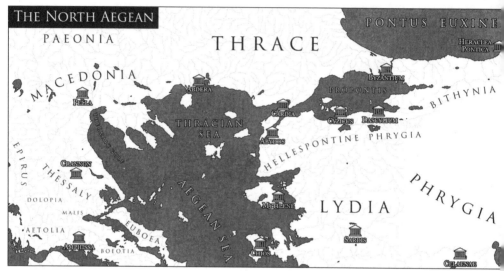

The North Aegean. Antipater and Craterus headed from Macedonia, through southern Thrace, to the western shoreline of the Hellespont (opposite Abydos).

Betrayal

By the height of spring (roughly mid to late April 320) Antipater, Craterus, Autodicus and their army had traversed southern Thrace and reached the Hellespont's western shoreline. But how would they cross? Perdiccas and Eumenes had good reason to believe that their defence would hold. Cleitus and his fleet controlled the straits. So long as this threat remained alive, Antipater was all too aware that any attempt to cross would meet with disaster. But Antipater was determined; he was shrewd. Antigonus' successes in western Asia Minor had already proven that the loyalty of many of Perdiccas' adjutants was fragile. Antipater knew that the offer of a lavish prize could bribe many ambitious figures over to their cause during this tumultuous time. Those senior figures who had outlived Alexander the Great expected rich rewards for their invaluable service – in exchange for loyalty they expected gifts, high positions and, most importantly, steady military successes. Cleitus was no exception. He had received supreme command over the royal fleet from Perdiccas. How could Antipater counter that?[24]

Without delay, Antipater dispatched envoys to Cleitus' camp across the Hellespont. Eumenes and his army, encamped elsewhere, were unaware. Cleitus listened to Antipater's overtures – voiced through his messenger. The fate of the defence depended upon Cleitus' response.

Cleitus' answer soon became apparent. Eumenes' heart must have dropped when he saw more than 100 ships sail out of port and head over to the strait's western shoreline to link up with Antipater's forces. Cleitus had decided to defect; Antipater's overtures had succeeded.[25]

But how?

Why did Cleitus decide to abandon the Perdiccans when he had known that his loyalty, his navy, was the keystone of their well-planned defence strategy? Why did he desert Eumenes when his navy could have easily halted Antipater's invasion in its tracks indefinitely? Why had he decided to throw away one of the most senior maritime positions in the empire to join his enemies? The man's past friendship with Craterus was well-known; the admiral and the general's joint efforts during the Lamian War had contributed significantly to the Macedonian victory. But nevertheless, Cleitus had surely not defected solely on the basis of past friendship with Craterus. Perdiccas, Eumenes and their adjutants – all clever commanders – had been convinced that the admiral was loyal and would fight for them. Other reasons must have contributed.[26]

Certainly news of Antigonus' success in western Asia Minor and the defections of Menander, Asander and the Ionian city-states may well have weakened Cleitus' resolve to oppose Antipater's forces. Everyone loves a winner. But Eumenes' defence plan was still strong and looked odds-on to succeed.

These factors, combined with Cleitus' stellar reputation at sea, meant that Antipater had needed something to further sweeten the deal if he were to convince this arrogant admiral to defect to their cause.[27] His envoys had therefore offered Cleitus a lavish bribe: a prime posting within the new order once Antipater and Craterus emerged victorious in the war. The man's past connections with western Asia Minor were well-known. So Antipater offered the admiral governorship over Lydia. By offering Cleitus such a wealth-laden, manpower rich region as reward for his new loyalty, Antipater was making the admiral an extraordinary offer. But the viceroy knew how vital securing Cleitus' support was for the success of his venture. It worked. Swayed by Antipater's promises, Cleitus abandoned Perdiccas' cause, placing his ships at Antipater's service and offering to transport their invasion force across the Hellespont without delay. For Antipater, the successful diplomacy was a decisive victory; for Eumenes, it was a catastrophic defeat.[28]

In one move, Cleitus' defection had violently tugged the linchpin out from Perdiccas' steady, carefully considered defence plan in the west. Without naval superiority, nothing prevented Antipater's army crossing uncontested onto Asian soil. Eumenes was helpless to stop it. So far Eumenes' situation in Asia Minor had encountered setbacks at almost every turn. The defections of Menander and Asander to his enemy's cause were irritating, but Cleitus' defection was a whole new level. It was devastating. All around Eumenes, the defence was collapsing like a pack of playing cards. The situation looked dire. And worse was to follow.[29]

Dissident subordinates

In either late April (or early May) 320 Cleitus' fleet sailed across the Hellespont once more, this time in the service of the enemy, transporting Antipater's army across the strait with impunity. Soon Antipater had established his full force on Asian soil, where further good news reached him. Neighbouring coastal cities had defected to the invaders – unable to contest the military strength Antipater, Craterus and Cleitus possessed on land and at sea. What was more, Antigonus reconvened with the army around this time, bearing further good news of more defections to Antipater's cause as he had progressed north along the coastline. As city-states flocked to Antipater's side, soon much of coastal Hellespontine Phrygia was in their hands. Among these new allies was Dionysius, the tyrant of Heraclea. Newly married to Craterus' former wife Amastris, Dionysius had emphatically pinned his colours to Antipater's mast, bringing a flotilla of ships to further bolster Cleitus' ranks.[30]

Eumenes looked on. He could do little else; Eumenes was powerless to prevent Antipater growing stronger with every passing day. Though suitable for guarding the Hellespont in tandem with Cleitus' fleet, his army was no match for Antipater's larger, more professional force on the open field. His own infantry, especially, stood little chance against the thousands upon thousands of Macedonian pikemen that had accompanied Antipater and Craterus to Asia Minor. With little choice Eumenes retreated from the Hellespont region, sending word to Perdiccas about this cruel reversal of fortune.[31]

Eumenes knew he had to adapt. Retreating from the Hellespont, he spread his forces to quarters across Phrygia, perhaps to better sustain his army or perhaps in preparation for guerrilla warfare. Whatever the reason, for the time being Eumenes kept only a portion of his army with him – a few thousand men at maximum.[32]

At the same time as he was dividing his forces, Eumenes sent messengers out to his leading adjutants in Asia Minor: to the Molossian Neoptolemus further east and to Alcetas in Pisidia. Both generals commanded thousands of soldiers that Eumenes recognised as being potentially invaluable in any upcoming, co-ordinated attempt to hinder Antipater's progress through Asia Minor.[33]

Eumenes requested that Alcetas and Neoptolemus hurry to his aid. He hoped that he would at least be able to depend upon the loyalty of the former – Alcetas was Perdiccas' brother after all. He was to be disappointed. It was not long before messengers returned from Alcetas bearing frustrating news:

> *Alcetas flatly refused to serve, because his Macedonians, he said, were ashamed to fight against Antipater, and loved Craterus so well, they were ready to receive him for their commander.* – Plutarch *Life of Eumenes* 5.2

Despite realising the severity of the situation, Alcetas had refused Eumenes' request for aid. His official excuse was that he doubted the loyalty of his Macedonians to oppose the beloved Craterus – a fear perhaps justified given the past disobedience the veterans had shown after Alcetas' murder of Cynane the previous summer. But problems still abound with the explanation. Although the recent insubordination of his soldiers during the Cynane fiasco almost certainly influenced Alcetas' response, Perdiccas' younger brother had an ulterior motive. For him it was a convenient excuse, designed so that he had a legitimate reason for not joining forces and submitting to Eumenes' authority. Alcetas resented Eumenes; he was envious at his supreme command. Rightly or wrongly, he feared that Eumenes' influence over Perdiccas was growing at the expense of his own. One can imagine his anger – he, a noble Macedonian aristocrat, being outranked by a former exile who he considered below him in social status. Outrage at the reproach he had received for his hard handling of the Cynane affair may also have influenced his judgement. Although his past dealing with Cynane gave Alcetas a plausible precedent to doubt the steadfast loyalty of his veterans, when confronted by not one but two famous Macedonian figures, he exploited this concern. He transformed it into an excuse that ensured he would not have to serve under his personal and political rival Eumenes.[34]

The man was too proud. Despite the severity of the situation, Perdiccas' brother was determined not to serve under Eumenes in any way, shape or form. Nevertheless, Alcetas did remain loyal to Perdiccas. He planned to oppose the invaders, but independently of Eumenes' authority.[35]

Disappointment must have gripped Eumenes as the messenger relayed Alcetas' flat refusal to reinforce the main defence. But there was some good news for Eumenes. Neoptolemus the Molossian, commanding a few thousand Macedonian veterans, had abided by Eumenes' order.[36] Inland from the Hellespont he had arrayed his forces close to those of Eumenes. For the moment their army camps remained separate and at a convenient distance, but for Eumenes the arrival of Neoptolemus with desperately needed high quality heavy infantry was welcome. Things, however, were not as cordial as Eumenes may have hoped. Neoptolemus held little love for Eumenes. He was aggrieved by the latter's success in Armenia at his own expense. Like Alcetas, he resented how he – once honoured as one of the bravest soldiers in Alexander the Great's all-conquering army – was now reduced to taking orders from the conqueror's former personal secretary. For the 'vainglorious' Neoptolemus, accepting commands from Eumenes must have been especially galling. Nevertheless, unlike Alcetas, Neoptolemus had swallowed his pride and marched to his superior's aid.[37]

Or so it seemed.

In fact, Neoptolemus had not swallowed his pride; he had not marched west to rescue Eumenes from this plight. A very different reason had influenced his decision to encamp a suitable distance away from Eumenes' headquarters. He planned to defect. For Eumenes the situation looked dire. Almost all of western Asia Minor was now in enemy hands; the royal fleet had abandoned the Perdiccan cause; Antipater, Craterus and at least 30,000 soldiers had landed in Asia. And now, with Eumenes still unaware, Neoptolemus aimed to hurl further misery upon him. He sought to follow in Menander, Asander and Cleitus' footsteps, switching his allegiance to the invaders. Unfair or no, Eumenes' non-Macedonian, secretarial background had sparked resentment among his subordinates. Both Alcetas and Neoptolemus were envious of Eumenes and his more senior position; neither were willing to serve under him. One had refused to serve outright behind the façade of a suitable excuse, the other plotted a great betrayal behind a façade of loyalty. Things were about to reach a head.[38]

Diplomacy

Messengers arrived at the camps of Eumenes and Neoptolemus. They came from Antipater, seeking further diplomatic successes. Just as he had done with Cleitus at the Hellespont, Antipater aimed to win over his opponents with lavish bribes and achieve another bloodless victory. Craterus was also involved in this diplomacy, his voice and position most evident in the message the envoy relayed to Eumenes.[39] Craterus had been a close companion of Eumenes during Alexander the Great's conquests. But the same could not be said of Antipater. Animosity reigned supreme between Eumenes and Antipater because of the latter's relationship with the former's nemesis: Hecataeus, the tyrant of Cardia. It was Hecataeus who had overseen Eumenes' exile all those years before; he was chiefly responsible for bringing down ruin upon Eumenes' family. But most important of all, Hecataeus was a loyal underling of Antipater – something Eumenes was loath to forget. If overtures to Eumenes were to succeed, Antipater knew he had to offer attractive terms through the voice of Craterus.[40]

Antipater used Craterus' mediation. If Eumenes abandoned Perdiccas and joined their ranks, the envoy announced that Craterus would help reconcile Eumenes with Antipater. What was more, if he defected, they would offer Eumenes similar power to that which Perdiccas had bestowed upon him months earlier. Switch sides and he would retain supreme command over almost all of Asia Minor, his position supported by a sizable army. It was a tempting offer. Once more Antipater and Craterus were willing to offer a foe lavish rewards to entice them over to their cause. This time, however, they were to be disappointed.

The envoy returned bearing Eumenes' refusal:

> *He could not so suddenly be reconciled to his old enemy Antipater, especially at a time when he saw him use his friends like enemies, but was ready to reconcile Craterus to Perdiccas, upon any just and equitable terms; but in case of any aggression, he would resist the injustice to his last breath, and would rather lose his life than betray his word.* – Plutarch *Life of Eumenes* 5.5

Despite his friendship with Craterus, Eumenes did not trust Antipater. He could not simply forgive the years of hostility that had existed between them, even if that meant coming to blows with Craterus. Defying the trend, Eumenes decided not to desert Perdiccas.

Neoptolemus proved less stubborn. This was the moment he had been waiting for. Resenting Eumenes' authority and no doubt aware that the situation looked bleak for Perdiccas' allies in Asia Minor, he was quick to accept Antipater's overtures to him. What these overtures were, we do not know. Perhaps the offer to join the winning side was enough. Whatever the offer, Neoptolemus hastily accepted, though he kept up the pretence of loyalty to Eumenes. Secret communications between the Molossian and Antipater ensued, centred around what they should do with the stubborn Eumenes. Still undesirous to fight a pitched battle and still harbouring hatred towards Eumenes, Antipater decided upon an infamous solution: murder. Neoptolemus was the perfect accomplice. Still hiding his planned treachery, he had direct access to Eumenes. He could see through the assassination. Neoptolemus needed little convincing to do the terrible deed, acting as Antipater's inside man when he next visited Eumenes' camp. The plan was agreed: Neoptolemus would find a way to kill Eumenes before deserting to the enemy.[41]

The plot, however, lacked the necessary secrecy. Eumenes' intelligence network soon uncovered the covert communications between Neoptolemus and Antipater's envoys. Eumenes discovered the treachery his supposed adjutant was secretly designing against him. Neoptolemus had proven even less dependable than Alcetas. Eumenes could not let this stand. He devised a plan to see that Neoptolemus paid the ultimate price for his intended treason.[42]

In roughly the middle of May messengers hurried across the plain, to Neoptolemus' base. Relaying Eumenes' orders, they summoned Neoptolemus to respond to rumours of his intended treason. The request provoked the intended response. Neoptolemus, rightly assuming that Eumenes had heard word of his secret dealings with Antipater, refused to obey. He rallied his men, drawing his soldiers up for battle on the plain opposite Eumenes' force and assuming a defensive position. Overall, the two armies were roughly equal in number. Neoptolemus' cavalry wing was lacking but it was his veteran infantrymen that he believed would be his key to victory. These Macedonians assumed their battlefield formations against Eumenes' Asian army. Their message was clear: if their foe wanted Neoptolemus, they would have to fight.[43]

Eumenes versus Neoptolemus

Eumenes responded to Neoptolemus' defensive preparations, drawing up his own army for battle. Mercenaries and Asian contingents filled its ranks, loyal to their leader. His infantry body matched Neoptolemus' in quantity, but quality was a different matter. Eumenes knew that their numbers could not outweigh their relative inexperience and the nigh impossible task they faced if they opposed Neoptolemus' grizzled veterans head on. What Eumenes did have, however, was a sizable advantage in cavalry. Many of his battle-proven Cappadocians remained with him and Eumenes aimed to take full advantage.[44]

Battle commenced. In the centre of the plain the infantry ranks collided, roughly equal in number but disparate in skill. It was not long before the tide of battle began to swing in favour of Neoptolemus' Macedonians, their wall of *sarissae* pikes carving through their enemy and forcing them back. Eumenes' footmen stood little chance, lacking the numbers and quality to efficiently challenge these masters of phalanx warfare. Soon they buckled, put to flight in the face of the enemy's unstoppable advance. Seeing their foe reduced to an undisciplined mess of fleeing soldiers, the veterans tasted victory. They laid down their *sarissae*, took out their swords and hurried to cut down the fleeing enemy and seize the spoils of war. Within no time at all the infantry fight had all but ended. But Eumenes had prepared for this. Having only a portion of his full army with him, a force that had not been designed with pitched battle in mind, Eumenes had known that his footmen stood little chance against the might of Neoptolemus' Macedonians. Nevertheless, they had played their part well in Eumenes' grand strategy. For Neoptolemus' veterans, carried away in pursuit of a routed enemy, victory appeared all but achieved. Eumenes would prove otherwise.[45]

Hundreds of Cappadocian cavalrymen descended on the disorganised Macedonian infantrymen, until then oblivious of this danger behind them. As the infantry fight had progressed, elsewhere on the field Eumenes had used his horsemen to devastating effect. With his Cappadocians he had charged Neoptolemus and his small contingent of horsemen. Undeterred by the size of Eumenes' cavalry wing, Neoptolemus had met the attack head on with his own horsemen. As the cavalry battle raged, the Molossian prince proved to those around him why he had gained such a stellar reputation for his bravery, fighting amid his men at the heart of the action against the Cappadocians. But even he could not prevent control of the engagement slipping away from his companions. Left and right the Cappadocians carved through Neoptolemus' retinue – the Molossian almost losing his life in the process. And then, disaster. Believing all was lost, Neoptolemus and what remained of his horsemen broke off from the clash. They fled to a safe distance and watched as Eumenes called off the pursuit.[46]

Eumenes had won the cavalry clash. Now he turned to ensure this victory proved decisive in determining the wider battle. As Neoptolemus peeled away in flight, Eumenes and his Cappadocians stormed the Molossian's unguarded baggage train with impunity. The possessions and families of Neoptolemus' soldiers were now at Eumenes' mercy – a useful bargaining chip. Eumenes, however, realised that the battle was not yet over. Far ahead Neoptolemus' veteran infantrymen, oblivious to their commander's defeat and the grave situation behind them, were still pursuing their routed enemy. Gathering all his cavalry Eumenes turned on the infantry.[47]

The Macedonian footmen had been in a euphoric mood. The enemy had broken; victory was theirs. But their euphoria was soon replaced by dread as the disorganised, pursuing veterans turned to see thousands of screaming cavalrymen bearing down upon them. In an instant the pursuant became the pursued: broken, disorganised and extremely vulnerable to a full-blooded cavalry charge on the open plain. Orders bellowed out towards them from among Eumenes' warriors, demanding they lay down their arms and take a sacred oath to serve under the Cardian from that moment on. It was a significant demand. Eumenes, however, possessed strong incentives to encourage their defection. He relayed news to the footmen that their baggage – families, possessions, everything they had acquired during their decade-long service in Asia – was now in his hands. That wasn't all. As Eumenes' demand filtered through the infantry ranks, so too did the gut-wrenching news that Neoptolemus, the leader they had placed great faith in, had deserted the field. He had abandoned his men to their fate, simply to save his own skin. In an instant, the Molossian noble's reputation transformed from one of courage to cowardice, at least in the eyes of the abandoned soldiers. It worked to Eumenes' benefit. Until recently these veterans had been happy to fight Eumenes and his Asian soldiers. But Eumenes' masterful strategy, combined with their own commander's flight, altered their perspective. They accepted Eumenes' call to surrender, pledging their services to the man of the hour for the wars to come.[48]

Eumenes had gained a remarkable victory. From the very start with his uncovering of Neoptolemus' planned betrayal to successfully winning over the enemy's infantry in the final stages, he had conducted the whole fight with great effect. Through a clever cavalry strategy, he had negated the infantry's superiority and decided the battle with his horsemen. It was also decisive. Having rallied as many cavalrymen as he could, Neoptolemus had fled the field. The rest of his army had either perished on the field or joined Eumenes' ranks. The Macedonian veterans, who until recently had been willing to oppose him with spear and shield, now served Eumenes' command – his victory had impressed them. Compared to the 'cowardly' Neoptolemus, Eumenes was a man these men, accustomed to military victories, were happy to follow. At least for now.[49]

Enjoying the fruits of his success, Eumenes sent word to Perdiccas about his victory – some good news amidst the dearth of setbacks and betrayals that had struck right at the heart of Perdiccan strategy. But this would by no means mark an end to the fighting. Further conflict loomed. Antipater and Craterus' army still remained untouched; Neoptolemus had escaped and Eumenes could count on retaliation. His victory over Neoptolemus was merely the beginning. Still, it was a good start.[50]

The council

Meanwhile Antipater and Craterus had started their march inland. Neoptolemus' imminent defection with his thousand strong force was anticipated. So when they saw this Molossian prince hurrying to their camp with a mere 300 horsemen, the sight was unexpected to say the least. His army all but lost, Neoptolemus had wasted little time riding across to unite with the invaders. But not before he had discovered the fate of his defeated army. Either with his own eye or from reports, he learned that his cherished infantrymen – the soldiers who had served under him for over a year – had joined Eumenes' ranks. For Neoptolemus this was difficult to bear, adding insult to injury on top of his recent defeat. But this despair soon transformed into a desperate determination. Neoptolemus was determined to reverse his current misfortune; determined to orchestrate a second clash with Eumenes and determined to crush his hated foe and reacquire the faith of his former footmen. As he hurried towards Antipater and Craterus' camp this deep-felt desire to overturn his disastrous defeat had become ingrained in Neoptolemus' mind. If he were to turn this aspiration into reality however, he needed help. He needed martial aid. He needed to convince Antipater and Craterus to march out and force a decisive battle.[51]

Antipater summoned a council of his most senior generals to discuss the new state of affairs. Himself, Craterus, Antigonus and Neoptolemus were all present, as was Dionysius, the tyrant of Heraclea who had recently arrived with maritime reinforcements.[52] Neoptolemus' recent reversal of fortune was relayed to those present: the stubborn Eumenes remained at large and had proven more of a challenge than expected. Neoptolemus did not dwell on his own failings however. Instead, he turned the council's attention to Eumenes. He derided the Cardian's ability; he derided the extent of Eumenes' control over his turncoat infantrymen. In complete contrast, Neoptolemus then turned to Craterus, lauding the latter's stellar military record. He exclaimed with confidence the undying love his former footmen had for Craterus – the man who they believed had always represented their concerns during the campaigns of Alexander the Great.

> ...for the Macedonians loved him so excessively, that if they saw but his hat, or heard his voice, they would all pass over in a body with their arms. – Plutarch Life of Eumenes 6.1

Neoptolemus proceeded to urge both Antipater and Craterus to come to his aid with the entire army and crush Eumenes. Failing that he asked that they at least send Craterus with a portion of the force. Whichever option they chose Neoptolemus reassured them a swift, easy victory would follow – Eumenes' men would desert in droves as soon as word spread that the legendary Craterus was coming against them. With that, Neoptolemus ended his address. Eulogising the proud Craterus was a clever tactic in the Molossian's desperate desire to orchestrate a second meeting between Eumenes and himself. The chances of Antipater sending the whole army were low – the viceroy's primary aim remained to reach Perdiccas and the royal army in Egypt as quickly as possible. Still Neoptolemus hoped that his arguments had proven enough to convince his allies to abandon all thoughts of negotiation with Eumenes, carried away by the promise of an easy victory.[53]

He was proved right. Convinced by Neoptolemus' persuasive speech Antipater agreed to his suggestion. The army would divide: Craterus would take a large portion and head off to surprise Eumenes' revelling force. Neoptolemus would accompany them – the general no doubt insisting that he be there when Eumenes met his untimely end. Antipater and the rest of the army would continue on their set course, traversing Asia Minor and laying the groundwork for the march's final leg towards Egypt. In Cilicia the forces would reconvene:

That way, they thought, once they had reunited the army, and once Ptolemy had been added to the alliance, they would be able to get the better of the Royal Army. – Diodorus 18.29.7

Meanwhile Cleitus would command the navy, leading it around the Asia Minor coastline bearing supplies and reuniting with the land force in Cilicia.[54]

The council's business did not end there. As these events were taking place Antipater and Craterus heard word that warfare had erupted in another theatre of the Eastern Mediterranean: on the island of Cyprus. Forces loyal to Ptolemy and Perdiccas were battling it out for control over this strategic island. Whoever controlled Cyprus could dictate naval operations in the east; whoever controlled the island could either sanction or strangle communication links between Anatolia and Egypt, the two geographic focal points of the war. Antigonus, who had likely received news of Cypriot conflict while campaigning in western Asia Minor, was selected to secure this strategic island for Antipater's cause. With a portion of the royal fleet and his 3,000 soldiers, he would head to the island and provide aid to Ptolemy's allied forces. Dionysius' Heracliote ships would aid Antigonus' cause, as would the ten Athenian vessels that had accompanied him throughout the war so far. Admiral Cleitus too may have been instructed to provide some of his ships to aid Antigonus' efforts, though Antipater would have needed a healthy supply of vessels to remain near him in Cilicia.[55]

By the time the council ended, Antipater and his subordinates had mapped out an adapted, concerted plan for the campaign. Cleitus, Antigonus and Dionysius gathered their ships and started sailing down to the Eastern Mediterranean at the head of their powerful armada. The land army divided in two. 22,000 men – over half of the invasion force – followed Craterus and Neoptolemus' lead out of the camp and commenced their hunt for Eumenes amid the Phrygian landscape.[56] Hardened Macedonian infantrymen formed the mainstay of this force.

(They were) famed for their prowess, on who he (Craterus) was chiefly relying for victory. – Diodorus 18.30.4

At its nucleus were Craterus' veterans, the soldiers who had accompanied both him and Alexander the Great throughout Asia during their long military careers. Complementing these veterans were the next generation of feared Macedonian phalangites – stalwarts to Antipater's cause and renowned in their own right. Mercenaries and allied light infantry complemented these renowned warriors.

2,000 cavalrymen would protect the flanks of Craterus' keystone infantry. Among them were the famed Macedonian heavy, shock Companion Cavalry, wielding their sturdy cornel wood *xyston* lances. The same type that Alexander the Great's troopers had used so effectively to overcome every Persian army that had opposed them. But Craterus also had another sizable, elite cavalry unit. Hundreds of renowned skirmisher cavalrymen also accompanied his army, equipped with javelins. Masters of the missile, these mercenaries were experts in the art of speedy, harassing cavalry tactics. These were the 'Tarentine' horsemen, designed to offer Craterus flexibility with a skilled light cavalry wing.[57]

Craterus' army was sizable and boasted some of the best units in the invasion army's ranks – more than enough to take on Eumenes' polyglot, largely-inexperienced enemy force. One can imagine the delight Neoptolemus expressed as he saw Craterus leading out this powerful outfit to oppose his hated rival. His plan to convince his allies to march to his aid had succeeded; now it was a matter of seeing this through and getting his revenge.

As for Antipater, the old viceroy pressed on toward Cilicia with the rest of the army. There he would await Craterus and Neoptolemus' victorious return, alongside the arrival of the fleet, and together they would march on Egypt.

At least, that was the plan.

Chasing Eumenes

Eumenes' Allies	Craterus' Allies
Phoenix	Neoptolemus
Pharnabazus	Pigres
Gorgias	Antipater
Alcetas	Antigonus
Cleopatra	Lysimachus
Hieronymus	Autodicus
Perdiccas	Menander
Xennias	Asander
	Dionysius of Heraclea
	Cleitus the White

The two armies parted ways. Craterus set off in pursuit of Eumenes – Neoptolemus and their men in tow. Neoptolemus had provided Craterus vital information that Eumenes' host was currently divided. Craterus hoped to exploit this. He aimed to catch Eumenes off-guard, springing a surprise on a weakened enemy still celebrating their recent success. He was to be disappointed.[58]

Eumenes had not lowered his guard. An effective intelligence network ensured he was quick to discover this new threat marching against his men. He acted decisively: a change in strategy. Any thoughts of fighting a guerrilla war were abandoned. Rather than refuse the pitched battle Craterus so desired, Eumenes would fight his mighty enemy on the open field. But if so, Eumenes was determined that the clash be on terms that best suited him and his army. It was his aim now to lure the world's most famous general to a battle of his choosing. This would be easier said than done.[59]

Without delay Eumenes carefully started to plan his strategy. Several issues had to be resolved before he could consider taking the field against Craterus. The first was his army itself. Large contingents of it were still scattered across the region – perhaps in anticipation of a pre-agreed harassment strategy. Eumenes addressed this quickly. From all quarters he gathered his men, reuniting them in one great force and organising an army that looked, on paper at least, a match for the enemy host marching against them. By the time Eumenes had finished assembling his soldiers, 28,000 men followed his command. Of these, Eumenes placed particular importance on his cavalry. Just as Craterus hoped that the key to victory would be his indomitable Macedonian heavy infantrymen, Eumenes intended his troopers to help him overcome the odds. 5,000 Asian horsemen served Eumenes' command, many battle-hardened with proven martial ability and fresh from their recent victory against Neoptolemus. They were Eumenes' elite soldiers and he planned to use them as best he could.[60]

23,000 infantrymen accompanied the cavalry – a mix of mercenaries and levies hailing from across Asia Minor and perhaps beyond. Their size was significant, outnumbering the footmen Craterus had at his disposal by some 3,000 soldiers. But this belied the skill their counterparts possessed. Though exceeding the opposition in quantity, in quality Eumenes' infantry were once again dwarfed by the ability of the thousands upon thousands of fresh, loyal Macedonian phalangites marching against them. Disciplined. Well-trained. Fuelled with belief that they were sons of the greatest fighting nation on earth. On paper, the infantry's similar numbers suggested a close-fought fight in the upcoming contest. In reality, the odds were stacked in favour of a complete mismatch.[61]

Eumenes predicted that his footmen would stand little chance in a prolonged engagement – their rout against Neoptolemus' veterans was proven testament to that. All the more reason, therefore, why Eumenes knew that the key to any chance of success depended upon his more capable cavalry squadrons, in which he outnumbered the enemy more than two to one. All the more reason why it was absolutely essential that Eumenes chose the battlefield and dictated the decisive cavalry clash he so desired against Craterus. Eumenes prepared to face Craterus on the open field. Just as Craterus hoped to surprise Eumenes, the latter now hoped to surprise him by seemingly offering the fight he so craved.

Concealing Craterus

Eumenes' preparations did not stop there. The question of maintaining army morale was also of paramount importance. Neoptolemus' eulogising of Craterus was based on truth; Eumenes was marching his men to fight against the world's most famous living military commander. Macedonian or no, Craterus' name carried huge weight as one of Alexander's greatest subordinates and the saviour of Macedon during the Lamian War. Eumenes rightly feared the psychological impact it could have on his troops. He doubted the strength of his soldiers' allegiance if they discovered who it was they were marching to fight against. Would his recently acquired Macedonian infantrymen defect, as Neoptolemus had confidently predicted? Would his local recruits and mercenaries hesitate and slip away from his army on the eve of battle, fearing the enemy commander and his stellar military record? The great weight Craterus' name carried stretched to all corners of Eumenes' force – Hellenic, Thracian and Asian. Their reaction to opposing him was untried and untested. Eumenes aimed to keep it that way and he prepared accordingly.[62]

From the outset that intelligence was relayed to him that Craterus was marching to fight him, Eumenes had taken drastic measures. He concealed the truth; he duped his own men. Not even his most loyal officers knew the truth about who they were going to fight.[63]

To trick his troops Eumenes had spread false information. To both his commanders and his men, he revealed that Neoptolemus was marching against them once more, resurgent with a new army. He also conceded that Neoptolemus was not alone commanding this force; another notable general accompanied him at the head of this new army. But rather than reveal this to be Craterus, Eumenes saw that news spread across his camp that this *strategos* was another, much less-feared commander. This was Pigres, an Asian commander in charge of Cappadocian and Paphlagonian cavalry who may have served as a mercenary adjutant of Neoptolemus.[64] Eumenes' fake news spread throughout his army; Craterus' presence in the enemy ranks was concealed with remarkable success. Now Eumenes had to maintain this deception; he had to keep his men oblivious. Ignorant. To this end, over the following days Eumenes led his soldiers by isolated routes; potentially ruinous announcements from enemy heralds were prevented at spear point; any attempted subterfuge within Eumenes' ranks by agents loyal to Craterus was either non-existent or snuffed out with great success. Over the following days Eumenes' 28,000 strong army were kept completely unaware that they were marching against Craterus, having heard nothing to make them doubt that the combined forces of Neoptolemus and Pigres were marching against them. Eumenes had orchestrated a remarkable deception.[65]

Athena vs Demeter

It had been just over a week since Neoptolemus and Eumenes had come to blows on the battlefield. Eumenes' army – still anticipating battle with Neoptolemus and Pigres – continued to edge closer. Fertile Phrygian plains dotted by intermittent small rises greeted them. Eumenes surveyed the landscape and recognised it as the battleground he had been looking for. The terrain was well-suited for cavalry warfare, while the low rolling hills also offered him the vital element of surprise. Here, he decided, he would fight Craterus. A later story would claim that a vision influenced Eumenes' decision:

> For he thought he saw two Alexanders ready to engage, each commanding his several phalanx, the one assisted by Athena, the other by Demeter; and that after a hot dispute, he on whose side Athena was, was beaten, and Demeter, gathering ears of corn, wove them into a crown for the victor. – Plutarch Life of Eumenes 6.5

Eumenes considered this a good omen – Demeter, the goddess of harvests, had evidently blessed this land. What was more subsequent reports from either spies or deserters that Craterus' watchword was 'Athena and Alexander' only stiffened Eumenes' resolve that this fertile landscape was the battle location he had been looking for. He halted his men and awaited Craterus' arrival, issuing to the camp his own auspicious watchword: 'Demeter and Alexander.'[66]

Craterus was quick to hear word that Eumenes and his army were close by, ready to give battle on the plain. Although his initial strategy to surprise his foe had failed, Craterus remained confident that his battle plan would succeed. Not only was Eumenes offering him a pitched battle, but Eumenes was offering it on a plain – the ideal terrain for his elite Macedonian phalanx. What was more, the small rises served as perfect vantage points from where Craterus could stand and strike astonishment into the opposition and watch as he saw them either defect or desert in droves, as Neoptolemus had confidently predicted. Craterus could not believe his luck. He accepted the challenge of a pitched battle. Conflict was imminent.

As his troops prepared for the clash Craterus convened an assembly, hoping to bolster the morale of his men with an inspiring speech. The man was an expert in martial motivation and by the time he finished speaking he had aroused his warriors' appetite for combat:

> *...promising that, in the event of victory, he would allow them the whole of the enemy's baggage train to plunder.* – Diodorus 18.30.2

Fuelled by the promise of war spoils and further encouragement from their legendary leader the Macedonians and their allies were fired up for battle, eager to show their loyalty to Craterus and prove to him why they deserved their reputation as the heirs of Alexander.[67]

Neoptolemus did not sit idly by in the meantime. He also wanted to get involved in the warrior rousing, sensing an opportunity to deride his foe and attain support from Craterus' men. In front of the Macedonian crowd, he took aim at Eumenes and his secretarial background:

> *Neoptolemus, who had been captain of Alexander's lifeguard, said that he had followed Alexander with shield and spear, but Eumenes only with pen and paper.* – Plutarch *Life of Eumenes* 1.3

In this arrogant show of contempt for Eumenes, Neoptolemus had conveniently left out all mention of his recent humiliation at the hands of this former secretary. He hoped to hoodwink the crowd, erasing his past failure from recent memory. But the Macedonians had not forgotten. As Neoptolemus had taken to the stage and started his attack on Eumenes, an unwelcome reaction greeted the Molossian. Rather than cheers, he was met with laughter. The military audience considered his attacks amusing. They weren't stupid. They knew of Neoptolemus' recent defeat; senior subordinate of Alexander the Great or no, he had developed an infamous reputation among the soldiers for his recent flight.

The Macedonians did not hide their dislike of Neoptolemus' opportunistic attempt to 'reshape historical memory'.[68] They laughed at the Molossian's 'pen and paper' jibe,

> *Knowing very well that, besides other marks of favour, the king (Alexander) had done Eumenes the honour to make him a kind of kinsmen to himself by marriage.* – Plutarch *Life of Eumenes* 1.3

The Macedonians were making a clear point. Their loyalty was to Craterus, not Neoptolemus. They were eager to fight and would happily follow the former into battle, once again fuelled by the Macedonian warrior *élan*. But they shared no similar love for Neoptolemus. Abandoning the field against Eumenes had destroyed his reputation.[69]

The assembly ended. The time for morale boosting speeches was over; their minds turned to battle. In the centre, row upon row of phalangites assembled and started to assume their positions within their larger tactical units. For much of his career, Craterus had served at the heart of these fearsome infantry battalions, helping guide them to victory at famous Alexandrian successes such as Gaugamela and Issus. But today his role was different. He aimed to surprise his foe with his distinguishable appearance, standing out with decorated steed, arms and armour and causing the opposition to lose heart in fighting such a famous adversary. He was also the army's figurehead. The commander-in-chief. It was custom that a man of his position assume command of the right wing with his best cavalry, imitating Alexander the Great's tactics at the head of his elite squadron. Neoptolemus occupied the opposite wing. The 300 of the cavalry that had escaped his past calamitous stand against Eumenes accompanied him. Both Craterus and Neoptolemus had left each other in high spirits. Both expected an easy victory – their foe losing all stomach for the fight as soon as they saw Craterus' figure standing aloof in the flesh. Time would tell how well-placed their confidence was.[70]

The battle

Craterus made the first move. At the head of his cavalry he sounded the advance, riding a long way forward to a position on his right wing. In the distance Neoptolemus mirrored his allies' movements, leading his own retinue forward on the opposite flank.[71]

For the moment there were no enemies in sight. A small, intervening hill between Craterus and the opposing army blocked any vision. Sounds of hooves and marching feet, however, must have echoed through the air, confirming reconnaissance reports that Eumenes was making ready to fight his foe.

The outlines of soldiers on the horizon soon confirmed the sounds. Craterus and his horsemen watched on as enemy troops started to crest the small hill, ready for battle. Far ahead of their own infantry phalanx Craterus' entourage stood – hundreds strong. The legendary general had placed himself in a risky position, vulnerable to an enemy strike attack. Although this must have crossed the commander's mind, Craterus was confident. He remained reassured by Neoptolemus' persuasive words. As soon as the enemy saw his cavalry guard, as soon as they saw this prestigious figure, adorned with beautiful arms, armour and steed, they would quickly conclude that this was the legendary Craterus. Their nerves would fail; desertion would spread as rapidly and as uncontrollably as a disease through the enemy ranks. Craterus expected his appearance to induce immediate defection. He was gravely mistaken.[72]

Craterus' expectation relied on the assumption that the enemy soldiers knew the truth about who they were marching to fight against. They didn't. Eumenes' deceptive strategy to conceal Craterus' name from his troops had worked with spectacular success. And now, his opponent would pay the price.[73]

As the enemy came into view, no soldiers rushed over to join Craterus; there was no mass panic as he had been led to expect. Although the enemy soldiers no doubt saw Craterus and his mounted entourage ahead, they were still too far away to recognise that this was Craterus. They assumed it was some other high-ranking enemy general, another figure who aimed to epitomise Alexander the Great in their charismatic leadership style. Perhaps they assumed this was Neoptolemus? Whatever their assumption, Eumenes' clever covert operations made sure that his soldiers did not recognise Craterus as they crested the hill. They pounced.

Confidence transformed into consternation. Hundreds of horsemen gave out their war cries and started descending down the hillside, making for Craterus and his isolated cavalry at breakneck speed. They weren't coming to change sides. They were galloping to engage, rapidly closing down the distance as the men committed to their cavalry charge.[74]

Eumenes' strategy

Eumenes had anticipated Craterus' intentions. He knew Craterus was confident; he knew Craterus presumed that Eumenes' force had heard word about who they were marching to fight. Eumenes was determined to make his enemy pay for such a blunder.

Having received good intelligence about his enemy's preparations, Eumenes had devised a plan that exploited enemy overconfidence. He had placed two squadrons of Asian cavalry on his left wing, directly opposite Craterus and his horsemen, equipped with traditional weapons such as the javelin. Almost no Macedonian troops were included within their ranks. In command Eumenes placed Pharnabazus, his trusted father-in-law and a veteran Greco-Persian military commander. Phoenix of Tenedos, another loyal adjutant, would share the leadership post.[75]

Their orders were simple: as soon as they saw the enemy in front of them, charge. Charge like never before, at full pelt. Surprise the enemy with the speed and fluidity that generations of horsemanship had drilled into ancient near eastern cultures. Close them down. Let none escape.

And so as soon as Pharnabazus and Phoenix crested the hill and saw this isolated enemy unit full of decorated horsemen ahead of them, they did not have to think twice. Immediately they sounded the charge and started hurrying their mounts with all haste toward the enemy. Craterus, 'paragon of military virtue', was caught by complete surprise. He had hoped to catch Eumenes off guard by boldly showing himself to the enemy troops and triggering mass desertion. Instead it was Eumenes who had caught him off guard, having anticipated his opponent's plan and made meticulous preparations to counter it as best he could. No-one deserted to Craterus; no-one thought it was him they were facing.[76]

Battle on the right

As he saw Pharnabazus and Phoenix's horsemen bearing down on his men, Craterus cursed Neoptolemus' name. The foolish Molossian had made Craterus overconfident of victory, carried away by Neoptolemus' flattery and the man's adamant desire for revenge against Eumenes. But Craterus did not dwell on this less than ideal situation. He portrayed himself as an heir of Alexander. He ensured he acted like one. The general turned to his men, riling them up for battle with boundless charisma and encouragement. His troopers cheered, ready to ride with their general and prove their warrior expertise. Craterus sounded the counter-charge. Living up to his fearless, stellar reputation he led the attack, his best men following close behind.[77]

One can only imagine the terrible scene as Pharnabazus and Phoenix's squadrons crashed at full speed into Craterus and his elite entourage's counter charging formation. A swirling, dense mass of horses and men. Soldiers throwing javelins, lunging spears and landing deadly strikes on their enemy. Dismounted riders and light infantry weaving their way in and out at the heart of the engagement, looking to strike at targets from below. Blood and guts all around. Spears shattering. A chaotic, seething mass of men and mounts.[78]

Craterus was in the thickest of the fighting. Now that he and his enemy were locked in a vicious melee with only victory on their mind, his reputation counted for little. There was no chance of desertion now. In the heart of battle, this legendary general fought with great courage. Standing out in his ornate armour, he imitated the great Alexander in his heroism, leading from the front and willingly sharing in the risks of his men, inspiring his comrades to overcome the odds and win Eumenes' carefully coordinated cavalry fight. He threw off his traditional *kausia* hat, hoping to make himself all the more recognisable to friend and foe alike.[79]

But fame also brought great risk. Craterus' fine appearance evoked importance. To the enemy swirling around him, this was evidently a man of high standing within the enemy army. All of a sudden, Craterus' panoply had turned him into a prime target. Again and again enemies came at Craterus, hoping to strike him down. Again and again Craterus parried the attacks. But then, catastrophe.[80]

In the heat of battle Craterus fell underneath the swirling, dense mass of horsemen, never to rise again. Various accounts survive about how he fell. Diodorus recorded that his horse merely stumbled amid the fighting, causing its prestigious rider to fall and be ingloriously trampled to death beneath hooves belonging to the mounts of friend and foe alike. Plutarch, another ancient writer living hundreds of years later, said differently. In his account Craterus was wounded by a 'Thracian' and fell to the ground. Arrian recorded a similar account, stating that the general was felled by a group of Paphlagonians who had centred their attention on downing the commander. [81]

Though far from certain, a mix of the two main narratives seems plausible. Craterus' standout appearance in the midst of a desperate melee no doubt made him a key target for enemy horsemen. Once one of them finally dealt the critical blow, the esteemed Macedonian general fell to the floor – either dead or dying – and there experienced the grim reality of what happened to those who ended up prostrated beneath hundreds of horse hooves, their riders too preoccupied with a vicious life-or-death struggle to notice what, or who, they were riding on.

As Eumenes' Asian cavalry saw Craterus crash to the ground they pressed their advantage, their morale boosted by the severe blow they had dealt their enemy. For Craterus' entourage, seeing their beloved leader fall was catastrophic. Disheartened and dismayed, more and more were cut to pieces in the face of the renewed onslaught. Soon it proved too much:

Overwhelmed by the enemy, they were forced to retreat for safety to the infantry phalanx – Diodorus 18.30.6

As Pharnabazus and Phoenix's cavalry pressed on, a dead or dying Craterus lay amid fallen men and horses in what had until recently been the scene of the vicious engagement. A soldier from Eumenes' retinue shielded his trampled person, having recognised the body amidst the maelstrom. His name was Gorgias, a veteran Macedonian general. Once a renowned commander under Alexander the Great, once friend and battlefield companion of Craterus, Gorgias now served Eumenes' command. He had been one of only a few Macedonians to accompany Pharnabazus and Phoenix on that flank. Recognising his friend as the fight diminished, Gorgias had dismounted while the rest had pressed ahead and decided to guard the body from further harm.[82]

Craterus was down, but the battle was far from over. Concurrent with the fight on the right, another cavalry clash had raged at the opposite end of the line. A clash no less ferocious that was similarly set to reach an epic climax.

Battle on the left

Neoptolemus had not been idle on the left flank as he witnessed Pharnazabus' horsemen descending on Craterus' entourage from a distance. At the same time, he had faced his own life-or-death struggle. Another enemy cavalry force – smaller in size to that attacking Craterus but roughly equal in number to Neoptolemus' squadron – were charging across the battlefield towards him and his men with undying speed. As Neoptolemus readied his men to meet the charge head on, he was quick to recognise who was leading the enemy force. It was Eumenes.

Eumenes had a score to settle with the turncoat Neoptolemus. Deploying with 300 of his best Cappadocian cavalry, he had positioned himself at the opposite end of the army line to Pharnabazus and Phoenix. Despite the distance, these two cavalry wings had worked in tandem – Pharnabazus and Phoenix charging Craterus and Eumenes charging Neoptolemus simultaneously for the most effective attack. Surprise had gripped both Craterus and Neoptolemus as they and their men viewed the hordes of cavalry rushing against them. Eumenes had outwitted them both. He had exploited their overconfidence and brought them to a battle of his choosing. He had his cavalry clash.[83]

Neoptolemus would not refuse battle with his hated Eumenes. Fuelled with more determination than ever to avenge his previous disgrace, he seized the chance and sounded the attack. The distance between the two forces decreased rapidly – both sides having reached full speed. Led by hated enemies, neither force backed down in the ferocity of their charges:

> (They) showed clearly what men can do when driven by love of glory. – Diodorus 18.31.1

The lines clashed. Two formations of horsemen crashed into each other at full speed, neither backing down. What ensued was a series of engagements, both Eumenes and Neoptolemus breaking away with small segments of their force as they searched for weak points in the meshed lines. Like Craterus on the opposite flank, both these commanders believed in the art of conspicuous leadership. With splendid arms and shining armour they rode their sturdy Nisaean horses into battle once more, re-entering the fray in their search for one another. Both were intent on eradicating their most hated enemy with their own hand and gaining the glory such an action would give them.[84]

For a time these two foes fought in different locations, aiding and inspiring their men as best they could. But then, amidst the chaotic struggle, their eyes met. They caught sight of each other, their powerful steeds and wealthy panoplies confirming they had both located their 'target'. In a scene that would not look out of place in an Epic movie, both generals drew their swords, aimed their horses and charged with all their might.[85]

Single combat was no novel concept for the generals of Alexander the Great. Homeric precedents had inspired these men since childhood; 'noble' duels between figures such as Hector and Achilles, Hector and Ajax or Diomedes and Aeneas motivated generals and commanders to slay leading enemies by their own hand. But for Eumenes and Neoptolemus there was added stimulus. Animosity between the two allies-turned-enemies ensured that both desired to decide the clash by slaying the other. Imbued with mutual hatred that boasted parallels with those legendary heroes clashing before the walls of Troy, the duel proved no less significant. Its outcome would decide the fight.[86]

Eumenes' ally Hieronymus later recorded the duel in colourful detail:[87]

At first, they went at each other with their swords, but then the duel became unusual, and in fact quite extraordinary, because they were so carried away by their passion and their loathing of each other that they let the reins drop from their left hands and grabbed hold of each other. As they grappled, their horses ran out from under them, carried forward by their impetus, and the two men fell to the ground. – Diodorus 18.31.2

As horsemen swirled around them, the now dismounted enemies still kept their gaze on each other.

Eumenes fighting Neoptolemus.

The abruptness and violence of the fall meant that both of them struggled to stand, especially since they were impeded by their armour, but it was Eumenes who found his feet first and got in the first blow, when he struck Neoptolemus behind the knee. It was a bad wound, and Neoptolemus collapsed. He lay disabled on the ground, with the wound making it impossible for him to get to his feet. Yet his mental courage was stronger than his physical impairment, and he raised himself on to his knee and wounded his adversary three times, in the arm and thighs. None of the blows was fatal, however, and with his wounds still fresh Eumenes struck Neoptolemus a second time, in the neck, and killed him. – Diodorus 18.31.3–5

Eumenes had won. Neoptolemus was dead – his corpse stripped of its armour by the victor in true Homeric fashion.[88]

The battle still raged. Molossian and Cappadocian troopers had not stopped fighting simply to see two generals duel. They were preoccupied with their own survival, fighting hard to tip the balance in their favour. But just like with Craterus' fall on the opposing flank, the morale impact of Neoptolemus' demise quickly started to become apparent. Shouts soon spread among the fighting ranks that the Molossian had fallen. The hearts of Eumenes' Cappadocians were hardened whilst their leaderless enemy began to lose faith. Until then the fighting had been evenly matched, many falling on either side. But now, with this 'glorious' personal victory behind him, Eumenes pressed the advantage. Bringing the full force of his entourage down upon their enemy, they started to make progress. And when they saw, in the distance, the remnants of Craterus' cavalry breaking off back to their infantry phalanx, Neoptolemus' horsemen resolved to do likewise. They buckled and fled. Eumenes had won the cavalry battle on both flanks.[89]

The infantry

Meanwhile, Craterus' infantry phalanx remained untouched. 20,000 strong, these men were ready for battle, expectant of an easy victory and encouraged by promises of abundant loot. Imagine their shock as they witnessed the exhausted remains of their cavalry return to their ranks, seeking safety behind the pikemen's long *sarissae*. But what was worse was the news these broken horsemen brought with them. Craterus, their beloved general who only hours before had been inspiring them for the upcoming engagement with great confidence and charisma, had fallen. Neoptolemus too. But it was the former's loss that hurt the infantrymen the most. In their eyes Craterus had been their general. He had looked after them; they had been proud to call him their commander. But now he was dead.

Craterus' loyal subordinates commanding the phalanx were professionals. Despite being aggrieved by their general's loss, they realised that they still had a battle on their hands. 20,000 infantrymen remained ready – the vast majority being highly-trained, highly-disciplined Macedonians. The battalion commanders steadied the men. The fight was not over yet.[90]

In the meantime trumpets echoed across the plain, recalling the victorious cavalry squadrons. Eumenes, Pharnabazus and Phoenix regrouped. The commanders took stock of their recent success. On the site of the victory Eumenes ordered the erecting of a trophy. He also ensured that their fallen comrades received the proper burial rites – the followers who had sacrificed their lives to help bring Eumenes victory. The wound-ridden bodies of Craterus and Neoptolemus were also retrieved. Honours were heaped high upon Craterus; Eumenes was quick to emphasise their past friendship and how rotten fate had forced them to fight on the battlefield. For his hated enemy Neoptolemus, Eumenes may have also arranged honours – Neoptolemus' royal status could hardly be pushed aside. So Eumenes made orders that the remains of both enemy commanders be looked after for eventual return to their families.[91]

Having issued men to oversee these dutiful post-battle tasks, Eumenes turned his mind to the follow-up fight. Craterus' infantry and cavalry remnants remained visible in the distance, ready to give battle on the plain. Though shaken by the news of Craterus' death, their commanders had stiffened their resolve. Eumenes knew he still had to deal with this formidable force. With his full cavalry contingent he advanced, hoping to coerce them into submission just as he had done with Neoptolemus' infantry ten days earlier. But Craterus' footmen – renowned for their prowess – would not be an easy nut to crack. Whereas Neoptolemus' veterans had numbered a couple of thousand, Craterus' amounted to more than five times that. Whereas Neoptolemus' veterans had been dispersed and caught up in the frenzy of pursuit, Craterus' were disciplined, in tight formation and fully aware of the danger they were in. As Eumenes approached, the officers mounted an effective defence:

> They advanced in close battle order in order to make the most fearful impression on the cavalrymen with the troops behind them (those who were cavalry) firing javelins in order to throw back the assault of the cavalry through the continuous barrage of missiles. – PSI XII 1284[92]

Eumenes and his Cappadocians struggled to break through this barrier. What remained of Craterus' Tarentine missile cavalry rained down a hail of javelins upon their opponents from behind the safety of the phalanx line. The defence proved highly successful, Craterus' soldiers proving to Eumenes why they deserved such a fearsome reputation. Buoyed by their success, the commanders grew in confidence. Keep this defence up and perhaps they might fend off the opposition long enough to escape the plain and commence their retreat towards Antipater and his army.

Eumenes rethought his strategy. The enemy had proven they were still a major threat. Their confidence was high; they believed they were invincible. Eumenes wanted to crush this. Once more he would remove this Macedonian aura of invincibility; once more he would show them that they were not as untouchable as they believed.[93]

The infantry readied themselves for the next attack, expecting Eumenes to try again. But no full-blooded follow up cavalry assault came. Instead, a solitary enemy horsemen approached their ranks. It was an emissary.

His name was Xennias, a loyal supporter of Eumenes who hailed from the Macedonian homelands and still retained the region's rough Hellenic dialect. Eumenes hoped that the man's familiar accent would convey trust and help his opponents fully understand the terms he was offering them.

The infantry listened as Xennias announced Eumenes' intended course of action:

> He (Eumenes) would not fight them face to face, but would follow closely with cavalry and light-armed units, barring them from provisions. – PSI XII 1284

Xennias then announced Eumenes' hammer blow:

> They (the Macedonians), even if they imagined themselves invincible, would not long endure against famine. – PSI XII 1284

The threat was painfully clear. Either resist and starve or submit and survive.

Craterus' officers contemplated Eumenes' plan of attack. Several days distant from Antipater, lacking supplies and deficient in enough cavalry to defend their foragers, this new strategy could prove catastrophic. And Eumenes had the resources to see it through.

This was no empty threat. Hunger would eat away at the Macedonian forces, whittling this fearsome army away and leaving it vulnerable to complete annihilation at Eumenes' hand. Once again Eumenes had found the weak spot in the seemingly impenetrable Macedonian armour and hammered his advantage home. Staring at an inglorious end, the commanders reconsidered their options. It was time to submit.[94]

Alongside the threat Xennias conveyed, the messenger had also offered the Macedonians terms. Ever keen for more quality manpower, Eumenes encouraged them to enlist within his army and bolster its ranks. The enemy agreed. They had little choice if they were to survive. Begrudgingly the soldiers swore their new allegiance, taking oaths of loyalty to serve amid

Eumenes' ranks for the rest of the campaign. But casting away the soldiers' previous fealty was more easily said than done. The officers' bonds with Antipater and Craterus were strong; they were the ones who had advocated that the two generals march to war against Perdiccas' regime. Many of their men were veterans of Lamia, Crannon and Aetolia. One oath of allegiance could not wipe away the vast amounts of past combat they had seen in the service of Antipater.[95]

Eumenes was delighted. Craterus' veterans had now agreed to serve him, following in the footsteps of Neoptolemus' soldiers before them. In return Eumenes hoped to strengthen the loyalty of his new soldiers. He allowed them to head into the neighbouring lands to replenish supplies: to forage and raid local villages. Together the remains of Craterus' army headed off to gather provisions for the campaigns ahead....[96]

An extraordinary success

As soon as hostilities had come to an end messengers rushed out of Eumenes' camp, riding hard for Egypt to bring word to Perdiccas of his commander's extraordinary victory. No-one could deny the unprecedented scale of its success. On a battlefield of his choosing, in a battle that suited his cavalry strengths, Eumenes had outwitted his famous foes. Craterus and Neoptolemus were dead. Eumenes had orchestrated the former's demise; he had slain the latter by his own hand in a duel that echoed the famous single combats fought outside the walls of Homeric Troy. His reputation had reached a whole new level.[97]

But Eumenes was not one to revel in victory. He understood the love the Macedonians had held for Craterus. What would happen when they, including Neoptolemus' former infantrymen, discovered that they had marched to fight Craterus in battle? Without delay Eumenes made sure he paid great public homage to his former friend turned foe. A magnificent funeral was arranged – Eumenes emphasising his past friendship with Craterus and cursing those who had forced them to oppose each other in hostile battle lines. He blamed the fight on Neoptolemus and his incessant desire for revenge, the man who had used wicked words to convince Craterus to march against Eumenes. Very quickly Neoptolemus became 'the villain of the story', Craterus became the tragic hero and Eumenes 'the reluctant victor'. Despite some evident grumblings, Neoptolemus' former veterans remained loyal to Eumenes.[98]

The same could not be said of Craterus' infantrymen.

Oath breakers

Oaths of loyalty only went so far; the defeated force could not so easily throw off their past allegiance to the cause of Craterus and Antipater. And so it proved. Not long after providing his new soldiers leave to rest and replenish, Eumenes and his men awoke one morning to find these men nowhere in sight.

> *As soon as they were rested and had stocked up on provisions, they left one night and surreptitiously made their way to Antipater.* – Diodorus 18.32.3

Craterus' commanders were unperturbed. Rested and well-supplied, they now had the capability to ward off Eumenes' threatened plan of action and re-join Antipater's forces. The perks of returning to Antipater's side far outweighed any benefits serving Eumenes might offer. These commanders were Antipater's men; these soldiers were Antipater's men. They had agreed to Eumenes' offer to end hostilities to free themselves from a sticky situation. Now, they betrayed him.[99]

Eumenes vowed vengeance. Seeking to repay the faithless act with interest, he planned to eradicate this stain on his recent success. The pursuit was on.

It was not long before Eumenes' more mobile forces reached the rear of the retreating army, laden with supplies for the march. But Craterus' commanders had anticipated the move. As Eumenes and his cavalry skirted around the enemy force, the Macedonians returned to their tried and tested formation to combat this threat. Once more it worked superbly, Eumenes finding himself unable to crack this disciplined, rearguard action that combined a line of *sarissae* pikes with a storm of deadly javelins. Outwitted and suffering from the wounds he had received while duelling Neoptolemus, it was not long before Eumenes realised that this was a fight he could not win. Well-supplied and well-prepared to resist, the Macedonian defence proved too strong. The pursuit was abandoned. For Eumenes it must have been a bitter blow. The man who prided himself on his cleverness had been 'out-tricked' by what remained of Craterus' army. Thousands of distinguished troops were now on the march to regroup with Antipater – a bitter blow. Still, this could not diminish the significance of Eumenes' victory. Craterus was dead; Eumenes' reputation was greatly enhanced. Although a series of betrayals had made them unable to delay the invasion army, the Perdiccan forces that remained had landed a huge blow by killing their foe's greatest commander. Eumenes prepared for further engagements that were sure to come.[100]

Setback

Antipater was shocked. News of Craterus' death had been quick to reach him and his army marching towards Cilicia. What Antipater had been convinced would be an easy victory for his son-in-law had proved a catastrophe. Once again, his venerable daughter Phila, now pregnant back in Macedonia with Craterus' child, was a widow. The keystone of Antipater's plan to make the famous general master of all imperial lands east of the Hellespont had irreversibly shattered. And what was worse Eumenes was still at large, championing a victorious army with unmatched cavalry power. Still, some good news was to follow.

Not long after news of the terrible defeat, another armed force came into sight. It was the remnants of Craterus' army, come to re-join Antipater having successfully fought off Eumenes' pursuit. For Antipater, this was a reassuring event amid a great setback. Thousands of mostly Macedonian infantrymen, as well as what remained of the cavalry, re-joined the main army. For Antipater, the return of these loyal, seasoned troops was welcome, although it did little to hide the scale of the disaster. Now only he, septuagenarian Antipater, remained to lead the force. They pressed on.[101]

All of a sudden, the war against Perdiccas' forces had taken a turn for the worse. Encouraged by their string of initial successes, Antipater and Craterus had grown careless. Carried away by Neoptolemus, they had divided their forces in enemy territory. They had underestimated their foe: his ability, his knowledge of the local landscape, his military intelligence. They had paid a wicked price. All of a sudden, the tide of war was starting to turn back in Perdiccas' favour. And what was more, further troubling news had recently arrived about events elsewhere. Not in Asia Minor. Not in Egypt. But to the west. In the meantime, fighting had erupted across the Aegean near the heart of Antipater's European territories. Antipater's most frustrating foe had returned with a vengeance. The Aetolians were back.

Further Reading

Primary Sources

Arrian *Events After Alexander* 10B.7,R25.1 – 10B.10, R25.8, 9.26B-9.27 & *PSI XII* 1284.

Diodorus Siculus 18.29–18.33.1.

Nepos *Eumenes*

Plutarch *Life of Eumenes*

Secondary Sources

Anson, E. (2015), *Eumenes of Cardia*, Leiden, 111–121.

Billows, R. A. (1990), *Antigonos the One-Eyed and the Creation of the Hellenistic State*, London, 62–67.

Bosworth, A. B. (1978), 'Eumenes, Neoptolemus and *PSI* XII 1284', *GRBS* 19 (3), 227–237.

Meeus, A. (2009), 'Kleopatra and the Diadochoi', in P. Van Nuffelen (ed.), *Faces of Hellenism: Studies in the History of the Eastern Mediterranean (4th Century BC – 5th Century AD)*, 63–92.

Roisman, J. (2012), *Alexander's Veterans and the Early Wars of the Successors*, Austin, 122–136.

Chapter 14

Polyperchon's Finest Hour

Allies of Perdiccas	Allies of Antipater
The Aetolians	Polyperchon
Alexander of Aetolia	Polycles
Menon of Thessaly (the Pharsalian)	The Locrians
King Aeacides of Molossia (possibly)	The Acarnanians

At the same time that Craterus and Eumenes were involved in their titanic showdown in Asia Minor, to the west Macedon was under threat. If Antipater had thought that the front lines of this great war would be confined to enemy lands east of the Aegean, he was much mistaken. As soon as he crossed the Hellespont a secret pact, struck between Antipater's enemies, revealed itself.

The powerful nation of Aetolia had taken up Perdiccas' cause and launched an offensive, leaving a trail of destruction as they stormed their way through Antipater's territory. Thousands of soldiers filled its ranks, many fuelled with historic animosity toward Macedon. A dashing Thessalian commander was their figurehead, inciting his homeland to revolt once more.

A new theatre for conflict had emerged on the Greek mainland. Antipater was facing his own two-front war. What could he do? Hundreds of miles away to the east he was powerless to help. His enemies had struck when he was at his most vulnerable. Much depended on Antipater's meagre forces that remained in Europe: if they failed to contain this new threat the consequences could be catastrophic. The victor of this war in the west could decisively alter the course of the whole conflict.

Divine deliverance

In late 321 the Aetolians were rejoicing. Antipater's abrupt withdrawal from their homeland had saved the desperate defenders from almost-certain devastation. The Aetolians celebrated the end of the invasion and their seemingly divine deliverance from the very jaws of defeat:

> *...as though one of the gods had taken pity on them for their courage.* – Diodorus 18.25.2

But an air of uncertainty and foreboding remained. The Aetolians may have weathered the invasion, but they were far from safe. The circumstances surrounding the premature end to hostilities had made it painstakingly obvious that this cessation of fighting was no long-term peace. It was merely a temporary truce. A ceasefire. Antipater was adamant in this. He vowed to his army that they would one day return to Aetolia and bring these despised people to heel. A public decree was drawn up, setting in stone a pledge that sooner or later Macedonian might would eradicate the Aetolian menace.[1] Permanently:

> *...they were determined to subdue them later, and to move them all, with their households, to the remotest part of Asia where no people lived.* – Diodorus 18.25.5

The decree was brutal. Unforgiving. It served to reassure the Macedonian troops that their hated foe would not remain free forever. But, understandably, it also had a profound impact on the Aetolians.

Antipater had made no effort to hide the terrible punishment he intended to inflict on the Aetolians when he returned to Europe. It cannot have been long before the content of this infamous decree became known throughout Aetolia, particularly among the upper echelons of the Aetolian League. The threat of a second invasion, no matter how far off in the future, was terrifying. Once again it appeared that their whole way of life was under threat. What the Aetolians did have, however, was time. By deciding to first cross the Hellespont to fight Perdiccas, Antipater and Craterus had offered them a precious window to prepare. The Aetolians were sure to use it.

Rather than simply sit and await a second invasion, the League considered their options: how could they best safeguard their independence against a superpower that possessed the most powerful army of the age? Aetolian animosity towards Antipater remained clear to see for those on the international stage. It soon attracted the attention of a powerful figure.[2]

My enemy's enemy

In the early months of 320 ships arrived off Aetolian shores. Perdiccas' envoys approached Aetolian League officials. These messengers offered the League a proposal: co-operation against Antipater, their common foe. Perdiccas suggested to the Aetolians a pre-emptive and potentially decisive course of action. He wanted them to seize the opportunity Antipater's imminent departure from Macedonia would bring; he wanted them to take the offensive.

Perdiccas was taking no chances. At the time that he sent his envoys to Aetolia, he and his adjutants remained confident that their combined land-sea Hellespont defence would stand strong in the face of Antipater and Craterus.

Nevertheless, he wanted a backup plan. If Eumenes and Cleitus' Hellespont defence faltered and the invasion army successfully crossed into Asia, this was when he intended the Aetolians to intervene. In this eventuality, the envoys requested that the Aetolians divert Antipater's attention by launching an unprecedented invasion of Thessaly, threatening Macedonian heartlands.[3]

For Perdiccas, the advantages of securing this 'plan B' agreement were obvious. Opening up a second front so close to Macedonia proper would distract Antipater and Craterus' attention away from events in Asia, alleviating pressure on Perdiccas' forces. For the Aetolians too, this proposed pact offered them opportunity. 'My enemy's enemy is my friend.' Rather than sit back and await the second invasion Antipater had so publicly forecast, Perdiccas' offer allowed the Aetolians to take the fight to Antipater, striking at the heart of his influence when he was at his weakest. Potential for plunder was another powerful incentive, as was the opportunity to further expand Aetolian influence into neighbouring Locris. Future relations with Perdiccas must have also crossed the League's mind: their assistance could help tilt this titanic civil war in Perdiccas' favour, leaving them on good terms with the potential victor. Not only that but it had been Perdiccas' actions across the Aegean that set in motion a series of events that culminated in Antigonus' arrival at Antipater's Aetolian camp half a year earlier. It had been Perdiccas' imperial actions that inadvertently saved Aetolia from Macedonian conquest.[4]

The only question was manpower. Although the Aetolians had ample hardened soldiers available, Perdiccas was asking them to embark upon a course of action that would undoubtedly put them on a collision course with Antipater's forces left behind in Europe – still thousands strong. If the Aetolians were to take the offensive and bring the fight to Macedon, they wanted clear martial superiority. They wanted more men.

Perdiccas could not offer the Aetolians any of his soldiers – the regent was stretched as it was. What he could offer his new ally, however, was the next best thing: money. Diving into the seemingly limitless wealth Perdiccas had at his disposal, his envoys offered the Aetolians enough money to sustain a formidable army of Aetolians, allies and mercenaries alike. Perdiccas would subsidise the operation. Backed by their warriors and thousands of hardened mercenaries this Aetolian army could wreak havoc, becoming more than a match for the meagre Macedonian forces left west of the Hellespont. Antipater's forces would be sandwiched between two powerful enemies. With Perdiccas' financial aid, the likelihood of victory had increased dramatically, convincing the League that this martial cause had a high chance of success.[5]

Armed with these facts the Aetolians accepted Perdiccas' overtures. Severing the ceasefire with Antipater did not concern them. Why should it? The latter had already made perfectly clear that he intended to end it upon his return.

Better then that the Aetolians land the first blow and decisively derail his intent. The pact was finalised. If Antipater did manage to cross into Asia, the Aetolians would strike. Antipater would have his own two-front war to worry about.[6]

Readying the army

In the spring of 320, when they discovered that Antipater and Craterus had set forth for the Hellespont, the Aetolians started mobilising. Thousands of warriors in the prime of life were summoned for service once more. Soon the Aetolian army numbered 12,400 men – 12,000 footmen and 400 cavalry. We can presume that some of these men equipped themselves as light infantry, fighting just as they had done against Antipater and Craterus' Macedonians in the Aetolian highlands a year earlier. Yet it seems that these men were in a minority. After all the Aetolians were not preparing for another defensive, highland standoff. They were preparing for a provocative, full-blooded offensive.[7]

As a result thousands of elite Aetolian warriors altered their equipment, trading the throwing spear for a more durable thrusting one. They donned their heavier hoplite arms and armour, more suitable for pitched battle. Professional and flexible they adapted from light infantry to heavily-armed hoplites with relative ease – boasting skills in both fighting styles.[8]

Small contingents of allies and mercenaries must have accompanied the ranks, as did exiles who had sought refuge within Aetolia's borders at the end of the Lamian War. By the time mobilisation had ended, the Aetolian army looked very different to the force that had taken to the hills a year earlier to combat Antipater's invasion. At the same time recruiters headed further afield to muster more mercenaries. The 'sellspear' hoplite haven at Taenarum remained free of Macedonian control. Reinforcements were on the way.[9]

Alexander, a leading Aetolian who presumably hailed from one of the region's most prominent noble families, was assigned command of the expedition. A leading Thessalian provided assistance, an exile with experience few could match in fighting Macedonians. Menon had returned to the fold.[10]

After his cuirassiers' reversal at Crannon, this dashing cavalry commander had been among those leading figures who sought refuge in Aetolia at the end of the Lamian War. No-one could deny that the exiled Menon's presence brought benefits to the Aetolians. Not only did he harbour deep hostility to Macedon, but he boasted a famous name among his countrymen. In particular Menon was a renowned figure among the Thessalian elite: he had been the highest-ranking confederate Greek cavalry commander during the Lamian War; it was this Pharsalian noble who had led the decisive charge against the legendary Leonnatus that ended in the latter's demise. Menon planned to use his fame to his advantage, hoping to rally thousands of Thessalians to the Aetolian cause as they marched north with unprecedented strength. Indeed, the Pharsalian's connections stretched much further than Thessaly. He was father-in-law to the cavalry-rich Molossian King Aeacides to the northwest, and to the south thousands of veteran mercenaries that shared his hatred toward Macedon resided at Taenarum. For the Aetolians, Menon was an invaluable ally.[11]

The offensive begins

At the height of spring 320 Admiral Cleitus the White's defection to Antipater paved the way for the latter and his 30,000 men to cross the Hellespont. It also inadvertently triggered the Aetolian attack. Alexander led his army onto the offensive. They headed east, leaving the Aetolian homeland and crossing into neighbouring Locris. Their aim: to exploit Macedonian weakness for personal gain. Whereas Perdiccas predominantly sought a diversion, the Aetolians sought security, glory and loot.[12]

The expedition's main aim was an invasion of Thessaly, but sound strategic reasoning meant that Alexander could not simply 'blitzkrieg' his army so far north straightaway. He had to secure his overland supply lines; he had to protect his rear; he had to eradicate any enemy forces stationed *en route* that could derail the whole expedition. Thessaly was not the army's first destination. Amphissa was.

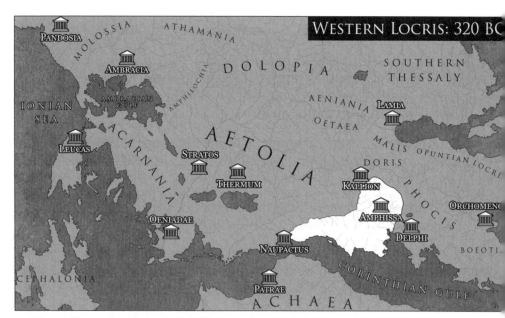

Western Locris (highlighted) 320. The region covered the territory directly to the east of Aetolia.

Amphissa dominated the lands immediately east of Aetolia. Its strategic value was significant: situated along one of the sanctuary's arterial transport routes, the city controlled access to Delphi, centre of the Greek World, from the northwest – from Aetolia. Most importantly for Alexander and his soldiers, however, was Amphissa's acropolis. At that time, it appears that this defensive bastion was serving as a military headquarters for the region's Macedonian garrison. Antipater had imposed this meagre force within Western Locris, perhaps with the purpose of watching over the Aetolians in the wake of his invasion's premature conclusion. A certain Polycles commanded the force. For Alexander and his Aetolians, this unknown Macedonian general posed a serious threat. If they simply passed him and his force by – no matter how small their numbers – this army could completely derail their plan of action, attacking them in their rear and assaulting Aetolian lines of communication as they advanced deeper and deeper into Thessaly. What was more, Polycles' forces could land punitive strikes at Aetolia itself, creating a dreaded second front for Alexander's army. For the Aetolian expedition, removing the threat Polycles posed was paramount. Everything else was secondary. Without delay they marched on Amphissa and assaulted the city. At the same time Aetolian warbands ravaged the farmland and stormed nearby towns in their search for plunder.[13]

Polycles and his Macedonians had been elsewhere when they discovered the grave Aetolian threat facing Amphissa and its local Locrian defenders.[14] They did not remain untouched for long. As soon as the Aetolians discovered Polycles' location they advanced to meet him on the battlefield, determined to eradicate all of Antipater's forces from Western Locris and secure Aetolia's eastern border. Polycles' army cannot have been more than a couple of thousand strong, Macedonians and mercenaries presumably forming the mainstay of his military strength. Yet the commander did not refuse the fight, despite his army being gravely outnumbered. The man was an experienced general, tasked with maintaining control over Locris, but even he was unable to overcome the great odds set against him. In battle somewhere near Amphissa, Polycles' army was defeated. Many of his men were slain – Polycles among the fallen. For those who survived slaughter the Aetolians looked to make financial gain, either selling or ransoming their captives. The threat posed by Polycles' force was removed; Aetolia's eastern border was secure; the road north lay open.[15]

Alexander's victorious army pressed north. Once again an Aetolian army, several thousand strong, crossed the Sperchius River and advanced into Thessaly.[16]

Inducing the Thessalians

It was not long before large swathes of southern and central Thessaly had joined the uprising. Menon's presence had helped the invaders persuade many city-states to join with the Aetolians. Nevertheless, these communities faced a stark choice. There were no major Macedonian forces in sight and reports of the Aetolians' plundering antics in Western Locris must have preceded their arrival north of the Sperchius. For these Thessalian city-states it was either side with the invaders or suffer the same dismal fate of Amphissa and its neighbouring lands.[17]

Once the cities were united behind Alexander and his Aetolians, reinforcements followed. Thousands of new soldiers swelled the army's ranks. Anti-Macedonian sentiment was widespread; Antipater's forces in Europe were weak; Alexander and Menon boasted a force many thousands strong. Within no time at all the strength of the Aetolian army had more than doubled in size: from 12,400 to 26,500 soldiers: 25,000 infantry and 1,500 cavalry.[18]

13,000 footmen had joined their ranks. Thousands of Thessalian infantrymen were among this number, lacking in quality but drawn to the cause having been convinced that Macedon was weak and convinced that now was the perfect time to take the offensive. Companies of soldiers from neighbouring regions may have also marched to join Alexander's ranks, but the majority of infantrymen were mercenaries. Menon and the Aetolians had made good use of the money Perdiccas had provided them. As Alexander and

The western theatre of the First War of the Successors.

his men had rampaged through Locris, clearing the way to Thessaly, allied recruiters had been enlisting thousands of veteran footmen to their cause. Elite mercenary hoplites were in no short supply on the Greek mainland at the time, nor were there a lack of professional soldiers who housed animosity toward the Macedonians. Veterans of the Lamian War abounded.[19]

Following the defeat at Crannon almost two years earlier, Antiphilus and the Athenians had disbanded their mercenary infantry force – thousands of veteran footmen that had successfully held off their Macedonian counterparts during the clash in northern Thessaly. Once more these men had returned to Taenarum, their mercenary haven at the southern tip of the Peloponnese. Now these hoplites found themselves marching to oppose the Macedonians in Thessaly once more. Thousands headed north, uniting with Alexander and Menon's Thessalian-Aetolian army north of the Sperchius to form a truly formidable force. Menon, a veteran of Crannon himself, was no doubt aware of the quality of these footmen; likewise these new arrivals would have been well aware of him. Linked by their past service and common hatred of Antipater they were natural allies in this fight.[20]

Alexander's infantry force was diverse and commendable, comprising heavy-armed infantry, skilled light infantry and zealous levies. His cavalry force, however, was lacking. Almost ninety-five per cent of the army was infantry; merely 1,500 cavalry complemented its ranks. Nevertheless, despite their relatively low quantity, these horsemen exuded quality. Over 1,000 of these horsemen were the famed Thessalian cavalrymen, enlisted from among the region's highly-trained aristocracy. For many of these horsemen, the opportunity to serve under Menon once more must have been a decisive factor in convincing them to join his ranks. But at the same time 1,000 Thessalian horsemen was a low turnout, lower than Menon might have expected. More than 3,000 Thessalians had followed him into battle at Crannon. Now less than one third of that number rallied to his cause. Unlike the thousands of Thessalian levies, the region's aristocracy were evidently more cautious at joining the invaders: they were reluctant to join a second war with Antipater, no matter how good the odds may have looked. Haunted by memories of being on the losing side of the Lamian War, they decided against joining the conflict, against joining Menon, against sending troops. Nevertheless 1,000 highly-skilled Thessalian cavalrymen was better than nothing.[21]

All things considered, things looked good for Menon and Alexander. They had crushed all opposition so far; they had the largest army on the Greek mainland; much of central and southern Thessaly – including Menon's home city of Pharsalus – had been persuaded to make a common cause against Antipater. Every passing day, as they proceeded to persuade more Thessalian communities join them, their strength was increasing. And what next? An advance into northern Thessaly, generally more loyal to Macedon due to its closer geographical proximity, would seem a logical next step. Nothing would then prevent them marching into Macedon proper and providing Antipater with one of the most distressing conundrums in the viceroy's long history. War, however, is never one-sided. As these events developed, Macedonian high command had not been idle.[22]

Enter Polyperchon

Polyperchon boasted a career that few west of the Aegean Sea could rival. Already in his 60s by the time of this Aetolian-led incursion into Thessaly, this seasoned general had spent much of his military career campaigning in the East. For much of Alexander the Great's reign, he had served within the king's army as a prominent infantry general: commander of the Tymphaean phalanx battalion. A native of Tymphaea himself, Polyperchon had retained control over his battalion for almost ten years. From fighting at the heart of the phalanx line on the dusty plain of Gaugamela to keeping the peace in ancient Bactria, Polyperchon and his battalion performed diverse but vital duties throughout Alexander the Great's campaigns.[23]

Over the course of these campaigns Polyperchon established strong links with fellow infantry commanders: Meleager, Gorgias, Attalus and Coenus for instance. Of them all, however, the man who had the closest working relationship with him was Craterus. In battle and on the march these two seasoned generals worked in tandem to help bring about success, something Alexander was sure to note. When the king sent Craterus back to Europe with his 10,000 discharged veterans in 324, Polyperchon accompanied him as second in command, a not-insubstantial role considering Craterus' ill-health at the time. But Craterus did recover and Polyperchon's harmonious role as Craterus' 'chief adjutant' remained. He followed his commander to Europe and presumably played a significant, untold part in the Lamian War, opposing Menon and his forces at the climactic Battle of Crannon. Polyperchon remained by Craterus' side until the end of the Lamian War, proving his worth to Antipater and further aiding his seniors in the key decisions they brought to their council. When Antigonus' warnings about Perdiccas' grand imperial ambitious were relayed to Antipater and Craterus' generals in Aetolia, it is not difficult to fathom that Polyperchon was among those unnamed officers who adamantly advocated war against the regent.[24]

Polyperchon's loyalty to Antipater and Craterus' cause was clear, but he himself did not accompany them on their return to Asia. As Antipater had headed east, the viceroy had entrusted his European possessions to this adjutant, placing them in good hands. What had happened next must have astonished Polyperchon and all those who remained with him. The brunt, if not all, of the fighting during this great war had been expected to occur in Asia. But within months of Antipater and Craterus' departure, Polyperchon found himself opposed by a great army across Macedon's southern border. The interim governor faced a huge task to defend his homeland against one of the most significant threats in Macedon's recent history.[25]

Polyperchon's army was meagre: perhaps 13,000 men at most. Trained Macedonian troops were in relatively short supply – the best soldiers had accompanied Craterus and Antipater to Asia. The most senior Macedonian figure west of the Aegean faced a manpower problem for the upcoming fight. Polyperchon was no fool – Polycles' demise was clear evidence how thousands of Aetolian warriors could annihilate enemy armies smaller in number. And that had been before c.15,000 more soldiers had reinforced the Aetolian army, including a sizable core of professional soldiers who had already proven their mettle against the Macedonian phalanx. All evidence pointed to Polyperchon, supposedly the most powerful figure west of the Aegean Sea, lacking the military manpower to tackle the full enemy army head on. If he marched south now, the commander could not guarantee victory. He had to find a way to somehow slice the odds more in his favour.[26]

Then, a masterstroke.

Polyperchon's skills stretched far beyond the battlefield. The man was also an adept diplomat. To help alleviate the current crisis he sought a valuable ally. But who? To the east Lysimachus lacked any sufficient manpower with which to aid him; to the west King Aeacides of Molossia had family links to Menon and may have already placed his support behind the Aetolian forces. Nevertheless, Polyperchon still had one clear option of alliance. There was one group of people who shared the Macedonians' deep-rooted hatred of the Aetolians, who would be equally eager to ruin any chance of their success in this unprecedented offensive. Who were these people? None other than Aetolia's western neighbours: the Acarnanians.[27]

The Acarnanians

Athens and Thebes. Croton and Sybaris. Sparta and Messene. Neighbouring Hellenic communities had several precedents for being erstwhile enemies. The Aetolians and the Acarnanians were no different. Minor border wars between the two erupted regularly. Land disputes and raiding were common. Frontline towns were frequently annexed, none more so than the strategic maritime city of Oeniadae, situated near the mouth of the Achelous River.[28]

The region of Acarnania (highlighted) 320. It was located to the west of Aetolia.

Animosity between the two peoples was mutual, but in the late fourth century the Aetolians were clearly dominant. Their expedition to Thessaly, however, offered the Acarnanians an opportunity to exact some sweet revenge and reclaim lost land. Just as the Aetolians had sensed Macedonian weakness with Antipater's departure and taken the offensive, now the Acarnanians in turn sensed Aetolian weakness with their army's departure. The Aetolian heartlands were vulnerable to an attack.[29]

The Acarnanians aimed to seize this opportunity with both hands, but initially they bided their time. For months they waited, keeping tabs on the Aetolian army's progress further and further north – farther and farther away from their homelands. Only when Alexander and his men were deep in the heart of Thessaly did they strike. An attack was mounted. Acarnanian warriors crossed the border into Aetolia and unleashed hell. They ravaged farmlands; they assaulted the lightly defended lowland towns. Raiding was rife. Panic spread across the region.[30]

The Acarnanians had been ruthless in their timing of this invasion, but it was no chance occurrence. The Acarnanians had not orchestrated this grand strategy alone. Polyperchon, it seems, had masterminded the whole affair. The Macedonian governor was well-aware of Aetolian-Acarnanian animosity and he had used it to his advantage, opening diplomatic channels and encouraging a major strike upon Aetolian heartlands at the most opportune time. The Acarnanians had required little convincing. This was a golden opportunity for them to exact revenge on their hated foe and hinder any progress the Aetolians had so far made in their expedition.[31] 'My enemy's enemy is my friend.' Perdiccas and the Aetolians had used this stratagem in their fight against Antipater. Now Polyperchon was using the same tactic against them.[32]

Knowing that he lacked the numbers to take on the combined Thessalian-Aetolian-mercenary army, Polyperchon hoped the Acarnanian assault would trigger its division. With an Acarnanian invasion, the Aetolians suddenly had a new front to deal with along their homeland's western border. A prime Aetolian weakness, the League could do little else but turn their attention away from further aggressive military movements in faraway Thessaly.

Divide.....

Polyperchon hoped his diplomatic strategy would divide his foe and so it proved. As Acarnanian warbands ravaged Aetolian borderlands, messengers from the Aetolian League hurried with all haste to Alexander in Thessaly, ordering that he return at once with the army to chase away this new threat. The League had taken up Perdiccas' cause with great enthusiasm but defending their homeland triumphed over everything else, even if that meant dividing their expedition's forces.

For Polyperchon and his Macedonians, Acarnanian intervention offered them a vital reprieve. As soon as Alexander received word of the Acarnanian invasion and the League's orders for the army, he readied all his Aetolian warriors to prepare for a homeward march. For Menon it must have looked like history repeating itself. Two years earlier during the opening stages of the Siege of Lamia – the high point of their revolt against Antipater – he had looked on powerless as the Aetolian contingent had similarly separated from the main anti-Macedonian army and returned home to deal with their own 'domestic matters', never to return. Now Alexander was doing something very similar. Thousands of Aetolians would be leaving the expedition when everything was seemingly going to plan.[33]

Alexander reassured Menon. He vowed to his ally that the Aetolians would return to Thessaly as soon as they had eradicated this Acarnanian threat and freed their homeland from danger. Once again, however, doubt must have crossed Menon's mind. The commander only had to think back to the dark days before Crannon. Then, just as in 320, Menon had remained hopeful that the Aetolians would return from their homelands to turn the tide of the war just in time for this great battle, only for them never to appear. The Aetolians had proven unreliable in the past. Would they prove so again?

There was, however, some good news. Not all of the 12,400 soldiers that Alexander had brought up to Thessaly would depart with him. Mercenaries and other non-Aetolian soldiers remained with Menon to complement Thessalian ranks as best they could. With that the Aetolian citizen force departed, hurrying back to their homeland to counter this new Acarnanian threat.[34]

…and conquer

Polyperchon was delighted. His successful diplomacy had brought the intended consequences. His enemy were divided. Weakened. Now he aimed to seize this window of opportunity. For as long as the Aetolian-Thessalian forces had been united, the veteran commander had retained his forces behind Macedonian borders. But now, with enemy forces in Thessaly a shadow of their former strength, he attacked. Mustering all available soldiers he marched into Thessaly, throwing the gauntlet down to Menon and his army for the decisive clash.[35]

Reinforcements from loyal northern Thessalian communities presumably swelled Polyperchon's forces *en route*. By the time his army had closed in on Menon's and pitched battle was imminent, the interim governor's military might was considerable: a Macedonian-Thessalian hybrid force. Still, in numbers Menon's army was equal to the enemy's. Alexander's Aetolian departure had cost them comfortable martial superiority, but Menon still favoured his chances in a pitched battle against Polyperchon in his native region. His army's collapse at Crannon must have haunted his decision, but his previous victories against Antipater near Themopylae and his annihilation of Leonnatus' elite horsemen near Lake Xynias offered comfort. As too did the great rewards that could come with defeating Polyperchon. If he could win here, the road to a relatively unguarded Macedon would open. Thessalian cities still loyal to Macedon would find themselves under increasing pressure to switch sides; more soldiers would join his ranks; the Aetolians would return; Macedonian hegemony over Thessaly and mainland Greece in general would crumble. The fruits victory could offer Menon were remarkable and tantalisingly close. But the stakes, as always with battle, were high.[36]

What followed was annihilation. In the ensuing pitched battle Polyperchon's home defence army completely outmatched their foe. All across the battlefield, Menon's soldiers were pushed back. Those who attempted to make a stand were cut to pieces – cavalry, levies and mercenaries alike. For Menon the fight proved disastrous. If he had thought Crannon was a catastrophic loss, the widescale destruction of his army in the field against Polyperchon's well-oiled war machine was a military tragedy unlike any witnessed during the Lamian War. Most of his men did not live to see the sun set, and neither did Menon.

The Thessalian commander was among the dead, presumably falling in the battle's cavalry clash. For this famous general it was a sudden but expected end: dying in battle leading his countrymen in an opportune attempt to liberate them from Macedonian overlordship.[37]

Polyperchon and his men celebrated their success. One of Macedon's most feared foes west of the Hellespont, the slayer of the legendary Leonnatus, was dead.

Any remnants of resistance melted away, as Polyperchon's force wiped out all enemies that remained on the field. The scale of his victory was astounding. Substantial Thessalian cavalry support from the loyal local aristocracy must have provided him the edge in cavalry, allowing his forces to cut down large swathes of the retreating enemy force with devastating results. Menon was dead; most of his army were dead. Polyperchon had irrevocably broken the back of the Thessalian insurgency. History repeated itself. Just as after the Battle of Crannon some two years earlier, as soon as Pharsalus and the other Thessalian cities that had sided against Polyperchon heard word of Menon's crushing defeat, they sued for peace. They submitted to Polyperchon, pledging their allegiance to Antipater. Thessaly was once again in Macedonian hands.[38]

Polyperchon's allied Acarnanians were not so fortunate. The Aetolian army's return to their homeland to combat this aggression proved decisive. The raiding warbands were repelled and chased back to their own lands. Cowing the Acarnanians into submission, Aetolian supremacy over their western neighbours was reaffirmed, but their victory proved a Pyrrhic one.[39]

Polyperchon's finest hour

By the time Alexander and his countrymen had warded off the Acarnanian threat it was too late to rejoin the Thessalian expedition. Word reached them of Menon's catastrophic defeat; Thessaly was now in Macedonian control. Rather than return to a now-hostile land and face the very real prospect of experiencing a similarly crushing defeat at Polyperchon's hands, the Aetolians recalculated their situation. A return to Thessaly was called off. They would look to their own defences, not marching their warriors outside their borders again. At least not for now…

The Aetolians could not shirk responsibility for Menon's demise. Their withdrawal had proven decisive to Polyperchon's success. But take nothing away from the latter's strategic brilliance. Through shrewd diplomacy and a decisive assault against a divided foe he had crushed a grave new threat that could have created a deadly second front for Antipater and his allies in his war against Perdiccas. He had risen to the occasion in a high-stakes campaign that, if it had failed, could have struck at the heart of Macedon's European possessions and wreaked unparalleled damage in the Empire's western lands. For Polyperchon, this was his finest hour.

And yet the Aetolians and their League continued to remain free of Macedonian control. Polyperchon may have gained success in Thessaly, but he lacked the resources to march into Aetolian heartlands and conduct his own costly highland campaign against such a fierce enemy. Antipater and Craterus had tried and failed with 30,000 men – Polyperchon among their ranks. There was little chance he could fare any better now with roughly half that manpower.[40] Once again Aetolian aggression went unpunished; the list of Macedonian grievances against these people was steadily growing. The Aetolian League remained free and as powerful as ever; the Acarnanians had been cowed into submission once more after a brief but effective revenge strike. Threat of a second Macedonian invasion of Aetolia remained as real as ever. One thing, however, was certain. The Aetolians would fight tooth and nail to preserve their independence, their way of life.

Perdiccas' plan to distract Antipater through this new European theatre of war had been a sound strategy. Thanks to his funds, combined with the energetic participation of the Aetolians, Menon and other anti-Macedonian allies, the offensive had nearly gained unprecedented success. But just as everything was going to plan, this threat was extinguished. Polyperchon's own clever diplomacy foiled the strategy. This veteran statesman, left behind to defend the homeland and seemingly at the swansong of his military career, had proven the unsung hero of Antipater's cause. He was the man who had caused Perdiccas' plan to crumble. Eyes once again turned to developments further east, to Perdiccas and the royal army at the banks of the Nile. How this great war would progress depended on events in Egypt. Its climax was about to materialise.

Further Reading

Primary Source
Diodorus Siculus 18.18.1–6.

Secondary Sources
Grainger, J.D. (1999), *The League of the Aitolians*, Leiden, 65–70.
Mendels, D. (1984), 'Aetolia 331–301: Frustration, Political Power and Survival', *Historia* 33 (2), 129–180.
Rzepka, J. (2009), 'The Aetolian Elite Warriors and Fifth-Century Roots of the Hellenistic Confederacy', *Akme. Studia Historica* 4, 7–31.
Westlake, H. D. (1949), 'The Aftermath of the Lamian War', *The Classical Review* 63 (3), 87–90.

Chapter 15

Perdiccas vs Ptolemy: The Invasion of Egypt

Perdiccas' Allies	Ptolemy and Antipater's Allies
Philoxenus	Philotas
Docimus	Archon
Aristonous	Nicocreon of Salamis
Sosigenes	Laomedon
Medius of Larissa	Arrhidaeus (the general)
Amyntas	Antigonus
Peithon	Craterus (recently deceased)
The Ruler of Marion (possibly Stasioecus)	Asander
Seleucus	Cleitus the White
Antigenes	Menander
Attalus	Neoptolemus (recently deceased)
King Arrhidaeus III	Dionysius of Heraclea
Peithagoras	
Eumenes	

ssyrians, Nubians and Persians. Over the centuries Egypt had witnessed countless invasions, led by kings and commanders determined to conquer the bountiful land that boasted thousands of years of remarkable history.

Now another was to try his luck.

Since his accession as regent three years earlier Perdiccas had overcome many diverse challenges: from defying a death squad to crushing the hardened hillmen at Isaura. On and off the battlefield this illustrious commander had gained successes, strengthening his power and stirring him to marry into the royal family. But Ptolemy had sought to put a stop to Perdiccas' imperial ambition, by removing the plan's 'keystone' when he seized Alexander's elaborate funeral carriage and its precious cargo. Perdiccas would now strike back, determined to remove Ptolemy from power once and for all.

On a stage brimming with betrayal, bribery, siegeworks, subterfuge, trickery and intrepid tactical manoeuvres the scene was set for their feud to reach its grand climax along the banks of the River Nile.

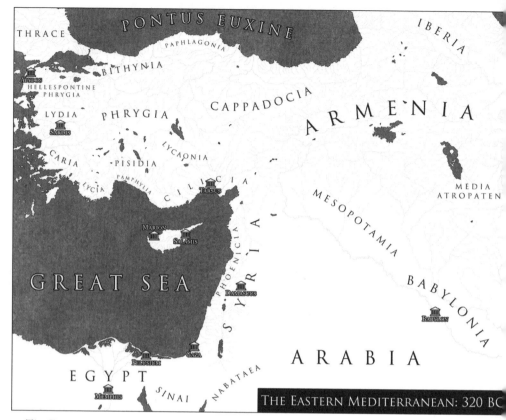

The Eastern Mediterranean: 320. The Taurus Mountains divided Cilicia from neighbouring regions to the north and west such as Lycaonia and eastern Pisidia.

Preparations

Cilicia had seen its fair share of sizable armies march through its lands. Since 323, both Craterus and Perdiccas had spent significant time in this plentiful region, replenishing their forces for upcoming campaigns. Now, in the early spring of 320, the latter and his royal army arrived in Cilicia once more, having crossed the Taurus Mountains. Traversing the region, they established their base near the coast, reconvening with Attalus' fleet in preparation for the upcoming march to Egypt. Before he could set off, however, there were other serious matters that required Perdiccas' attention.[1]

The first issue was Philotas, the Macedonian governor of Cilicia. This former infantry commander boasted a fine reputation, as a distinguished veteran of Alexander the Great's campaign. Philotas' high standing and subsequent allying with Perdiccas in the chaos that immediately followed Alexander's death ensured that he was confirmed as governor of Cilicia in the Babylon Settlement. Fast forward three years, however, and matters had changed.

Craterus and Philotas were known associates. The two had fought side by side in command of infantry battalions during Alexander the Great's campaigns; Craterus had spent several months in the latter's province in 323 / 322. These links made Perdiccas wary. He feared Philotas' defection in the upcoming war, an act that would sever land communications between his forces in Egypt and Eumenes' forces in the north.[2] He could not take that risk. Perdiccas embraced his powers as regent and rescinded the decision made at Babylon three years earlier. Philotas' demotion was confirmed. The governor's rule over Cilicia was at an end.[3]

For Philotas this ruthless political move was a clear breach of the Babylon Settlement, but the ambitious Macedonian's hostile feelings counted for little. Lacking the strength to oppose Perdiccas, he deserted, intent on joining Antipater and the opposition forces.[4]

So Philotas fled. Another seasoned general, alienated by Perdiccas' humiliating actions, had opted for betrayal. In his stead Perdiccas selected the Macedonian Philoxenus. The man boasted no illustrious history of achievements, unlike the other great governors of the time. During Alexander the Great's campaigns he had served as a mercenary, on board one of the Macedonian ships. Philoxenus' relative obscurity however, was exactly what Perdiccas wanted. The surprise selection of Philoxenus to this important position undeniably placed him in Perdiccas' debt. Cilicia was in the hands of a governor beholden to Perdiccas, a scenario Perdiccas may well have aimed to replicate across the empire.[5]

Punishing a plotter

Philotas was not the only appointed governor that Perdiccas wished to remove. There was another that he was determined to punish for past disobedience: Archon, the governor of Babylonia.

Ever since Alexander the Great's funeral carriage had been escorted out of Babylon in mid-321, Archon had remained on the periphery of the political spotlight. As the likes of Antipater, Craterus, Eumenes, Perdiccas and Ptolemy prepared for the great war Archon had remained aloof in Babylonia, managing this wealthy province and perhaps delighted that the fighting would occur far away from Babylon. If Archon had hoped to escape the ire of Perdiccas however, the man was much mistaken.

Perdiccas was no fool. He knew that Ptolemy's infamous collusion with Arrhidaeus, that had resulted in their successful theft of Alexander the Great's precious funeral cortège, must have taken months of meticulous planning. The plot must have started back in Babylon; communications between Arrhidaeus and Ptolemy almost certainly could not have happened without Archon's knowledge. Significant or no, Perdiccas rightly suspected that the governor of Babylonia had played a role in the great funeral carriage heist. Now he plotted his revenge. An expeditionary force was assembled, consisting of soldiers segmented from the royal army. Rather than continue south with the rest of their comrades this elite task force would head east, returning to the wealthy heartlands of the now extinct Achaemenid Empire. It was a strong force, no doubt full of veterans, affirming Perdiccas' desire to see Archon pay for his past deeds.[6]

In overall command Perdiccas placed Docimus, an until then unheard-of Macedonian commander seeking to make his mark in the new regime. Once again, as with Philoxenus, more prestigious adjutants were overlooked in preference of a commander that Perdiccas knew would be in his debt for this new prominent position.[7]

Not only did Perdiccas appoint Docimus as the expedition's supreme commander but he also instructed Docimus to assume control over Babylonia and become this wealthy province's new governor in place of Archon. Archon was to suffer an embarrassing demotion; this renowned Macedonian commander was to become the new organiser of war revenues – a position beneath Docimus. At least, that was the official story.

In fact, Perdiccas had no intention of letting Archon retain any position of power:

He secretly commanded Docimus, if he might get to Babylon and take over the satrapy, to get rid of Archon – Arrian *Events After Alexander* 10A.3, R24.3

Perdiccas expected trouble. Archon would almost certainly not go quietly. But Perdiccas had prepared for this. If Docimus encountered resistance, then his strong army would seize control by force. Acceptance or resistance, whatever Archon's reaction his days controlling this wealthy gateway to the eastern provinces were numbered.

His orders assigned, the expeditionary force having gathered, Docimus quit the royal army and set forth for the Euphrates.

The Cypriot front

Conundrums kept on coming for Perdiccas. As he was addressing the problems of Philotas and Archon, another critical issue had materialised. Ships had reached the Cilician shoreline bearing word that another military front had opened on the large island that dominated the Eastern Mediterranean.

Throughout antiquity Cyprus' fractured political landscape ensured that it frequently became a theatre for bitter warfare. Powerful petty kings controlled vast tracts of the island, some boasting friendly relations with their neighbours, others holding bitter animosity. Certain Cypriot monarchs were more powerful than others and in 320 the strongest was King Nicocreon of Salamis, ruler of the island's north-eastern sector. For ten years, Nicocreon had enjoyed supremacy on the island. Now he decided to use the great war that was brewing between Perdiccas and Ptolemy to his advantage. He struck an alliance with the latter, building on the good relations Ptolemy had forged with him over the past years. Nicocreon acted and others followed. Less powerful Cypriot monarchs, vassals of Nicocreon, copied their overlord's actions: Pasicrates of Soli, Nicocles of Paphos and Androcles of Amathus. Others did not, retaining allegiance to Perdiccas and his regime. Soon Cyprus' most powerful figures had become sucked into this great Macedonian civil war. Fighting was quick to follow.[8]

Hoping to increase his power on the island, Nicocreon struck first. Together with his vassals, a huge armada was assembled – 200 ships. In full strength they gathered outside the stronghold of Marion and laid siege to this powerful Perdiccan-aligned city. Things looked dire for Marion and its people, but all hope was not lost. Stasioecus, the city's governor, sent out a call for aid. Ships bearing news of their difficult situation sailed across the sea to Cilicia, heading straight for Perdiccas and the royal camp. For Perdiccas it was another headache he had to deal with. Nevertheless, this was not something he could ignore. Cyprus' strategic importance in the Eastern Mediterranean was significant. Whoever controlled this island ruled the surrounding waters; whoever ruled these waters dominated maritime communication routes between Egypt and Asia Minor. Perdiccas could not allow the island to fall into enemy hands. Upon receiving word of the troubles in Cyprus, he made provisions for the rapid assemblance of a new fleet. Fortunately for him he had some of the world's best seafarers at his command. These were the Phoenicians, a people whose homeland dominated a large swathe of the Levantine shoreline.[9]

Triremes and supply ships were emptied from Phoenician shipyards and gathered for Perdiccas' Cypriot expedition. It was not long before Perdiccas had gathered this significant secondary naval force, manned by experienced Phoenician sailors and reinforced by a large number of troop transports and merchant supply ships.

The triremes, after all, formed but the naval wing of this expedition. As the troop transports indicated, this armada was also to escort an accompanying land force to the island. Once more Perdiccas was forced to siphon off part of the royal army for this Cypriot expedition: 800 mercenaries and 500 cavalry received fresh orders to prepare for fighting across the Cilician Sea. Small numbers at first glimpse, but we can presume that Perdiccas expected their number to be significantly swelled by local allied Cypriot forces. Their role, however, would be

Phoenicia (white) in the Eastern Mediterranean with four of its main maritime cities: Tyre, Sidon, Byblos and Aradus.

secondary to the fleet. The maritime strength of Nicocreon and the island's other powerful magnates made clear that the decisive showdown would occur at sea.[10]

Several seasoned *strategoi* were appointed for the expedition, each tasked with command over a certain force. Sosigenes, an admiral from the renowned maritime city of Rhodes, received command of the Phoenician navy. Meanwhile Medius, a Thessalian, was appointed leader of the mercenaries while a certain Amyntas took charge of the cavalry. All were capable leaders, appointed to lead certain segments of this combined armed force. But they also required an overall commander-in-chief. Someone to oversee the expedition on land and at sea. For this post Perdiccas required a faithful and capable adjutant. Someone in whom he could place his full trust.[11]

Aristonous was his man. Since the immediate aftermath of Alexander the Great's death this former bodyguard of Alexander had loyally served Perdiccas, remaining by the regent's side for the past three years. Now Perdiccas rewarded his ally with command of the Cypriot expedition, placing it in his capable hands. Not long after Docimus' departure Aristonous and his own expeditionary force left the royal camp, sailing away to turn the tide of the Cypriot war in Perdiccas' favour.[12]

Perdiccas could now finally focus his attention on Egypt. Logistical needs for the upcoming march were addressed. Food and water were stockpiled along the route in advance. Meanwhile Attalus' fleet would hug the Levantine Sea's eastern shoreline, provisioning the royal army as they progressed through the harsh terrain that divided Egypt from Palestine. Having addressed these issues, the royal army set off for Egypt.[13]

Docimus in Babylon

By the time Perdiccas and the army finally left Cilicia, in c. early April 320, Docimus was already well on his way toward Babylonia. The as-of-yet relatively untested commander did not know what to expect upon his arrival. How would Archon react? He soon found out.

Archon chose war. Having heard word of Docimus' upcoming arrival and the non-negotiable nature of his mission, this incumbent governor decided upon defiance. He gathered his officers, informing them of Perdiccas' provocative attempt to remove him from his position; he ordered them to gather their men and prevent Docimus from taking command of the region. Across Babylonia, Archon's soldiers prepared to resist Docimus' impending arrival from strong defensive locations. Babylonians, mercenaries and maybe even a handful of Macedonians formed the basis of Archon's intended resistance. Yet he must have known that the enemy's force was powerful – Perdiccas had anticipated the governor's hostile reaction. Perhaps lacking the quality of troops to contend with Docimus' army on the open field Archon advocated guerrilla warfare, centred around skirmishes and resistance from well-fortified bastions.[14]

Meanwhile, as Archon was laying out this strategy of resistance, Docimus and his army entered Babylonia. Thanks to Archon's actions the region brimmed with hostility, yet Docimus remained undeterred. He and his army made a beeline for Babylon, taking control of the powerful Asian metropolis which almost three years earlier had witnessed the death of Alexander and its chaotic aftermath. Babylon, the heart of Archon's magisterial power, was his. As a consequence, many Babylonians switched sides, swelling Docimus' ranks, but the fighting continued.[15]

Docimus was quick to press on, marching out to confront Archon and cut the head off the enemy snake. Perdiccas' general may have been relatively untested, but the man showed no signs of being a callow commander. In fact he proved quite the opposite, as Docimus carried out this campaign with extraordinary success. Although Archon and his men managed to fend off Docimus' assaults for a time, thanks to their position's strong defences, it was not long before their fortunes took a terrible turn. Archon's luck ran out. As he was leading a small attack on some of Docimus' troops, the governor turned resistance leader was overwhelmed and received several severe wounds. He died not long after, following in the tragic footsteps of Leonnatus and Craterus as a victim of a fierce cavalry skirmish.[16]

Archon was dead and any Babylonian resistance that remained expired with him. A triumphant Docimus returned to Babylon and commenced his rule as the region's new governor. Perdiccas had an ally in the east once more.

Cyprus

If the story of events in Babylonia was one of ultimate success for the Perdiccans, the Cypriot campaign proved more disappointing. Initially the arrival of Aristonous and his forces must have shifted the balance of power on the island back in Perdiccas' favour. The arrival of a further player, however, ensured that this superiority proved only temporary. It was Antigonus.

Reaching Cyprus at the height of 320, Antigonus' arrival dramatically shifted the balance of power yet again. He had brought with him a powerful force. His mercenaries, with him since his departure from Europe all those months before, provided Antigonus the strength for a lengthy land campaign. But it was at sea that Antigonus had the greatest power. His navy included warships from Cleitus the White's turncoat fleet, reinforced by vessels supplied by the city-states of Heraclea Pontica and Athens. Together with Nicocreon and his Cypriot allies, Antigonus now had an armada that could take on Aristonous and his own forces. Neither side was willing to cede control of the island to the other and it seems that a clash at sea followed between the two fleets. Antigonus prevailed, his Athenian and Heracliote allies later boasting of the central roles their ships had played in attaining this decisive victory. The Perdiccan fleet was crippled; Antigonus ruled the waves. Nevertheless Aristonous and his land army would keep fighting, determined to resist Antigonus' mercenary army until they received word of Perdiccas' success in Egypt. The campaign would continue.[17]

March to Pelusium

As these events around Cyprus and in Babylonia were unfolding, Perdiccas had been making good progress toward Egypt. The royal army's road to Damascus had encountered no major problems although a temporary halt at this Syrian administrative capital was necessary. Laomedon, the region's incumbent governor, had likely accompanied Ptolemy to Egypt with Alexander the Great's funeral cortège. Given Perdiccas' previous actions it is not farfetched to suggest he appointed a new governor to the province, loyal to him, before he resumed his journey to Egypt.[18]

From Damascus to Pelusium Perdiccas and the royal army marched, hugging the coast while crossing the harsh Sinai Desert and encountering no major logistical problems thanks to Attalus' accompanying fleet. By the time they reached Pelusium, the traditional gateway to Egypt for armies invading from the east, it was already May. They pitched camp close to the city. Meanwhile Attalus' fleet established itself close to the mouth of Pelusium's namesake branch of the Nile River. Perdiccas and his army had reached the borders of Egypt. They had reached the Nile. Now they had to cross it.[19]

Fortress Egypt

Map of Lower Egypt highlighting the Pelusiac Nile Branch.

Ptolemy had prepared for a defensive war. Neither at land nor at sea had the governor wished to risk a potentially suicidal pitched battle east of the Nile River. And with good reason. Both his army and navy were significantly fewer in number than Perdiccas' invasion force. His strategy had always been to build on Egypt's natural defensive strength and turn it into an impregnable fortress. Ever since arriving in the province two years earlier he had dedicated time to this task, rightly predicting that a Perdiccan attempt to remove him from this wealthy satrapy would come sooner or later.[20]

By 320 Ptolemy's Egypt had transformed into a bastion of defensive strength. Thousands of battle-hardened mercenaries were in Ptolemy's employ, funded by the province's vast treasury; potential internal troubles had been dealt with; Cyrene and large tracts of Cyprus were in allied hands. An alliance with Antipater had been agreed, to be sealed with a marriage between Ptolemy and the viceroy's daughter Eurydice at the end of hostilities. Closer to home Ptolemy had some notable supporters: Laomedon and Arrhidaeus, Perdiccas' most wanted, were within his ranks. All this was mightily impressive, but most important for Ptolemy's defensive preparations were the crucial line of strongholds that protected his eastern border. Along the length of the Pelusiac Nile branch he had either erected or improved existing fortifications. Their task: to prevent Perdiccas' army from crossing at all costs. Ptolemy's mercenaries formed the strong garrisons that resided within these forts, each of which was equipped with state-of-the-art artillery. Along the northern and western banks of the Pelusiac Nile branch these garrisoned bastions formed a powerful line, but it was not only along this waterway that Ptolemy had prepared defences. To prevent any amphibious invasion attempt from Attalus' powerful armada, more forts may have dotted Egypt's Mediterranean shoreline.[21]

The lion's share of Ptolemy's forces were located in these garrisons, strategically situated to defend important positions. As for Ptolemy, he took up position with a more mobile central army. This force would shadow Perdiccas' movements from the opposite bank, reacting to his moves and acting as a rapid response unit that could reinforce any of Ptolemy's garrisons that were attacked by Perdiccas' forces. As Ptolemy received word of Perdiccas' arrival near Pelusium, he knew that his extensive defensive preparations would soon face the ultimate test. After years of planning, the hour had finally arrived.

Perdiccas faced a considerable challenge if he were to breach Ptolemy's defences and the story goes that the omens did not offer him any comfort. Among Perdiccas' ranks was Peithagoras, a renowned diviner who had long served the Macedonian royal court. Now, as Perdiccas looked to initiate his Egyptian campaign, the regent had asked Peithagoras to conduct a ceremony and reveal what sign the state of the sacrificial animal's liver indicated. The result was far from reassuring. Three years earlier, when Alexander the Great had entered Babylon, Peithagoras had conducted a similar sacrifice and revealed a victim's liver that had no lobe. This was a terrible sign, portending disaster. It proved so. Within months Alexander had died and the age of his successors had started. Now, three years later, the chief beneficiary of Alexander's death received a no-less foreboding sign. Once more the victim's liver had no lobe; once more this seer forecast disaster for his Macedonian superior. Nevertheless, Perdiccas remained undeterred, determined to prove the divination wrong.[22]

The trial

Hoping to bolster the morale of his men on the eve of the Egyptian Campaign, Perdiccas announced a public trial. He himself would take centre stage in the proceedings, personally pressing charges against the trial's defendant. Who? None other than Ptolemy.

A message was sent across the river, inviting Ptolemy to venture to the royal camp and plead his case in front of the enemy soldiers. Ptolemy accepted the offer, perhaps agreeing to walk into the lion's den on condition that hostages be exchanged beforehand. Perdiccas agreed and his former comrade hurried over to the regent's camp for a public war of words.[23]

But why did Perdiccas do this? What did he hope to gain from this trial? And what drove Ptolemy to accept? In one word – justification. Once more Perdiccas wanted to justify to his veterans why they were embarking on this Egyptian campaign. For Ptolemy it was a case of justifying his past actions, in so doing refuting the treasonous charges he no doubt knew formed the mainstay of Perdiccas' accusatory ammunition. Both commanders had close relationships with the soldiers; both hoped to use this to help sway their martial audience to favour their argument. Their oratorical eloquence was proven – both Ptolemy and Perdiccas had delivered emphatic speeches to this audience back in Babylon years earlier. Now these two enemies would clash with their rhetoric once more in the hope of a decisive verbal victory.[24]

Perdiccas launched the assault. Many charges were laid at Ptolemy's feet. The stealing of Alexander's body, imperial ambition and blatant defiance of royal authority – presumable accusations that Perdiccas delivered against the defendant. Yet Ptolemy had prepared his defence well. Every charge Perdiccas pressed upon him he eloquently refuted, turning his opponent's charges against him and making them appear ill-founded. Perhaps he justified the stealing of Alexander's body because he intended to fulfil the dead king's wish that he be buried at Siwa in Libya? Perhaps he publicly reaffirmed his loyalty to the kings to refute the charge that he was conspiring for the kingship? Perhaps he appealed to his audience's shared nationality. Their shared past. They were all Macedonians. They had all endured the harsh conditions of Alexander the Great's campaigns. Were they really ready to fight against fellow countrymen in bloody civil war?[25]

Whatever Ptolemy's arguments, they proved very effective. By the end of the trial his words had won the clear support of his audience – much to Perdiccas' horror. The regent's popularity with the royal rank and file had led him to believe that they would support him wholeheartedly. Once more, however, these veteran soldiers had shattered that belief, emphatically hammering home how they would not cower from voicing an unpopular opinion if offered the chance. Perdiccas should have known better than to expect blind loyalty from these 'mercenary' footmen.[26]

Nevertheless, the trial's importance was limited. Ptolemy departed the camp still expecting imminent conflict. Perdiccas would carry on the war. Peithon, Seleucus, Antigenes and the rest of his officers remained supportive. His troops, not wishing to back up their thoughts with action, would follow him. Ptolemy's verbal victory was unexpected and remarkable, yet ultimately its significance was small. Within no time at all Perdiccas' plan to breach the Nile got underway.[27]

Perdiccas' forces included significant maritime strength. Already his navy had proven its logistical capability in provisioning the army for the final part of their arduous march to Egypt. Now he hoped to utilise the fleet further for the main event. He ordered his engineers to set to work dredging an old, silted up canal. Removing waste from the bottom of the waterway would allow ships from Attalus' armada to accompany the royal army as they progressed, not only aiding the army with supplies but also providing a maritime platform for assaults on Ptolemaic fortifications that covered Egypt's eastern tributaries. Perdiccas' engineers, the heirs of famous Alexandrian inventors such as Diades and Poseidonius, wasted no time constructing the riverbank contraptions needed to remove waste from the canal floor. As soon as these works were complete, the dredging commenced.[28]

Progress, however, proved short-lived. Not long after these engines began to dredge the canal they were destroyed, victims of a fast-flowing current after the river violently burst its banks and ruined the contraptions. In an instant any headway Perdiccas had made was swept away with the water. His plan had ended in total failure; morale among his officer corps was dented.[29]

Ptolemy pounced. Whether he had played a covert role in the bursting of the canal's bank is unclear, albeit possible. Regardless he was sure to take advantage of the disillusion this setback amplified among his enemy's subordinates.

Spies loyal to Ptolemy had long-infiltrated Perdiccas' army and these agents now sought to encourage disaffected enemy officers to take the ultimate leap and defect. Promises and rich rewards were offered to the most alienated of Perdiccas' subordinates. Betrayal through bribery – an all-too common military method in this period dominated by ambitious self-seeking *strategoi*.[30] It worked. As the canal dredging disaster hit home, the news of officerial defections to the enemy must have heaped insult upon injury for Perdiccas. This demoralising setback was merely the latest to be added to a litany of grievances harboured by these subordinates. Other demoralising factors must have influenced their decision to desert, none more so than the recent depressing news from the north: western Asia Minor was lost. Asander had defected; Menander had defected;

Cleitus had defected; Antipater and Craterus had crossed the Hellespont unopposed; Eumenes had been forced to retreat without a fight. Such a chain of allied setbacks only compounded the misery among Perdiccas' adjutants – figures who until recently had been assured that the Hellespont defence could stand strong indefinitely. Dissatisfaction with Perdiccas increased, focusing too on the man's arrogant and suspicious nature. It was those dissatisfied subordinates that Ptolemy's spies targeted. It was they who defected.[31]

Perdiccas was quick to react to this growing sense of disillusionment. Embracing the flexible leadership style that had served Alexander the Great so well before him, he started showing generosity to those with wavering loyalty. Keen to regain their trust he reassured them that their ultimate victory remained certain. Some were offered gifts; to others Perdiccas made extravagant promises. Perdiccas intended such magnanimity to trump any similar gestures these officers might receive from Ptolemy. It worked. Perdiccas' tactful behaviour and generosity repaired the damage, stemming the flow of defections and restoring confidence in his campaign throughout the officer corps. Like Ptolemy, at times Perdiccas had proven he could be brutal. A man of blood. But he could also be magnanimous. All depended upon the situation these generals found themselves in and how they could best resolve it. Flexibility was key.[32]

A new strategy

It was not long before a renewed sense of confidence flowed through Perdiccas' forces – a feeling greatly aided by another more recent report from Asia Minor. It had come from Eumenes. Overcoming recent setbacks Eumenes had gained a victory, decisively defeating the traitor Neoptolemus in battle. Finally, Perdiccas' allies had a success in the north! This emboldened Perdiccas. His army's morale flying high once more, he devised an ambitious new strategy to break Ptolemy's defences.[33]

He would launch a surprise attack. Ptolemy's preparations to fend off this invasion were thorough, but they were not fool proof. His garrisons paled in size and strength against Perdiccas' Macedonian veterans – several thousand strong. If Perdiccas could assault one of these garrisons and seize it quickly before his enemy knew what was happening, the result could prove decisive. He would have his vital crossing point. But launching such a surprise attack was easier said than done. Ptolemy's agents had infiltrated Perdiccas' camp, intent on hindering his plans wherever possible. If this new plan of action was to succeed, Perdiccas needed secrecy. He had to prevent word of his movements reaching Ptolemy long enough for him and his much slower force to gain enough of a head start over a shadowing enemy. He was determined to take every care to ensure its success – to ensure that word of his new plan was not relayed to his foe prematurely. No-one was informed; neither his officers nor his men knew any clear detail about Perdiccas' bold strategy.[34]

One afternoon in early June, Perdiccas put this plan into effect. He gathered his officers, ordering them to ready the men and prepare to break camp. Hoping to steal a considerable march on Ptolemy's force, Perdiccas had opted for a night march. But their destination remained a secret to everyone except Perdiccas. Carrying limited supplies, that evening the royal army departed their camp near Pelusium and headed west; Attalus and the fleet remained behind.[35]

All through the night Perdiccas' force marched, keeping close to the southern bank of the River Nile's Pelusiac branch. Men, horses and elephants kept up a fast pace for hours on end, such was Perdiccas' determination to reach his destination before the sun rose once more. He succeeded. During the night's final hours Perdiccas' army pitched camp close to the river bank, some 10km west of their set-off point. Finally, as the sun started to rise, their destination became clear.[36]

A shallow crossing was located nearby, protected by a palisaded fort that overlooked the river's opposite bank. Suddenly Perdiccas' strategy was revealed. *This* was where he intended to cross. This was where he aimed to strike the decisive blow.

The fort itself was called 'The Camel Fort'. A strong surrounding wooden palisade topped with a parapet formed its central defence, the nearest side of which was situated metres from the waterway. If the Perdiccan army was to cross here, they *had* to take the fort. It could not be bypassed.[37]

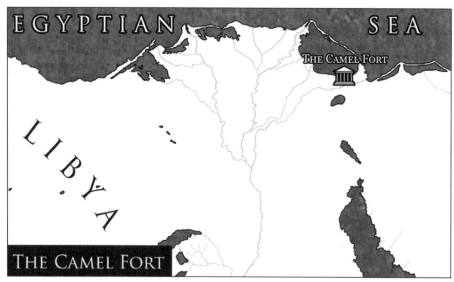

An approximate location of the Camel Fort. The fort must have been c.10–15km from Perdiccas' camp near Pelusium.

Perdiccas wasted little time. Ptolemy's arrival was a matter of when, not if. It would not take long for Perdiccas' opponent to make up the distance and arrive at the fort with his more mobile force, when he inevitably discovered that his enemy had stolen this considerable march on him. Perdiccas had planned for a surprise attack. So far, his strategy had worked; Ptolemy was nowhere in sight. But he had to move quickly. There was still the garrison to take care of.

The attack commenced at daybreak – roughly 5 a.m. Fatigue must have gripped many of the attacking soldiers, barely rested from their recent night march. Time, however, was of the essence if Perdiccas' strategy was to succeed without a hitch. Quickly the soldiers chosen to assault the fort formed up and prepared to ford the Nile.[38]

In first went the elephants, light infantry presumably advancing with them to offer the large beasts the necessary protection from the fort's defenders as they proceeded to clear a path to the palisade. Behind them came the Silver Shields, Alexander the Great's veteran shield bearers wielding spear and shield. They were the best assault infantry in the known world – seasoned stormers of powerful fortifications such as Isaura, Halicarnassus, Tyre and the countless rock fortresses of the distant east filled their ranks. Bearing ladders, it was these expert defence-takers that were going to assault the Fort's walls. For any defending mercenary it was a frightening sight, the gleaming of their enemy's silver armour giving them no doubt which legendary unit they were about to fight. As they had done with the elephants, archers and other light infantry covered the hypaspists' advance, once again shooting arrows and aiming other projectiles. 'Covering fire' to try and keep enemy heads down.[39]

Behind the infantry and forming the rear of the assault force was an elite cavalry squadron. These horsemen would struggle to storm the Fort directly, but Perdiccas had a different purpose for them. Consisting of some of the finest cavalrymen in the empire, this skilled squadron was to form a human blockade between the fort and the expected direction of Ptolemy's hurrying relief force. The quality of these horsemen reassured Perdiccas that this squadron would prove more than a match for fending off his foe.[40]

Perdiccas had been quick to initiate the assault. He had devised a careful strategy to counter his enemy's expected arrival. But it was not quick enough.

As the assault party started to cross the Nile, Ptolemy's mounted force came into view on the opposite bank. The governor had been caught off-guard by Perdiccas' surprise night march, but he had reacted with utmost haste as soon as he learned of his enemy's movements. By the time Ptolemy and his small force had reached the Fort the attackers were still fording the Nile – barely halfway across. The fort's gates were opened and Ptolemy's relief threw themselves inside. A psychological victory for the defenders. Loud trumpet calls and shouts reverberated across the river, putting Perdiccas and the attackers in no doubt that Ptolemy had arrived. The element of surprise had evaporated.[41]

Perdiccas was forced to adapt. The cavalry's mission, now null and void, was abandoned. Still the assault would continue. Ptolemy's arrival was unwelcome, but not disastrous. His reinforcing troops must have been relatively few in number and the impact of their arrival on Perdiccas' assaulting troops morale had proven negligible. Perdiccas' Macedonian veterans pressed on – 'nothing daunted'. They had survived the storming of countless powerful strongholds throughout their long military careers, overcoming much greater odds than those Ptolemy's forces appeared to pose on the Nile's northern bank this early morning of June 320. Boldly they continued the advance alongside the elephants and light infantry.[42]

The assault force completed the river crossing without problem and soon both men and beasts were positioned on the small stretch of shoreline outside the palisade, ready to attack. The Silver Shields placed their ladders in position and started to ascend; light infantry targeted defenders who dared raise their heads above the parapet; the elephants acted as battering rams, intent on tearing down another stretch of wall with their tusks. The multi-pronged assault was a fierce proposition for those guarding the fort. The combination of fending off mighty Indian war elephants, combined with the thought of fighting hand to hand with the world's most renowned assault infantry, must have been terrifying.[43]

'Cometh the hour. Cometh the man.' Ptolemy knew he needed to inspire his defenders and harden their resolve. And what better method than an act of fearless conspicuous leadership, worthy of Alexander the Great. In full view of his leading adjutants and many of the defenders, Ptolemy leapt up onto the parapet in full view of the enemy soldiers in his elaborate armour. Grabbing a pike and positioning himself above the front Indian elephant and its 'mahout' (driver):

> *...he put out the eyes of the leading elephant and wounded the mahout mounted on it, and then he turned to those who were climbing up the ladders. Disdainfully he struck at them and sent them tumbling down into the river in their armour, sorely wounded.* – Diodorus 18.34.2

So Diodorus tells us. Through this remarkable and risky Homeric tale of heroism Ptolemy filled his defenders with renewed vigour to counter Perdiccas' attacking forces. It certainly was a great story for later writers to relay about the clash, but would this have actually happened? Elements of fiction in the story seem certain.[44] Ptolemy's standing atop the bulwarks, pike in hand and in full conspicuous view of enemy sharpshooters. His subsequent skewering of the elephant's eyes single-handedly. These events seem fantastical in their nature. Nevertheless, despite this fictional Homeric colouring, we similarly have no reason to doubt that the story has its basis in truth. Just as Alexander the Great and many other prominent Macedonian generals had done before him, Ptolemy did inspire his men at the Camel Fort by leading from the front and fighting in the midst of the vicious battle for the walls alongside mercenaries, friends and officers alike. Though he probably did not personally blind the lead elephant in such a show of splendid bravery, Ptolemy's charismatic leadership did embolden his soldiers to emerge from behind their bulwarks and oppose the beasts below. Our surviving sources may exaggerate Ptolemy's heroism in the defence, but let this not conceal the charismatic leadership he evidently showed during this intense fight.[45]

Meanwhile, elsewhere along the wall, a vicious melee had erupted between the Silver Shields and the defenders. Establishing a small 'bridgehead' at the top of their ladders these veteran soldiers refused to give up. They shared Perdiccas' determination to take the fort, embracing years of experience to maintain discipline during the attack and assault the stronghold in relays. As the fight for the wall continued Perdiccas himself had crossed the river, following in Ptolemy's footsteps and inspiring his soldiers onward in the assault. Fatigue increased on either side, but the unbending resolve of both generals ensured the fighting continued. The Silver Shields gave Perdiccas everything they had for hours on end, but they came up against an equally determined defence. Embracing a 'last stand' mentality, Ptolemy continued to inspire his men to oppose the attackers with all they could – a gargantuan effort. He fought 'like a hero', knowing the high price defeat would cost him. If Ptolemy was to maintain his rule over Egypt his men *had* to win at the Camel Fort. If they faltered and the fort was lost, Ptolemy's defence line would be irreversibly punctured. Perdiccas' troops would cross the vital eastern branch of the Nile and the royal army, jubilant in their success, would press on to complete the conquest of Egypt.[46]

Both Perdiccas and Ptolemy realised the strategic importance of the Fort. Both were loath to give in and offer the other victory. This reciprocal refusal to give in brought a bloody consequence:

Thanks to the incredible determination of these two generals there was severe loss of life on both sides, because Ptolemy's men had the advantage of height, while Perdiccas had superior numbers. – Diodorus 18.34.5

Soon, dead Macedonians and mercenaries littered the Camel Fort's parapet and the tiny stretch of land below.

From daybreak to nightfall on this long summer's day, the fighting continued. For an age dominated by short but violent clashes its length was extraordinary. Such was the determination of Ptolemy and Perdiccas to see their forces triumph. Finally, the coming of night brought a conclusion to the fighting. Perdiccas ordered his exhausted soldiers back across the river, realising that further effort was futile for the time being. The Camel Fort had held; the heroic effort of Ptolemy and his solders had stood firm against the best their enemy could throw at them. At least for now.[47]

Rest and persistence, following a day of fierce fighting, would seem to be Perdiccas' two greatest allies. Many of his soldiers had been deprived of sleep for more than a day. Once rested up, these troops could try again. Precedents such as storming the stronghold of Isaura stressed the advantages of persisting with the siege and whittling away their foe over several days. But Perdiccas, for whatever reason, believed differently. As the sun rose the next morning, Ptolemy and his men looked out across the waterway to see Perdiccas' royal army marching away. Rather than persist with the siege Perdiccas had opted to pursue a new plan of action.[48]

March to Memphis

Having broken camp at the dead of night the royal army and its entourage headed south. For a few weeks they marched, traversing the c.200km distance between the Camel Fort and Memphis, the traditional Egyptian capital. Perdiccas had a plan. Reports had informed him of advantageous topography that could benefit any attacking army looking to conquer this city from across the Nile. Directly to the east of Memphis, a large island capable of accommodating and offering security to his sizable army divided the River in two. What was more, no fort protected this point in the Nile. Presumably Ptolemy had considered it too far upriver for the island to be in need of physical defences. Perdiccas had a lifeline. If he could cross his army to this island, then the road to Memphis, his ultimate goal, would lie open. And what a prize awaited him within the city. It was there that Ptolemy had elaborately interred Alexander the Great's body.[49]

Memphis was within sight for Perdiccas. With supplies running low he had to make his move quickly. Reaching the island would be no easy task however. Ptolemy had avoided placing defences there for good reason. This was not a natural crossing point, especially for a heavily-armed military force. The Nile was much deeper here than it had been at the Camel Fort further downriver. The current, too, was significantly stronger – so much so that any attempt to cross would prove a perilous venture without proper preparation. Perdiccas' plan was risky, but just about possible. Succeed and the rewards would be great,

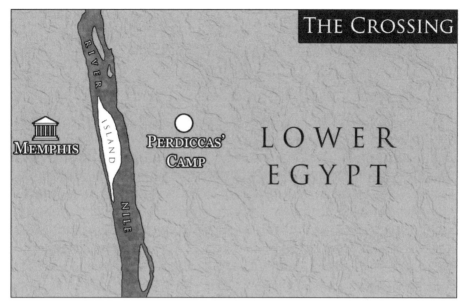

A rough map highlighting the position of Memphis, Perdiccas' army and the large island, according to the account of Diodorus Siculus. The large island (highlighted) was situated directly east of Memphis.

successfully turning Ptolemy's well-prepared Nile defences and striking at the heart of his foe's influence. Following in Alexander's footsteps, if this risky plan paid off it would be a masterstroke. If....[50]

The crossing

Not long after reaching the Nile's eastern bank opposite the island, Perdiccas ordered the crossing to commence. His Macedonians remained loyal and once again formed the invaluable vanguard of this venture. They waded into the river, embarking on a crossing very different to the one they had accomplished two weeks earlier:

> *The water came up to their chins, and its buffeting of their bodies as they crossed threatened to knock them off their feet, especially since they were hampered by their arms and armour.* – Diodorus 18.34.7

The Nile's strong current, combined with its depth, made the crossing particularly arduous for the soldiers. Perdiccas needed to address this issue. The quicker his army completed the crossing the better. Fortunately for him, his past mentor offered him a perfect precedent.

Alexander the Great had proven no stranger to overcoming mighty river obstacles. From the Jaxartes to the Hydaspes, the Macedonian king had seen his men succeed in crossing some truly wretched waterways. His solutions were varied but for Perdiccas there was one method Alexander used that seemed particularly relevant for the current crossing.[51]

Alexander and the Tigris

Eleven years earlier, Alexander the Great and his army had reached the unguarded western bank of the Tigris, a river that was both deep and fast-flowing.

The Roman historian Curtius recalled:

> *...Alexander sent a few cavalrymen ahead to attempt a crossing of the river (Tigris). At the start the water level reached the top part of the horses' chest; then, at mid-channel, it came up to their necks, and it is a fact that no other eastern river moves with such violence, receiving as it does the waters of many torrents and actually sweeping rocks along.* – Curtius 4.9.15–16

Certainly the Tigris' swift flow was highly dangerous for any traversing army. Alexander however, determined to cross, had quickly devised an effective solution. North and south of his intended crossing point he placed a line of horsemen in the river. The horsemen upriver slowed the current, while those positioned downriver formed a barrier to collect infantrymen that had either lost their footing on the slippery rocks or had been swept off their feet by the current as they crossed. The strategy worked. Alexander's infantry successfully crossed the potentially perilous Tigris, flanked by their cavalry barriers. The Tigris had been overcome.[52]

'One-upping Alexander'

The Tigris episode's parallels to Perdiccas' current predicament seemed obvious: the Nile's significant depth, the strong current and the lack of enemy defences. So he decided to recreate Alexander's Tigris solution. In fact, he went one better.[53]

Emulating Alexander, Perdiccas placed a line of cavalry downriver, their purpose to catch any soldiers that lost their footing during the crossing. Upriver, however, Perdiccas innovated. To stem the current's flow, he did not intend to use a similar line of horses. He wanted his largest animals. His elephants.[54]

As the powerful ungulate shield took linear shape north and south of the crossing, Perdiccas' mood must have turned from one of concern to elation. The water level started to fall; the current was easing. Perdiccas' men took full advantage. Hundreds completed the crossing without issue. Before long more than 2,000 veteran troops had reached the island and formed a powerful vanguard contingent. The plan was working.[55]

But something was wrong. Gradually, as the first wave of soldiers successfully reached the island, the water's subdued nature started to reverse. Once more the Nile's depth began to increase; once more the current crept toward becoming a lethal obstacle. Elephants and horses remained in position. The shield had not faltered but no longer was it effectively stemming the Nile's fast flow.

For no apparent reason, the river had become far deeper and, with their bodies completely submerged, the men were little short of helpless. – Diodorus 18.35.2

Perdiccas, his officers and soldiers were stunned. Why was this happening? Had a wave of extra rainfall upstream caused it? The sudden change suggested no. Was Ptolemy somehow at work, his subordinates having deviously unblocked a silted-up canal further upriver? Once again, the answer was no.[56]

The reason lay much closer to the royal army.

Perdiccas had hoped that by placing his elephants north of the crossing he would go one further than his military mentor Alexander at the Tigris. He had believed that these powerful beasts would prove more effective at blocking the current. To an extent this was true. There was logic in his thinking. What Perdiccas hadn't taken into account, however, was the elephants' heavy weight. This helped bring about an unexpected terrible side effect below the surface.

Sand covered the bottom of the Nile, easily displaced when disturbed. So as the elephants had started to take up their positions in this beast barrier, as they began to dig their feet into the river floor, combined with the thousands of armour-clad infantrymen wading through the water, gradually this sediment had started to shift. Slowly the Nile's sandy layer began to ebb away and be carried downstream. As it did, gradually the base of the river began to get deeper and deeper. The subaqueous ground seemed to be sinking around the soldiers' eyes much to their and Perdiccas' despair, its cause unknown. Soon so much sand had been displaced that those soldiers still in the midst of crossing found their bodies completely submerged. So high was the water level, that they were soon forced to carry their arms, armour and provisions above their head. Still the Nile continued to deepen – the soldiers and animals proving the unintended central culprits in this calamity.[57]

The writing was on the wall. Completing the crossing quickly turned from just being merely hazardous to near-suicidal for Perdiccas' soldiers. Not long before Perdiccas had been in a jubilant mood, seeing his strategy seemingly bearing fruit: a breakthrough! Now he panicked. Unable to perform further crossings his army was divided. More than 2,000 of his best soldiers had reached the island along with their officers. Make no mistake, this was a strong, disciplined forward contingent – capable of holding its own against enemy attacks until Perdiccas and his officers devised a solution to the current issue. So long as Perdiccas did not order anything rash there was still time to resolve the current crisis.[58] Ptolemy refused to give him any. The man was a master of exploiting weakness. If he were to survive this invasion, he had to seize every opportunity Perdiccas presented him with. So when he received news of his enemy's current predicament near Memphis, he pounced.

The ruse

As Perdiccas and his officers were contemplating a solution to the current crossing fiasco, hearts dropped. A huge dust cloud had appeared on the horizon beyond the opposite bank. It was Ptolemy, the opaque natural screen indicating that a large body of enemy troopers were accompanying him on a rapid dash towards the island. The size of this force was unclear, but the sheer scale of the accompanying dust cloud was enough to strike grave concern into Perdiccas. Should he risk leaving his valuable Macedonian vanguard, isolated on the island, to face what looked like a giant enemy force on their own? Ptolemy's timely arrival with unprecedented manpower forced Perdiccas to make a quick decision.[59]

Looks, however, can be deceiving. Ptolemy's dust cloud was not what it seemed. Its size indicated that a large mass of men and horses were heading for the Nile. But this threat was a chimera. It was a ruse.

Ptolemy's army was nowhere near as powerful as the dust cloud suggested. In actual fact, his approaching force was relatively small. Its chances of success against Perdiccas in the open field were close to zero. Even against Perdiccas' isolated island force, the likelihood of Ptolemy winning a pitched battle against these hardened veterans looked slim. Ptolemy was therefore desperate to avoid fighting his foe on the open field, and yet if Perdiccas successfully completed his crossing near Memphis such a scenario would seemingly become all but inevitable. He had to somehow panic Perdiccas into a disastrous mistake. So he designed this ruse. Far away from the Memphis crossing Ptolemy gathered his army's baggage, along with a bizarre mixture of domestic animals: goats, swine and oxen. Possessions, supplies and equipment were tied to these animal auxiliaries – laid down behind the beasts of burden to be dragged along the dusty floor. Then, once preparations were ready, a group of herdsmen and horsemen started driving the animals forward, towards the Nile. The result was extraordinary.[60]

The amount of dust the animals raised from the ground was huge, evoking an approaching horde of men and horses to any viewing this spectacle from a distance. Ptolemy had created a phantom army. Its effect was instant.

Perdiccas panicked. Seeing this huge dust cloud in the distance, he fell for Ptolemy's ruse. In his mind a large enemy army was coming with enough force to overwhelm his soldiers on the island – a huge moral victory in the making for his enemies. This Perdiccas could not allow, but what could he do? He couldn't send men to their support – by then the Nile was more treacherous than ever. Unless he ordered something drastic quickly, he believed 2,000 of his best soldiers would be exposed to an overwhelming attack. Having fallen completely for Ptolemy's ruse Perdiccas decided upon a drastic course of action. It was unpopular. It was rash. It would almost certainly end in significant loss of life. But Perdiccas believed he had no choice.[61]

Orders were shouted across to the islanders that they return to the Nile's eastern bank. Buglers and signallers confirmed the order to the vanguard's officers, affirming Perdiccas' drastic decision that they make a second perilous crossing of the Nile with haste. Quickly these officers relayed Perdiccas' instructions to their men as they prepared to cross the dangerous waterway once more. Many of these men had overcome various natural challenges before then. Some had crossed the ambush-ridden passes of the Zagros Mountains, the harsh hinterlands of Bactria and Sogdia, the Hindu Kush, the Indus Valley and the Gedrosian Desert. Now these stranded men faced their latest geographic challenge: a return journey across the deep, fast-flowing Nile River. Clasping their arms and armour the Macedonians plunged into the water.[62]

Perdiccas expected to lose men in this return crossing, but he could not have anticipated its terrible scale. In front of his eyes he watched on as hundreds of his armoured soldiers were swallowed up by the river, never to raise their heads above water again. Of those who managed to avoid drowning, some of the better swimmers did complete the crossing, having sacrificed much of their equipment. The rest were not so fortunate. Carried away by the current, some were washed up half-dead on Ptolemy's side of the river. Others experienced a much more gruesome end:

> ….*most of them were carried a long way downstream and were eaten by river-dwelling creatures.* – Diodorus 18.35.6

Crocodiles devoured these soldiers – a horrific sight for their comrades watching on haplessly from the eastern bank. It was a terrible end for these prestigious soldiers. They had served with Alexander the Great. They had survived numerous hard-fought battles, faced off against many frightening foes and journeyed to the edges of the known world, only now to be eaten alive by the carnivorous creatures of the Nile. All thanks to a terrible decision taken by Perdiccas, the general they had trusted with their lives.[63]

By the time Perdiccas' disastrous retreat order had been carried through more than 2,000 of his soldiers had lost their lives: drowned or devoured.

Macedonian veterans, combined with a handful of their officers, formed a significant portion of the casualties. The death total resembled a disastrous military defeat. Perdiccas had sent his soldiers into battle against the Nile and lost decisively. To add insult to injury it must have been then that the true size of Ptolemy's force became apparent, as his small army arrived at the opposite bank to mop up Perdiccas' stranded, washed up soldiers. Ptolemy's ruse had worked superbly. Perdiccas was back to square one. His army was still not across the Nile. They had lost 2,000 men and achieved nothing in return. Ptolemy had duped Perdiccas into making one of the most catastrophic tactical errors in the whole of antiquity.[64]

Retribution

Anger swept through Perdiccas' camp. The regent's actions and their consequences at the river had caused the deaths of hundreds of their comrades. And for what? Absolutely nothing. Violent rage erupted among the Macedonian veterans still in Perdiccas' employ. Twelve months earlier these soldiers had lauded Perdiccas' name, bathing in the afterglow of his successive, spoil-filled victories in Asia Minor. But now things were different. This morale-crushing defeat against the Nile proved the decisive trigger that turned Macedonian opinion against Perdiccas. The veteran soldiers had remained loyal to him after Ptolemy successfully acquitted himself at the show trial; they had remained loyal to him after the failure to dredge the canal; they had still believed in him after their setback at the Camel Fort. But Perdiccas' self-inflicted catastrophe near Memphis was one failure too far. In their long history of service these veteran soldiers had never witnessed such an abject series of failures. All their comrades who had perished for Perdiccas on his Egyptian vendetta against Ptolemy had died for nothing. What was more, they could not retrieve the bodies of many of these dead soldiers. They could not fulfil the all-important burial rites. Only the blood of those who had been devoured by the river-dwelling creatures downriver remained visible in the Nile. This lack of material remains only magnified the horrific death these men had suffered, further incensing the veterans' desire for vengeance against Perdiccas. Once more Ptolemy sensed opportunity.[65]

The bodies of many of Perdiccas' Macedonians who had lost their lives in the terrible river crossing had been devoured by Nile Crocodiles, but not all. The corpses of some drowned individuals remained intact, having been washed up on the river's western bank.

These waterlogged bodies required burial rites – a task every soldier expected their commanding officer to oversee. The political power of this process was highly significant; whoever oversaw the burial rites for these soldiers could claim victory over his enemy. Ptolemy, once again, pounced. Quickly he collected the washed-up corpses and took them to his camp. A public funeral for these fallen soldiers was arranged, presumably in full view of Perdiccas' camp across the river. Ptolemy oversaw the honorific cremation of the bodies, providing each fallen soldier the honours worthy of a proper funeral. To hammer home his 'generosity' Ptolemy then had these remains ferried across the river to friends and family of the fallen. He was returning the enemy's war dead.[66] A generous act indeed, though no doubt one Ptolemy primarily did for a political purpose. Once again, his success further emphasised Perdiccas' failings as a leader. Forced to depend upon Ptolemy's generosity to receive these cremated remains, it hammered home Perdiccas' inability to provide the same rites. Ptolemy's action sent a very clear message to Perdiccas' soldiers: it was only thanks to him that they had received the remains of fallen friends. Once more it highlighted Perdiccas' failings.[67] Ptolemy symbolised victory; Perdiccas represented defeat:

> ...the more the Macedonians on Perdiccas' side became disaffected with him, the more they were inclined to give their allegiance to Ptolemy. – Diodorus 18.36.2

Finally, after what must have seemed an age for Perdiccas, night descended. At the start of the day he had been confident in his ambitious plan, backed by officers and soldiers that were willing to do his bidding and ensure the success of the crossing. How things had changed. As the sun set, lamentations seized the royal camp. The soldiers mourned the tragic demise of their fallen comrades, keen to heap the blame high upon Perdiccas with loud shouts and curses. They refused to hide their rage. Perdiccas' popularity with the Macedonian rank and file had reached its lowest, but it was not just among the infantry that this hatred festered.[68]

Many of Perdiccas' officers had always considered their superior an arrogant man. Nevertheless over the years most had remained loyal, convinced that their best chance of future prominence in this new world order depended upon siding with the all-powerful Perdiccas and gaining his favour. This loyalty, however, was conditional on success. It depended upon the officers remaining confident that they were siding with the victor – a winning general whose success would best serve their own interests. This conditional loyalty affected ambitious subordinates across the empire, but at this moment in time it was particularly prevalent among the upper echelons of Perdiccas' officer corps. Deep unconditional allegiance to Perdiccas was non-existent.[69]

It was then, as Perdiccas' fortunes crumbled in the wake of this terrible disaster, that this unspoken oath of conditional loyalty reared its ugly head.

Similar to what had happened weeks earlier at Pelusium, senior defections to Ptolemy were considered – the latter's agents once more orchestrating potential betrayal. Again, it did not take long for Perdiccas to discover that this treasonous inclination had returned. In the past he had carefully resolved the crisis through courteous actions: reassurance, gifts and kind words. This time however, he took a very different approach. Such a diplomatic response was far from Perdiccas' mind. Enraged, he treated any who were inclined to defect severely. Blasting his adjutants once more he revealed his infamous arrogance, presumably highlighting his close relationship with Alexander the Great that no-one south of Asia Minor could rival. It was not a clever move, only deepening the resentment and hatred Perdiccas' lieutenants were rapidly developing for their leader. Perdiccas departed but the issue was far from resolved. The night was still young.[70]

All across the camp the unending shouts and curses of the Macedonian rank and file confirmed to their seniors how widespread the dissatisfaction with Perdiccas was. In the dead of night, roughly 100 of these officers met to decide what they should do. It was no insignificant gathering. At its head was Peithon, the illustrious former bodyguard of Alexander the Great who had ventured from Babylon to Bactria to Asia Minor to Egypt over the past three years. He held more status – possessed more prestige – than any other subordinate still in Perdiccas' camp. If Peithon was conducting this meeting to decide their commander's fate, this was serious.[71]

Peithon's presence was emphatic, but he was not the only senior subordinate present at the gathering. Other notable figures stood among the crowd. Antigenes, veteran commander of the elite Silver Shields, had lost faith in Perdiccas' cause. So too had Seleucus. Since the days of Babylon the latter had loyally accompanied Perdiccas, serving as the regent's second in command. But, like the other officers, the strength of Seleucus' allegiance was conditional. His loyalty to Perdiccas ultimately depended upon Perdiccas' continued success. And now, with that success floundering, Seleucus too had decided to cross the floor and join this covert gathering of dissident officers. Angered by Perdiccas' behaviour, distressed by his catastrophic failure to cross the Nile and emboldened by the soldiers' open hostility towards him, the officers soon opted to take the next drastic step: mutiny.[72]

That same night a small band of commanders made their way through the camp towards Perdiccas' tent – Peithon at their head. A group of Macedonian troopers had swelled their ranks, united in mutiny. Once the nucleus of Perdiccas' support, now even these esteemed cavalrymen had decided to abandon the regent to his fate. Having encountered no resistance Peithon, Seleucus, Antigenes and several others entered Perdiccas' tent – intent on a dreadful deed.[73]

Three years earlier Perdiccas had survived an assassination attempt by the skin of his teeth, using his eloquent speech to scare off a death squad and spare himself execution. There would be no escape this time, however. Resolved to their treachery, Antigenes took out his sword and dealt the first blow. Peithon, Seleucus and the rest followed suit landing deadly strikes against Perdiccas. Before long, all that remained of Perdiccas was a punctured corpse.

So Perdiccas lost both his leadership and his life, after having been at the helm for three years. – Diodorus 18.36.7

Perdiccas was dead. Throughout his extraordinary career, this general had regularly proven his Alexander-like character and his exceptional ability to command on the battlefield. His rise to becoming Alexander the Great's second in command was no mere accident.[74]

For three years following Alexander's death, he had dominated, crushing revolts, controlling dissident subordinates, gaining victories and even making an ambitious play for the throne. In the end, however, a decline in political and military fortunes, combined with his ruling over an unstable empire dominated by such a multitude of ambitious men and women keen to see his fall, culminated in his demise near the Nile's eastern bank.

The 'great war' had resulted in the deaths of two major figures. Both Craterus and Perdiccas had met their end during the struggle. Of the 'big three' at the start of the conflict, only the elderly Antipater remained alive. Alexander's leading adjutants had fallen. More peripheral generals and statesmen could now exploit this power vacuum and assume prominent positions in an imperial reshuffle.

Chapter 16

The Aftermath

Perdiccas' allies	Ptolemy's allies
Alcetas	King Philip Arrhidaeus III
Atalante	Peithon
Attalus	Arrhidaeus (the general)
Eumenes	Seleucus
Pharnabazus	Antigenes
Polemon	Antigonus
Docimus	Antipater
Aristonous	Dionysius of Heraclea
Phoenix	Polemaeus
Sosigenes	
Medius of Larissa	

News was quick to reach Ptolemy of Perdiccas' demise. It was expected. Ptolemy had played his part in the assassination, albeit from afar. Just as he had before at Pelusium, once again he had used his infiltrated agents to communicate messages between himself and dissident enemy officers. One officer in particular had been central to Ptolemy's dealings.[1]

Of all Perdiccas' adjutants few, if any, could rival the illustrious and valiant reputation of Peithon. This former bodyguard of Alexander the Great had benefitted from Perdiccas' rise: governorship over wealthy Media, a significant military command in the east and a high position at the heart of the new regime upon his return. But with Perdiccas' fortunes in Egypt running low and Peithon's selfish desire to side with a winner, he too had considered defection.

Still the man's decision to mutiny could not be guaranteed without added incentives. He required a bribe if he were to defect – a significant one at that. Peithon knew his worth. His high standing within the army would give any mutiny validity. Ptolemy knew it too, so to convince Peithon to take the all-important step and lead the officerial rising against Perdiccas, he had offered this potential turncoat an attractive offer. Taking advantage of Peithon's self-centred ambitious nature, Ptolemy's agents relayed assurances that he would receive a prominent position in the new imperial order, that was bound to emerge after Perdiccas' demise.[2]

Peithon was convinced. Believing betrayal would best suit his own fortunes he threw away his past allegiance to Perdiccas and agreed to defect, going on to lead the mutiny later that night which culminated in Perdiccas' killing. Peithon and his comrades had murdered Perdiccas, but Ptolemy's role in orchestrating this infamous act was vital. The Perdiccan turncoats had simply done his dirty work for him.

Tying up loose ends

Perdiccas was dead; Ptolemy was alive. The latter had won the great duel that had waged between them on and off the battlefield for years. But the crisis was far from over for Ptolemy. The royal army remained in Egypt and he was now very much in Peithon's debt. Several issues still had to be resolved.

The next day Ptolemy crossed over the Nile, a train of provisions and an entourage of officers accompanying his ride to the enemy camp. No resistance greeted his arrival, as he proceeded past any defences to the base's royal heart. His first duty was to visit the two monarchs: Philip Arrhidaeus III and the infant Alexander IV. Gifts were bestowed upon both of them, Ptolemy taking all measures to show great respect for his official overlords. Once more Ptolemy was tackling Perdiccas' past verbal accusations against him head on. He was desperate to show that he was not attempting to assume the kingship but was in fact a dutiful and loyal subject. Hostile criticism that he was a traitor, these acts emphasised, was unfounded. Untrue.[3]

Actions speak louder than words and it may well have been during this initial audience that Ptolemy went one step further to emphasise his loyalty to the kings. He vowed to honour Philip III in a new sanctuary, still visible today within the Temple of Karnak. For Ptolemy, publicly showing his allegiance to the kings was the first of several vital tasks he needed to fulfil at the royal camp, dramatically refuting past Perdiccan smears that he had any desire to seize the kingship from the two monarchs. It worked. Having showered the two regal figureheads with honours, Ptolemy turned his attention to the real power-holders within the camp.[4]

Later that day a crowd of senior officers piled into a secluded, agreed meeting place to determine what was to happen next. Ptolemy was present, as was Peithon, Seleucus and the rest of the conspirators. Several of Ptolemy's high-standing subordinates also stood by their general's side: Laomedon and Arrhidaeus among them. Days before many of these figures had been in open arms against one

Philip III as pharaoh on a relief in Karnak. Ptolemy may have built this sanctuary after defeating Perdiccas.

another. Now they came together in this council of conspirators to decide the fate of the empire once more. With Perdiccas' death, the Babylon Settlement that many of these figures had personally agreed upon three years earlier was null and void. This 'Nile Settlement' would rectify the problem, at least until a more permanent arrangement could be agreed with Antipater.[5]

Just as at Babylon, the question of custodianship over the monarchy dominated the meeting. Perdiccas was dead. Who was to become *prostates* – the new regent – in the dead man's place? Despite being the man of the moment, Ptolemy did not want the position. Leaving Egypt in another's hands to march away with the royal army and lead a rather 'nomadic' lifestyle for the next several years sorting out imperial loose ends was not his intention. Besides, assuming such a position in this unstable world was filled with risk, bound to put the holder on a collision course with other senior figures in the empire. For Ptolemy, the constant troubles Perdiccas had faced highlighted how the office of regent could be a poisoned chalice. Ptolemy's future lay in Egypt. So if not Ptolemy, who was to assume this senior position?[6]

Others at the council were more willing to take on the risks the regency had to offer. Despite its inherent risks, Perdiccas had proven how powerful a figure holding this position could become if this authority fell into the hands of one ambitious person. Ptolemy knew full well that this council of conspirators was filled with such figures. So he proposed a radical alternative: a *du-prostates*. A two-man regency.

Addressing the council Ptolemy announced his suggestion, along with the two candidates he proposed for the positions: Peithon and Arrhidaeus.[7]

Ptolemy had little choice in proposing the former. Peithon's high-standing, his ambition and his leading role in Perdiccas' downfall had ensured that he could not be ignored. *This* was his reward for agreeing to betray Perdiccas. Nevertheless Ptolemy did not want Peithon to potentially become the next all-powerful regent – the new Perdiccas. This must have been one of Ptolemy's chief fears and it may well have been to prevent this ambitious officer assuming such a powerful position that Ptolemy advocated a joint regency.[8]

Arrhidaeus appears a clear counter to Peithon. He was a man of proven loyalty to Ptolemy, having fought for him against Perdiccas during the previous campaign. He would serve as Ptolemy's man at the heart of the royal government. At least for the time being. Further talks with Antipater and Craterus were yet to be arranged. Until then, at least, Peithon and Arrhidaeus would assume leading positions within the empire.

As all this was agreed, those in the council remained strikingly silent on one issue. What about Alexander's body? What of this highly symbolic corpse, the target of Ptolemy's successful heist and Perdiccas' failed invasion. Any requests for it going to Macedon, by kings or commanders, were thrown out. Alexander's body would remain in Egypt, far away from the royal tombs at Aegae and far away from Siwa. It belonged to Ptolemy.[9]

The commander's conclave dispersed, signalling to the awaiting soldiers that its members had reached agreement and now sought their seal of approval for this new imperial settlement. Quickly the soldiers gathered for this public assembly, eager to hear Ptolemy speak. Vivid memories of the Nile catastrophe remained among the Macedonian audience; great hatred towards the recently deceased Perdiccas lingered. For Ptolemy, with animosity toward his dead enemy still high, this was the perfect time to clear his name and justify his actions to the rank and file.[10]

As acting head of the royal army, Peithon paved the way for Ptolemy to speak and the audience's former enemy stood up to address the crowd. Mobilising his eloquent words once more he honoured the Macedonian soldiers, at the same time justifying his past actions against them during the conflict. It was after all, many of the men in this audience that Ptolemy and his fellow defenders had desperately fought against in the bitter day-long battle at the Camel Fort weeks earlier. At the same time Ptolemy directly addressed those adjutants who had been close friends of Perdiccas: senior figures who had not joined the mutiny. Large Perdiccan armies and navies remained dotted around the Eastern Mediterranean: the forces of Alcetas, Aristonous, Attalus, Docimus and Eumenes for instance. Hoping to strike a deal with the powerful Perdiccan forces that remained, Ptolemy reassured those present that they would not suffer retribution. It was time to end this civil war, Ptolemy stressed, a notion that presumably went down well with the Macedonian rank and file.[11]

Ptolemy did not stop there. Supplies in the royal camp were running low, something he and his bountiful grain reserves could exploit to garner further support. Having justified his actions, he promised the army ample provisions of grain, alleviating them of their current food shortage. Cheers erupted throughout the assembly. Ptolemy had addressed the most basic, but most important of needs for an army on campaign. His provision promise made him a saviour in his audience's eyes – the man who would ensure they stave off starvation and experience an end to recent hardships.[12]

All across his audience Ptolemy's popularity was clear to see. The governor had successfully cleared his name and won the Macedonian veterans' support. Now he turned his attention to the conclave's decisions, intent on getting the soldiers' stamp of approval.

Three years earlier at Babylon, Ptolemy had left a similar conclave, having seemingly agreed to the plan of action Perdiccas had proposed for the empire. As soon as he had noticed the hostile reception to Perdiccas' proposal in the subsequent soldier assembly, however, he changed his mind. He went back on his word and proposed his own radical solution, sowing the seeds for his great rivalry with Perdiccas. Ptolemy had a reputation for breaking past promises if he believed it best suited his own agenda. But not this day in June 320. He resisted the temptation to triumph himself as the new regent in front of jubilant soldiers. Instead, sticking to the strategy he and the other officers had agreed beforehand, he proposed Peithon and Arrhidaeus as the two new regents of empire. Enthusiastically the soldiers accepted this proposal, affirming their superiors' choice of 'plenipotentiary custodians of the kings'. Peithon and Arrhidaeus addressed the rejoicing crowd, before bringing the assembly to a close. From initially paying homage to the kings to winning the support of the Macedonian rank and file, Ptolemy's visit to the royal camp in the wake of Perdiccas' demise had been a great success.[13]

But an unexpected twist was about to materialise. Little news had reached the camps of either Ptolemy or Perdiccas about the war in the north over the past couple of weeks. A report of Eumenes' victory over Neoptolemus had reached the royal army around fourteen days earlier, but nothing significant had arrived since. This was all about to change. The next day, a messenger finally arrived at the royal camp, bearing news of a second titanic clash in the north and its extraordinary outcome.

Craterus was dead. Neoptolemus was dead. Eumenes had won a crushing victory and now threatened to cut Antipater off from the north. It was extraordinary news, with Plutarch and Diodorus famously quoting the same source that:

> If the news had arrived two days earlier, before Perdiccas' death, his great good fortune would have deterred anyone from laying hands on him.[14] – Diodorus 18.37.1

How great a difference a couple of days made.

Ptolemy, the two new regents and other senior officers convened a new council. Craterus' death was extraordinary – another of Alexander's most senior adjutants had lost his life in this civil war. There was little sense in mourning – none of these generals had seen Craterus for almost four years. But the man's name, his stellar reputation, still carried great weight – particularly among the Macedonian veterans. The commanders sensed opportunity.

The purge

Previously these *strategoi* had agreed on a policy of reconciliation with the leading Perdiccans dispersed across western Asia. Only the previous day Ptolemy had given those still present in the royal camp public reassurance that they had nothing to fear. Now, however, they changed their minds. It was time for a purge of potentially troublesome Perdiccans, and Craterus' death provided them the perfect pretext under which to announce it.[15]

Hastily another assembly was gathered and the generals announced to the soldiers the distressing news. Carefully the commanders construed the tale of Craterus' demise so as to stir their audience into an enraged frenzy. Soon these soldiers cried out for blood. They wanted vengeance.[16]

The generals then delivered the hammer blow. They started condemning leading Perdiccan figures to death. Eumenes, Alcetas, Attalus, Docimus, Pharnabazus, Phoenix, Polemon and many others were denounced and sentenced to die. By the time the sentencing ended some fifty leading Perdiccan officers had been condemned to death. It was a politically-motivated purge of Perdiccas' supporters throughout the empire – Ptolemy and his cronies had colourfully described Craterus' demise to send the soldiers into an anarchical state.[17]

As soon as the assembly ended, these soldiers hurried to carry through the executions. The red mist had well and truly descended as they embarked on a murderous killing spree against the condemned that remained in the camp. Only recently these men had been reassured by the new senior officers that they were in no danger of retribution. Barely twenty-four hours later and they were being ruthlessly butchered as those same generals stood idly by, condoning this politically-advantageous purge. Some did escape, fleeing north for the Mediterranean coast as quickly as they could. Many others did not.

The Macedonian murderers became uncontrollable, fired up to kill all those who had been close companions of the still-hated Perdiccas. But they went far further than expected. Condemned or no, figures in the camp who had been close to the recently deceased Perdiccas became targets. Even his sister Atalante.

Atalante had remained by her brother's side for the whole duration of his Egyptian campaign. Since joining Perdiccas in Pisidia over a year earlier she had become a mother, having recently given birth to two daughters. But now she and her family were incredibly isolated. Her brother had been ruthlessly murdered days earlier; her other sibling Alcetas was hundreds of miles away fighting in Asia Minor; her husband Attalus had remained with the fleet near Pelusium. She was alone, isolated among a crowd of Perdiccas-hating butchers.

It is unlikely that Atalante had been among those figures the generals had condemned to death. But her familial links to Perdiccas could not be concealed. She was a well-known face within the army, having remained with them for at least a year. This didn't save her. As bands of blood-seeking soldiers purged the camp of Perdiccas' closest friends, Atalante was murdered in cold blood. It was a merciless and terrible act, the soldiers leaving her two infant daughters without a mother. The children, at least, were spared.[18]

Reaction

In one swift act the royal camp was mercilessly emptied of Perdiccas' friends and family. Yet the fight would continue. No longer expecting mercy if they surrendered to the new regime, the powerful Perdiccan generals elsewhere in the empire would continue to fight. For Alcetas especially, brother to two murdered siblings, any chance of reconciliation was destroyed.

Attalus, still stationed at Pelusium with the fleet, was among the first to hear reports of the ruthless camp purge. News of the deaths of his wife and brother-in-law, the capture of his infant daughters and his recent condemnation by the new regime, must have left him distraught. Delaying no further he ordered the fleet to leave harbour and head for pastures new, determined to continue the struggle with this powerful armada.[19]

Leaving Egypt

Back near Memphis the bloody purge was over. Resupplied with abundant provisions Peithon, Arrhidaeus, the kings and their forces prepared to march north and leave Egypt for good. Their destination was Syria, intent on linking up with Antipater's army to decide the fate of the empire.[20]

Ptolemy looked on as he saw these tens of thousands of men commence their journey out of Egypt. Relief must have flowed through him as he saw the invasion force leave. He had survived. Egypt was his: spear-won land thanks to his victory over Perdiccas. Safe from invasion he looked to build on this success, on and off the battlefield. He looked to consolidate. Not only was trouble brewing to the west in Cyrene, but Perdiccas' invasion had revealed Egypt's vulnerability from the east. The experience had frightened Ptolemy and he quickly turned his attention to protecting his Egyptian heartlands from future invasion. Stronger defences, however, required expansion. Cyprus, Syria and Phoenicia – all powerful bases from where adversaries might spring a second invasion of Egypt. Military action remained on Ptolemy's mind.[21]

Away from the battlefield too Ptolemy would consolidate his position. Not long after Perdiccas' death he started to write his famous history of Alexander the Great and his campaigns. Throughout it he purposely derided Perdiccas' name, depicting him as an unruly adjutant and concealing some of the general's greatest achievements. At the same time, Ptolemy would boost his own story, telling fictitious tales and adding exaggerated Homeric achievements that promoted his standing with the dead Alexander. Deriding Perdiccas and promoting Ptolemy, this work soon became a powerful piece of propaganda.[22]

So the First War of the Successors came to an end, its final climactic act witnessing the downfall of Perdiccas after three years ruling the empire. But this imperial rule was more idealistic than realistic; dissent toward the general's superior position had always been present among several ambitious subordinates. Through various methods – execution, coercion, bribery – Perdiccas had tried to keep these troublesome forces under control. But to no avail. His successes fuelled his ambition for the kingship, yet with every step closer to this ultimate goal more obstacles had arisen, laid down by hostile, ambitious figures determined to derail Perdiccas' grand plans at whatever cost. Ultimately their actions succeeded and almost exactly three years after Alexander the Great had given his second in command his signet ring during his dying days, Perdiccas' punctured body lay lifeless by the Nile. His allies who survived the purge transformed from representatives of the empire's legitimate ruling body to condemned traitors, waging a war of resistance in Asia Minor. Their tales, however, were far from over. For Eumenes, Alcetas, Attalus, Docimus and many others, their stories were only just beginning.

Epilogue

From Babylonia to Thessaly and from Asia Minor to Egypt, the First War of the Successors had been fought across several theatres. Thousands had perished, several notable figures among the dead. In Europe Macedon's hated foe Menon had met his end in a disastrous battle against Polyperchon; in Babylonia Archon succumbed to his wounds; in Asia Minor Neoptolemus lost his duel and his life. But the deaths of Perdiccas and Craterus outshone all others. Together, alongside Antipater, these two men had dominated the immediate aftermath of Alexander the Great's death. Their prestige had exceeded that of Ptolemy, Antigonus and the many other governors and subordinates that dominated the empire. It was Craterus and Perdiccas that a new world order had initially been centred around. But now these two titans were dead, paving the way for the rise of more peripheral figures to become major players in deciding the future shape of Alexander's empire. Peithon, Seleucus and Ptolemy for instance.

And then there was Antigonus. Since his naval victory near Cyprus it seems this one-eyed general had pressed his advantage, subsequently forcing the Perdiccan land forces on the island under Aristonous to surrender. His Cypriot expedition had proven highly successful, further increasing the man's standing. Of Perdiccas' commanders the Rhodian admiral Sosigenes managed to escape. Both Medius of Larissa and Aristonous, however, were captured. With Aristonous' surrender another of Perdiccas' most loyal allies had found himself at their enemy's mercy, but the former's future proved more fortunate. Perhaps embracing his independence, taking note of Aristonous' esteemed renown or seizing the general before hearing word of the Perdiccan purge, Antigonus had allowed Aristonous to go free on condition that he return to Macedonia, retire and take no further action in the fighting.[1]

Antigonus went on to display further generosity to friend and foe alike. He welcomed Medius into his entourage – a shrewd appointment as it would turn out. Meanwhile to his erstwhile ally Dionysius, the general rewarded the tyrant with a marriage agreement, uniting their two houses through the wedding of Antigonus' nephew Polemaeus to Dionysius' daughter.[2]

Antigonus had risked much in his efforts to convince Antipater and Craterus to wage war on Perdiccas, but the ultimate benefits for him were extraordinary. Not only did he benefit from military successes, but he also gained from the high-standing casualties of the war. The demise of Perdiccas and Craterus paved the way for the rise of new dominant figures. Antigonus was determined to be among those men. Receiving word that a new settlement was to be decided in Syria, he sailed over to exert his newfound influence on the imperial stage. From landless fugitive to leading commander, the Great Macedonian War had proven very beneficial to Antigonus. Nevertheless new challenges were already starting to emerge. Antigonus' greatest challenge was still to come.[3]

Further Reading

Primary Sources

Arrian *Events After Alexander* 10A.2, R24.2 – 10A.6, R24.6 and 9.28 – 9.30
Diodorus Siculus 18.33.1–18.37.4
Frontinus *Stratagems* 4.7.20
Polyaenus 4.19

Secondary Sources

Anson, E. M. (2003), 'The Dating of Perdiccas' Death and the Assembly at Triparadeisus', *GRBS* 43, 373–390.

Errington, R. M. (1970), 'From Babylon to Triparadeisos: 323–320 BC' *The Journal of Hellenic Studies* 90, 64–67.

Hauben, H. (1974), 'An Athenian Naval Victory in 321 BC', *Zeitschrift für Papyrologie und Epigraphik* 13, 61–64.

Roisman, J. (2012), *Alexander's Veterans and the Early Wars of the Successors*, Austin, 93–111.

Roisman, J. (2014), 'Perdikkas's Invasion of Egypt', in H. Hauben and A. Meeus (eds.), *The Age of the Successors and the Creation of the Hellenistic Kingdoms (323–276 BC)*, 455–474.

Worthington, I. (2016), *Ptolemy I: King and Pharaoh of Egypt*, New York, 95–100.

Who's Who

Alexander the Great: King Alexander III of Macedon, who conquered the Persian Empire and forged a kingdom that stretched from Greece to the Indus Valley. It is the immediate aftermath of his death that this book focuses on.

Alexander IV: Son of Alexander the Great and Roxana. Proclaimed king by Perdiccas after the death of Alexander, probably in 322.

Adea: Daughter of Cynane and Amyntas. Object of Cynane's ambitious power play in 321. Later adopted the Macedonian name Eurydice, becoming Adea-Eurydice. Wife of King Philip Arrhidaeus III.

Aeacides: King of Epirus. Married to Phthia, the daughter of Menon. Ally of Olympias.

Agathocles: Father of Lysimachus, Alcimachus, Philip and Autodicus. Became a favourite of King Philip II of Macedon at his court, which ensured that his sons grew up at the heart of the Macedonian Kingdom.

Agis III: Spartan king who led an unsuccessful revolt against Macedon (and Antipater) in 331.

Alcetas: Younger brother of Perdiccas; brother of Atalante. Veteran of Alexander the Great's campaigns; served and advised Perdiccas after Alexander's death.

Alcimachus: Son of Agathocles; older brother of Lysimachus, Philip and Autodicus. A prominent commander in Alexander the Great's army at the start of the Persian expedition, though all references to him abruptly vanish after 334.

Alexander the Aetolian: Aetolian general who commanded the force that invaded Locris and Thessaly in 320.

Amastris: Persian princess, who had been given in marriage to Craterus by Alexander the Great. Discarded by Craterus in 322, when he married Antipater's daughter Phila. Amastris was given to Dionysius of Heraclea, to secure his support in the war against Perdiccas.

Amyntas: Macedonian, who commanded the cavalry during Aristonous' expedition to Cyprus in early 320. Otherwise unknown.

Amyntas IV: Son of Perdiccas III; nephew of Philip II and cousin of Alexander the Great. Married to Cynane in c.336, who bore him a daughter: Adea. Murdered by Alexander the Great in 335, who considered Amyntas a threat to his rule.

Androcles: Cypriot. King of Amathus. Subject/ally of Nicocreon.

Andromachus: Commander in Alexander the Great's army. Part of the expeditionary force that was annihilated by Spitamenes at the Polytimetus River, alongside Caranus, Pharnuches and Menedemus.

Andromenes: Father of Attalus and Polemon; father-in-law of Atalante.

Antigenes: Commander of the Silver Shields. Veteran Macedonian soldier and general who fought in armies of Philip II, Alexander and Perdiccas.

Antigonus 'the One-eyed': Veteran commander and governor. Governed the important region of Phrygia (central Anatolia) for much of Alexander the Great's reign. Father of Demetrius; husband of Stratonice. Hostile to Perdiccas.

Antipater: Alexander the Great's viceroy in Europe. Controlled Macedonia's 'European' territories while Alexander campaigned in Asia. Already late into his 70s when Alexander died, he played a major role in the Lamian War and the early years of the Wars of the Successors.

Antiphilus: Athenian commander that replaced Leosthenes as commander-in-chief of the anti-Macedonian land forces following Leosthenes' death outside Lamia at the height of the Lamian War.

Apries: Egyptian pharaoh who led an attack against the Hellenic colony of Cyrene in c.570 at the request of a neighbouring Libyan king. Defeated by the Cyreneans.

Archias: From the Italiote-Greek city of Thurii. An ancient bounty hunter in the service of Antipater. With a band of Thracians, he hunted down Hypereides and Demosthenes at the end of the Lamian War. Later accompanied Antipater's children Iollas and Nicaea to Perdiccas' camp in central Anatolia.

Archon: Veteran of Alexander the Great's campaigns. Made governor of Babylonia just before the death of Alexander the Great. Played a key role during the heist of Alexander's body.

Ares: Famously the god of war, Ares was also guardian of agriculture and the embodiment of virility and aggression.

Ariarathes: Iranian satrap (governor) and later King of Cappadocia. Never submitted to Alexander the Great. Would fight the forces of Perdiccas and Eumenes after Alexander the Great's death.

Ariarathes, son of Olophernes: Son of Olophernes; adopted son of Ariarathes I. Managed to avoid being brutally executed by Perdiccas in 322.

Aristides: Athenian general who fought at the Battle of Marathon and at Plataea. Flourished in the early fifth century.

Aristonous: Veteran general of Alexander the Great. One of the King's 'bodyguards' (advisors). Prominent supporter of Perdiccas after Alexander's death.

Aristotle: Famous philosopher from the city of Stageira; student of Plato; taught Alexander the Great when Alexander was still a prince. Adopted Nicanor.

Arrhidaeus: Macedonian commander. Present at Babylon when Alexander the Great died. Instructed with overseeing the construction of Alexander's funeral cortège.

Arrian: second century AD Greek historian, living under Roman rule. Famous for his history on Alexander the Great and his campaigns. Also the author of *Events After Alexander*, which has only survived through fragments.

Asander: Son of Agathon from Beroea; Macedonian; satrap of Caria in 323; friend of Antigonus and Menander.

Asclepiades: Brought the first news of Alexander the Great's death to Athens.

Asclepiodorus: Athenian diplomat who secured an alliance between the Phocians and Athenians at the beginning of the Lamian War. The Athenians would honour this diplomat's efforts by setting up an elaborate 'stele' (stone slab) in his honour.

Atalante: Sister of Perdiccas and Alcetas. Married to Attalus in 321 to fulfil a diplomatic agreement struck by Perdiccas. Accompanied her brother to Egypt in 320. Mother of two.

Athena: Goddess of wisdom, arts, trade and strategy.

Athenaeus: Greek rhetorician and grammarian, flourishing about the end of the second and beginning of the third century AD.

Athenodorus: Leader of a group of Greek mercenaries stationed in Bactria that planned to march home to Greece when they heard a rumour of Alexander the Great's death in India in early 325. Murdered by the rival mercenary leader Biton before this march could begin.

Atropates: Persian governor of Media. Father-in-law of Perdiccas. His territory was greatly diminished in the Babylon Settlement, with much of it being handed over to Peithon, son of Crateuas. Became the ruler of Media Minor, later known as Media Atropatene.

Attalus: Macedonian general and veteran of Alexander the Great's campaigns. Son of Andromenes; brother of Polemon. Husband of Atalante and ally of Perdiccas after Alexander's death.

Audata: Illyrian. Related to the veteran Dardanian chieftain Bardylis. Married King Philip II of Macedon in 358 to seal an honourable peace between the Macedonian and Dardanian kingdoms. Mother of Cynane. Adopted the proper Macedonian name Eurydice.

Autodicus: Son of Agathocles; youngest brother of Lysimachus. Joined Antipater on his campaign to Asia against Perdiccas in 320.

Balacrus: Veteran Macedonian general and former bodyguard/advisor of Alexander the Great who was made governor of Cilicia in 333. Killed by highland raiders in 324. Married to Phila, Antipater's daughter.

Bardylis: Bardylis was the king of the Dardanians, an Illyrian tribe, ruling from 393–358. In his lifetime he turned the Dardanians into a leading power in Central Europe, improving the economic and military systems of his kingdom. After many successful campaigns he and his army were eventually defeated in 358 by Philip II of Macedon at the Battle of Lyncus Plain. When he died Bardylis was over 90 years old – something almost unheard of back in the fourth century.

Barsine: Wife first of Mentor of Rhodes and then Mentor's younger brother Memnon. Lover of Alexander the Great. Her daughter (from her marriage with Mentor) was married to Nearchus, Alexander's top admiral.

Bessus: Persian commander in the army of King Darius III. Later betrayed Darius, leaving him to die by the roadside. Seized the Persian crown for himself and attempted to raise a fresh army to counter Alexander in Bactria but his call for support fell on deaf ears. Pursued by Alexander and eventually handed over to him. Crucified by Alexander.

Biton: Mercenary Greek commander. Murdered Athenodorus and then led 3,000 soldiers on a homeward-bound journey towards the Aegean and mainland Greece. Their fate remains unclear, though I believe they probably never reached the Mediterranean.

Callimedon: Athenian. Fled Athens when its citizens declared war on Macedon in 323. Aided the Macedonian ambassadors during the Lamian War. Called 'the spiny lobster' because of his love of that food.

Caranus: Commander in Alexander the Great's army. Part of the expeditionary force that was annihilated by Spitamenes at the Polytimetus River, alongside Andromachus, Pharnuches and Menedemus.

Cersebleptes: Odrysian king who fought, and was ultimately defeated by, King Philip II of Macedon between 343 and 341.

Cleitus 'the Black': Senior subordinate of Alexander the Great. Commanded the Royal Squadron (*basilike ile*). Murdered by Alexander during a drunken argument in Maracanda in 328.

Cleitus 'the White': Macedonian commander; veteran of Alexander the Great's campaigns. Admiral of the powerful Macedonian fleet that was constructed in the Eastern Mediterranean between 324 and 322. Played a key role in the Lamian War and in the First War of the Successors.

Cleomenes: Greek administrator from the Hellenic colony of Naucratis in Egypt (by the Nile Delta). Governor of Egypt until Alexander the Great's death. Famed for his decadence and corruption.

Cleopatra: Daughter of Philip II and Olympias; sister of Alexander the Great. Formed a powerful mother-daughter team with Olympias after Alexander's death, trying to secure herself a powerful husband. Ally of Perdiccas

Coenus: Macedonian commander who served with Alexander the Great. A trusted advisor and capable leader, he was a senior figure within the Macedonian army. Spoke on behalf of the Macedonian troops at the Hyphasis River in India, who were refusing to march with Alexander any further east. Died not long after from illness. Some believe Alexander had Coenus murdered in revenge for his intervention at the Hyphasis, but illness is most likely.

Cornelius Nepos: Roman biographer writing during the first century BC. Included works on two prominent figures between 323 and 320: Eumenes and Phocion.

Cotys I: Odrysian king. Strengthened his kingdom and threatened Macedonia during the early years of King Philip II's reign.

Craterus: One of Alexander the Great's chief generals. Commanded the Macedonian infantry; loved by the troops. Ordered back to Macedon in 324 with 10,000 veteran soldiers. Was in Cilicia (southeast Anatolia) when Alexander died. Prominent figure after Alexander's death.

Curtius: First century AD Roman writer, famous for writing a history of Alexander the Great's campaigns. Included within his work is a detailed description of the turmoil that engulfed Babylon after Alexander's death.

Cynane: Half-sister of Alexander the Great, Cleopatra and Arrhidaeus (and others); daughter of Philip II and Audata. Mother of Adea. Raised in the arts of war by her mother; accompanied Philip II on campaigns against the Illyrians and supposedly killed an Illyrian queen. Became renowned as a Macedonian 'Amazon'. Widow of Alexander the Great's murdered cousin Amyntas. Strived to see her daughter Adea married to King Philip Arrhidaeus III in 321.

Darius I: Great King of Persia between 522 and 486. Famous for his expansion of the Persian Empire, including into Thrace and Macedonia. Launched a failed amphibious Persian attack on Athens in 490, which culminated in the Battle of Marathon.

Darius III: Great King of Persia who was defeated by Alexander the Great at the battles of Issus and Gaugamela. Later murdered by his general Bessus. Father of Stateira, who later married Alexander.

Demades: Athenian. Fought against the Macedonians at Chaeronea in 338 but later struck up good terms with both Alexander the Great and Antipater. Alongside Phocion he was more cautious of Athens declaring war on Macedon in the wake of Alexander's death.

Demeter: Goddess of agriculture, grain, women, motherhood and marriage; and the lawgiver.

Demetrius: Son of Antigonus and Stratonice. Rather insignificant in the early years after Alexander's death.

Demosthenes: Renowned as Athens' greatest statesman/orator of the fourth century. Hostile to Macedonian overlordship. Was at the forefront of Athenian affairs between 324 and 323.

Diades: One of Alexander the Great's best military engineers. His siege engines were key to many of Alexander's successful sieges, especially the momentous Siege of Tyre. Diades became known as the 'man who took Tyre.'

Dinarchus: Athenian. Ally of Hypereides. Hostile to Macedonian overlordship. Ferociously denounced Demosthenes during the latter's trial in early 323.

Diodorus Siculus: Siciliote Greek historian who wrote his monumental universal history in the first century BC. The main source for the events after Alexander the Great's death.

Dionysius of Heraclea: Tyrant of Heraclea Pontica. Ally of Antipater, Antigonus and Craterus during the First Successor War. Aided Antigonus with the naval campaign off Cyprus.

Docimus: Ally of Perdiccas. Would lead an expedition to Babylonia against Archon in 320.

Drypetis: Sister of Stateira; daughter of Darius III. Married Hephaestion in 324. Murdered by Roxana alongside Stateira following Alexander the Great's death in June 323.

Epicydes: Hailed from the city of Olynthus. Made governor of Taucheira in North Africa (Cyrenaica) by Ophellas. Subordinate to Ophellas.

Euetion: Athenian admiral during the Lamian War. Commanded Athenian naval forces at Amorgos.

Eumenes: The personal secretary of Alexander the Great who played a leading role in administering imperial affairs. He also commanded cavalry during Alexander's campaigns. Hailed from the Hellenic city of Cardia, near the Hellespont. Became a key figure after Alexander the Great's death. Ally and advisor of Perdiccas.

Euphron of Sicyon: Citizen of Sicyon, a city in the northern Peloponnese. Drove the Macedonian garrison out of Sicyon in late 323, affirming his city's new alliance with Athens against Macedon. Honoured in Athens.

Gorgias: Macedonian commander. Veteran of Alexander the Great's campaigns. Ally of Perdiccas and Eumenes.

Harpalus: Macedonian. Boyhood friend of Alexander the Great. Was Alexander's treasurer in Central Asia until fleeing west in early 324. Tried to instigate a revolt against Alexander in Athens, but was foiled by Demosthenes. Amassed a powerful mercenary army that was ultimately used by Thibron.

Hecataeus: Tyrant of Cardia. Ally of Antipater; enemy of Eumenes.

Hephaestion: One of Alexander the Great's closest companions and lover. Senior figure in Alexander's army. Died of illness in 324, at Ecbatana. His death helped pave the way for the rise of Perdiccas during Alexander's final years.

Heracles: Illegitimate son of Alexander the Great and Barsine.

Hieronymus: Hailed from the city of Cardia, near the Hellespont. Ally of Eumenes and author of a detailed history about the Successor Wars.

Hypereides: Athenian orator. One of the staunchest anti-Macedonian, pro-war figures in Athens. Leading statesman during the Lamian War; enemy of Antipater.

Iollas: Son of Antipater; brother of Cassander, Phila, Nicaea and others. Was present in Babylon when Alexander the Great died. Accompanied Nicaea to Asia in 321, alongside Archias, to secure marriage alliance between Perdiccas and the house of Antipater.

Justin: Second century AD Latin writer who wrote an epitome of the work of Pompeius Trogus. An unreliable source who writes about the aftermath of Alexander's death in Book 13.

Langarus: King of the Agrianes, a Paeonian tribe situated along the upper, mountainous reaches of the Strymon River. An ally of King Philip II, Langarus and his Agrianians aided their Macedonian neighbours in a series of expansionist conflicts. Alexander offered Langarus his half-sister Cynane in marriage, to strengthen the ties between the Macedonians and the Agrianians. Died *en route* to marry Cynane in 335.

Laomedon: Commander in Alexander the Great's army. Originally from the city of Mytilene on Lesbos. Friend, and later accomplice of Ptolemy. Made governor of Syria at Babylon in 323.

Leonnatus: A leading general and favourite of Alexander the Great, who boasted almost-legendary status by the time of Alexander's death in 323. Charismatic and confident, he marched to Antipater's aid during the Lamian War.

Leosthenes: 'The Athenian Alexander'. Former mercenary who had served in Asia during Alexander the Great's campaigns. Returned to mainland Greece in the 320s and became a figurehead for the Athenians during the Lamian War. Bold, charismatic but also arrogant.

Letodorus: Commander in Philon's mercenary army. Bribed by Peithon to betray Philon and join the Macedonians with 3,000 soldiers.

Lycurgus: Athenian statesman who revitalised Athens between 336 and 324 with military, social and economic reforms. Strongly opposed and hostile to Macedonian overlordship.

Lysimachus: Advisor/comrade of Alexander the Great. Renowned for his fearlessness, but also for his recklessness. Present at Babylon when Alexander died and received governorship over Macedonian-controlled Thrace.

Lysippus: A famous Sicyonian sculptor. Was tasked with crafting bronze sculptures dedicated to Apollo at Delphi by Craterus in 322/321. The sculptures depicted Alexander the Great and Craterus hunting.

Medius of Larissa: Thessalian noble and friend of Alexander the Great. It was supposedly at his drinking party that Alexander the Great fell ill in mid-323. Supporter of Perdiccas after Alexander's death. Accompanied Aristonous to Cyprus in 320.

Meleager: Infantry commander in Alexander the Great's army. Played a significant role in the immediate aftermath of Alexander's death.

Memnon of Heraclea: Ancient writer, remembered for his history of his home city of Heraclea Pontica. He refers to events and figures in the aftermath of Alexander the Great in his work.

Memnon of Rhodes: One of Alexander the Great's most formidable foes. Fought Alexander at the Battle of the River Granicus and continued to resist him until his death in 333. Had married Barsine following the death of his elder brother Mentor in c.340.

Menander: Governor of Lydia; Macedonian; friend of Antigonus.

Menedemus: Commander in Alexander the Great's army. Part of the expeditionary force that was annihilated by Spitamenes at the Polytimetus River, alongside Caranus, Pharnuches and Andromachus.

Menon: Thessalian; belonged to a leading family in Pharsalus. Fought with Alexander the Great in Asia, but led the elite Thessalian cavalry contingent against the Macedonians during the Lamian War. A brilliant cavalry commander; grandfather of Pyrrhus.

Mentor of Rhodes: High-standing Rhodian mercenary general who fought in Persian service during the mid-fourth century. Older brother of Memnon; husband of Barsine, his niece; his daughter married Nearchus in 324.

Micion: Macedonian naval commander. Led a raid on Attica in 323/322, during the Lamian War, but was repulsed (and killed) by Phocion's home guard.

Miltiades: Athenian general at the Battle of Marathon in 490. He held command the day the battle was fought and was lauded as the mastermind behind this decisive Athenian victory.

Mnasicles: Cretan mercenary commander who served with Thibron in North Africa. He may have served in Alexander the Great's army in Asia before then. Ultimately betrayed Thibron and became one of his greatest enemies.

Nearchus: Cretan who travelled to Macedonia and gained favour with King Philip II of Macedon. Went with Alexander the Great to Asia. Initially served as Alexander's governor of Lycia and Pamphylia in southern Anatolia, but later rejoined Alexander's army and became his chief admiral. Oversaw the Macedonian fleet's voyage to the Persian Gulf from the Indus River delta, which survives today in his Indica. Married a daughter of Barsine and consequently became related through marriage to Alexander the Great's illegitimate son Heracles. Present at Babylon when Alexander died.

Nectanebo II: Last native ruler of ancient Egypt. Fled to Ethiopia following the Persian King Artaxerxes III's successful conquest of Egypt in 343/342. His sarcophagus may have been used to temporarily house Alexander's body when Ptolemy took it to Memphis.

Neoptolemus: Member of the Molossian royal family (the Aeacidae) who accompanied Alexander the Great to Asia. Renowned for his bravery; first to storm the walls of Gaza in 332. Initially supported Perdiccas, but later joined Antipater. Enemy of Eumenes.

Nicaea: Daugher of Antipater; married Perdiccas in 321 but later discarded by the latter.

Nicanor: Hailed from Stageira, in the Chalcidice. Adopted son of Aristotle. Sent to Greece by Alexander the Great in 324 to announce the Exiles Decree.

Nicocles: Cypriot. King of Paphos. Subject to/ally of Nicocreon.

Nicocreon: King of Salamis, on Cyprus' eastern shoreline. The most powerful ruler on Cyprus, who possessed a strong fleet. Friend of Ptolemy.

Olophernes: Member of the Iranian family that ruled Cappadocia. Brother of Ariarathes. Gained great renown fighting with his Cappadocian contingent for the Persian King Artaxerxes III during the King's Egyptian campaign. Died in c.340. His son, also called Ariarathes, was adopted by his brother (Ariarathes I).

Olympias: Mother of Alexander the Great and Cleopatra; enemy of Antipater. Hoped to align herself with certain powerful figures in the aftermath of her son's death. Formed a formidable mother-daughter political team with Cleopatra.

Ophellas: Macedonian officer and veteran of Alexander the Great's campaigns. Friend of Ptolemy; accompanied Ptolemy to Egypt in 323/322. Would see action against Thibron in Cyrenaica.

Oxyartes: Sogdian chieftain. Initially aided Spitamenes in his revolt against Alexander. Later came to an understanding with Alexander when his daughter Roxana married Alexander as part of a diplomatic agreement. Became a powerful ruler in the north-eastern corner of Alexander's Empire, centred around the Hindu Kush.

Parmenion: One of Philip II's and Alexander's most able adjutants. Alongside Antipater, Parmenion was one of King Philip II's top advisors. Killed on Alexander the Great's orders in 330.

Pasicrates: Cypriot. King of Soli. Subject to/ally of Nicocreon.

Peithagoras: A renowned diviner who had long served the Macedonian royal court. Accompanied Perdiccas to Egypt.

Peithon: Son of Crateuas; general of Alexander the Great; one of Alexander's 'bodyguards'. Present at Babylon when Alexander died. Over the next three years he travelled across much of Alexander's empire with various armies: from Bactria to Anatolia to Egypt.

Peithon, Son of Agenor: Macedonian commander. Made governor of the lower Indus in 325. Remained governor of the province (with more land added) at the Babylon Settlement.

Perdiccas: One of Alexander the Great's leading subordinates and a close advisor. Hailed from one of Macedonia's most noble families. Prominent figure in the immediate years after Alexander the Great's death. One of the central figures of this book. Sometimes referred to as 'the regent' or 'the chiliarch' (Chapter 1).

Pericles: Athens' greatest statesman. Ruled Athens in all but name in the years up to the outbreak of the Peloponnesian War (mid-fifth century). The most prominent victim of the Great Plague of Athens.

Peucestas: Rose to prominence at the end of Alexander the Great's reign, after protecting an injured Alexander when they were storming an Indian citadel. Governor of Persia. Present in Babylon when Alexander died, having recently brought 20,000 Persian reinforcements to bolster the royal army.

Pharnabazus: Persian noble who fought against Alexander the Great. Later reconciled with the Macedonians and fought alongside Perdiccas and Eumenes.

Pharnuches: Interpreter in Alexander the Great's army. Part of the expeditionary force that was annihilated by Spitamenes at the Polytimetus River, alongside Andromachus, Caranus and Menedemus.

Phila: Daughter of Antipater. Renowned for her virtue and sage advice. Married to Balacrus, the Macedonian governor of Cilicia, until Balacrus' death in 324. Would then marry Craterus, after she returned to Europe with him in 322.

Philinna of Larissa: Thessalian noblewoman who was married to King Philip II in the 350s. The mother of Arrhidaeus, Alexander the Great's older half-brother.

Philip, satrap of Bactria-Sogdia: Macedonian governor of Bactria and Sogdiana. Retained his satrapy in the Babylon Settlement.

Philip II: Father of Alexander the Great, Arrhidaeus, Cleopatra, Cynane and several others. Transformed the Kingdom of Macedon from a domain on the brink of complete collapse to the dominant power in the Central Mediterranean. Assassinated in 336; succeeded by Alexander.

Philip Arrhidaeus III / Arrhidaeus: Older half-brother of Alexander the Great. Though we don't know what illness he suffered from, it was severe enough that he was not capable of ruling/making decisions without help. This weakness was exploited by Alexander's generals, who used Arrhidaeus as a pawn.

Philip, son of Agathocles: Son of Agathocles; brother of Alcimachus, Lysimachus and Autodicus. Remembered for his extraordinary end, collapsing and dying from exhaustion after running c.60 miles (according to Curtius Rufus) and then fighting in a skirmish alongside Alexander the Great in modern day Uzbekistan.

Philocles: Athenian *strategos* (general) in charge of the Piraeus (Athens' harbour) and the nearby stronghold of Munychia in 324. It was Philocles that admitted Harpalus into Athens.

Philon: Commander of the Greek mercenaries in Bactria that decided to march home following Alexander the Great's death. Originally from the region of Aenis, just west of Thermopylae.

Philotas: Macedonian commander in Alexander the Great's army. Commanded an infantry battalion. Made governor of Cilicia just before Alexander's death, replacing the murdered Balacrus. Friend of Craterus.

Philoxenus: Macedonian official in Asia Minor for much of Alexander the Great's reign. Demanded Harpalus' extradition from Athens in 324.

Phocion: Veteran Athenian statesman. Almost 80 years old when Alexander the Great died but still an active figure on the Athenian political front. More wary of war with Macedon compared to many of his fellow statesmen. Respected by both Athenians and Macedonians.

Phoenix of Tenedos: Hellenic commander and ally of Eumenes.

Phrataphernes: Persian noble who surrendered to Alexander the Great after Darius III's death. Alexander allowed Phrataphernes to remain governor over Hyrcania and Parthia, a position he held for the rest of Alexander's reign. He also retained this satrapy at the Babylon Settlement of 323.

Phthia: Daughter of Menon; married King Aeacides of Epirus; mother of Pyrrhus.

Pigres: Asian commander in charge of Cappadocian and Paphlagonian cavalry who may have served as a mercenary adjutant of Neoptolemus. Eumenes duped his soldiers into thinking that Pigres was marching against them, instead of Craterus, during the First War of the Successors.

Plato: Philosopher who thrived in the early 4th century. Student of Socrates; teacher of Aristotle.

Plutarch: Greek biographer writing in the first/second centuries AD. Among his biographies was one on Eumenes, a major source for the immediate aftermath of Alexander the Great's death.

Polemaeus: Nephew of Antigonus 'the One-eyed'; married Dionysius of Heraclea's daughter at the end of the First War of the Successors.

Polemon: Younger brother of Attalus; son of Andromenes. Joined his brother on his mission to retrieve Alexander's body from Ptolemy's grasp.

Polyaenus: Macedonian historian, writing in the second century AD. His book of stratagems includes a few tactical manoeuvres made by leading figures between 323 and 320: Antipater, Perdiccas and Ptolemy for instance.

Polycles: Macedonian garrison commander. Subordinate of Antipater. Fought the Aetolians in 320.

Polyperchon: Veteran Macedonian commander who served with Alexander the Great. Commanded the Tymphaean phalanx battalion (Polyperchon came from Tymphaea in southwest Macedonia). Accompanied Craterus back west in 324; governed Macedonia when Antipater and Craterus headed for Asia in 320.

Porus: Indian king who ruled in the Punjab region of the Indus River Valley. Fought Alexander the Great at the Battle of the Hydaspes River and was defeated. Reconciled with Alexander and retained control over his kingdom. Autonomous in all but name, he retained control of his kingdom at the Babylon Settlement.

Poseidonius: A prominent member of Alexander's engineering corps; would design his own modified siege tower for Alexander.

Ptolemy: General and friend of Alexander the Great. Became one of Alexander's bodyguards/closest advisors alongside the likes of Perdiccas and Leonnatus. Became governor of Egypt and the chief adversary of Perdiccas after Alexander's death.

Pytheas: Athenian. Fled Athens when the city declared war on Macedonia. Supported Antipater and Macedonian ambassadorial teams during the Lamian War. Had a war of words with Demosthenes in one particular Arcadian city as both Macedon and Athens vied for the city's support.

Roxana: Daughter of the Sogdian chief Oxyartes; wife of Alexander the Great. Was married to Alexander to quell the Sogdian Revolt. Mother of Alexander IV. Ally of Perdiccas.

Seleucus: Macedonian commander and veteran of Alexander the Great's campaigns. Commanded the hypaspists at the time of Alexander's death. Became an ally of Perdiccas and his second in command.

Seuthes III: Ruler of the Odrysian Kingdom in central Thrace (in modern Bulgaria). Declared his kingdom's independence from Macedonian rule late in Alexander the Great's reign. Chief enemy of Lysimachus after Alexander the Great's death.

Sibyritus: Macedonian who was the governor of Arachosia and Gedrosia when Alexander the Great died. Retained his position at the Babylon Settlement.

Sippias: Antipater's subordinate in Macedonia in 323. Managed Macedonia while Antipater marched south to fight Leosthenes and quell the 'Greek' revolt.

Sitalkes: Odrysian king who ruled between 431 and 424. Son of Teres I. Was supposedly able to call upon an army 150,000 strong.

Sosigenes: Rhodian admiral. Accompanied Aristonous' expeditionary force to Cyprus in early 320.

Spitamenes: Sogdian chief and leader of the Sogdian Revolt against Alexander the Great. Was ultimately defeated by Alexander and murdered by his allies (possibly by his wife).

Stasanor: Cypriot Greek from Soli. Governor of Aria and Drangiana at the time of Alexander the Great's death. He was also present at Babylon on 11 June 323. Retained control over his satrapy during the Babylon Settlement.

Stateira: Persian princess. Daughter of Darius III. Wife of Alexander the Great. Murdered by Roxana, with Perdiccas' support, in 323 after Alexander's death. Roxana feared that Stateira was pregnant and would give birth to a son who could rival her own for the Macedonian throne.

Stratocles: Athenian statesman. Proclaimed to the Athenians that Euetion and his fleet had won a great victory against the Macedonians at Amorgos in late June 322. Even though they had suffered a dismal defeat...

Taxiles: Indian king who ruled in the Punjab region of the Indus River Valley. Allied with Alexander the Great; enemy of King Porus. Ruled his kingdom with relative independence from Macedon.

Thibron: Spartan mercenary general who accompanied Harpalus west from Babylon when he fled in early 324. Later murdered Harpalus and attempted to conquer the rich Hellenic cities of Cyrenaica in North Africa.

Tlepolemus: Macedonian; son of Pythophanes and companion of Alexander the Great. Alexander appointed Tlepolemus governor of Carmania in 325 and he retained his satrapy in the Babylon Settlement.

Xennias: Macedonian, who served with Eumenes of Cardia during the First War of the Successors.

Zeus: Supreme King of the gods. God of the sky and thunder.

Zopyrion: Macedonian *strategos* of Thrace between 329 and 324. Led a disastrous expedition north of the Danube River which was utterly destroyed – Zopyrion among the dead.

Notes

Chapter 1: The End of an Era

1. Curtius 10.5.5; Arrian *Anabasis* 7.26.3; Diodorus 17.117.4. Though a great story this is fictional, as Alexander was mute during his last hours. Waterfield (2019), 473; Meeus (2008), 66; Grant (2019), 26.
2. Curtius 10.5.4. Anson (2015), 63; Rathmann (2005), 26.
3. Arrian *Anabasis*, 6.28.4; Curtius 10.7.8.
4. Thebes: Arrian, *Anabasis* 1.8.1–3 and Diodorus 17.12.3–4. Persian Gate: Arrian, *Anabasis* 3.18.5.
5. Arrian, *Anabasis* 6.15.1.
6. Arrian *Anabasis* 7.12.1–4 and 7.14.1.
7. Arrian, *Anabasis* 7.14.10. Heckel (2006), 198: 'in effect he (Perdiccas) was Alexander's second in command.'
8. Errington (1970), 49.
9. Worthington (2016), 11.
10. Throughout Alexander's genocidal Indian campaign, Ptolemy had commanded portions of the army during several missions in and around the Indus Valley, receiving a near-fatal wound from a poisoned arrow in the process. This being said, it is difficult to dissect the fact from fiction about Ptolemy's role during the Indian Campaign, as much of the information that survives originally comes from Ptolemy's own writing, which is evidently filled with fiction to suit his own agenda.
11. According to Curtius, Leonnatus and Aristonous were also present when Peucestas famously saved Alexander during the Siege of Multan in February 325.
12. Curtius 10.5.9–14 & 35–36.
13. Curtius 10.5.15.
14. Curtius 10.6.1–2. See also Anson (2015), 62 and Worthington (2016), 75. I agree with the likes of Anson (2015), 66, Errington (1970), 49–54, Meeus (2008), 41–2 and Worthington (2016), 75 that Curtius' version of events in Babylon after Alexander's death is the most plausible, compared to those of Justin and Diodorus. For the opposite view see Bosworth (2002), 29–63.
15. Curtius 10.6.2; Justin 13.2.2; Anson (2015), 63; Worthington (2016), 75.
16. Roisman (2012), 63.
17. For the impact/significance of the marriage in quelling the Sogdian Revolt, see chapter 4. Alexander had also instated his new father-in-law as governor of Paropamisadae, the vital province dominated by the Hindu Kush. Bosworth (1980), 11.
18. Metz Epitome 70, in Heckel and Yardley (2004), 204.
19. Curtius 10.6.4–9; Justin 13.2.5.
20. Anson (2015), 62.
21. Meeus (2008), 47.
22. Curtius 10.6.16; Errington (1970), 50.
23. For example: Arrian *Anabasis* 7.4.6.
24. Curtius 10.6.10–12; Justin 13.2.7, although Justin mistakenly associates this proposal with Meleager.
25. Worthington (2016), 75.

26. Anson (2015), 64; Meeus (2008), 42: '...it can be safely assumed that the resentment toward what was seen as blurring the lines between conquered and conqueror was authentic...' See also Justin 13.2.9.

27. Curtius 10.6.10–12.

28. Curtius 10.6.13–15; Justin 13.2.11–12.

29. Anson (2015), 64 for this possibility. Though not certain, I am inclined to believe that Ptolemy initially supported the idea to await the birth of Roxana's child, especially seeing his later support for this policy after the infantry championed Arrhidaeus.

30. Meeus (2008), 50 & (2014), 270; Errington (1970), 51; Worthington (2016), 76–77.

31. Curtius 9.5.14–18. Arrian *Anabasis* 6.10.1–4, however, makes no mention of Aristonous during this episode.

32. Roisman (2012), 62: 'For Curtius' speeches, the prudent scholar will accept as historically valid only the speaker's identity and his core argument.'

33. Curtius 10.6.18.

34. Curtius 10.6.18–20.

35. Errington (1970), 51; Heckel / Yardley (2001), 3. Xref Heckel (2016), 164.

36. Anson (2015), 64–65; Errington (1970), 50.

37. Curtius 10.6.19. For the importance of strong relationships in the Macedonian succession see Mitchell (2007), 61–74. Also Anson (1985), 303–316 and Anson (1991), 237.

38. Curtius 8.12.18; Heckel (2006), 160.

39. Curtius 10.6.23–24; Errington (1970), 51.

40. Anson (2015), 67. 'While it has been claimed that such a minor individual would not dare make a suggestion in a meeting dominated by the great commanders, this was not a normal situation.'

41. Also Justin 13.2.8 although, once again, Justin has wrongly credited this proposal to Meleager.

42. Alexander had never seen his older half-brother as a threat during his reign. When Alexander ascended the kingship in 336, for example, and immediately put in motion a ruthless purge of possible, rival claimants, Arrhidaeus emerged unscathed. Indeed it seems that Alexander had some degree of brotherly affection for his step-brother, perhaps even taking him on campaign.

43. Curtius 10.7.3–7.

44. Curtius 10.7.8–9; Errington (1970), 52.

45. Errington (1970), 52.

46. Curtius 10.7.8–9.

47. Justin 13.2.13; Meeus (2008) 53.

48. Curtius 10.6.21. This decision to announce a male heir no matter what is not mentioned by our sources, but the newfound universal agreement among the generals makes it likely that this was agreed as a suitable 'failsafe'.

49. Curtius 10.7.10–12.

50. Curtius 10.14–18; Diodorus 18.2.3; Justin 13.31–4.

51. Curtius 10.7.19.

52. Curtius 10.7.20–21. Bosworth (2002), 45.

53. Curtius 10.8.1–4; Justin 13.3.7–8.

54. Anson (2015), 70.

55. Bosworth (1980), 16.

56. *Epigoni:* Arrian *Anabasis* 7.6.1; Curtius 8.5.1; Diodorus 17.108.1–2; Plutarch *Alexander* 71.1; Macedonian resentment: Arrian *Anabasis* 7.8.1–3. Bosworth (1980), 2 & 17–18.

57. Diodorus 17.110.2; Arrian 5.12.2; Anson (2015), 70.

58. Curtius 10.8.5–8.

59. The anger the soldiers express when they hear word that Meleager had made an attempt on Perdiccas' life only confirms that the house of Perdiccas and Alcetas was held in high respect by their men. Bosworth (2002), 44 and 46. It may well have been Alcetas and his

infantry battalion that had supported conferring supreme command on Perdiccas earlier during the crisis (Curtius 10.7.12).

60. Plutarch *Eumenes*, 3.1; Anson (2015), 68 for being Perdiccas' agent.
61. Curtius 10.8.7–14.
62. Curtius 10.8.15.
63. Heckel (1978), 377–82; Heckel (2006), 63; Heckel (2016), 195–7; Diodorus 18.37.2.
64. Attalus commanded the Tymphaean phalanx battalion, which likely followed their general when he defected to Perdiccas. See Heckel (2016), 194–197.
65. Curtius 10.8.16.
66. Curtius 10.8.16–22 claims that this impassioned plea was made by Arrhidaeus, but Bosworth (2002), 49 has convincingly rejected this as a later attempt by Ptolemy to remove any noteworthy achievement by Perdiccas from the history books. 'It is the most striking incidence of propaganda in the whole episode.'
67. Joint kingship: Arrian, *Events After Alexander* 1.1; Justin 13.4.3; Meeus (2008), 53. Recognising Arrhidaeus: Errington (1970), 54; Curtius 10.8.15.
68. Anson (1992), 39; Meeus (2008), 55. For further discussion see Meeus (2009), 287–310.
69. Arrian, *Events After Alexander* 1.3; Justin 13.4.5; Anson (1992), 42.
70. Anson (2015), 71; Arrian, *Events After Alexander* 1.3; Justin 13.4.5.
71. Arrian, *Events After Alexander* 1.3; Justin 13.4.5; Curtius 8.22; Errington (1970), 56. For the alternate view that Meleager's position was equal to Perdiccas' see Meeus (2008), 58.
72. Justin 13.4.4.
73. The most notable loser was Leonnatus, who we shall cover in a subsequent chapter.
74. Arrian, *Anabasis* 1.14.3. Anson (2015) 72; Errington (1970), 55. The battalions of Craterus and Meleager are noted fighting next to each other on the right side of the infantry line at the Battle of the Granicus River. Craterus went on to be overall commander of the infantry battalions.
75. Curtius 10.9.8–11.
76. If we believe the entire army was present, there would have been at least 70,000 soldiers at this event. We know, for instance, that there were at least 50,000 Persian infantry in Babylon at the time of Alexander the Great's death – Arrian, *Anabasis*; 7.6.1 & 7.23.1-4; Anson (2015) 70. It is more likely that the reconciliation event was only attended by a portion of the royal army, including the Macedonian infantry, the cavalry and the elephants.
77. Curtius 10.9.13–15.
78. Curtius 10.9.18 says there were 300, Diodorus 18.4.7 claims there were 30. I am more inclined to believe the latter figure, as 300 seems excessive. Although Perdiccas was capable of being extremely brutal when he thought it necessary.
79. Curtius 10.9.7–19; Meeus (2008), 58; Errington (1970), 56.
80. Curtius 10.9.20–21.
81. Whether Seleucus was a staunch ally of Perdiccas at this time is debated. I am of the opinion that at this time he was, or at least that he portrayed himself as a loyal subordinate for his own benefit. Perdiccas' power at this time revolved around his control of the royal army. He would not have undermined it so quickly by instating someone who he doubted as his chief adjutant. See Heckel (2006) 247 but note Anson (1988) 476: 'Loyalty and friendship with these men were political commodities to be retained so long as they were useful.'
82. The view of Anson (2015), 75 and Meeus (2008), 68–76. For the opposing view, that Perdiccas dominated proceedings, see Bosworth (2002), 57–58 and Worthington (2016), 79. Mercenaries in Alexander the Great's Empire: Badian (1961) 26–29 and chapters 2 and 4 of this book.
83. See Worthington (2016) 80 and 83–86.
84. Anson (2015) 75. Bosworth (2002), 57–63; Errington (1970), 57-8.
85. Diodorus 18.3.5; Curtius 10.5.4; Meeus (2008), 67.

86. These were Ptolemy, Laomedon, Asander, Leonnatus, Lysimachus, Peithon, Eumenes and Craterus.
87. For the Babylon Settlement see Curtius 10.10.1–4, Diodorus 18.3, Arrian, *Events After Alexander* 1.5–1.7 and Justin 13.10–23 (Justin's account is muddled and unreliable).
88. Curtius 10.10.3; Plutarch *Eumenes*, 3.2.
89. It is unlikely all the new appointments left the city immediately. Ptolemy, for instance, appears to have remained in Babylon for a small amount of time. See Worthington (2015), 89. Peithon meanwhile also remained at Babylon for a few months (see Chapter 4).
90. Diodorus 18.4.1–6. These last plans are only mentioned in Diodorus.
91. Bosworth (2002), 31; Meeus (2008), 63 & 78.
92. Errington (1970), 59. See Bosworth (1980), 2–3 for the possibility that Perdiccas may have included fictitious proposals among Alexander's Last Plans to ensure the Macedonians rejected them.

Chapter 2: The Lamian War: Part One

1. Pseudo Plutarch *Lives of the Attic Orators* VII 841c-842a; Lawton (2003), 123–4; Worthington (2000), 100.
2. Macedonia's uncontested supremacy in Greece emerged after Agis III's failed revolt in 331 – Curtius 6.1.1-21.
3. Lycurgus *Against Leocrates*; Diodorus 17.15; Pseudo Plutarch *Lives of the Attic Orators* VII 841e; Lawton (2003), 124; Mari (2003), 83.
4. Pseudo Plutarch *Lives of the Attic Orators* VII 842f; Habicht (1997), 22–3.
5. Pseudo Plutarch *Lives of the Attic Orators* VII 841b & 841c; Diodorus 18.11.3; Green (2003), 1.
6. Plutarch *Life of Phocion* 21.1; IG II² 1629.783–812; Not all of these triremes were suitable for battle however, as Morrison (1987), 90 n.12 states. Indeed, some 200 of them would never leave the Athenian harbour in the ensuing war, either due to lack of crews or damage. I include a more in-depth analysis of the ships in a later chapter.
7. Lycurgus *Against Leocrates*; Demosthenes *On the Crown*; IG II² 349; Lawton (2003), 124–5.
8. Plutarch *Life of Phocion* 17; Worthington (2000), 100.
9. I follow the view of Habicht (1997), 31 and others that this Nicanor was the adopted son of Aristotle.
10. Bosworth (1988), 223; Grainger (1999), 56. Early 324: Worthington (1986), 63 & 65.
11. Aristotle *Rhetoric* 1384b 24; Diodorus 18.8.7; Plutarch *Life of Alexander* 49.15.
12. For Athenian and Aetolian ethnic cleansing see Habicht (1996), 398. Athenaeus 12.538b; Plutarch *Life of Alexander* 49.15; Grainger (2019), 65 for Alexander being influenced by figures sympathetic to these exiles and the story of Gorgus of Iasus, the keeper of Alexander's armoury.
13. Worthington (1986), 65.
14. Hypereides *State Prosecution of Demosthenes* 18. A feeling further aided by the emergence of rumours that Alexander wished them to worship him as a god.
15. Dinarchus *Against Demosthenes* 58 & 94.
16. Curtius 10.2.1; Diodorus 17.108.6.
17. Athenaeus 13,586d & 596a-b; Diodorus 17.108.5–6. Worthington (1994), 47.
18. Harpalus was, at the end of the day, a Macedonian. They probably feared having a Macedonian, who possessed a large army, within their walls.
19. Diodorus 17.108.7.
20. Dinarchus *Against Philocles* 1–2; Pseudo Plutarch *Lives of the Attic Orators* VII 86a; Plutarch *Life of Demosthenes* 25.3; Worthington (1994), 47.
21. What was more, according to Hypereides, Harpalus also promised allies. 'Enigmatic satraps,' who would provide their support in any upcoming revolt – Hypereides *State Prosecution of Demosthenes* 19.

22. Diodorus 17.108.7; Hypereides *State Prosecution of Demosthenes* 17–19; Plutarch *Life of Demosthenes* 25.2; Worthington (2000), 103–4.
23. Diodorus 17.108.7; Hypereides *State Prosecution of Demosthenes* 8.
24. Hypereides *State Prosecution of Demosthenes* 19; Worthington (2000), 103–4.
25. Worthington (1994), 48; Worthington (2000), 103–4.
26. Hypereides *State Prosecution of Demosthenes* 8–9 & 19; Worthington (1984), 139; Worthington (1986), 66.
27. Worthington (1986), 66.
28. Diodorus 18.8.5; Dinarchus *Against Demosthenes* 81–2; Worthington (2000), 104.
29. Hypereides *State Prosecution Against Demosthenes* 19; Worthington (2000), 104.
30. Hypereides *State Prosecution Against Demosthenes* 11–12. Argument of Worthington (1986), 67; Worthington (2000), 104–5.
31. Diodorus 17.108.7; Plutarch *Life of Demosthenes* 25.6; Chapter 5.
32. Pseudo Plutarch *Lives of the Attic Orators* VII 842d; Hypereides *State Prosecution Against Demosthenes* 31–2.
33. Dinarchus *Against Demosthenes* 94; Hypereides *State Prosecution Against Demosthenes* 21; Mari (2003), 85.
34. Worthington (1986), 139; Worthington (2000), 105.
35. Hypereides *State Prosecution of Demosthenes* 31. Mari (2003), 84.
36. Arrian 1.9, 1.10.2–6 & 6.17.1–2; Diodorus 17.15.3–5. Worthington (1994), 49; Worthington (2000), 104.
37. Hypereides *State Prosecution of Demosthenes* 19. At the forefront were the Aetolians, who were similarly fearful of Alexander's return. The Athenian embassy hoped to retain control of Samos; the Aetolian embassy hoped to retain control of Oeniadae – Grainger (1999), 55.
38. Dinarchus *Against Demosthenes* 45; Worthington (1986), 68.
39. Worthington (1984), 142–3.
40. Demosthenes *Letters* 3.31–2; Dinarchus *Against Aristogiton* 15; Plutarch *Life of Phocion* 26.2.
41. Dinarchus *Against Demosthenes* 1; Plutarch *Life of Demosthenes* 26.1–2.
42. See Worthington (2001), 129–31.
43. See also Mari (2003), 85.
44. Plutarch *Life of Demosthenes* 26.2; Worthington (2000), 106: 'The verdict was political, designed to remove Demosthenes from the political scene.'
45. Worthington (2000), 106.
46. Errington (1975), 51–7; Habicht (1997), 34; Worthington (1984), 142.
47. Diodorus 17.106.3 & 17.111.1.
48. Diodorus 18.8.2; Grainger (1999), 56; Griffith (1935), 34; Worthington (2000), 102.
49. Diodorus 17.111.1–2. Leading figures supposedly accompanied them – disgraced Persian governors hoping to escape Alexander's wrath. We don't know who they were.
50. Diodorus 15.95; Polyaenus 6.2.1–2; Heckel (2006), 151.
51. Diodorus 17.111.1–3; *IG* II² 1631; Pausanias 1.25.5; Badian (1961) 27 & 38 for this 'ferry service' occurring early in 324; Worthington (1987), 489–91 for the academic debate surrounding this.
52. Diodorus 18.9.2–3; Pseudo Plutarch *Lives of the Attic Orators* IX 848e; Griffith (1935), 35. Although the text in Pseudo Plutarch mentions a certain Chares in command at Taenarum, I agree with Griffith that this is likely to be an error for Leosthenes.
53. Plutarch *Life of Phocion* 22.3.
54. Diodorus 18.9.4; Plutarch *Life of Phocion* 22.3–4.
55. Diodorus 16.42.7 & 17.15.1–2; Plutarch *Life of Phocion* 14.7, 17.1–3 & 21.1.
56. Plutarch *Life of Phocion* 17.4–6; Heckel (2006), 221.
57. Diodorus 18.9.1.
58. Diodorus 18.9.4–5.
59. Diodorus 18.9.5; Grainger (1999), 57.

60. Diodorus 18.10.1; Plutarch *Life of Phocion* 23.1.
61. Diodorus 18.10.1; Green (2003), 2.
62. The soldiers were impetuous. Many men of property were not inclined to fund the war and the city had recently been hit by the Harpalus affair.
63. Diodorus 18.10.2. The debate on trireme and quadrireme numbers: see Morrison (1987), 89–93 vs. the likes of Bosworth (2003), 15–16. I am more inclined to believe Morrison's argument. Ships were not a problem for the Athenians. Thanks largely to Lycurgus' reforms, by the time of this decree the dockyards at the Piraeus housed more than 400 war vessels – 360 triremes and 50 quadriremes. The issue was finding enough trained crews to man them. Lacking enough trained rowers, only a portion of the warships at Athens' disposal were mobilised – Green (2003), 1–4.
64. Diodorus 18.10.2.
65. Words of Diodorus 18.10.2.
66. The Athenians would honour Asclepiodorus' efforts by setting up an elaborate 'stele' (stone slab) in his honour.
67. Diodorus 18.11.1; IG II^2 367; Bosworth (2003), 18–19; Lawton (2003), 126.
68. Worthington (1989), 81. Figures recalled by the Athenians included the recently-disgraced Philocles.
69. The Aetolian army was commanded by Aetolian generals chosen by the League, but it would be Leosthenes who served as the army's commander in chief.
70. Diodorus 18.9.5; Grainger (1999), 57–8.
71. Ever since the ascendancy of King Philip II of Macedon in 359 – and perhaps before then – Antipater had been a significant force in Macedonian politics. Alongside Parmenion, Antipater was one of Philip's most influential advisors – a vital part of the Macedonian triumvirate. His influence had only increased further following Philip's unexpected death in 336.
72. Diodorus 17.62.5–63.4.
73. Grainger (2019), 76. Indeed, it was perhaps for this very reason that Antipater had defied one of Alexander the Great's last orders to him, instructing that he send reinforcements to Asia. Consequently, he retained a strong army in Macedonia.
74. Diodorus 18.12.2.
75. Diodorus 18.12.2; Grainger (2019), 79.
76. Diodorus 18.12.1; Plutarch *Life of Demosthenes* 27.2.
77. Diodorus 18.12.2.
78. Green (2003), 1.
79. Griffith (1935), 36 argues that Phocion's 'short course' comment was targeted at the Athenian levies, not the veteran mercenaries.
80. Diodorus 18.11.5.
81. Grainger (2019), 78.
82. Diodorus 18.11.5.
83. Strabo 10.1.13; Sekunda (1984) 19–20; Strootman (2011), 53–4 & 60–2.
84. Diodorus 18.12.3 & 18.15.2.
85. Why did the Thessalians desert? Grainger (2019), 80 provides two reasons: partly to gain freedom from Macedonian control, but partly also so that, once they had gained this freedom, the Thessalian nobility (who provided the region's famous cavalry) could exploit their peasants without interference.
86. The idea that they were fighting for 'Greek freedom' is a misnomer, but it was employed by the likes of Hypereides to increase support for the revolt.
87. Herodotus 7.201; Pausanias 10.21.2–22.4. Grainger (2019), 80.
88. Diodorus 18.12.4.
89. Polyaenus 4.4.2.
90. Perhaps the garrison had gone out to fight with Antipater south of the Sperchius? Or perhaps the Lamians evicted it after hearing word of Antipater's defeat?

91. Polyaenus 4.4.2. Some historians, for instance Bennett and Roberts (2008), 15, argue that the Lamians always remained loyal to the Macedonians and dismiss Polyaenus' anecdote on the Lamian cavalry at the Sperchius outright. I disagree. Leosthenes had just won a major victory after all and the Lamians may well have thought that Antipater's army would be annihilated if they prevented him from crossing the Sperchius. The alternative possibility is that Polyaenus' account is complete fiction, aimed to conceal Antipater's defeat and retreat with this clever stratagem.

92. Diodorus 18.12.4; Polyaenus 4.4.2. See note 91. Grainger (2019), 80 n.23: 'no doubt it (Lamia) changed sides when Antipater took over.'

93. Diodorus 18.12.4; Grainger (2019), 83; Heckel (2016), 299–300. See Chapter 6.

94. Diodorus 18.13.1.

95. Perhaps this was why the Athenian general was initially so keen to storm Lamia as soon as possible.

96. Diodorus 18.13.2; Grainger (1999), 60–1. There is an alternative argument that Aetolian soldiers were light-armed and that they thought themselves unneeded for the siege, so they asked to return home. This seems unlikely, seeing how most soldiers were probably equipped as hoplites rather than light infantry – Rzepka (2009), 23–27. Here I have followed the argument of Grainger. For a different argument, that the Aetolians faced an invasion by the Acarnanians against Oeniadae, see Bosworth (2003), 17–18.

97. Diodorus 18.13.3.

98. Athenaeus 3.100c-e and 3.104d-e; Plutarch *Life of Demosthenes* 27.2–3.

99. Demosthenes *Letters* 6; Diodorus 18.11.2; Justin 13.5.10; Plutarch *Life of Demosthenes* 27.3; *IG* II² 448; Worthington (2003), 585–9. See also Wallace (2014), 602–607.

100. Diodorus 18.11.2; Justin 13.5.10; Plutarch *Comparison of Demosthenes and Cicero* 4.2–3; Plutarch *Life of Demosthenes* 27.4–5.

101. Plutarch *Life of Demosthenes* 27.6.

102. Plutarch *Life of Phocion* 23.4.

103. Diodorus 18.18.3; Plutarch *Life of Phocion* 26.4.

104. Diodorus 18.3.5.

105. Diodorus 18.13.5; Justin 13.5.12; Plutarch *Life of Phocion* 23.2–24.1.

Chapter 3: The Thracian Test

1. For Lysimachus' family background: Arrian *Anabasis* 6.28.4; Porphyry FGH III.F.4.4; Lund (1992), 2; Heckel (2006), 153. Many of the Macedonian nobility had perished fighting the Illyrians in 360.

2. Alcimachus: Arrian *Anabasis*, 1.18.1; Philip: Curtius 8.2.32–39; Justin 15.3.12.

3. Curtius 8.1.15–16.

4. In India, Lysimachus was among those who fought in the vanguard alongside Alexander at the Battle of the Hydaspes River; a little later he received a wound while leading an assault on the Indian stronghold at Sangala (Arrian *Anabasis*, 5.13.1 & 5.24.5).

5. I believe Lysimachus' reckless streak was noticed by Alexander and that it is not sheer coincidence that Alexander never seems to have entrusted this bodyguard with a senior military command. As a soldier, he was fearless and inspirational. As a general, however, he was frequently unreliable and liable to his own, rash decisions. Alexander needed subordinates who were brave and charismatic, but he also depended upon their sound judgement in the heat of battle. Lysimachus' reckless nature is affirmed by his impetuous decision to combat the lion single-handed, as well as by his future actions fighting Seuthes in Thrace (Arrian *Events After Alexander*, 1.10). See also Lund (1992), 8.

6. Lund (1992), 3; Heckel (2006), 153.

7. Arrian *Anabasis*, 6.28.4; Heckel (2006), 154–55.

8. Highland swordsmen and skirmishers: Thucydides 2.96.1–3. 'People devoted to Ares!': Euripides *Hecuba*, 1089–90. 'Swarm of locusts': Aristophanes *Acharnians* 149–150.

9. Herodotus 5.10.1 and 9.89; Webber (2011), 1–3.

10. Diodorus 16.71.2; Arrian *Anabasis*, 1.1.4–4.8. For an overview of Philip's conquests/establishments in Thrace see Delev (2015), 5–7 & Archibald (1998), 234–236. For Alexander's activity in Thrace see Delev (2015), 7–8.
11. Diodorus 17.17.4.
12. Arrian *Anabasis* 1.28.4 & 3.12.4; Archibald (1998), 305; Heckel (2006), 251.
13. Thucydides 2.95–98. At first 150,000 men might seem an evident exaggeration, but the Thracians were renowned as one of the most numerous peoples in antiquity, second only to the Indians (Herodotus, 5.3). Thucydides' claim is likely correct, that the Odrysian Empire was able to field remarkably large armies in the late fifth century. See Webber (2003), 529.
14. Diodorus 16.71; Delev (2015), 2–7; Dimitrov and Cicikova (1978), 3. For more detail on the devolved nature of Odrysian administration by 360 see Archibald (1998), 216.
15. Xydopoulos (2010), 217.
16. Xydopoulos (2010), 219; Archibald (1998), 307.
17. Justin 12.2.16–17.
18. It is possible that Antipater had sent Zopyrion some of Agis III's defeated mercenary hoplites to serve garrison duty on the northern frontier. Other less-experienced hoplites may have joined Zopyrion from coastal city-states.
19. Curtius 10.1.43–45; Macrobius *Saturnalia*, 1.11.33 and Justin 12.2.16–17.
20. Curtius 10.1.43–45; Xydopoulos (2010) 216; Lund (1992), 23.
21. Webber (2010), 14.
22. Xydopoulos (2010), 215; Delev (2015), 10; Dimitrov and Cicikova (1978), 4 and 31–34; Archibald (1998), 307.
23. Diodorus 18.14.2; Archibald (1998), 307.
24. Lund (1992), 19–21.
25. Arrian *Events After Alexander* 1.7; Delev (2015), 11. For the belief that Lysimachus was still nominally subordinate to Antipater see Heckel (2006), 155 and Lund (1992), 54.
26. Lund (1992), 19.
27. Anson (2015), 80–82 for the argument that Lysimachus' army was made up of mercenaries and not Macedonians. Considering the abundant number of mercenaries/Asian troops in Babylon at the time of Alexander the Great's death, this argument seems convincing to me.
28. Bosworth (2002), 80. We know that a substantial number of these mercenaries were brought to Babylon, before Alexander died, by the likes of Menander – Arrian, *Anabasis* 7.23.1-3. Whether these soldiers had been trained to fight in the Macedonian manner is not explicitly stated but is certainly possible, especially when we consider the similar case of the *Epigoni*, later examples of non-Macedonian phalanxes (Diodorus 19.14.5) and the likelihood that Macedonian training programmes had been created in Asia Minor during Alexander's reign.
29. The size of his force when he departed is unclear but, given the speed with which he reached Europe, presumably it numbered in the few thousands.
30. Archibald (1998), 309.
31. Though Macedonian over lordship over much of the Thracian hinterland north of the Haemus River had been lost, several Thracian tribes situated nearer the Black Sea and Aegean remained within the Macedonian sphere – tribes such as the Thynii and Apsinthii. Mercenaries from across the region – hostile to the Odrysians for one reason or another and desiring plunder – may well have offered their services to the Macedonian general, for a charge. For Lysimachus, skilled Thracian light infantry were a welcome addition to his force.
32. Diodorus 18.14.2. I follow Anson's belief that the number of Macedonians Lysimachus had in his army was very low – Anson (2015), 80–82. He may have been reinforced by some Macedonians from frontier settlements like Philippopolis as he advanced into Odrysian territory: Archibald (1998), 309.

33. Diodorus 18.14.2; Lund (1992), 25. The battle site being on the Thracian plain identified by Saitta (1955), 63.
34. Diodorus 18.14.2; Lund (1992), 24. Archibald (1998), 246–7 and 299.
35. Webber (2011), 42, 86, 87 & 97; Webber (2003), 530.
36. Webber (2011), 93. See Webber (2003), 530–552 for a comprehensive paper on Odrysian cavalry arms, tactics and equipment.
37. Mobility was a key component of Thracian warfare throughout antiquity. For an overview of the Thracian peltast see Webber (2011), 108–112. Seuthes' infantry may have also used larger light shields. See Webber (2011), 53–55.
38. Each warrior could carry a bundle of javelins. Aided by a throwing device called an *amentum*, they could throw javelins 'beyond the usual 35–60m'. Webber (2011), 70–71; Webber (2003), 549.
39. Lund (1992), 24: 'A likely source of infantry is the tribes of the Haemus mountains.'
40. Herodotus 7.111.1 (on the Satrae tribe, who the Bessi belonged to) The Bessi had a history of hostility with Macedon: Theopompus fr.217; Polyaenus 4.4.1; Archibald (1998), 235. They were close to Seuthes' kingdom and were outside Macedon's influence at this time. It is very possible that Bessi warriors were serving in Seuthes' army. Another tribe may have been the *Dii*, famed for their swordsmen and who had served in Odrysian armies before. (Thuc. 2.92).
41. Sekunda (1983), 275–88; Webber (2011), 61–69.
42. Diodorus 18.14.2.
43. Archaeological evidence at Vetren may suggest that Lysimachus had embarked on a campaign of terror to bring Seuthes to the battle he wanted. Archibald (1998), 308–9.
44. Polyaenus 7.38; Webber (2011), 83: 'the lack of a solid heavy infantry core for the army, combined with the loose organisation of the state, and the constant in-fighting, are the major reasons for the success of later invasions of Thrace.' Also see Webber (2003), 529.
45. An unfazed Lysimachus was no stranger to fighting foes when drastically outnumbered, after his many years spent campaigning alongside Alexander the Great. He may well have used tactics learned from these clashes to his advantage in this battle.
46. For Lysimachus being defeated in a second clash, Arrian *Events After Alexander*, 1.10. I believe Diodorus refers to the first battle, while Photius' summary of Arrian refers to the second clash. The discovery of Seuthopolis all but affirms Seuthes was not subjugated by Lysimachus. See also Lund (1992), 27; Archibald (1998), 309. Arrian wrongly states that Lysimachus was killed fighting Seuthes. For the belief that there was no second clash see Heckel (2006), 248.
47. Evidence of this meeting in literature is sparse, but archaeological discoveries affirm the signing of this non-aggression pact. Most interesting is an uncovered, contemporary Thracian fresco, discovered within the entrance chamber of a monumental Odrysian tomb, dating to c.320. It seems to portray Macedonian nobles – wearing their traditional *kausia* hats on one side. Mounted and dismounted Thracians oppose them. Perhaps this depiction is an actual representation of the meeting and striking of agreement between Seuthes and Lysimachus in 323 / 322? See Webber (2011), 14 and 28–29.
48. Lund (1992), 27.
49. Lund (1992), 27.
50. Seuthes' founding of Seuthopolis and his Hellenisation attempts had probably started before 323, but Lysimachus' treaty likely catalysed this keystone domestic policy. See Delev (2015), 11.
51. Xydopoulos (2010), 219; Dimitrov and Cicikova (1978),14.
52. Dimitrov and Cicikova (1978), 42 and 57–58; Hoddinott (1981), 122–124; Webber (2011), 153; Xydopoulos (2010), 220. I must note that we do also see several features more characteristic of the original Thracian culture at Seuthopolis, for instance in Thracian tomb architecture and burial customs and in the retaining of the traditional fortified palace at Seuthopolis' core. Although Hellenisation is evident, certain features of Thracian culture remained.

53. Dimitrov and Cicikova (1978), 4–5.
54. Lund (1992) 54; Archibald (1998), 309.
55. Euripides *Hecuba*, 1089–90; Justin 15.3.15.

Chapter 4: The Bactrian Revolt

1. Ammianus Marcellinus 23.6.55–57; Arrian, *Anabasis* 3.29.2–3; Curtius 7.4.26–31; Strabo 11.7.3. For a detailed run down of Bactria's development before Alexander the Great's arrival, see Holt (1989), 27 and 32–44.
2. Curtius 7.4.27–29 and 7.5.1–16. For more on the climate and the logistics for operating in this part of the ancient world, see Engels (1978), 99–102.
3. There remains some debate whether ancient Maracanda is today's Samarkand, though it appears likely.
4. Ammianus 23.6.59 (the Dymas was probably the Polytimetus River); Arrian, *Anabasis* 4.5.3; Curtius 7.7.2 (Curtius here incorrectly calls the Jaxartes the Tanais) and 7.10.1–3. For an overview of Bactria and Sogdia's geography see Holt (1989), 11–24. See also Holt (1989), 24–25.
5. Bessus had murdered King Darius III in July 330, as they fled east from Alexander.
6. For Alexander's campaign against Bessus see Arrian *Anabasis* 3.25.3–30.5; Curtius 7.4–5. For an overview see Holt (1989), 48–51.
7. Arrian *Anabasis* 3.29.6–30.5; Curtius 7.5.36–7.
8. Arrian, *Anabasis* 4.1.3–4, 4.4.1; Curtius 7.6.25–27; Justin 12.5.2.
9. Holt (1989), 54–57.
10. Arrian, *Anabasis* 4.5.1–6.2; Curtius 7.7.31–39.
11. Curtius 7.7.39; Holt (1989), 78–9: 'The fact that Alexander's Greek mercenaries blamed Macedonian commanders for the debacle is clear in the sources.' This is despite Alexander's best efforts to cover up the disaster.
12. Significant events include Alexander's severe wound suffered during the Siege of Cyropolis, his infamous killing of Cleitus at Maracanda, the Pages Conspiracy and the costly storming of several rock fortresses across Sogdia. I have decided only to cover the Polytimetus River disaster in detail due to its relevance to the mercenary hoplites in Alexander's army. For a detailed account of these events, see Goldsworthy (2020), 387–402.
13. Curtius 6.1.1–21; Diodorus 17.62.1–63.4; Holt (1989), 78–9.
14. Arrian *Anabasis*, 3.23.8–9.
15. Arrian *Anabasis*, 4.22. For the argument that these mercenary settlers were disgruntled, anti-Macedonian mercenaries see Holt (1989), 79–81; Iliakis (2013), 182–3 and 186–7. See also Griffith (1935), 24–25.
16. The first revolt: Curtius 9.7.1–11; Diodorus 17.99.5–6. For an analysis, see Holt (1989), 82–86 and Iliakis (2013), 187–90.
17. Diodorus 18.7.1–2.
18. Holt (1989), 88: 'It is possible, too, that mercenaries from surrounding satrapies also joined in the new rebellion'.
19. Diodorus 18.7.1–2.
20. Curtius 10.2.8. Anson (2015), 70: 'there appears no good reason to question Curtius' figure (of 15,000 Macedonians).'
21. Diodorus 18.7.3.
22. Already Perdiccas had despatched a large number of mercenaries to aid Eumenes and Leonnatus in their Cappadocian campaign. He had also provided Lysimachus a substantial mercenary force to help assert his authority in Thrace (see Chapter 3).
23. Diodorus 18.7.3. A test of loyalty perhaps, testing their obedience to Perdiccas' new regime?
24. Arrian, *Anabasis* 7.5.6; *Indica* 18.6.
25. Diodorus 18.7.4.

26. The fact that Peithon was now the governor of the most powerful satrapy in the east, with bountiful manpower reserves, was another likely reason why Perdiccas chose him to command the expedition.

27. Although Diodorus claims that Peithon was not among the satraps ordered to provide soldiers for the expedition, I find it difficult to believe that the manpower-rich province of Media did not supply the lion share of the forces Peithon ended up commanding. If Peithon had remained in Babylon between Alexander's death and Perdiccas sending him east on this expedition, which seems almost certain given the small time-frame, perhaps Atropates, the previous Median governor, had remained as an 'interim' satrap over the whole of Media until Peithon's arrival. Atropates' close relations with Perdiccas, combined with his vast influence over Media, means he was almost certainly a key satrap who Perdiccas expected Peithon to receive troops from. Though Diodorus omits his name, it seems very likely this Persian governor played a key role in mustering a sizable contingent of Medians in little time for Peithon's expedition. This is not to mention the renowned ability of Median cavalry in the fourth century. Peithon would have been foolish not to enlist a sizable contingent of them.

28. Diodorus 18.7.5; Bosworth (2002), 61–2; Iliakis (2013), 192. The satraps in the eastern provinces had evidently answered the call to supply soldiers. An entry from a Babylonian astronomical diary seems to suggest that Peithon departed in either December 323 or January 322.

29. The root for this hatred is the conflict between Eumenes and Peithon, which I will discuss in the next book.

30. Holt (1989), 90; Roisman (2012), 84–5.

31. If Perdiccas had doubted Peithon's loyalty in the slightest, then he surely would have appointed either Alcetas, Aristonous, Seleucus or Attalus as the commander of the expedition instead.

32. Diodorus 18.7.2.

33. If we consider other battles of the period (for instance the Battle of Gaugamela – Arrian *Anabasis* 3.11.8-9), Peithon likely positioned his 3,000 elite Macedonian footmen on the right side of the infantry line. Next to them were soldiers from the various eastern satrapies: Medians, Persians, Drangianians, Arachosians, Mardians and Parthians. Cavalry must have covered the flanks. For shouting before engaging see Onasander XXIX.

34. Diodorus 18.7.6.

35. Diodorus 18.20.1. Resentment/hostility towards Philon is likely what led Letodorus to be targeted by Peithon's spy.

36. Diodorus 18.7.5–6.

37. Our source makes no mention that Peithon made any attempt at a lengthy cavalry pursuit and suggests that a large proportion of the defeated force had survived the battle.

38. Though they may have regained a degree of composure, this appears tenuous. Diodorus makes clear that discipline had completely broken down among the mercenaries' ranks during the battle, implying fear had taken hold. Any composure those that regrouped may have regained would quickly shatter if they had to fight a second, futile prolonged combat with Peithon's victorious army.

39. A likely place where these men had regrouped was their baggage train. Though they had little stomach to fight, this camp contained all they held dear – their families and possessions. The mercenaries would be loath to let them fall into their enemy's hands.

40. Given the size of Philon's army initially and subsequent events, it seems likely that not all the rebels who had fled regrouped at their baggage camp. But it appears a significant number were present to hear Peithon's proposal. They must have also been disheartened at having had to abandon the field and leave their fallen comrades without burial.

41. Diodorus 18.7.8.

42. Diodorus 18.7.8–9. Holt (1989), 90 believes only Letodorus' 3,000 turncoats were slain. Yet Diodorus makes clear that the victims of the massacre were the 'defeated Greek

rebels' and not Letodorus' contingent. I am more inclined to believe Heckel (2006), 151 that Letodorus' 3,000 survived the massacre.

43. According to Diodorus, the reason Perdiccas issued such a brutal order is because he was suspicious of Peithon and his sinister ambitions to recruit the defeated mercenaries to carve out his own kingdom in the east. This reason however, as I have explained above, is almost certainly fictional, especially as Peithon avoided any punishment from Perdiccas when he returned to the royal army.

44. Roisman (2012), 84–6. Though the idea that Peithon had a traitorous ulterior motive is fictional, the idea that he had intended the reconciliation to achieve a more peaceful resolution is very possible. The Macedonians needed as many garrison troops as possible to remain in Bactria-Sogdia and help maintain this frontier. Peithon's mission would then appear all the more successful. The Macedonians however, keen for spoils, had other ideas.

45. Holt (1989), 90–91. For, what I would argue is, the best modern account of Hellenistic Bactria see Frank Holt's *Thundering Zeus: The Making of Hellenistic* Bactria (1999).

46. Strabo 11.7.1; Holt (1989), 89: 'Only the spade is likely to clarify the problem'.

47. Heckel (2006), 151. Xref Holt (1989) 90, who believes Letodorus' 3,000 soldiers were the ones massacred by Peithon's Macedonians.

Chapter 5: The Spartan Adventurer

1. Arrian 6.27.3–4; Curtius 10.1.1. See Badian (1969), 16–25 for an alternate argument that a paranoid Alexander was deliberating purging himself of possible threats.

2. Hypereides *State Prosecution of Demosthenes* 8 & 17–19. For a full list of references, see Chapter 2, particularly notes 16–23.

3. Athenaeus 12.538b.

4. Hypereides *State Prosecution Against Demosthenes* 11–12. Argument of Worthington (1986), 67; Worthington (2000), 104–5.

5. Diodorus 17.108–7–8.

6. Arrian *Events After Alexander*, 9.16; Curtius 10.2.3; Diodorus 18.19.2 For a slightly different version of events see Pausanias 2.33.4.

7. Arrian *Events After Alexander* 9.16. Arrian claims Thibron had 6,000 men, although Diodorus (18.19.2) claims Thibron had 7,000.

8. Arrian *Events After Alexander* 9.16; Diodorus 18.19.3.

9. Herodotus 4.156–8. Stucchi, Robinson and Descoeudres (1989), 73–74. It appears people from settlements including Sparta, Thera, Samos, Lindus and Crete also sailed, but it was the Therans who were the dominant force.

10. The ancient Greeks viewed Libya as one of the World's three continents: Asia, Europe and Libya.

11. It is possible the Gilgammes, the local Libyan tribe, wanted the Greek settlers off their land.

12. For the full story of Cyrene's founding see Herodotus 4.150–9. For discussion on its veracity, see Stucchi, Robinson and Descoeudres (1989), 73–84.

13. Herodotus 2.161 and 4.159.

14. Pindar *Pythian* 9.5.

15. Arrian *Indica* 43.13; Herodotus 4.199.

16. SEG IX 2; Kingsley (1986), 165–177.

17. Herodotus 4.169; Pindar *Pythian* 4.15; Holland (2013) 674.

18. Pindar *Pythian* 5.55.

19. Worthington (2016), 93.

20. Arrian *Events After Alexander* 9.16; Diodorus 18.19.3. Arrian claims that Thibron's assistance was also requested by exiles from the nearby city of Barca.

21. Waterfield (2019), 480: 'Since Cyrene was one of the largest and most prosperous Greek cities of the Mediterranean, this was a bold plan.'

22. Diodorus 18.19.3.

23. The function of Cyrenean chariots has been debated in academic circles. See Anderson (1965), 349–352; (1975), 175–187 and Greenhalgh (1973), 16. I am more inclined to believe they served the role I have described: Aeneas Tacticus 16.14 for their purpose as troop transports; Diodorus 20.41.1 for there being three people in every chariot. We also have a relief from the Temple of Zeus at Cyrene, showing a transport, or war, chariot, with a cabin carrying three figures. In this case the archaeology seems to confirm the literature that there were three people per war chariot. See Stucchi, Robinson and Descoeudres (1989), 80. Also Polyaenus 7.28.1.
24. I cannot give a precise value, given it is based on modern estimates.
25. Diodorus 18.19.3–4.
26. Diodorus 18.19.5.
27. Diodorus 18.19.4. For the fifty vehicles, I am basing this number on the total number of vehicles Ophellas later had at his disposal when he controlled Cyrene (Diodorus 20.41.1).
28. Diodorus 18.19.5; Thucydides 7.50.2.
29. Diodorus 18.20.3.
30. Newell (1938), 3–4.
31. Heckel (2006) 169. We know nothing else about his background but it is possible that he had previously served among Alexander the Great's famed, mercenary Cretan contingent.
32. Diodorus 18.20.1. Animosity between supposedly allied, ambitious military leaders is a hallmark of this period.
33. Diodorus 18.20.2.
34. Diodorus 18.20.2; Hornblower (1981), 122. It appears Diodorus' source for Thibron's venture is a mercenary source, likely someone who served in Thibron's army.
35. Diodorus 18.20.3.
36. Diodorus 18.20.4. It appears that Thibron believed he would be able to retain hold of Apollonia, because he had kept his men's baggage there. For some reason, he seems to have believed Apollonia was unlikely to be attacked.
37. Diodorus 18.20.5.
38. The Cyrenean raiding army had possibly sought refuge within allied Taucheira.
39. Diodorus 18.20.6. That the Taucheirans were harshly treated by Thibron and his mercenaries is suggested by later events (the Taucheiran demands for violent retribution against Thibron). See page 120.
40. The recapture of Apollonia is explained as a primary reason for the food shortage, but the devastating Cyrenean *chevauchee* against their neighbouring city-states must also have played its part.
41. Diodorus 18.21.1.
42. This is contrary to the argument of Bosworth (1988), 291–2, who supports an earlier chronology and believes these mercenaries were recruited before Leosthenes set off for the Lamian War. Diodorus' wording, implying that there were still 2,500 mercenaries at Taenarum, suggests that this is not the case.
43. Diodorus 18.21.1–2. It is not difficult to presume that the material wealth of Cyrenaica was emphasised to these mercenaries.
44. Diodorus 18.21.2.
45. Diodorus 18.21.3.
46. Diodorus 18.20.3 for allied Cyrenean city-states. We know that at least the cities of Barca and Euhesperides remained on Thibron's side. If we consider Thibron's original 6,000 soldiers, his 2,500 reinforcements, alongside an unknown number of casualties and allied units, I will take an educated guess that Thibron's army numbered between 5–15,000.
47. Diodorus 18.21.4.
48. Mnasicles' presence at the decisive battle is unclear. He does not appear to have been one of the army's generals but, given his non-Cyrenean birth, this does not necessarily mean he had not taken part in it.
49. Diodorus 18.21.5. Contrarily, it appears Thibron had established good logistical supply networks with his allies in western Cyrenaica, aided further by his pillaging of fertile, Cyrenean countryside.

50. Diodorus 18.21.6.
51. Though not explicitly said, it seems likely that Mnasicles was among those who fled to Egypt. He would not have received mercy from Thibron.
52. Worthington (2016), 89, for Ptolemy arriving in 322.
53. Arrian *Anabasis* 7.23.6–8; Pseudo-Aristotle *Oeconomicus* 1352a-b; Badian (1961), 19.
54. Pausanias 1.6.3; Pseudo-Aristotle *Oeconomicus* 1352a-b; Worthington (2016), 90–1. When exactly Cleomenes was murdered we do not know, but I am more inclined to believe he was executed not long after Ptolemy's arrival at Memphis.
55. Diodorus 18.14.1.
56. Diodorus 18.14.2; Meeus (2014), 271–2; Worthington (2016), 91.
57. Curtius 4.8.4; Bosworth (2002), 81–2 strongly suggests the 4,000 soldiers left in Egypt were mercenaries, considering the region's harmonious subjugation.
58. Worthington (2016), 89.
59. Diodorus 18.33.3.
60. Arrian *Events After Alexander* 10A.6; Justin 13.6.19; Errington (1970), 65. I am more inclined to believe that formal alliances with at least some of these Cypriot kings – notably Nicocreon and Pasicrates of Soli – came later, when war was about to break out against Perdiccas. See Meeus (2014) 271–2 and Worthington (2016), 92 as examples of the opposite argument that Ptolemy struck an alliance with these Cypriot kings in 322.
61. Diodorus 18.21.7. Ptolemy was certainly aware of many of these developments, though the oligarchs may have provided him fresh information.
62. Diodorus 18.21.7; FGH, no.239, B(10). Worthington (2016), 92. The Parian Marble entry confirms that Ophellas must have been sent to Cyrene after June 322 BC.
63. Diodorus 18.21.7.
64. Diodorus 18.21.8.
65. Arrian *Events After Alexander* 9.18; Diodorus 18.21.9. The word Arrian uses is 'hung up'. I follow Goralski's (1989), 90 belief that this means Thibron was probably crucified, rather than being lynched.
66. SEG 9.1.1–46; Austin (2012), 69–70; FGH, no.239, B(11). Worthington (2016), 93 & 103–4.
67. Arrian *Events After Alexander* 9.19; Diodorus 18.21.9, 19.79.1–4 and 20.40.1. Thibron's defeated mercenaries may well have been enlisted in Ophellas' garrison force.

Chapter 6: The Lamian War: Part Two

1. Antiphilus had likely served among Athenian ranks at the Battle of Chaeronea all those years before.
2. Diodorus 18.13.6; Plutarch, *Life of Phocion* 24.1. Habicht (1997), 38.
3. Prior to fighting in the Lamian War, it is possible Menon had served in the elite Pharsalian contingent that had headed east with Alexander the Great on his Persian campaign back in 334. Arrian *Anabasis* 3.11.10.
4. Plutarch *Life of Pyrrhus* 1.3; *Life of Phocion* 25.3. Menon's daughter was called Phthia. The powerful king she married was Aeacides of Molossia. They were the parents of Pyrrhus.
5. Plutarch, *Life of Phocion* 24.2.
6. Ashton (1980) i.70, mentioned in Bosworth (2003), 21 (n.66).
7. Strabo 10.1.6. Bosworth (2003), 21.
8. Plutarch *Life of Phocion*, 25.1. Heckel (2006), 167 for Micion possibly also being the commander of Antipater's fleet.
9. Plutarch *Life of Phocion* 25.1–2.
10. Diodorus 18.12.1.
11. Justin 13.5.13.
12. Diodorus 18.14.4.
13. Arrian *Anabasis* 4.25.3, 6.10.1–2 & 7.5.5. Leonnatus then went on to gain an emphatic victory against the Oreitae. Curtius 9.10.19.

14. Curtius 10.7.8; Diodorus 18.3.1; Arrian, *Events After Alexander* 1.2 & 1.6. Anson (2015), 83. See Chapter 1.
15. Plutarch *Life of Eumenes* 3.3. Bosworth (2002), 78; Roisman (2012) 111: 'Scholars largely agree that Leonnatus took no (Macedonian) veterans with him...' This being said, I do believe Leonnatus had a small number of Macedonian companions, who served among his elite cavalry, his *agema*. It was Macedonian phalanx troops that he lacked.
16. Diodorus 18.12.1. Diodorus mistakenly calls Leonnatus, 'Philotas'. Anson (2015), 83; Errington (1970), 60.
17. Diodorus 18.14.4; Plutarch *Life of Eumenes* 3.9; Justin 13.5.14. Carney (2006), 65.
18. Heckel (2016), 119 & 121; Sprawski (2008), 12–13.
19. Plutarch *Life of Eumenes* 3.3.
20. Plutarch *Life of Eumenes* 3.4–6.
21. For March 322: Heckel (2016), 299; Walek (1924), 28.
22. The Athenians may have found safe anchorage at Sestos, a city-state on the European side of the Hellespont that had once been an Athenian possession.
23. Diodorus 18.14.5. Anson (2015), 84; Grainger (2019), 83; Heckel (2016), 299–300; Wrightson (2014), 525. For the naval battles of the Lamian War, I am convinced by Wrightson's argument in regard to chronology and the number of battles (one before Cleitus' arrival, three fought by Cleitus).
24. *Suda* Λ 249 in Heckel (2016), 120–1; Romm (2011), 137; Sprawski (2008), 12–4.
25. Diodorus 18.14.5. Sprawski (2008), 14: 'Cleopatra's favour may have also been of significance; she may have cared about her future husband gathering appropriately large forces.'
26. Diodorus 18.14.5.
27. *Suda* Λ 249, in Heckel (2016), 120–1; Karunanithy (2013), 62–3; Sprawski (2008), 16.
28. For the following (Leonnatus' campaign in Thessaly), I have found the arguments of Sprawski (2008), 9–31 convincing and follow his arguments for the campaign.
29. Sprawski (2008), 26.
30. Diodorus 18.15.1; Sprawski (2008), 26
31. For the battle site being the plain near Lake Xynias, see Sprawski (2008), 26–7. See also Heckel (2006), 150 for the battle happening not far north of Lamia.
32. Diodorus 18.15.2. Diodorus seems to indicate that Menon had just his 2,000 Thessalians with him at this clash.
33. Sprawski (2008), 28.
34. Arrian, *Events After Alexander* 1.9B; Diodorus 18.15.3; Justin 13.5.14; Plutarch, *Life of Phocion* 25.3.
35. Diodorus 18.5.4.
36. Sprawski (2008), 28.
37. Diodorus 18.15.5; Justin 13.5.15–16. Sprawski (2008), 28.
38. Diodorus 18.15.6.
39. Diodorus 18.15.7.
40. Diodorus 18.12.1.
41. *Suda* K 2335, in Heckel (2016), 149.
42. Arrian *Anabasis*, 7.12.1–4; Heckel (2016), 141.
43. Diodorus 18.22.1. Heckel (2006), 98. Balacrus, the previous governor of Cilicia, had recently died fighting the Isaurians. Harpalus had also spent some time in the province.
44. Diodorus 18.4.4; Justin 13.5.7. Ashton (1993), 128–9. This is also mentioned in Chapter 1. Anson (2015), 85, for Alexander approving Craterus' prolonged stay in Cilicia.
45. *Suda* K 2335, in Heckel (2016), 149; Anson (2012), 53; Anson (2015), 85–6; Grainger (2019), 81; Heckel (2016), 141–2.
46. Craterus would not have set off during the winter months, especially without the fleet. Grainger (2019), 83: '...winter was no time to sail in the Mediterranean'.
47. Grainger (2019), 85–6; Heckel (2016), 144.

48. Diodorus 18.16.1 and 18.16.4; Bosworth (2002), 60; Errington (1970), 61; Heckel (2016), 300.
49. For the agreed belief that Craterus left Cilicia in spring 322 see Anson (2015), 86; Bosworth (2002), 60 as examples.
50. Diodorus 18.4.4; Morrison (1987), 91.
51. Murray (2012), 8–9 & 54.
52. Arrian *Anabasis* 2.21.3–4; Curtius 4.3.14–5; Diodorus 17.43.4. Murray (2012), 4. Boarding parties equipped with grappling hooks and well-versed in the art of maritime melee combat likely also served among the ship's crew, providing them further potential to serve as competent boarding vessels.
53. Phoenician and Cypriot 'fours' and 'fives' at the Siege of Tyre: Arrian *Anabasis* 2.20.1–3; Curtius 4.3.14–5; Murray (2012) 94–100. Persian wealth: Murray (2012), 68: 'Alexander's successors drew from their stores of Persian treasure to build larger and heavier warships.' Helmsmen: Murray (2012), 30.
54. Plutarch *Moralia* 338a.
55. Heckel (2016), 302; Wrightson (2014), 526–7.
56. Diodorus 18.15.8. For the debate about how many ships the Athenians had overall in their battle fleet before Amorgos see Ashton (1977) 1–11 and Morrison (1987) 90–92. Epigraphic evidence from the Athenian naval yard in 323/322 seems to suggest that just under 1/3 of Euetion's fleet at Amorgos were quadriremes. For the number 49 see line 174 of *IG* ii2.1631 and Ashton (1977) 5. The rest of Euetion's fleet were triremes. What happened to the seven quinqueremes (fives) mentioned in the Athenian fleet in 325/4 we don't know.
57. Bosworth (2003), 16.
58. Date credibly proposed by Ashton (1977) 11. For why the battle was fought off Amorgos see Wrightson (2014), 528–530. I find his argument about the order of the Lamian War's naval battles convincing.
59. We are told this on the Parian Marble (*FGrH* 239 B9).
60. See Morrison (1987) 93–94 for how Athenian losses do not appear heavy. I am in agreement, particularly because of how we hear the Athenians were able to drag their wrecked ships back to Athens. For an example of the opposite argument, see Bosworth (2003), 14–22.
61. Plutarch *Moralia* 338a. For the significance of Amorgos see Ashton (1977), 1; Heckel (2016), 301–2. Bosworth (2003), 14–22 correctly identifies the importance of Amorgos, but I find his argument that Amorgos was the last battle fought at sea, unconvincing. Although I agree with Ashton that the sea battle off Amorgos was very significant, I disagree that the Athenians lost a lot of ships. It was significant because it paved the way for Cleitus to reach the Hellespont and unite with Antipater's navy.
62. Plutarch, *Life of Demetrius* 11.3.
63. *IG* II2 505; Wrightson (2014), 523–4.
64. *IG* II2 493; Heckel (2006), 37; Wrightson (2014), 519 and 523.
65. Diodorus 18.16.4–5.
66. See also Justin 13.5.17.
67. Diodorus 18.17.3.
68. At one of Alexander the Great's most important battles, Issus in 333, it was this cavalry force that had critically fended off the much larger Persian horse long enough for the Macedonian king to gain victory for instance. Arrian *Anabasis* 2.11.1–3.
69. Diodorus 18.17.3.
70. Bennett & Roberts (2010), 37.
71. Diodorus 18.17.4.
72. Grainger (2019), 88. There would have been Asian cavalrymen among Antipater and Craterus' horsemen too.
73. Diodorus 18.17.4.

74. Diodorus 18.17.5.
75. Diodorus 18.17.5; Plutarch, *Life of Phocion* 26.1.
76. Diodorus 18.17.6–8. Grainger (2019), 89 for Antipater and Craterus detaching significant portions of their army to besiege the various Thessalian cities.
77. See Chapter 14. Polybius 9.29.1–6 & 30.3.
78. Diodorus 18.17.8; Plutarch, *Life of Phocion* 26.1.
79. Bosworth (2003), 21–22; Wrightson (2014), 532.
80. Wrightson (2014), 532–3.
81. Diodorus 18.15.9. Debate continues among scholars as to whether this battle was fought by the Echinades Islands or the Lichades Islands. I believe the former is most likely. See Bosworth (2003) 17–18; Wrightson (2014), 530–534. For the Lichades see Morrison (1987), 94–5. Heckel (2016) 302–4 evaluates both possibilities.
82. Diodorus 18.18.1–2; Plutarch, *Life of Phocion* 26.3.
83. Diodorus 18.18.3; Plutarch, *Life of Phocion* 27.4–5.
84. Plutarch *Life of Phocion*, 30.2; Green (2003), 5.
85. It was also these citizens that had manned the Athenian fleet. Disenfranchising them was a clever way through which Antipater could neutralise 'Athens' naval aggressiveness'. Green (2003), 2.
86. Diodorus 18.18.4–5; Plutarch, *Life of Phocion* 28.4.
87. Antipater's activity in Thrace: Polyaenus 4.4.1; Theopompus *FGrH* 115 F.
88. Pliny *Natural History*, 4.41; Strabo 7.6.2. Baynham (2003), 25; Jones (1937), 4–5.
89. Diodorus 18.18.4; Plutarch *Life of Phocion* 28.4. Meeus (2008), 65. For an in-depth paper on the removal of these disenfranchised Athenians see Baynham (2003), 23–29. See also Chapter 3, for Lysimchus in Thrace.
90. Plutarch *Life of Phocion* 28.1.
91. Diodorus 18.18.5; Plutarch *Life of Phocion* 28.1–2; Green (2003), 2. Celebrating a military victory feels an abnormal concept now, but this was not the case in antiquity.
92. Plutarch, *Life of Phocion* 27.3; *Life of Demosthenes* 28.2.
93. Plutarch, *Life of Phocion* 26.2; *Life of Demosthenes* 28.2.
94. Plutarch, *Life of Demosthenes* 28.3–4.
95. Polybius 9.29.2; *Syll.3* 317; *IG* II2.448; Austin (2006), 74–5.
96. Plutarch *Life of Demosthenes*, 28.4; Polybius 9.29.4. Heckel (2006), 141.
97. Plutarch *Life of Demosthenes* 29.
98. Plutarch *Comparison of Demosthenes and Cicero* 1–5.

Chapter 7: The Rise of Perdiccas

1. Examples: Antipater's delayed response to Perdiccas' marriage request. Ptolemy in Egypt killing Cleomenes. Leonnatus crossing to Europe to pursue his own imperial goals. Antigonus refusing Perdiccas' orders. Craterus' obstinance.
2. Justin 13.1.
3. Arrian *Indica* 18.7; Nepos *Eumenes* 1.1; Plutarch *Life of Eumenes* 1.1–2; Anson (2015), 42.
4. Nepos *Eumenes* 1.4–6; 13.1; Anson (2015), 43–4.
5. Diodorus 18.58.2; Nepos *Eumenes* 6.1–2 & 13.1; Anson (2015), 50–2.
6. Nepos *Eumenes* 1.6 & 13.1.
7. Arrian *Indica* 18.4.
8. Arrian *Anabasis* 5.24.6; Plutarch *Life of Eumenes* 1.2–2.5. For a detailed write up of Eumenes' early life, see Anson (2015), 41–57.
9. This is not to say that he hadn't been in the wars and hadn't commanded, but the sheer military experience of those present in Babylon in mid-323 belittled anyone with even moderate experience of battle.
10. Plutarch *Life of Eumenes* 3.1.
11. Paphlagonia: Xenophon *Hellenica* 4.1.3–15; Jones (1937), 148. Cappadocia: Strabo 12.1.1–3 & 12.2.7–10; Iossif & Lorber (2010), 445–6; Jones (1937),178–9. Volcanic 'red earth' became one of the finest sources of dyes in the ancient Mediterranean. Cappadocia

was largely treeless, the exception being the plentiful forests below Mount Argaeus. See also Panichi (2005) 200–15, especially 202.

12. Curtius 4.5.13. Jones (1937), 148.
13. Diodorus 31.19.2.
14. Diodorus 31.19.3–4.
15. Diodorus 18.16.1.
16. Curtius 4.1.34; Anson (1988), 473. 'Were Ariarathes present in Asia Minor, and there is no good evidence that he was not, he must have remained neutral in the struggle.'
17. Strabo 12.1.2. Anson (1988), 474–5; Anson (2015), 79.
18. Diodorus 18.16.2. For Ariarathes' own drachms, minted at Sinope and Gaziura, see Simonetta (1961), 11.
19. Curtius 10.10.3. Eumenes initially refused the posting.
20. Anson (2015) 80 (n42) & 82.
21. Plutarch *Life of Eumenes* 3.5.
22. Plutarch *Life of Eumenes* 3.2. For the late summer, see Anson (2015), 79. Especially n.41.
23. Billows (1990), 15–22.
24. Billows (1990), 27–9 for Antigonus losing an eye at the Siege of Perinthus (340). But see Heckel (2016), 308 (n1). The evidence is too vague to claim with any certainty Antigonus could be the Antigenes or Atarrhias that Plutarch mentions lost his eye at Perinthus. Though widely-believed, as I do too, that Antigonus lost his eye during Philip II's reign, I must also note that there is a possibility Antigonus did lose it later, perhaps in the 333/332 Persian counter-attack in Anatolia.
25. Arrian *Anabasis* 1.29.3; Diodorus 17.17.3; Billows (1990), 40–1.
26. Arrian *Anabasis* 1.29.3; Curtius 3.1.8. For an overview of Antigonus' role as satrap (governor) of Phrygia, see Anson (1988), 471–7.
27. Anson (1988), 471; Billows (1990), 42. Protecting the great roads through Asia Minor was especially critical during the early years of Alexander's campaigning, when the Persian navy was still a dominant force in the Mediterranean.
28. For Antigonus recruiting native forces see Anson (1988), 475.
29. Curtius 4.1.34–5. Anson (1988), 474 and Billows (1990), 44–5 argue for 3 battles by Antigonus. Heckel (2004), 33 for just one battle.
30. Curtius 4.5.13; Billows (1990), 45–6.
31. Anson (1988), 473–5; Anson (2015), 79.
32. Plutarch *Life of Eumenes* 3.3.
33. Anson (1988), 476; Anson (2015), 79 and 82. See also Billows (1990), 57–8.
34. Leonnatus' western venture is explained in the previous chapter. Plutarch *Life of Eumenes* 3.3–5.
35. Based on the presumption preparations for the Cappadocian campaign were taking place in Hellespontine Phrygia. 2,000 is a rough estimate. Xenophon says the distance from Sardis to Cunaxa is 535 parasangs = c.2,000 miles.
36. Plutarch *Life of Eumenes* 3.6.
37. Bosworth (2002), 60, especially n.115, for Perdiccas' contact with Craterus. Errington (1970), 60.
38. Heckel (2016), 173. 'The Kappadokian campaign gave Perdikkas an opportunity to gain prestige: he would complete the conquest of Alexander's Empire.'
39. Plutarch *Life of Eumenes* 3.6.
40. Examples of units in the royal army: Arrian *Anabasis* 5.12.2, 7.8.1–3 & 7.11.2–3; Curtius 10.9.18; Diodorus 17.110.2. Anson (2015) 70.
41. *IG* ii2. 402. I am more inclined to believe Bosworth's argument that the infant Alexander was proclaimed later, because of the inscription fragment referenced above. Bosworth (1993), 422: 'The infant Alexander was proclaimed king, as we are specifically informed, but there is no indication whether the proclamation came at birth or sometime later, when the child had survived the neonatal period.' See also Errington (1970), 58.

42. Bosworth (2002), 9–10: 'There is no record of his (Craterus) meeting Perdiccas and it is most likely that the regent had invaded Cappadocia from the east, via Armenia. Macedonian authority in Armenia was likewise dubious and Perdiccas may well have hoped to reassert recognition of Macedonian suzerainty *en route* to Ariarathes' domain.' The other aspect to consider is that if Perdiccas approached Cappadocia via Cilicia, he would have to march his army through the Cilician Gates, which Ariarathes could use to his advantage. Iossif & Lorber (2010), 445–6 highlights the strategic importance of holding the Cilician Gates. All this being said, it is still very much possible that Perdiccas did approach Cappadocia via Cilicia.

43. I here believe the argument of Bosworth (2003) 10, 60 and Errington (1970), 60–1 that Craterus' departure from Cilicia was linked with Perdiccas' westward march. See Heckel (2016), 173 for more caution in linking the two events.

44. Diodorus 18.16.1–2.

45. Diodorus 18.16.2; Strabo 11.13.8; Jones (1937), 178–9; Panichi (2005) 200. Most of these horsemen presumably preferred to fight as light cavalry (the large majority likely did not have the money for lots of armour), equipped with weapons such as javelins.

46. Arrian *Events After Alexander* 1.11; Diodorus 18.16.2.

47. Appian *Mithridatic Wars* 8; Arrian *Events After Alexander* 1.11; Diodorus 18.13.3; Lucian *Octogenarians*, 13. For a muddled, alternate version see Justin 13.6.1.

48. Diodorus 31.19.4–5. Anson (1990), 125–8; Anson (2015), 88–90. Neoptolemus' army likely numbered a few thousand – see Bosworth (2002), 81. It also seems plausible that Perdiccas expected Neoptolemus to receive cavalry from local 'allies' in western Armenia. Surely he would not have sent this strong infantry force, devoid of horsemen, unless he expected cavalry reinforcements.

49. Appian *Mithridatic Wars* 8; Diodorus 18.16.3; Plutarch *Life of Eumenes* 3.6.

50. Anson (2015), 87. 'The fact that Eumenes was given such broad discretionary powers was a measure of Perdiccas' confidence in Eumenes' loyalty to him personally.'

51. Bosworth (1993), 422–3.

52. Bosworth (1993), 420–7 and Bosworth (2002), 9 for the argument that Perdiccas proclaimed Alexander king in 322, after the Cappadocian campaign.

53. Bosworth (1993), 424–5.

54. Plutarch *Life of Eumenes* 3.7–4.1. Errington (1970), 76. I am convinced by Anson's version of events that Perdiccas spent the winter in Cilicia after he left Cappadocia and commenced his campaign against the Isaurians the following spring. It would make sense, therefore, that it was then that Perdiccas enlisted the Silver Shields. See Anson (2015) 88–9. Heckel (2016), 311 meanwhile, believes Perdiccas collected the Silver Shields in Cilicia when he was *en route* to Egypt, in early 320.

55. Anson (2015), 89 (n.89). 'It is also very possible that, despite claims to the contrary, these troops did not wish to leave Asia'.

56. Anson (2015), 88–9. For alternative arguments when Perdiccas enlisted the Silver Shields, see Heckel (2016), 311 and Bosworth (2002), 33.

57. Peithon re-joining with Perdiccas Bosworth (2002), 61 (n121). Roisman (2012), 89 for how Peithon's army would have been laden with loot. Diodorus 14.20.4 – says it takes roughly four months for an army to march from Bactria to Cilicia.

58. Presumably Neoptolemus was wintering in Armenia. Anson (1990), 128; Anson (2015), 89–90. Also see Bosworth (1978), 232–4.

59. Plutarch *Life of Eumenes* 4.1.

60. Jones (1936), 127; Lenski (1999), 416.

61. Strabo 12.6.3; Jones (1936), 127; Lenski (1999), 416, 439, 446 and 450.

62. Alexander had to retain control of Cilicia at all costs. If not, his communications with the west would be utterly severed.

63. Bosworth (2002), 11 (n.24); Heckel (2006), 68–9.

64. Curtius 4.5.13; Diodorus 18.22.1. Heckel (2006), 69. Bosworth (1974) 58–64 for Balacrus dying earlier, but it seems much more likely that Balacrus died in 324 (Antonius Diogenes, in Photius *Bibliotheca* 166).

65. Bosworth (2002), 11 (n.24).
66. Lenski (1999), 415. For agreement that the Isaurian campaign occurred in spring 321, see Errington (1970), 77.
67. Syme (1986), 162.
68. Ladder teams – we know ladders were used by the Macedonians for storming settlements with immediate attacks (Arrian *Anabasis* 4.2.3). It is also possible that Perdiccas used his elephants to attack the walls, just as he would do at the Camel Fort – Diodorus 18.34.2.
69. Diodorus 18.22.2.
70. The terrain was ill-suited for a huge army, particularly one possessing both elephants and the extensive royal baggage train.
71. Diodorus 18.22.2. Lenski (1999), 446–55.
72. For a comparative assault example, see Diodorus 18.34.4.
73. Justin 13.6. Justin's narrative confuses Perdiccas' campaign against Ariarathes with the assault on Isaura. I'm inclined to believe the wound Justin mentions Perdiccas suffers when fighting Ariarathes actually occurred when assaulting Isaura.
74. Diodorus 18.22.4.
75. Diodorus 18.22.4–7.
76. Diodorus 18.22.8.
77. Lenski (1999), 418 and 455.

Chapter 8: Consolidation

1. Diodorus 18.25.6 for Perdiccas being in Pisidia.
2. Anson (2015), 93–4; Anson (1988), 476–7; Billows (1990), 58–9.
3. Arrian *Events After Alexander* 9.20.
4. Anson (1988), 477; Anson (2015), 94.
5. Plutarch *Life of Eumenes* 4.
6. Anson (2015), 90.
7. Note Karunanithy (2013) 73: 'Eumenes appears to have purchased large numbers of suitable mounts from independent dealers.'
8. Plutarch *Life of Eumenes* 4.1. Anson (2015), 91–2. For the opposing argument, that Eumenes' arrival with cavalry sparked animosity with the Macedonian veterans, see Roisman (2012), 121 & Bosworth (2005), 686. I find it more likely that the Macedonians were relieved to have much-needed cavalry aid in this hated land. Comparisons with the harsh reaction to Alexander's new Asian recruits in 324 seem unfounded. Neoptolemus' Macedonians had been on the frontier, fighting a difficult campaign. Much-needed cavalry relief would have been welcome. The evidence for Eumenes leaving his Cappadocians in Armenia is that they are not with Eumenes when he receives units from Perdiccas at the onset of the First Successor War (Diodorus 18.29.3). It is likely that sometime between Eumenes leaving them in Armenia in spring 321 and his reuniting with them in spring 320, the Cappadocians were disbanded, returning to their homes for the winter months of 321/320. There were probably also some Armenians, among Eumenes' 6,300 cavalry.
9. Anson (2015), 98.
10. Diodorus 18.37.2; Heckel (1978) 377–82; Heckel (2016), 176, 197.
11. Arrian *Events After Alexander*, 9:21.
12. Heckel (2016) 34.
13. Arrian *Events After Alexander*, 9:21; Diodorus 18.23.1.
14. Diodorus 18.23.2. Anson (2015), 94 for Antipater being preoccupied with the Lamian War. See also Chapters 2 and 6. Examples of Perdiccas' 'aloofness': Leonnatus, Antigonus and Craterus ignoring orders, governors doing their own thing (Ptolemy), insurrection (Bactria and arguably Pisidia and Cappadocia), Perdiccas remaining in Babylon until spring of 322.
15. Already Antipater had attempted to affirm his loyalty to Perdiccas after hearing of the latter's victory in Cappadocia, leaving certain decisions surrounding the fate of recently-defeated Athens to the regent (such as the question of Samos – Diodorus 18.18.6–9).

Having then returned to Macedonia, Antipater had finally focused his attention on an alliance with Perdiccas, sending Nicaea and her entourage to the regent at the turn of 322/321.

16. Arrian *Events After Alexander*, 9:21; Diodorus 18.23.1.
17. Carney (1988), 399; (2000), 124–5; (2006), 65–6.
18. Diodorus 18.23.3. For Perdiccas' royal blood, see Chapter 1. For more on Cleopatra's importance, particularly to Perdiccas, see Meeus (2009), 71–80.
19. Justin 13.6.4; Carney (2006), 66 – Olympias and Cleopatra's attempt to 'stymie' Antipater's marital plans.
20. Arrian *Events After Alexander*, 9:21. Anson (2015), 97; Heckel (2016), 173–4.
21. Justin 13.6.6. So my argument is a mix of Anson (2015), 97–8 and Heckel (2016), 174–5. Alcetas does envisage Perdiccas taking the throne and marrying Cleopatra in the near future, but he advises Perdiccas marry Nicaea now so as not to anger Antipater before everything was ready with his grand plan (discussed in Chapter 12). Justin suggests this was also done (keeping Antipater on side) so Perdiccas could acquire fresh Macedonian recruits from Europe, which is definitely possible. See also Meeus (2009), 79.
22. Arrian *Events After Alexander*, 9:21. Anson (2015), 96–9. For Hecataeus and Eumenes' animosity, see Chapter 6.
23. Arrian *Events After Alexander*, 9:21; Diodorus 18.23.3; Justin 13.6.6, although Justin wrongly states that Perdiccas did not marry Nicaea.

Chapter 9: The Macedonian Amazon

1. Athenaeus 557 c; Carney (2006) 22; Grant (2019), 227; Heckel (2006) 64. Olympias was Molossian by birth.
2. Polyaenus 8.60; Carney (2000), 69; Grant (2019), 228; Macurdy (1927), 210. Grant and Carney both agree that Cynane was likely born in the mid to late 350s.
3. I am convinced by David Grant's argument in his recent book that the bones in the antechamber of Tomb II belong to Cynane. For the limp, see Grant (2019), 135–9.
4. Grant (2019), 229.
5. Arrian *Events After Alexander* 9.22; Polyaenus 8.60; Justin 12.6.14.
6. Arrian *Anabasis* 1.5.4–5; Polyaenus 8.60.
7. Athenaeus 13.560 f; Polyaenus 8.60.
8. Diodorus 18.23.1; Plutarch *Life of Eumenes* 3.5; Roisman (2012), 90; Chapter 8, n17.
9. Arrian *Events After Alexander* 9.23; Carney (2000), 129–130; Roisman (2012), 91.
10. Carney (2000), 70; Macurdy (1927), 201–2 & 213–4.
11. Anson (2015), 100; Pomeroy (1990), 6; Roisman (2012), 90.
12. Polyaenus 8.60; Chapter 8.
13. Roisman (2012), 90–1.
14. Polyaenus 8.60.
15. Polyaenus 8.60; Heckel (2006), 101 for Ephesus although there is no clear evidence it occurred around this area of western Asia Minor.
16. Polyaenus 8.60; Grant (2019), 54. We have a later example of royal women leading their armies in striking sets of armour to try and amaze the soldiers – Athenaeus 13.560 f. This is the ceremonial attire found in the Tomb II antechamber at Vergina, which likely belonged to Cynane. I am happy to stretch my neck out here and suggest that Cynane may have been wearing this armour to awe Alcetas' Macedonians in the summer of 321.
17. Grant (2019), 228.
18. Arrian *Events After Alexander* 9.22; Diodorus 19.52.5; Polyaenus 8.60.
19. Errington (1970), 64; Roisman (2012), 91–2.
20. Arrian *Events After Alexander* 9.23; Roisman (2012), 91.
21. Grant (2012), 232.
22. Anson (2015), 100–1.
23. Arrian *Events After Alexander* 9.23.
24. Arrian *Events After Alexander* 9.23; Diodorus 19.52.5; Polyaenus 8.60.

25. Arrian *Events After Alexander* 9.24; Roisman (2012), 90–1.
26. Anson (2015), 101. Unlike Anson, however, I do not believe that this was a major turning point for Perdiccas. Subsequent events suggest the damage to Perdiccas' authority was limited – see Roisman (2012), 92.

Chapter 10: Antigonus' Flight

1. Diodorus 18.23.4.
2. Diodorus 18.23.4.
3. Diodorus 18.23.4. Waterfield (2019), 480. It was Perdiccas who had decided to return Samos to the Samians, following Athens' defeat in the Lamian War.
4. Anson (1988), 477: 'The flight of Antigonus to Europe, despite subsequent events, was one of the few successes of Perdiccan policy.'
5. Anson (2015), 102.
6. Diodorus 18.23.3; Carney (2000), 125 & 131.
7. Diodorus 18.25.3; Anson (2015), 102–4. Arrian *Events After Alexander* 9.26A is evidence that Perdiccas' intention to marry Cleopatra was only fully confirmed in early 320. When Antigonus left Asia, this was still only a rumour, albeit a strong one.
8. Arrian *Events After Alexander* 9.24 implies that Antigonus did head to Macedonia. But Diodorus 18.25.3 suggests that Antipater and Craterus were campaigning along with the main Macedonian army in Aetolia when Antigonus reached them. If we believe this, then Antigonus' route from Athens to Aetolia would not have taken him anywhere near Macedonia. The latter seems most credible to me, so I have gone with the belief that Antigonus went to Aetolia, rather than Macedonia.

Chapter 11: The Aetolian War

1. *Suda* K 2335, in Heckel (2016), 149.
2. Diodorus 18.16.5; Roisman (2012), 113–4.
3. Diodorus 18.18.7. Grainger (2019), 85–6; Heckel (2016), 146; Karunanithy (2013), 120. We have a precedent for largesse being distributed to the soldiers alongside marriage ceremonies with Alexander at Susa: Arrian *Anabasis* 7.5.1–3. See also Plutarch Life of Alexander 71.8–9, which mentions how Alexander had ordered Antipater to honour Craterus' Macedonian veterans when they returned to Macedon. As these veterans immediately participated in the Lamian War, the marriage between Phila and Craterus back in Macedon seems to have been the earliest time that Antipater could have fulfilled this order. It therefore seems likely that Antipater also honoured the soldiers at the marriage of Craterus and Phila.
4. Roisman (2012), 116–7.
5. Diodorus 18.18.7; *Suda* K 2335, in Heckel (2016), 149. See also Roisman (2012), 113.
6. Anson (1992), 43; Errington (1970), 61–2. I do not believe Craterus was meant to contest Perdiccas' power, but to rule alongside him as an equal somewhere else. The previous triumvirate Antipater had been involved in was the one formed between himself, King Philip II and Parmenion.
7. See Chapter 2.
8. Polybius 9.29.1–4 & 30.3; Mendels (1984), 154.
9. For more on the Aetolian League's constitution see Grainger (1999), 169–187.
10. Argument put forward by Grainger (1999), 51–2. For the opposing argument, that the Aetolians restored their League without Antipater's permission, see Heckel (2016), 41 (n.58).
11. There is no suggestion that there were negotiations in the primary sources but see Grainger (1999), 62 for its likelihood.
12. Diodorus 18.24.1; Mendels (1984), 154; Roisman (2012), 117.
13. Grainger (1999) 62.
14. Diodorus 18.24.2.
15. Diodorus 18.24.2; Grainger (1999), 63.

16. Grainger (1999) 63; Rzepka (2009), 23–27. Rzepka puts forward a convincing argument that 7,000 Aetolian soldiers were professionals who could act either as hoplites or as light infantry.
17. Diodorus 18.25.1.
18. Diodorus 18.25.1.
19. Argument of Grainger (1999), 63.
20. Diodorus 18.25.1; Heckel (2016) 149.
21. Grainger (1999), 63.
22. Anson (2015), 104.
23. Arrian *Events After Alexander* 9.24.
24. For the opposing argument, that the murder of Cynane did not cause Antipater or Craterus much concern, see Anson (2015), 103.
25. See Chapter 10; Diodorus 18.25.3; Anson (2015), 104.
26. Diodorus 18.25.4.
27. Diodorus 18.25.4.
28. Diodorus 18.25.4–5; Justin 13.6.9; Roisman (2012), 117.
29. Diodorus 18.25.5 & 18.38.2.
30. Grainger (1999), 63.
31. Heckel (2016), 147–8.
32. It is not clear when Craterus commissioned these sculptures. Heckel (2016), 147–8 argues that it occurred during the wedding celebrations after the Lamian War in 322 BC, back in Macedon. This certainly seems plausible.
33. Arrian *Events After Alexander* 10B.7,R25.1.
34. Diodorus 18.38.6; Justin 13.6.9. Based on the assumption that Polyperchon is one of the officers who unanimously voted for war with Perdiccas.
35. Diodorus 18.25.5; Roisman (2012), 118. I follow Roisman's argument that the decree was finalised in Macedonia.
36. Roisman (2012), 118.
37. Roisman (2012), 118.

Chapter 12: The Greatest Heist in History
1. Curtius 10.10.9–13; Erskine (2002), 168.
2. Plutarch *Life of Alexander* 34.1.
3. Erskine (2002), 171; Saunders (2006), 36.
4. Pliny *Natural History* 13.9.41; Miller (1986), 410–411. For a detailed examination of the funeral carriage, see Miller (1986), 401–412.
5. Erskine (2002), 163–79.
6. Diodorus 18.27.3–5; Erskine (2002), 170.
7. Karunanithy (2013), 59–61; Erskine (2002), 168–9.
8. Erskine (2002), 171; Roisman (2012), 92; Saunders (2006), 36–7
9. Anson (2003), 383 for September 321.
10. Diodorus 18.28.1–2.
11. Diodorus 18.3.5; Curtius 10.5.4; Meeus (2008), 67–8.
12. Diodorus 18.25.4 (hostility with Ptolemy); Erskine (2002), 170.
13. Meeus (2008), 67–8.
14. Diodorus 18.25.3; Anson (2015), 104: 'Perdiccas prepared to march to Macedonia with the army, the kings and Alexander's body in spring of 320.'
15. Erskine (2002), 171; Chapter 9.
16. Anson (2015), 102; Billows (1990), 61; Heckel (2016), 178.
17. Heckel (2016), 178.
18. Arrian *Events After Alexander* 9.25; Anson (2015), 105 for the long-term planning of this plot. Given the importance of Syria in this heist and Laomedon's friendly relations with Ptolemy, I am convinced that Laomedon was involved in the heist.
19. Anson (2015), 105; Heckel (2016), 178.

20. Arrian *Events After Alexander* 9.25.
21. Arrian *Events After Alexander* 9.25; Erskine (2002), 170. Heckel (2016), 178. A mixture of cavalry and light infantry seems likely, given the necessity for speed to catch up with the funeral cortège. Engels (1978), 155 highlights how light units could march between 40 and 50 miles in a day.
22. Diodorus 18.14.1 & 18.28.3; Erskine (2002), 170.
23. Arrian *Events After Alexander* 9.25.
24. Saunders (2006), 40.
25. Curtius 10.10.20; Diodorus 18.28.3–5, wrongly stating the body was taken to Alexandria straightaway; Pausanias 1.6.3; Anson (2015), 106; Chugg (2002), 14–20; Jacoby *FGH* 239 B(11).
26. Billows (1990), 61 argues that Attalus and Polemon were sent to meet the body in eastern Syria. I am less convinced as Arrian seems to imply that Perdiccas only sent them out after he had received word that the funeral carriage had changed course and because Attalus and Polemon only reached the carriage after it had passed Damascus i.e. after Ptolemy and his army had reinforced Arrhidaeus' escort.
27. Diodorus 18.25.6. Note Justin 13.6.11–12 who states that some in the council at first recommended Perdiccas head to Macedonia, where he could gain the support of Alexander the Great's mother Olympias.
28. JÖAI 16 (1913), p. 235 no. IIn; Justin 13.6.16; Hauben (1977), 87–8. Justin claims that Cleitus sailed to the Hellespont from Cilicia. I do not believe this is likely due to the short timeframe of events – why would Perdiccas have waited until he had reached Cilicia to dispatch so vital a tool as his fleet to guard the Hellespont? Given Justin's tendency for muddle ups, I believe this is a confusion with Cleitus' sailing from there in 322 to aid Craterus. The Ephesus inscription seems to affirm that Cleitus was in fact in western Asia Minor at the time Perdiccas held his council in Pisidia. See also Anson (2015) 107–8.
29. The inscription from Ephesus (JÖAI 16) suggests Cleitus was working alongside, and had good relations with, Perdiccas' brother Alcetas. Anson (2015), 108.
30. Anson (2015), 108 convincingly argues that this is the strategy.
31. Arrian *Anabasis* 2.27.6.
32. See Chapter 9.
33. Anson (2015), 108–9.
34. Diodorus 18.25.6; 18.29.1–2.
35. Diodorus 18.29.1–2.
36. Diodorus 18.29.2; Justin 13.6.15; Plutarch *Eumenes* 5.1–2. Anson (2015), 109 for Alcetas and Neoptolemus' forces being a second line.
37. Grainger (1999), 65; Heckel (2016), 206; Simpson (1958), 358; Westlake (1949), 89. I am convinced by the argument that Perdiccas, having so much wealth at his disposal, would have offered to subsidise the Aetolians. Another powerful ally on the Greek mainland was Demades, the Athenian statesman. Demades had grown disillusioned with Antipater's authority and had been communicating with Perdiccas. I will explain this story in the next book.
38. Heckel (2016), 179; Roisman (2012), 94–5.
39. Arrian *Events After Alexander* 10A.1,R24.1; Erskine (2002), 171; Roisman (2012), 94–5.
40. Hauben (1977), 105–6.
41. Attalus' daughters are mentioned a few years later with Olympias (Diodorus 19.35.5). Heckel (2016), 195.
42. Billows (1990), 64.

Chapter 13: The Fight for Asia Minor

1. It appears from the later clash with Craterus that at least some of Eumenes' cavalrymen did not hail from Cappadocia – Arrian *Events After Alexander* 9.27.
2. Diodorus 18.29.3; 18.30.5; Nepos *Eumenes* 3.3. Nepos highlights how Eumenes' troops lacked experience and were recently recruited.

3. Anson (2015), 111; Billows (1990), 62.

4. Arrian *Events After Alexander* 9.26A; Heckel (2016), 178. Eumenes was a known friend of Cleopatra and her mother Olympias. Indeed it may well have been Eumenes who had acted as go-between for Perdiccas and Cleopatra earlier that year. Eumenes may have already played a decisive role in convincing Cleopatra to remain in Sardis and to persist with Perdiccas. See Anson (2015), 104 and Heckel (2006), 90.

5. Arrian *Events After Alexander* 9.26A; Carney (2000), 125.

6. Arrian *Events After Alexander* 10B.7,R25.1. Antigonus is following in the footsteps of Attalus and Parmenion.

7. Billows (1990), 63; Hauben (1977), 90.

8. Arrian *Events After Alexander* 10B.7,R25.1.

9. Arrian *Events After Alexander* R25.2; SEG IX 2; Meeus (2009), 79.

10. Arrian *Events After Alexander* R25.2. Menander probably hoped that by siding with Antigonus and aiding him in the war to come, he would have a good chance of being rewarded with his old position.

11. Arrian *Events After Alexander* 9.26A – R25.3.

12. Arrian *Events After Alexander* R25.4.

13. Arrian *Events After Alexander* R25.5.

14. Arrian *Events After Alexander* R25.6; Meeus (2009), 79.

15. Arrian *Events After Alexander* R25.7.

16. Arrian *Events After Alexander* R25.8.

17. Anson (2015) 112; Billows (1990), 65.

18. Anson (2015), 111; Billows (1990), 64–5.

19. Arrian *Events After Alexander* 9.26A. We know Antigonus relayed information about Eumenes' actions in Sardis so we can assume he also sent word to Antipater of his martial achievements. They were, after all, allies in this fight. Another incentive for Antipater was that, as far as we know, his daughter Nicaea was still trapped at the heart of Perdiccas' regime.

20. Arrian *Events After Alexander* 9.26A; Diodorus 18.29.7; Billows (1990), 63; Bosworth (1978), 233. Why 30,000: we know that Antipater had a similarly sized army for his campaign against the Aetolians. We also know that Craterus takes 22,000 men to fight Eumenes. This 22,000-strong force is described as half of the whole army. If an accurate translation, Antipater's army could have consisted of as many as 40,000 men, although we must remember that he would have had to leave a sizable garrison back in Macedonia with Polyperchon.

21. Diodorus 18.18.4.

22. Lund (1992), 53–4.

23. Arrian *Events After Alexander* 9.38. for Autodicus accompanying Antipater's army.

24. Justin 13.6.16.

25. Arrian *Events After Alexander* 9.26B.

26. See Chapter 6.

27. Plutarch *Moralia* 338a.

28. JÖAI 16 (1913), p. 235 no. IIn. Arrian *Events After Alexander* 9.37 – Cleitus later received control over Lydia at Triparadeisus. On the basis that bribery was a common method employed by all the Successors (e.g. Peithon with Letodorus or Ptolemy with Perdiccas' officers near Pelusium), I believe this appointment was promised to secure Cleitus' vital defection at the Hellespont.

29. Anson (2015), 112; Hauben (1977), 107–8.

30. Arrian *Events After Alexander* 9.26B; Memnon *History of Heraclea* 4.3–4. Anson (2015), 112; Billows (1990), 66. Dionysius' support secured through marriage to Amastris, Craterus' former wife. Once again, here Antipater is using diplomatic means to gain allies. It was a political union.

31. Nepos *Eumenes* 3.3.

32. For Eumenes being in Phrygia and the strategy of guerrilla warfare: Anson (2015), 109 & 118; Roisman (2012), 122.

33. Diodorus 18.29.2–4; Justin 13.6.15; Plutarch *Life of Eumenes* 5.2. We can only estimate the number of Macedonian soldiers Alcetas and Neoptolemus had, but presumably they both had sizable contingents of around 2,000 veterans. See Bosworth (2002), 81 and 90 for instance.

34. Anson (2015) 114; Heckel (2016), 181; Roisman (2012), 123–4.

35. Roisman (2012), 123 n.13: 'As Perdiccas' brother, Alcetas was *prima facie*, the least likely to desert him'. Perhaps Alcetas aimed to muster his own army with which he could oppose Antipater independently of Eumenes?

36. For the amount of Macedonians serving under Neoptolemus, see n.33.

37. Arrian Anabasis 2.27; Diodorus 18.29.4; Plutarch *Life of Eumenes* 5.2; Anson (2015), 114.

38. Diodorus 18.29.4; Plutarch *Life of Eumenes* 5.2. Anson (2015), 114.

39. Arrian *Events After Alexander* 9.26B; Plutarch *Life of Eumenes* 5.4.

40. Plutarch *Life of Eumenes* 5.4. Chapter 6.

41. Arrian *Events After Alexander* 9.26B; Diodorus 18.29.4; Justin 13.8.3; Plutarch *Life of Eumenes* 5.2.

42. Arrian *Events After Alexander* 9.27; Diodorus 18.29.4; Justin 13.8.4; Plutarch *Life of Eumenes* 5.2.

43. Diodorus 18.29.4; Plutarch *Life of Eumenes* 5.2. Why mid-late May 320: Anson (2003), 390. Mid-late May seems a credible date for the battle as it is in June that messengers reached Perdiccas in Egypt, informing him of Eumenes' victory further north.

44. For Neoptolemus' 'superior' forces see Arrian *Events After Alexander* 9.27; Diodorus 18.30.5.

45. Plutarch *Life of Eumenes*, 5.3.

46. Diodorus 18.29.4; Plutarch *Life of Eumenes* 5.3.

47. Plutarch *Life of Eumenes* 5.3.

48. Diodorus 18.29.5; Plutarch *Life of Eumenes* 5.3; Roisman (2012), 125.

49. Roisman (2012), 125.

50. Diodorus 18.33.1.

51. Arrian *Events After Alexander* 9.27; Diodorus 18.19.6; Justin 14.8.5; Plutarch *Life of Eumenes* 5.4. Roisman (2012), 125–6.

52. This is not stated in the sources, but I believe that Dionysius was at the meeting, alongside Antigonus. This seems possible as we later find Dionysius aiding Antigonus on Cyprus – Memnon *History of Heraclea* 4.6. For Antigonus' presence see Billows (1990), 66.

53. Diodorus 18.29.7; Plutarch *Life of Eumenes* 6.1–2. What was more neither Antipater nor Craterus could deny the logistical challenge Eumenes posed. Though they did have control of the sea, the possibility of Eumenes waging a guerrilla war in Anatolia would threaten their overland supply routes as they headed deeper and deeper into Asia. This was not to mention Alcetas' forces, which remained untouched elsewhere in Anatolia. Eumenes and Alcetas posed a significant logistical challenge for Antipater.

54. Arrian *Events After Alexander* 9.27; Diodorus 18.29.7; Justin 14.8.5; Plutarch *Life of Eumenes* 6.3.

55. Arrian *Events After Alexander* 9.30; Memnon *History of Heraclea* 4.6. Billows (1990), 66–7; Hauben (1974), 61–4; Hauben (1977), 113–4. A large fleet would be invaluable for Antipater, especially as he was marching against Perdiccas, who had Attalus' fleet at his disposal. This is not to mention the need for supply ships.

56. Diodorus 18.30.4; Justin 14.8.5; Plutarch *Life of Eumenes* 6.3. Diodorus says it is half the force. The size of the army sent against Eumenes adds further credence to the idea that Antipater feared the logistical threat Eumenes posed if he was allowed to wage a guerrilla war with relative impunity in Asia Minor. Antipater wanted Eumenes dealt with before he marched on Egypt.

57. Diodorus 18.30.4; *PSI XII* 1284. Diodorus 19.29.2. We know that Antigonus has Tarentines later on when fighting Eumenes, so it is possible that Antipater also had this troop type.

58. Plutarch *Life of Eumenes* 6.3.
59. Plutarch *Life of Eumenes* 6.3; Anson (2015), 119.
60. Diodorus 18.30.1 & 18.30.5. The episode shares similarities with Diodorus 19.39.1, when Eumenes gathers his army from all quarters in preparation for his final clash against Antigonus.
61. Diodorus 18.30.5; Nepos *Eumenes* 3.3. Anson (2015), 119; Roisman (2012), 128. It appears light infantry were not included in this count, at least not in Craterus' army count.
62. Arrian *Events After Alexander* 9.27; Nepos *Eumenes* 3.4; Roisman (2012), 128.
63. Plutarch *Life of Eumenes* 6.4 & 6.7.
64. Anson (2015), 119.
65. Arrian *Events After Alexander* 9.27; Nepos *Eumenes* 3.5–6; Plutarch *Life of Eumenes* 6.4. Anson (1990), 127; Roisman (2012), 128. Eumenes' military intelligence must have been nothing less than astounding that he managed to successfully conceal Craterus' name for several days.
66. Plutarch *Life of Eumenes* 6.6.
67. Diodorus 18.30.3. Craterus' speech must have included more than just promise of plunder, but this is all that survives in Diodorus. See Roisman (2012), 128.
68. Roisman (2012), 127. I am more inclined to believe Roisman's argument that this episode occurred on the eve of Craterus' battle with Eumenes, not in Armenia as Anson (2015), 91 suggests.
69. Roisman (2012), 127.
70. Diodorus 18.30.3–5; Plutarch *Life of Eumenes* 6.1. It seems that the majority of Craterus' 1,500 cavalry accompanied Craterus on the right wing. Neoptolemus may have had more than just 300 horsemen, provided by Craterus, though this is not stated.
71. Diodorus 18.30.5.
72. Roisman (2012), 129.
73. Nepos *Eumenes* 3.6.
74. Plutarch *Life of Eumenes* 7.2.
75. Plutarch *Life of Eumenes* 7.1. Phoenix and Pharnabazus commanded one squadron each. There seem to have been a handful of loyal Macedonian captains. For instance Gorgias.
76. Plutarch *Life of Eumenes* 7.2; Karunanithy (2013), 120.
77. Diodorus 18.30.5; Plutarch *Life of Eumenes* 7.2.
78. Diodorus 18.30.5.; Plutarch *Life of Eumenes* 7.3.
79. Arrian *Events After Alexander* 9.27.
80. Plutarch *Life of Eumenes* 7.3. A good comparison is Pyrrhus' elaborate armour at the Battle of Heraclea – Plutarch *Life of Pyrrhus* 17.2.
81. Arrian *Events After Alexander* 9.27; Diodorus 18.30.5; Plutarch *Life of Eumenes* 7.3. Presumably when Plutarch says a 'Thracian', he means a cavalryman equipped in the Thracian style of warfare. Craterus' assailant was probably a Paphlagonian or a Cappadocian.
82. Justin 12.12.8; Plutarch *Life of Eumenes* 7.4. Roisman (2012), 130. I agree with Roisman that this is more likely Gorgias of Alexander the Great's campaigns. For the possibility that this is another Gorgias, see Heckel (2006), 127.
83. Nepos *Eumenes* 3.6; Plutarch *Life of Eumenes* 7.2.
84. Plutarch *Life of Eumenes* 7.4; Roisman (2012), 130.
85. Diodorus 18.31.2; Plutarch *Life of Eumenes* 7.4. Karunanity (2013), 116–7.
86. Arrian *Anabasis* 3.28.3; Curtius 4.9.25 & 7.4.32–38. Roisman (2012), 130.
87. Hornblower (1981), 194–6. Serving among Eumenes' retinue, Hieronymus may well have witnessed the duel first hand.
88. Plutarch *Life of Eumenes* 7.7.
89. Diodorus 18.32.1.
90. Diodorus 18.30.4; Roisman (2012), 132.
91. Diodorus 18.32.2; Nepos *Eumenes* 4.4. Nothing survives about what Eumenes ordered for the deceased enemy troopers. Given the importance of burial rites at this time and

Eumenes' desire to win over enemy troops, it seems very likely that they also received proper burial rites.

92. I agree with the argument that this fragment dates to the aftermath of this battle. See Anson (2015), 121; Roisman (2012), 131–2. For the opposing argument see Bosworth (1978), 227–37.
93. *PSI XII* 1284.
94. Roisman (2012), 132.
95. Diodorus 18.32.3.
96. Diodorus 18.32.3.
97. Nepos *Eumenes* 3.6; Plutarch *Life of Eumenes* 8.1.
98. Nepos *Eumenes* 4.4; Plutarch *Life of Eumenes* 7.8 & 8.1; Roisman (2012), 130–1.
99. Anson (2015), 121; Roisman (2012), 134.
100. Diodorus 18.32.4; Justin 14.8.9; Roisman (2012), 133.
101. Arrian *Events After Alexander* 9.27; Diodorus 18.33.1.

Chapter 14: Polyperchon's Finest Hour
1. See Chapter 11.
2. Westlake (1949), 89.
3. Diodorus 18.38.1
4. Diodorus 18.31.1; Heckel (2016), 205; Mendels (1984), 155–6; Westlake (1949), 89.
5. Heckel (2016), 206; Simpson (1958), 358; Westlake (1949), 89.
6. Grainger (2019), 66.
7. Diodorus 18.38.1.
8. Rzepka (2009), 25 for this argument, who lays it out very credibly especially as it now appears Aetolian urbanisation occurred long before the end of the fourth century. Also see Pausanias 10.20.4 for Aetolians at Thermopylae in 279 fighting as hoplites. For their march into Thessaly, expecting a pitched battle, it seems credible to suggest they would have fought as heavy infantry.
9. Polybius 9.29.1–4 & 9.30.3; Westlake (1949), 88–9. Possible sources for the cavalry include Aetolian urban cities like Naupactus (which may well have already been in Aetolia's possession) or the Molossian king Aeacides. It seems possible Aeacides aided the Aetolians in this venture. He was related to Olympias, who was intent on destroying Antipater's power and was an ally of Perdiccas.
10. Diodorus 18.31.1.
11. Polybius 9.29.1–4 & 9.30.3. Westlake (1949), 88–90. Chapter 6. Although it is nowhere explicitly stated that Menon found refuge with the Aetolians, his close cooperation with them suggests this is possible. Either Menon had found refuge in Aetolia or he had found refuge in nearby Molossia.
12. Diodorus 18.38.1–2; Mendels (1984), 155–6.
13. Diodorus 18.38.1–2; Heckel (2016) 205; Mendels (1984), 155–156; Waterfield (2019), 482.
14. Diodorus' wording seems to suggest that Polycles' force was not at Amphissa when the Aetolians assaulted it, though a small garrison must have remained there.
15. Diodorus 18.38.2; Bosworth (2002), 85–6 for the composition of Polycles' force. Antipater may have provided Polycles mercenaries and some Macedonians for the garrison, but we have no concrete evidence for the total number of troops. 2,000 is generous.
16. For the two possible routes the Aetolians could have taken to reach Thessaly, see Grainger (1999) 67.
17. Diodorus 18.38.3.
18. Diodorus 18.38.3.
19. Grainger (1999) 67; Westlake (1949) 88–9. If the Aetolians did march to Thessaly through Ainis and Dolopia, as Grainger suggests, then we can presume Alexander had also been reinforced with Ainianians and Dolopians. 'Both had been allies of Aetolia in the Lamian War.'

20. Waterfield (2019), 482; Westlake (1949), 88–9. Here I follow Westlake's argument, agreed with by Waterfield, that the Aetolian army included a large number of mercenaries. For the opposing view, that Thessalian recruits formed the majority of the infantry force, see Grainger (2019), 106.
21. Westlake (1949), 88.
22. Bosworth (2002), 86; Grainger (2019), 106.
23. Arrian *Anabasis* 3.11.9 & 4.16.1.
24. Arrian *Anabasis* 7.12.4.
25. Diodorus 18.38.6; Justin 13.6.9.
26. Bosworth (2002), 86; Grainger (2019), 106.
27. Waterfield (2019), 482.
28. Diodorus 18.8.6.
29. Grainger (1999), 106.
30. Diodorus 18.38.4.
31. Mendels (1984), 156.
32. Heckel (2016), 206 (n.32).
33. Diodorus 18.38.5.
34. Diodorus 18.38.5; Westlake (1949), 90.
35. Diodorus 18.35.6; Bosworth (2002), 86.
36. Westlake (1949), 90.
37. Diodorus 18.38.6.
38. Diodorus 18.36.6; Westlake (1949), 90.
39. Diodorus 18.36.5.
40. Grainger (2019), 107 suggests 1/3.

Chapter 15: Perdiccas vs Ptolemy: The Invasion of Egypt

1. Arrian *Events After Alexander* 10A.2,R24.2. Perdiccas' subsequent dispatching of a fleet to Cyprus suggests he was near the coast.
2. Perdiccas' previous visit to Cilicia the year before had proven uneventful. Philotas had shown obedience and Perdiccas had not needed to make any radical changes. Now, however, things were different. It seems Philotas had not done enough to convince Perdiccas of his loyalty in the upcoming struggle and the risk of losing the strategically vital land of Cilicia to treachery was too great to be ignored.
3. Arrian *Anabasis* 4.24.10; Arrian *Events After Alexander* 1.5 & 10A.2,R24.2; Justin 13.6.16. See also Heckel (2006), 219.
4. Heckel (2006), 219. Philotas later ends up in the service of Antigonus and, although not definitively stated, it is likely he fled to Antipater and Craterus after his demotion.
5. Arrian *Events After Alexander* 10A.2,R24.2; Grainger (2019), 104. Of prominent figures giving governorships to friends, see Antigonus (Diodorus 18.50.5).
6. Arrian *Events After Alexander* 10.A.3,R24.3; Roisman (2012), 93.
7. Arrian *Events After Alexander* 10.A.3,R24.3; Grainger (2019),104.
8. Arrian *Events After Alexander* 10.A.6,R24.6; Errington (1970), 69 (n.135).
9. Arrian *Events After Alexander* 10.A.6,R24.; Diodorus 19.62.6; Hauben (1977), 113–4.
10. Arrian *Events After Alexander* 10.A.6,R24.
11. Arrian *Events After Alexander* 10.A.6,R24.
12. Heckel (2006), 50.
13. Anson (2015), 110.
14. Arrian *Events After Alexander* 10.A.4,R24.4.
15. Arrian *Events After Alexander* 10.A.4,R24.5. Note how Docimus may have rewarded his soldiers here. The Greek is unclear but given their mercenary nature and Babylon's great wealth it makes sense.
16. Arrian *Events After Alexander* 10.A.4,R24.5.
17. Memnon *History of Heraclea* 4.6; Hauben (1974), 61–4; Hauben (1977), 90–1 & 110–5; Grainger (2019), 105. Where I disagree with Hauben is I believe this battle took place in 320 (when Archippos was still archon at Athens), rather than 321.

18. See also St Jerome *Chronological Tables* 121.1 for Perdiccas' founding of a city *en route*.
19. Arrian *Events After Alexander* 9.28; Diodorus 18.33.1; Anson (2015), 110; Anson (2003), 390.
20. Diodorus 18.14.1–2 & 18.29.1; Bennett & Roberts (2008), 32; Heckel (2006), 202.
21. Diodorus 18.14.1–2, 18.28.5, 18.29.6 & 18.33.3; Pausanias 1.6.3; Chapters 5 and 12. For defences on the Mediterranean shoreline see, for instance, the garrisons Ptolemy had prepared to fend off an amphibious invasion by Antigonus and Demetrius in 306 – Diodorus 20.75.1–5.
22. Arrian *Anabasis* 7.18.
23. Arrian *Events After Alexander* 9.28; Roisman (2012), 95–7. For hostages possibly being exchanged, we have a comparable story in Plutarch *Life of Eumenes* 12.3.
24. Chapter 1; Roisman (2012), 96–7.
25. Arrian *Events After Alexander* 9.28; Anson (2015), 122; Roisman (2012), 97.
26. Arrian *Events After Alexander* 9.28; Roisman (2012), 97.
27. Anson (2015), 122; Anson (1991), 240–1; Roisman (2012), 97.
28. Diodorus 18.33.2; Bennett & Roberts (2008), 32; Roisman (2012), 97.
29. Diodorus 18.33.2.
30. Bribery examples: Attalus (Chapter 1), Letodorus (Chapter 4), Cleitus the White (Chapter 13); Bennett & Roberts (2008), 32; Errington (1970), 65; Roisman (2012), 98; Worthington (2016), 96.
31. Diodorus 18.33.2; Anson (2015), 123; Roisman (2012), 97–8. Although the dredging disaster was the trigger for defections, it seems likely that this was preceded by dire reports from Asia Minor. I find Anson's argument that the preceding army assembly was a key cause of these defections unconvincing.
32. Diodorus 18.33.3–5; Roisman (2012), 98.
33. Diodorus 18.33.1; Anson (2015), 118; Roisman (2012), 108. Diodorus seems to suggest that Perdiccas received this report before he reached Pelusium, but this does not make sense. It makes more sense to suggest that Perdiccas received this information later in the campaign, probably just before he set out for the Camel Fort. Perdiccas' 'more daring' actions as a result of receiving this news can be explained as his decision to launch a surprise attack at the Camel Fort.
34. Diodorus 18.33.5; Roisman (2012), 99. All the indications suggest that Ptolemy's army was situated close by on the opposite side of the river.
35. June 320: Anson (2003), 390. I follow, and have followed throughout this book, the much more convincing low chronology for these first three years following Alexander's death. See also Boiy (2007), 199–207.
36. Diodorus 18.33.6. For roughly 10km: an average daily march for an army with elephants was less than 10 miles. Less at night. See Engels (1978), 155.
37. Diodorus 18.33.6 and 34.2. Roisman (2012), 98; Worthington (2016), 96. I do not follow the arguments of either Roisman or Worthington that the Camel Fort was near Memphis. Not only does Diodorus imply that Perdiccas reached the Fort within a night of leaving Pelusium, but the shallow water level and the fact that the crossing was guarded suggests that the Fort was near the mouth of the Pelusiac Nile Branch.
38. Diodorus 18.33.6. Anson (2003), 375 & 383–4. The Babylonian Chronicle places the battle in either May or June 320. Early June seems more likely, when the sun rises at around 5 a.m.
39. Diodorus 18.33.6; Roisman (2012), 99. Interestingly, there is no mention of Ptolemy's forces having artillery at the Camel Fort. Perhaps this was why Perdiccas selected this fort for the assault.
40. Diodorus 18.33.6.
41. Diodorus 18.34.1.
42. Diodorus 18.34.1–2.
43. Diodorus 18.34.2; Roisman (2012), 100.

44. Bosworth (2002), 255. Hornblower (1982). 40–41, for Diodorus using an earlier pro-Ptolemaic source.
45. Bosworth (2002), 255; Worthington (2016), 96.
46. Diodorus 18.34.4–5. It would fit with Perdiccas' character that he had crossed the river to help inspire his men.
47. Diodorus 18.34.5.
48. Diodorus 18.34.6. Roisman (2012), 100.
49. Diodorus 18.34.6; Pausanias 1.6.3; Anson (2003) 381 & 384–5 (n.49). The crossing from the island to the Nile's western bank was not an issue.
50. Low provisions: Diodorus 18.36.6.
51. Arrian *Anabasis* 4.4.2–5; 5.13.1–4.
52. Curtius 4.9.17–21.
53. Bennett & Roberts (2008), 32.
54. Diodorus 18.35.1.
55. Diodorus 18.35.1–2.
56. Diodorus 18.35.3.
57. Diodorus 18.35.4.
58. More than 2,000 soldiers: Diodorus 18.36.1; Roisman (2012), 101.
59. Diodorus 18.35.5.
60. Frontinus *Stratagems* 4.7.20; Polyaenus 4.19; Bosworth (2002), 87.
61. Diodorus 18.35.5; Roisman (2012), 101. Access to the island from the west bank was still possible.
62. Asclepiodotus *Tactics* 2.9. Diodorus 18.35.6.
63. Diodorus 18.35.6. Perhaps hippos were also among the 'river dwelling creatures' Diodorus mentions.
64. Diodorus 18.36.1; Frontinus *Stratagems* 4.7.20; Polyaenus 4.19. Griffith (1935), 41 highlights that Diodorus never explicitly says that the losses consisted solely of Macedonians and it is likely a large number of those that perished were mercenaries. Nevertheless the immediate reaction in the Macedonian camp suggests many Macedonians were among the dead.
65. Bennett & Roberts (2008), 33; Bosworth (2002), 14; Roisman (2012), 102.
66. Diodorus 18.36.1.
67. Roisman (2012), 102.
68. Diodorus 18.36.3.
69. Perdiccas' arrogance: Arrian *Events After Alexander* 9.28; Justin 13.8.2; *Suda* Π 1040, in Heckel (2016), 183–4.
70. Arrian *Events After Alexander* 9.28; *Suda* Π 1040, in Heckel (2016), 183–4.
71. Diodorus 18.36.4–5; Roisman (2012), 103.
72. Diodorus 18.36.5 & 18.39.6. Nepos *Eumenes* 5.1; Heckel (2006), 247.
73. Diodorus 18.36.5.
74. Diodorus 18.39.6. Anson (2003), 373–390 – for Perdiccas' death in June 320.

Chapter 16: The Aftermath

1. Errington (1970), 65.
2. Errington (1970), 66: 'That such a man (Peithon) should lead a conspiracy against Perdiccas is quite comprehensible: that he did so without looking to his own advantage is unthinkable.'
3. Arrian *Events After Alexander* 9.29; Diodorus 18.36.6.
4. Worthington (2016), 98.
5. Arrian *Events After Alexander* 9.30; Anson (2015), 124; Anson (1991), 243.
6. Diodorus 18.36.6; Roisman (2012), 106–7.
7. Arrian Events After Alexander 9.30; Diodorus 18.36.6.
8. Diodorus 18.36.6; Errington (1970), 66.
9. Worthington (2016), 99.

10. Anson (2015), 124; Anson (2014), 69. Xref Roisman (2012), 105, who believes the assembly is spontaneous.
11. Arrian *Events After Alexander* 9.29; Diodorus 18.36.6; Anson (2015), 125; Errington (1970), 66.
12. Diodorus 18.36.6; Roisman (2012), 106.
13. Arrian *Events After Alexander* 9.30; Diodorus 18.36.7; Roisman (2012), 106–7. I agree with Roisman and do not believe Ptolemy was offered the regency. Opposing argument: Waterfield (2011), 65. Worthington (2016), 98 considers it.
14. Also Plutarch *Life of Eumenes* 8.2.
15. Arrian *Events After Alexander* 9.29.
16. Roisman (2012), 109 (n.60) believes there were two assemblies, following Briant (1973), 273–4 and Engel (1974) 122–4. Xref Anson (2015), 125 who believes there is only one.
17. Arrian *Events After Alexander* 9.30; Diodorus 18.37.2. Only Eumenes and Alcetas are specifically mentioned as being condemned, but we can presume the others were included on the list.
18. Diodorus 18.37.2; Anson (2015), 126. Atalante's daughters would soon be sent home to Macedonia. Our next (and only) reference to them comes in 316 when they are in Macedonia – Diodorus 19.35.5.
19. Diodorus 18.37.3.
20. Diodorus 18.39.1.
21. Diodorus 18.43.1; Waterfield (2011), 65; Worthington (2016), 99.
22. Arrian *Anabasis* 1.8.1 as an example. Erskine (2002), 173; Heckel (2016), 153–4.

Epilogue
1. Billows (1990), 68; Grainger (2019), 105; Waterfield (2011), 65.
2. Memnon *History of Heraclea* 4.6.
3. Arrian *Events After Alexander* 9.30.

Bibliography

Primary Sources

Armstrong, G.C and Tredennik, H. (1935), tr., *Aristotle: Metaphysics, Volume II*, London.
Bennett, C. E. (1925), tr., *Frontinus: Stratagems. Aqueducts of Rome*, London.
Bowra, C. M. (1969), tr., *Pindar: The Odes*, London.
Burtt, J. O. (1954), tr., *Minor Attic Orators, Volume II: Lycurgus. Dinarchus. Demades. Hypereides*, London.
Clough, A. H. (2010), ed., *Plutarch: Lives of the Noble Grecians and Romans*, Oxford.
De Witt, N. W. (1949), tr., *Demosthenes Orations 60–61: Funeral Speech. Erotic Essay. Exordia. Letters*, London.
Freeze, J. H. (2020), tr., *Aristotle: Art of Rhetoric*, London.
Goralski, W. J. (1989), tr., 'Arrian's Events After Alexander: Summary of Photius and Selected Fragments', *The Ancient World* 19, 81–108.
Gulick, C. B. (1929), tr., *Athenaeus: The Deiphnosophists III*, London.
Hammond, M. (2013), tr., *Arrian: Alexander the Great, the Anabasis and the Indica*, Oxford.
Harmon, A. H. (1913), tr., *Lucian: Phalaris. Hippias or The Bath. Dionysus. Heracles. Amber or The Swans. The Fly. Nigrinus. Demonax. The Hall. My Native Land. Octogenarians. A True Story. Slander. The Consonants at Law. The Carousal (Symposium) or The Lapiths*, London.
Henderson, J. (1928), ed., *Aeneas Tacticus, Asclepiodotus, Onasander*, London.
Henderson, J. (1988), ed. and tr., *Aristophanes: Acharnians. Knights*, London.
Holland, T. (2013), tr., *Herodotus: The Histories*, London.
Jones, H. L. (1928), tr, *Strabo: Geography, Volume V*, London.
Jones, W. H. S. (1918), tr., *Pausanias: Description of Greece, Volume I*, London.
Jones, W. H. S. (1935), tr., *Pausanias: Description of Greece, Volume IV*, London.
Kaster, R. A. (2011), tr., *Macrobius Saturnalia: Books 1–2*, London.
Keaveney, Arthur and Madden, John A., 'Memnon (434)', in: *Brill's New Jacoby*, General Editor: Ian Worthington (Macquarie University). Consulted online on 29 December 2020 <http://dx.doi.org/10.1163/1873-5363_bnj_a434> First published online: 2016
Kovacs, D. (1995), ed. and tr., *Euripides: Children of Heracles. Hippolytus. Andromache. Hecuba*, London.
McGing, B. (2019), ed. and tr., *Appian: Roman History, Volume III*, London.
Olson, S. D. (2007), ed. and tr., *Athenaeus: The Learned Banqueters, Volume I*, London.
Olson, S. D. (2010), ed. and tr., *Athenaeus: The Learned Banqueters, Volume VI*, London.
Paton, W. R. (2011), tr., *Polybius: The Histories, Volume IV*, London.
Rackham, H. (1945), tr., *Natural History, Volume IV: Books 12–16*, London.
Rolfe, J. C. (1929), tr., *Cornelius Nepos: On Great Generals. On Historians*, London.
Rolfe, J. C. (1940), tr., *Ammianus Marcellinus: History, Volume II*, London.
Shackleton Bailey, D. R. (2000), ed. and tr., *Valerius Maximus: Memorable Doings and Sayings, Volume II*, London.
Shepherd, R. (1793), tr., *Polyaenus: Stratagems of War*, Chicago.
Sickinger, James P., 'Marmor Parium (239)', in: *Brill's New Jacoby*, General Editor: Ian Worthington (Macquarie University). Consulted online on 29 December 2020 <http://dx.doi.org/10.1163/1873-5363_bnj_a239>

Vince, C. A. (1926), tr., *Demosthenes Orations 18–19: De Corona, De Falsa Legatione*, London.
Warner, R. (1954), tr., *Thucydides: History of the Peloponnesian War*, London.
Waterfield, R. (2015), tr., *Lives of the Attic Orators: Texts From Pseudo-Plutarch, Photius and the Suda*, Oxford.
Waterfield, R. (2019), tr., *Diodorus of Sicily: The Library, Books 16–20*, Oxford.
Whitehead, D. (2000), tr., *Hypereides: The Forensic Speeches*, Oxford.
Yardley, J. (2001), tr., *The History of Alexander: Quintus Curtius Rufus*, Chatham.
Yardley, J.C. (1994), tr., *Justin: Epitome of the Philippic History of Pompeius Trogus*, Atlanta.

Secondary Sources

Anderson, J. K. (1965), 'Homeric, British and Cyrenaic Chariots', *American Journal of Archaeology* 69 (4), 349–352.
Anderson, J. K. (1975), 'Greek Chariot-Borne and Mounted Infantry,' *American Journal of Archaeology* 79 (3), 175–187.
Anson, E. M. (1985), 'Macedonia's Alleged Constitutionalism', *The Classical Journal* 80 (4), 303–316.
Anson, E. M. (1988), 'Antigonus, the Satrap of Phrygia', *Historia* 37 (4), 471–477
Anson, E. M. (1990), 'Neoptolemus and Armenia', *Ancient History Bulletin* 4, 125–128.
Anson, E. M. (1991), 'The Evolution of the Macedonian Army Assembly (330–315 BC)', *Historia* 40 (2), 230–247.
Anson, E. M. (1992), 'Craterus and the Prostasia', *Classical Philology* 87 (1), 38–43.
Anson, E. M. (2003), 'The Dating of Perdiccas' Death and the Assembly at Triparadeisus', *GRBS* 43, 373–390.
Anson, E. M. (2012), 'The Macedonian patriot: The Diadoch Craterus', *Ancient History Bulletin* 26, 49–58.
Anson, E. M. (2014), *Alexander's Heirs: The Age of the Successors*, Chichester.
Anson, E. M. (2015), *Eumenes of Cardia*, Leiden
Archibald, Z. H. (1998), *The Odrysian Kingdom of Thrace: Orpheus Unmasked*, Oxford
Ashton, N. G. (1977), 'The Naumachia Near Amorgos in 322 B.C', *The Annual of the British School at Athens* 72, 1–11.
Ashton, N. G. (1993), 'Craterus from 323 to 321', *AM* 5, 125–131.
Austin, M. (2006), *The Hellenistic World from Alexander to the Roman Conquest: A Selection of Ancient Sources in Translation*, New York.
Badian, E. (1961), 'Harpalus', *Journal of Hellenic Studies* 81, 16–43.
Baynham, E. (2003), 'Antipater and Athens', in O. Palagia and S. V. Tracy (eds.), *The Macedonians in Athens: 322–229 BC*, Oxford, 23–29.
Bennett, B. and Roberts, M. (2008), *The Wars of Alexander's Successors 323–281 BC: Commanders and Campaigns*, Barnsley.
Billows, R. A. (1990), *Antigonos the One-Eyed and the Creation of the Hellenistic State*, London.
Bosworth, A. B. (1974), 'The Government of Syria under Alexander the Great', *The Classical Quarterly* 24 (1), 46–64.
Bosworth, A. B. (1978), 'Eumenes, Neoptolemus and *PSI* XII 1284', *Greek, Roman and Byzantine Studies* 19, 227–37.
Bosworth, A. B. (1980), 'Alexander and the Iranians', *The Journal of Hellenic Studies* 100, 1–21.
Bosworth, A. B. (1988), *Conquest and Empire: The Reign of Alexander the Great*, Cambridge.
Bosworth, A. B. (1993), 'Perdiccas and the Kings', *The Classical Quarterly* 43 (2), 420–427.
Bosworth, A. B. (2002), *The Legacy of Alexander: Politics, Warfare, and Propaganda under the Successors*, New York.
Bosworth, A. B. (2003), 'Why did Athens lose the Lamian War?', in O. Palagia and S. V. Tracy (eds.), *The Macedonians in Athens: 322–229 BC*, Oxford, 14–22.
Briant, P. (1973), *Antigone le Borgne*, Paris.

Carney, E. D. (1988), 'The Sisters of Alexander the Great: Royal Relicts', *Historia* 37 (4), 385–404.

Carney, E. D. (2000), *Women and Monarchy in Macedonia*, Norman.

Carney, E. D. (2006), *Olympias: Mother of Alexander the Great*, New York.

Chugg, A. (2002), 'The Sarcophagus of Alexander the Great?', *Greece and Rome* 49 (1), 8–26.

Delev, P. (2015), 'Thrace from the Assassination of Kotys I to Korupedium (360–281 BCE),' in J. Valeva et al. (eds.), *A Companion to Ancient Thrace*, Chichester, 48–58.

Dimitrov, D. P., and Cicikova, M. (1978), *The Thracian City of Seuthopolis*, Oxford.

Engel, R. (1974), 'Zwei Heersversammlungen in Memphis', *Hermes* 102, 122–124.

Engels, D. W. (1978), *Alexander the Great and the Logistics of the Macedonian Army*, London.

Errington, R. M. (1970), 'From Babylon to Triparadeisos: 323–320 BC' *The Journal of Hellenic Studies* 90, 49–77.

Errington, R. M. (1975), 'Samos and the Lamian War', *Chiron* 5, 51–58.

Erskine, A. (2002) 'Life after Death: Alexandria and the Body of Alexander', *Greece and Rome* 49 (2), 163–179.

Grainger, J.D. (1999), *The League of the Aitolians*, Leiden.

Grainger, J.D. (2019), *Antipater's Dynasty*, Barnsley.

Grant, D. (2019), *Unearthing the Family of Alexander the Great: The Remarkable Discovery of the Royal Tombs of Macedon*, Barnsley.

Green, P. (2003), 'Occupation and co-existence: the impact of Macedon on Athens, 323–307', in O. Palagia and S. V. Tracy (eds.), *The Macedonians in Athens: 322–229 BC*, Oxford, 1–7.

Greenhalgh, P. A. L. (1973), *Early Greek Warfare: Horsemen and Chariots in the Homeric and Archaic Ages*, Cambridge.

Griffith, G. T. (1935), *The Mercenaries of the Hellenistic World*, Cambridge.

Habicht, C. (1996), 'Athens, Samos and Alexander the Great', *Proceedings of the American Philosophical Society* 140 (3), 397–405.

Habicht, C. (1997), *Athens From Alexander to Antony*, Munich.

Hauben, H. (1974), 'An Athenian Naval Victory in 321 BC', *Zeitschrift fur Papyrologie und Epigraphik* 13, 61–64.

Hauben, H. (1977), 'The First War of the Successors (321 BC): Chronological and Historical Problems', *Ancient Society* 8, 85–120.

Heckel, W. (1978c), 'On Attalos and Atalante', *Classical Quarterly* 28, 377–82.

Heckel, W. (2006), *Who's Who in the Age of Alexander the Great*, Oxford.

Heckel, W. (2016), *Alexander's Marshals: A Study of the Makedonian Aristocracy and the Politics of Military Leadership*, Oxon.

Heckel, W. and Yardley, J. C. (2004), *Historical Sources in Translation: Alexander the Great*, Oxford.

Hoddinott, R. F. (1981), *The Thracians*, Over Wallop.

Holt, F. M. (1989), *Alexander the Great and Bactria*, Leiden.

Holt, F. M. (1999), *Thundering Zeus: The Making of Hellenistic Bactria*, Berkeley.

Hornblower, J. (1981), *Hieronymus of Cardia*, New York.

Iliakis, M. (2013), 'Greek Mercenary Revolts in Bactria: A Re-Appraisal', *Historia* 62 (2), 182–195.

Iossif, P. P. and Lorber, C. C. (2010), 'Hypaithros: A Numismatic Contribution to the Military History of Cappadocia,' *Historia* 59 (4), 432–447.

Jones, A. H. M. (1937), *Cities of the Eastern Roman Provinces*, New York.

Karunanithy, D. (2013), *The Macedonian War Machine: Neglected Aspects of the Armies of Philip, Alexander and the Successors 359–281 BC*, Barnsley.

Keil, J. (1913), 'Ephesische Burgerrechts- und Proxeniedekrete aus dem vierten und dritten Jahrhundert v. Chr.' *Jahreshefte des Osterreichischen Archaeologischen Insititutes in Wien* 16, 231–48.

Kingsley, B. M. (1986), 'Harpalos in the Megarid (333–331 BC) and the Grain Shipments from Cyrene (S.E.G. IX 2 + = Tod, Greek Hist. Inscr. II No.196', *Zeitschrift fur Papyrologie und Epigraphik* 66, 167–177.

Lawton, C. L. (2003), 'Athenian anti-Macedonian sentiment and democratic ideology in Attic document reliefs in the second half of the fourth century BC', in O. Palagia and S. V. Tracy (eds.), *The Macedonians in Athens: 322–229 BC*, Oxford, 117–127.

Lenski, N. (1999), 'Assimilation and Revolt in the Territory of Isauria, from the 1st Century BC to the 6th Century AD', *Journal of the Economic and Social History of the Orient* 42 (4), 413–465.

Lund, H. S. (1992), Lysimachus: A Study in Early Hellenistic Kingship, Abingdon.

Macurdy, G. H. (1927), 'Queen Eurydice and the Evidence for Woman Power in Early Macedonia', *The American Journal of Philology* 48 (3), 201–214.

Mari, M. (2003), 'Macedonians and anti-Macedonians in early Hellenistic Athens: reflections on ἀσέβεια', in O. Palagia and S. V. Tracy (eds.), *The Macedonians in Athens: 322–229 BC*, Oxford, 82–92.

Meeus, A. (2008), 'The Power Struggle of the Diadochoi in Babylon, 323 BC,' *Ancient Society* 38, 39–82.

Meeus, A. (2009A), 'Some Institutional Problems concerning the Succession to Alexander the Great: "Prostasia" and Chiliarchy', *Historia* 58 (3), 287–310.

Meeus, A. (2009B), 'Kleopatra and the Diadochoi', in P. Van Nuffelen (ed.), *Faces of Hellenism: Studies in the History of the Eastern Mediterranean (4th Century BC – 5th Century AD)*, 63–92.

Meeus, A. (2014), 'The Territorial Ambitions of Ptolemy I', in H. Hauben and A. Meeus (eds.), *The Age of the Successors and the Creation of the Hellenistic Kingdoms (323–276 BC)*, Leuven, 263–306.

Mendels, D. (1984), 'Aetolia 331–301: Frustration, Political Power and Survival', *Historia* 33 (2), 129–180.

Miller, S. G. (1986), 'Alexander's Funeral Cart', *Ancient Macedonia* 4, 401–412.

Mitchell, L. (2007), 'Born to Rule? Succession in the Argead Royal House,' in W. Heckel., L. Tritle and P. Wheatley (eds.), Alexander's Empire: Formulation to Decay, California, 61–74.

Morrison, J. S. (1987), 'Athenian Sea-Power in 323/2 BC: Dream and Reality', *The Journal of Hellenic Studies* 107, 88–97.

Murray, W. M. (2012), *The Age of Titans: The Rise and Fall of the Great Hellenistic Navies*, Oxford.

Newell, E.T. (1938), *Miscellanea Numismatica: Cyrene to India*, New York.

Panichi, S. (2005), 'Cappadocia Through Strabo's Eyes', in D. Dueck, H. Lindsay and S. Pothecary (eds.), *Strabo's Cultural Geography: The Making of a Kolossourgia*, 200–215.

Pomeroy, S. B. (1990), *Women in Hellenistic Egypt: From Alexander to Cleopatra*, Detroit.

Rathmann, M. (2005), *Perdikkas zwischen 323 und 320: Nachlassverwalter des Alexanderreiches oder Autokrat?*, Vienna.

Roisman, J. (2012), *Alexander's Veterans and the Early Wars of the Successors*, Austin.

Romm, J. (2011), *Ghost on the Throne: The Death of Alexander the Great and the Bloody Fight for his Empire*, New York.

Rzepka, J. (2009), 'The Aetolian Elite Warriors and Fifth-Century Roots of the Hellenistic Confederacy', *Akme. Studia Historica* 4 , 7–31.

Saitta, G. (1955), 'Lisimaco di Tracia', *Kokalos* 1, 62–152.

Saunders, N. J. (2006), *Alexander's Tomb: The Two Thousand Year Obsession to Find the Lost Conqueror*, New York, 33–48.

Sekunda, N. (1981), 'The rhomphaia: a Thracian weapon of the Hellenistic Period', in A. G. Poulter (ed.), *Ancient Bulgaria*, Nottingham, 278–288.

Sekunda, N. (1984), *The Army of Alexander the Great*, Oxford.

Simonetta, B. (1961), 'Notes on the Coinage of Cappadocian Kings', *The Numismatic Chronicle and Journal of the Royal Numismatic Society* 1, 9–50.

Simpson, R. H. (1958), 'Aetolian Policy in the Late Fourth Century B. C.', *L'antiquite Classique* 27 (2), 357–362.

Sprawski, S. (2008), 'Leonnatus' Campaign of 322 BC', *Electrum* 14, 9–31.

Strootman, R. (2011), 'Alexander's Thessalian Cavalry', *Talanta* XLII-XLIII, 51–67.

Stucchi, S., Robinson, E. G. D., and Descoeudres, J. (1989), 'Problems Concerning the Coming of the Greeks to Cyrenaica and the Relations with their Neighbours,' *Mediterranean Archaeology* 2, 73–84.

Syme, R. (1986), 'Isauria in Pliny,' *Anatolian Studies* 36, 159–164.

Walek, T. (1924), 'Les operations navales pendant la guerre lamiaque', *RP* 48, 23–30.

Wallace, S. (2014), 'History and Hindsight. The Importance of Euphron of Sikyon for the Athenian Democracy in 318/7', in H. Hauben and A. Meeus (eds.), The Age of the Successors and the Creation of the Hellenistic Kingdoms (323–276 BC), Leuven, 599–629.

Waterfield, R. (2011), *Dividing the Spoils: The War for Alexander the Great's Empire*, Oxford.

Webber, C. (2003), 'Odrysian Cavalry Arms, Equipment and Tactics', in L. Nikolova (ed.), *Early Symbolic Systems for Communication in Southeast Europe*, 529–544.

Webber, C. (2011), *The Gods of Battle: The Thracians at War: 1500 BC–AD 150*, Barnsley

Westlake, H. D. (1949), 'The Aftermath of the Lamian War', *The Classical Review* 63 (3), 87–90.

Worthington, I. (1984), 'IG II² 370 and the Date of the Athenian Alliance with Aetolia', *Zeitschrift fur Papyrologie und Epigraphik* 57, 139–144.

Worthington, I. (1986), 'The Chronology of the Harpalus Affair', *Symbolae Osloenses* 61 (1), 63–76.

Worthington, I. (1987), 'The Earlier Career of Leosthenes and I.G. II2 1631', *Historia* 36 (4), 489–491.

Worthington, I. (1989), 'Thoughts on the Identity of Deinarchus' Philocles (III against Philocles)', *Zeitschrift fur Papyrologie und Epigraphik* 79, 80–82.

Worthington, I. (1994), 'Alexander and Athens in 324/3 BC: On the Greek Attitude to the Macedonian Hegemony', *Mediterranean Archaeology* 7, 45–51.

Worthington, I. (2000), 'Demosthenes' (in)activity during the reign of Alexander the Great', in I. Worthington (ed.), *Demosthenes: Statesman and Orator*, Oxon, 90–113.

Worthington, I. (2001), 'Hypereides 5.32 and Alexander the Great's Statue', *Hermes* 129 (1), 129–131.

Worthington, I. (2003), 'The Authenticity of Demosthenes' Sixth Letter', *Mnemosyne* 56 (5), 585–589.

Worthington, I. (2016), *Ptolemy I: King and Pharaoh of Egypt*, New York.

Wrightson, G. (2014), 'The Naval Battles of 323 BCE' in H. Hauben and A. Meeus (eds.), *The Age of the Successors and the Creation of the Hellenistic Kingdoms (323–276 BC)*, Leuven, 517–535.

Xydopoulos, I. K. (2010), 'The Odrysian Kingdom after Philip II: Greek- and Self-perception', *Eirene* 46, 213–222.

Index